Text by Valerie Steele
and Colleen Hill

Foreword by
Daphne Guinness

with contributions by
Melissa Marra-Alvarez,
Emma McClendon,
Michelle McVicker,
Patricia Mears, and
Elizabeth Way

photographs by
Eileen Costa

and illustrations by
Robert Nippoldt

Shoes

The Collection of The Museum at FIT

TASCHEN

"High heels create artifice. It's the way you walk. You create a motion, a space – it's sinuous."

— MANOLO BLAHNÍK

Foreword

Daphne Guinness

IT IS SAID THAT ONE should never judge a book by its cover, but I believe footwear is a good indicator of character. Serge Gainsbourg's white Repetto Zizi oxfords, David Bowie's bespoke red space-platforms, the Ramones' Converse sneakers — all were visual clues to who these icons were and what they represented. A shoe speaks a thousand words about its wearer. Shoes are so much more than practical and protective accessories between us and the ground on which we walk.

Shoes have also long been a symbol of status. I recall my mother telling a friend of mine about the enduring allure of the red sole, an extravagance permitted by Louis XIV to his favored French courtiers. In fiction, shoes are the clue that attests to or betrays a person's true identity. Like all clothing, shoes offer us the chance to be who we want to be and to express who we really are.

People have always been fascinated by my footwear as they might be with a work of art or sculpture. They have become as much a part of me as the color of my hair. I've viewed shoes as important for as long as I can remember. I grew up between London and near Leicester, which had been home to a burgeoning leather trade in the 1800s, where the master shoemaker Thomas Crick pioneered many manufacturing techniques still used today. The other place that had a huge visual impact on my childhood was Cadaqués in Spain, where we all wore espadrilles. They were our summer uniform, worn every day, by everyone: locals, fishermen, artists (of which Dalí was best known), and, always, by dancers of the Sardana. I still wear them today. My mother was especially fascinated with shoes and would show shoe designers where local artisans who made them lived.

During my childhood in 1970s Britain, shoes were a clear indicator of young peoples' cultural tastes or allegiances. Skinheads wore Dr. Martens boots. Teddy boys and punks wore brothel creepers. Mods wore two-tone winklepickers and American penny loafers, and bad girls wore stilettos. Shoes defined you: they had tribal power. Tribes, though, were never my thing. Even then, I had a strong instinct for customization; I hankered for individuality. The magical idea of wearing something that no one else had always captivated me. This notion became more compelling as I pursued artistic endeavors.

Transforming physically is a big part of my performance in the music and film projects I've worked on, and shoes are possibly the most important element. My giant shoes have served me well in that respect. As a model I needed to be tall. As a singer I needed to be larger than life.

Some years ago, I was on a photo shoot wearing a pair of platform shoes with stiletto heels. One of the heels snapped, and in that moment fate delivered the notion that this was like a Chopine (the fifteenth-century shoes that Venetian women wore to avoid soggy feet). I had accidentally designed my first heel-less platforms: part glam rock, part Italian courtesan. They felt unique, distinctive, timeless — and somehow exactly the right fit for my own chameleonic identity. In the ensuing years, I went on to design and make more of these shoes in collaboration with Noritaka Tatehana and Massaro. They became part of my uniform, part of my being. They changed my life in the most positive ways. Shoe trends are revisited and recycled across cultures and their histories. The design I had stumbled upon is similar to a pedestal- or hoof-like design noted in eighteenth-century China for its stabilizing effect, and so I find it now. I have worn these shoes in many situations and on many terrains: from weddings and funerals to the slope of a volcano for a photo shoot with David LaChapelle. Surprisingly, gravity has very rarely got the better of me. I admit they don't work well on sand — although they do look great with a swimsuit.

Throughout history and across cultures, shoes have been an eternally compelling subject, a source of intrigue, and one shrouded in mysticism. They are rich in legend and feature heavily in cross-cultural folklore. The transformative effect of shoes is the stuff of fairy tales: glass slippers, magic slippers, and eternally dancing shoes (a punishment for vanity — of which ornate shoes are the ultimate symbol). Boots that magically shrink to fit their owner, old women who live in shoes, elves, and shoemakers, boots that bring feline fame and fortune. The tale of Cinderella describes the uniquely personal identity of footwear: the idea that there is only one foot to fit each shoe and that the shoe somehow chooses its owner. Would I lend a pair of shoes to a friend? Would they ask to borrow them? It seems too intimate.

The FIT collection is a stunning testament to the multifaceted history of the shoe. What a pleasure to observe with such clarity the trajectory shoes have taken, from the square toes of 1600s Europe to the square frontal heel of today's Noritaka Tatehana. To see traditional concepts of Western masculinity and femininity so plainly subverted in seventeenth-century men's shoes is to witness one example of how circular history really is. How interesting to observe society's changing relationship with our toes and our heels and our ankles, from concealment to revelation to emphasis. Shoes, we see, have the power to seduce. The ease with which they are removed is a direct reflection of our changing attitudes in propriety, as the mule demonstrates.

The shoe collection at FIT is a feast for the eyes for any shoe lover to behold, but its audience should be wider than that. Shoes are a language; they speak of our identity. They delight and shock, captivate, cajole, and appall. They heighten us, embolden us, dictate the very way we move.

The trajectory of footwear is a kaleidoscope of how people have lived, documenting their lifestyles, allegiances, and priorities. Shoes are an archive of our human narrative. They are also surely one of life's great joys.

Vorwort

Daphne Guinness

ES HEISST, MAN SOLLE EIN BUCH nie nach dem Umschlag beurteilen, doch ich glaube, dass Schuhe ein gutes Indiz für den Charakter sind. Serge Gainsbourgs weiße Zizi-Oxfords von Repetto, David Bowies maßgefertigte rote Plateauschuhe im Space-Look, die Converse-Sneaker der Ramones – sie alle lieferten visuelle Hinweise darauf, wer diese Ikonen waren und wofür sie standen. Ein Schuh sagt über seinen Träger mehr als 1 000 Worte. Schuhe sind so viel mehr als praktische Accessoires, die uns Schutz vor dem Boden bieten, auf dem wir gehen.

Schuhe sind seit Langem auch Statussymbole. Ich erinnere mich, wie meine Mutter einem Freund von mir die anhaltende Anziehungskraft der roten Absätze erklärte – jener Extravaganz, die Ludwig XIV. einst seinen bevorzugten Höflingen zugestand. In der Literatur geben Schuhe Aufschluss über die wahre oder falsche Identität einer Figur. Wie jedes Kleidungsstück bieten Schuhe uns die Möglichkeit, zu sein, wer wir sein wollen, und auszudrücken, wer wir wirklich sind.

Von meiner Fußbekleidung waren die Leute schon immer so fasziniert wie sonst vielleicht von einem Gemälde oder einer Skulptur. Schuhe machen mich heute genauso aus wie die Farbe meiner Haare, und sie sind mir wichtig, solange ich zurückdenken kann. Ich wuchs in der Gegend zwischen London und Leicester auf, wo im 19. Jahrhundert der Handel mit Lederwaren florierte und der Schuhmachermeister Thomas Crick viele Fertigungstechniken auf den Weg brachte, die noch heute angewandt werden. Der zweite Ort meiner Kindheit, der visuell enorm prägend war, ist Cadaqués in Spanien. Dort trugen wir alle Espadrilles. Sie waren unsere Sommeruniform. Jeder trug sie, jeden Tag: Einheimische, Fischer, Künstler (von denen Dalí der bekannteste war) und jeder, der die Sardana tanzte. Ich trage sie heute noch. Meine Mutter hatte ein besonderes Faible für Schuhe und führte

so manchen Schuhdesigner zu den Handwerkern im Ort, die Espadrilles herstellten.

Während meiner Kindheit im England der 1970er-Jahre waren Schuhe bei jungen Leuten ein klares Indiz für ihre kulturelle Ausrichtung oder Zugehörigkeit. Skinheads trugen Dr.-Martens-Springerstiefel. Teds und Punks trugen Creepers. Mods trugen spitze, zweifarbige Pikes oder amerikanische Pennyloafer, und böse Mädchen trugen Stilettos. Man definierte sich über Schuhe: Sie hatten die Macht von Stammeszeichen. Stammeszugehörigkeit war allerdings nie meine Sache. Schon damals stand mir der Sinn ganz nach exklusiv Gefertigtem; ich wollte Individualität. Die Vorstellung, etwas zu tragen, das niemand sonst hatte, zog mich schon immer magisch an. Noch unwiderstehlicher wurde dieser Gedanke, als ich mich künstlerischen Zielen zuwandte.

Körperliche Verwandlung spielt eine große Rolle in meiner Performance, wenn ich an Musik- und Filmprojekten arbeite, und Schuhe sind dabei das vielleicht wichtigste Element. Meine Riesenschuhe haben mir in dieser Hinsicht gute Dienste geleistet. Als Model musste ich groß sein. Als Sängerin musste ich überlebensgroß sein.

Vor einigen Jahren trug ich bei einem Fotoshooting Plateauschuhe mit Stilettoabsätzen. In dem Moment, als einer der Absätze abknickte, kam mir die Eingebung, dass der Schuh nun wie eine Chopine war (die Schuhe, die Venezianerinnen im 15. Jahrhundert trugen, um keine nassen Füße zu bekommen). Durch Zufall hatte ich meine ersten absatzlosen Plateauschuhe kreiert: halb Glamrock, halb italienische Kurtisane. Sie wirkten einzigartig, markant, zeitlos – und eigentlich wie geschaffen für mein chamäleonhaftes Ich. In den folgenden Jahren entwarf und fertigte ich in Zusammenarbeit mit Noritaka Tatehana und Massaro weitere solcher Schuhe. Sie wurden Teil meiner Uniform, Teil meines Seins. Sie veränderten mein Leben auf die allerbeste Weise. Schuhtrends werden in der Geschichte aller Kulturen immer wieder aufgegriffen und neu interpretiert. Das Design, über das ich gestolpert war, ähnelt einem sockel- oder hufartigen Schuhtypus, den man im China des 18. Jahrhunderts seiner stabilisierenden Wirkung wegen schätzte, und das tue ich heute auch. Ich habe diese Schuhe schon in vielen Situationen und in unterschiedlichstem Gelände getragen, auf Hochzeiten und Beerdigungen ebenso wie am Abhang eines Vulkans bei einem Shooting mit David LaChapelle. Erstaunlicherweise hat mich die Schwerkraft dabei nur sehr selten eingeholt. Ich gebe zu, dass sie für Sand nicht ideal sind – zum Badeanzug allerdings sehen sie fantastisch aus.

Zu allen Zeiten und in allen Kulturkreisen waren Schuhe ein ewig fesselndes Motiv, ein von Mystik umhüllter Quell der Faszination. Von vielerlei Sagen umwoben, spielen sie in der Folklore jeder Kultur eine wichtige Rolle. Weil sie Verwandlungen herbeiführen können, spenden Schuhe den Stoff für Märchen: gläserne Pantoffeln, Zauberschuhe und Schuhe, die nicht mehr aufhören zu tanzen (als Strafe für Eitelkeit – die wiederum von nichts besser symbolisiert wird als von prunkvollem Schuhwerk). Stiefel, die von Zauberhand zu passender Größe schrumpfen, Greisinnen, die in Schuhen hausen, Elfen und Schuster, Katerstiefel, die Ruhm und Reichtum bescheren. Das Märchen vom Aschenputtel beschreibt die einmalige individuelle Übereinstimmung von Schuh und Trägerin: die Vorstellung, dass jeder Schuh nur an einen Fuß passt und sich seinen Besitzer irgendwie selbst sucht. Würde ich Schuhe an Freundinnen verleihen? Würden sie mich um so etwas bitten? Das scheint zu intim zu sein.

Schuhe sind wie Spiegel des politischen und kulturellen Klimas. In Reaktion auf veränderte Verhaltensweisen waren Höhe und Form der Absätze über die Jahrhunderte hinweg immer wieder modischen Schwankungen unterworfen. Quer durch die Geschichte geben uns Schuhe Auskunft über die Gemütslage einer Gesellschaft: ihren Hang zur Extravaganz oder Genügsamkeit. Ob eine Generation auf Risiko setzt oder zu prüder Bescheidenheit zurückkehrt, lässt sich auch an den Schuhen erkennen.

Im Aufkommen robuster Sohlen, genau wie in unterschiedlichen Absatzarten, spiegelte sich der veränderte Lebensstil von Frauen wider. Es sind Beweise unserer Befreiung oder Begleiterscheinungen unserer Gefangenschaft, so wie die fort- oder rückschrittlichen Ansichten, die diesen Veränderungen vorausgehen.

Die Sammlung des Fashion Institute of Technology (FIT) ist ein atemberaubendes Zeugnis der facettenreichen Geschichte des Schuhs. Welch ein Vergnügen, den Entwicklungsweg von Schuhen in solcher Klarheit nachzuverfolgen, von den breiten Vorderkappen im Europa des 17. Jahrhunderts bis ins Heute zu Noritaka Tatehanas breitem Frontabsatz. Wie zyklisch die Geschichte verläuft, lässt sich gut an Herrenschuhen aus dem 17. Jahrhundert erkennen, die tradierte westliche Vorstellungen von Männlichkeit und Weiblichkeit untergraben. Wie spannend ist es zu beobachten, welchen Wandel das Verhältnis der Gesellschaft zu Zehen und Fersen und Knöcheln durchlaufen hat – vom Verbergen über die Enthüllung bis zur Betonung. Und wir erkennen das Verführungspotenzial von Schuhen. Die Leichtigkeit, mit der man sich ihrer entledigen kann, ist unmittelbarer Ausdruck unserer sich wandelnden Einstellung zur Schicklichkeit, wie am Beispiel von Mules zu sehen ist.

Für Liebhaber ist die Schuhsammlung des FIT ein Augenschmaus, doch wünschte man ihr ein breiteres Publikum. Schuhe sind eine Sprache; sie berichten von unserer Identität. Sie entzücken und schockieren, fesseln, schmeicheln, stoßen ab. Sie erhöhen uns, machen uns mutig, diktieren sogar die Art, wie wir uns bewegen.

Die Entwicklung von Fußbekleidung offenbart kaleidoskopartig, wie Menschen gelebt haben, dokumentiert ihren Alltag, ihre Loyalitäten und Prioritäten. Schuhe stellen ein Archiv des menschlichen Narrativs dar. Und sie zählen mit Sicherheit zu den großen Freuden des Lebens.

PAGE 4
Manolo Blahník
Ankle strap stiletto:
Black leather
England, 1998

PAGE 7
Ohne Titel
Sandal boot: Blue-and-white printed, embossed, and glazed leather
USA, spring 2015

PAGE 8
Jack Jacobus
Boot: Black-and-brown leather, red silk
Austria, 1895–1900

PAGE 11
Palter DeLiso, Inc.
T-strap evening shoe:
Black silk satin, gold-and-silver metallic kid
USA, ca. 1930

PREVIOUS
Salvatore Ferragamo
"Invisible" sandal:
Nylon, black suede
Italy, 1947

OPPOSITE
Raphael
Platform sandal:
Silver leather, wood
USA, 1972–73

Préface

Daphne Guinness

ON A BEAU DIRE QUE l'habit ne fait pas le moine, les chaussures reflètent tout de même assez bien le caractère de leur propriétaire. Les Repetto blanches de Serge Gainsbourg, les bottines compensées rouges de David Bowie et les Converse des Ramones étaient autant d'indices visuels révélateurs de la personnalité de ces icônes et de ce qu'elles représentaient. Nos chaussures en disent long sur nous. Elles sont bien plus que de simples accessoires fonctionnels protégeant nos pieds du sol que nous foulons.

Les chaussures sont depuis longtemps un marqueur social – je me souviens de ma mère parlant à l'une de mes amies de l'éternel attrait des semelles rouges, une extravagance que Louis XIV accordait à ses courtisans préférés. Dans les œuvres de fiction, elles servent d'indices confirmant ou trahissant la véritable identité d'un personnage. Et comme les vêtements, elles nous offrent la chance d'être ce que nous avons envie d'être et d'exprimer notre véritable personnalité.

Les gens ont toujours été fascinés par mes chaussures, comme ils peuvent l'être par une œuvre d'art ou une sculpture. Elles font désormais autant partie de moi que ma couleur de cheveux. Aussi loin que je m'en souvienne, j'ai toujours accordé de l'importance aux chaussures. J'ai grandi entre Londres et la région de Leicester, où le marché de la maroquinerie était florissant au XIXᵉ siècle, le maître cordonnier Thomas Crick y ayant d'ailleurs inventé de nombreuses techniques de fabrication encore utilisées de nos jours. Cadaqués en Espagne est l'autre lieu qui a exercé une immense influence visuelle sur moi pendant mon enfance. Nous y vivions tous en espadrilles. C'était notre uniforme estival. Tout le monde en portait, tous les jours : les gens du coin, les pêcheurs, les artistes (dont Dalí était le plus célèbre) et tous ceux qui dansaient la sardane. J'en porte encore aujourd'hui. Ma mère se passionnait pour les chaussures et aimait montrer aux autres créateurs là où elles étaient fabriquées par les artisans locaux.

J'ai grandi dans l'Angleterre des années 1970, quand les jeunes portaient des chaussures qui révélaient clairement leurs goûts et leurs allégeances culturelles : les skinheads portaient des Dr. Martens ; les Teddy Boys et les punks, des creepers ; les Mods, des chaussures bicolores à bout pointu et des mocassins américains ; les jeunes filles rebelles, des talons aiguilles. Vos chaussures vous définissaient : elles possédaient un pouvoir tribal. Je n'ai pourtant jamais été attirée par les tribus. À l'époque, j'avais déjà un fort penchant pour la customisation, car je cherchais à sortir du lot. J'ai toujours trouvé magique l'idée de porter des choses que personne d'autre ne possédait – un sentiment qui s'est encore accentué dans le cadre de mes projets artistiques.

La transformation physique représente une grande partie de ma performance dans mes projets musicaux et cinématographiques, et les souliers y jouent sans doute le rôle le plus important. Mes chaussures de géante m'ont bien servie à cet égard. En tant que mannequin, je devais être grande, mais en tant que chanteuse, je devais être immense.

Il y a quelques années, j'ai dû porter des escarpins compensés à talons aiguilles pour une séance photo. L'un des talons a cassé et c'est à ce moment-là que le destin m'a montré ce à quoi ressemblait une chopine (ces souliers que portaient les Vénitiennes du XVᵉ siècle pour garder les pieds au sec). Je venais accidentellement de créer mes premières compensées sans talons, à mi-chemin entre le *glam rock* et la courtisane italienne. Je les trouvais uniques, originales, intemporelles – et parfaitement adaptées à ma personnalité caméléonesque. Les années suivantes, j'ai créé d'autres modèles en collaboration avec Noritaka Tatehana et Massaro. Ces chaussures font aujourd'hui partie intégrante de mon uniforme et de mon identité. Elles ont changé ma vie de la façon la plus positive qui soit. Dans le domaine des chaussures, toutes les cultures ont revisité et recyclé les tendances tout au long de leur histoire. J'ai appris récemment que le soulier que j'avais créé par hasard est très proche d'un modèle en forme de piédestal ou de sabot d'animal réputé pour son effet stabilisateur dans la Chine du XVIIIe siècle. J'ai porté ces chaussures en toutes circonstances et sur tout type de terrain : à l'occasion de mariages et d'enterrements, et même sur les pentes d'un volcan devant l'objectif de David LaChapelle. Étonnamment, la gravité a très rarement eu raison de moi. J'admets toutefois que ces chaussures ne sont pas idéales pour marcher dans le sable – bien qu'elles fassent merveille avec un maillot de bain.

Au fil de l'histoire et dans toutes les cultures, les chaussures ont toujours été un sujet de fascination et une source d'intrigue auréolée de mysticisme. Elles sont entourées de légendes et occupent une place très importante dans tous les folklores. C'est dans les contes de fées que leur pouvoir transformateur se révèle : pantoufles de vair, souliers magiques, chaussons rouges dansant éternellement (pour punir la vanité, dont les belles chaussures sont le symbole ultime), bottes de sept lieues qui s'adaptent à la taille de celui qui les chausse, vieilles dames vivant dans des chaussures, elfes, cordonniers, bottes valant gloire et fortune à un félin... L'histoire de *Cendrillon* parle de l'identité personnelle des chaussures, c'est-à-dire de l'idée selon laquelle la chaussure ne peut aller qu'à un seul pied et choisit son ou sa propriétaire. Prêterais-je une paire de chaussures à une amie ? Oserait-elle me le demander ? Cela me semble trop intime.

Les chaussures reflètent aussi des climats politiques et culturels. La mode a évolué à travers les siècles en privilégiant successivement différentes hauteurs et formes de talons pour s'adapter à l'évolution des comportements. Les chaussures ont toujours été un langage exprimant le caractère d'une société, qu'elle prône l'extravagance ou la sobriété. Elles peuvent refléter la libération des mœurs d'une génération comme son retour à la décence et à la pudibonderie.

Le développement de semelles robustes et de différents types de talons correspondait au nouveau style de vie des femmes. Les chaussures illustrent notre émancipation ou notre captivité, ainsi que les attitudes progressistes ou régressives qui précèdent ces changements.

La collection du Fashion Institute of Technology (FIT) offre un témoignage éblouissant sur l'histoire des chaussures et ses multiples facettes. Des souliers à bouts carrés de l'Europe du XVIIe siècle à l'actuel talon carré frontal des modèles de Noritaka Tatehana, quel plaisir de pouvoir observer aussi clairement la trajectoire qu'elles ont empruntée ! Ces souliers pour homme du XVIIe siècle qui subvertissent si clairement les concepts occidentaux traditionnels de masculinité et de féminité illustrent la véritable circularité de l'histoire. Il est très intéressant d'explorer le rapport changeant de la société avec nos orteils, nos talons et nos chevilles, de la dissimulation au dévoilement jusqu'à la mise en valeur. Nous voyons bien que les chaussures ont un pouvoir de séduction. D'ailleurs, la facilité avec laquelle on les retire est le reflet direct de nos rapports fluctuants avec la bienséance, comme le prouvent les mules.

La collection du FIT est un régal pour les yeux de tous les amoureux des chaussures, mais son public devrait être plus large. Les chaussures sont un langage qui parle de notre identité. Elles ravissent, choquent, fascinent, enjôlent et atterrent. Elles nous grandissent, nous enhardissent et dictent jusqu'à notre façon de bouger.

L'évolution des chaussures révèle de manière kaléidoscopique comment les gens vivaient, documentant leur quotidien, leurs allégeances et leurs priorités. Les chaussures sont des archives du récit de l'humanité. Et elles comptent certainement parmi les grands plaisirs de la vie.

PREVIOUS
Louis Vuitton
Evening oxford:
Gold leather, silk, mink
France, fall 2004

**Zaha Hadid for
UN United Nude**
"Nova" shoe: Rose-gold
metallic chromed vinyl
France, 2013

The Power and Allure of Shoes

Valerie Steele

EVER SINCE *SEX AND THE CITY* depicted Carrie Bradshaw consuming high-fashion footwear, popular culture has been fixated on "women's intimate relationship" with shoes. A photograph of a woman's shoe closet appeared in a 2001 advertisement for the Citibank AAdvantage Card with the caption "Was it a fetish?" At *Shoe Obsession* (2013), one of The Museum at the Fashion Institute of Technology's most popular exhibitions, which featured more than 100 of the most extreme, extravagant, and expensive shoes of the twenty-first century, I overheard a visitor exclaim, "I've died and gone to shoe heaven!"

People are fascinated by shoes. Whenever I talk about the collection of The Museum at FIT, which has more than 50,000 garments and accessories by the world's greatest designers, it is always the figure of *4,000 pairs of shoes* that elicits the most excitement.

Shoes have played an important role in human society for millennia, but interest in them appears to have grown dramatically over the past few decades. Certainly, people have been *buying* more shoes: In 1995 the average American woman supposedly had 12 pairs of shoes, and the average man had six. Today, she is thought to have 27–30 pairs, while he has 12. Some women go far beyond the average with hundreds of pairs to their name while rarer collections number in the thousands — although former first lady of the Philippines Imelda Marcos ultimately admitted of her infamous collection: "I did not have 3,000 pairs of shoes. I had 1,060."

The book you hold in your hands features approximately 400 of our most intriguing pairs of shoes, including historical footwear as well as modern creations by shoe designers and fashion brands — from Azzedine Alaïa and Roger Vivier to Manolo Blahník and Vivienne Westwood.

In addition to analyzing the shoes in The Museum at FIT's collection, we explore the significance of shoes from prehistory to the present, in real life and in the cultural imagination. "People have probably been wearing shoes for about 40,000 years," says evolutionary biologist Daniel E. Lieberman, "although some suspect that Neanderthals remained shoeless." Being barefoot in Europe during the Ice Age seems "unimaginable," he told *Scientific American*, but "maybe our cousins, the Neanderthals, were able to handle it just fine." The Ice Age might have necessitated shoes, but even today in countries such as India and

PREVIOUS
An evening shoe
by Roger Viver for
Christian Dior features
a scalloped trim, floral
embroidery, and ribbon.
Paul Schutzer for *LIFE*,
1961.

Men's shoe: Black
leather, red painted
leather, green silk
Europe, 1640–70

Kenya, many people go their entire lives without wearing shoes. Indeed, scientific studies find benefits in going barefoot.

By the Neolithic era (10,000–2,000 BCE), however, humans in many parts of the world were wearing sandals and shoes made from straw, bark, papyrus leaves, yucca leaves, leather, fur, or wood. Shoes discovered in archaeological sites can be found in museums around the world. The History Museum of Armenia, for example, contains the Areni-1 shoe, a 5,500-year-old leather shoe that was discovered in near-perfect condition in a cave in Armenia. Even older, perhaps 10,000 years old, is a pair of sandals made of braided yucca leaves, which were found in the American Southwest. They reside at the private shoe museum SONS (Shoes or No Shoes) in Kruishoutem, Belgium.

Preserved in a glacier for 5,300 years, Ötzi the Iceman's shoes and clothes can be seen today in the South Tyrol Museum of Archaeology in Bolzano, Italy. According to experts who experimented with their reconstructions, Ötzi's shoes — made of deer hide (fur side in) and string netting, stuffed with dried grass — would have been quite effective in keeping his feet warm and protected from the rough terrain and harsh climate conditions of the Alps.

Yet protection from the elements and enhanced mobility, the original purpose of shoes, are obviously not the *only* reasons we wear shoes. They may not even be the most important reasons.

Throughout much of world history, shoes were the prerogative of an elite minority. In the Roman Empire, for example, professional shoemakers created finely crafted, decorated shoes for patricians of both sexes, while plebeians wore plain shoes, and slaves were explicitly forbidden from wearing shoes at all. Similarly, in eighteenth-century Haiti, where the majority of the Black population was enslaved, free Blacks were also prohibited from wearing shoes. Meanwhile, Roman soldiers wore heavy-soled, hobnailed sandal-boots that not only facilitated marching on rough terrain but also served as weapons.

Hook, Knowles & Co.
Evening shoe: Black
satin, glass beads
England, *ca.* 1910

FOLLOWING
In Hyacinthe Rigaud's
1701 painting *Portrait
of Louis XIV*, the "Sun
King" wears red-heeled
boots with diamond
buckles. Heels were
worn by aristocratic men
in the seventeenth and
eighteenth centuries, and
red heels, in particular,
were a status symbol.

Because shoes were symbolically associated with movement and journeys, Hermes-Mercury, the Greco-Roman god of travelers, was always depicted wearing boots or sandals with wings. Yet cross-culturally, shoes that *reduce* mobility have been among the most prestigious styles. Aphrodite, the Greek goddess of love and beauty, was depicted as early as the first century BCE wearing platform shoes, which are thought to have originated in Persia. Although men have worn some extreme shoes such as medieval poulaines (with very long toes), history provides many more examples of women's shoes that impede walking, from Chinese "lotus shoes" (for bound feet) to Venetian chopines (very high platform shoes worn by courtesans).

It was formerly believed that high heels, which entered Europe at the end of the sixteenth century, derived from chopines, but Elizabeth Semmelhack argues convincingly that, "The enthusiastic adoption of the heel by upper-class men argues against regarding it as a variant of the highly gendered chopine.... Instead, the origin of the heel is in the Near East where heeled footwear had been worn for centuries as a part of male equestrian and military attire." When Persia and France allied against the Ottoman Empire, heels suddenly became popular among aristocratic European men, who also appreciated how heels helped keep "a rider's feet in the stirrups."

By the early seventeenth century, upper-class European men had adopted the new style of riding boots with heels as well as shoes with stacked heels. As ordinary people began to wear the new heel, the wealthy and aristocratic adopted *high* heels. At Louis XIV's court the most important men wore shoes with red high heels. Women, as well as men, found the new high-heeled styles attractive and prestigious. As Giorgio Riello observes: "In the seventeenth and eighteenth centuries high heels conveyed meanings of wealth, power, and distinction in a hierarchical society, rather than the sexual connotations, which they came to assume in the early nineteenth century. High heels not only provided higher physical stature, but were also a self-inflicted sign of 'constrained mobility.' Only the members of the upper classes — men and women alike — could wear shoes that clearly symbolized an inability to walk."

Men and women wore different types of high-heeled shoes, made by different shoemakers. Men's heels were squared and sturdy, while women's heels tended to be higher, narrower, and tapered. As a result, women's high heels became associated with an unsteady gait. Although often mocked, this type of walk was also perceived as erotic. As a mideighteenth-century rhyme put it: "Mount on French heels when you go to a ball, / 'Tis the fashion to totter and show you can fall." Women's high heels also had the effect of making the foot look smaller, which resonated with widespread ideals of femininity, as expressed, for example, in Perrault's fairy tale "Cinderella" (1697).

The identification of high-heeled shoes with erotic femininity was a turning point in shoe design. Henceforth, men's and women's shoes, like fashion in general, would take divergent paths with very clear gender distinctions. By 1800, for example, when women's shoe fashion shifted from high heels to flat slippers, men increasingly adopted military-style boots, symbolizing, respectively, delicate women and powerful men. In her autobiography, George Sand recalled the flimsy French shoes of the 1830s: "On the Paris pavement, I was like a boat on ice. My delicate shoes cracked open in two days." Soon she began to dress as a man: "My boots delighted me . . . . With those steel-tipped heels I was solid on the sidewalk at last. I dashed back and forth across Paris."

Over the course of the nineteenth and early twentieth centuries, industrialization made fashionable shoe styles more widely available, and women acquired access to a greater variety of footwear — walking boots as well as evening shoes, high heels and low. Men also added to their footwear wardrobes, adopting laced and side-buttoned shoes and boots, which soon influenced women's footwear. The vulcanization of rubber made it possible to design sneakers — a new category of footwear with rubber soles, worn by men and women alike, initially for sports like tennis but increasingly for other aspects of modern life.

Today footwear continues to be perceived as strongly gendered. Research conducted in the late twentieth century indicates that people tend to categorize shoes as either "feminine and sexy," "masculine," "asexual and dowdy," or "young and casual." High heels are definitely classified as feminine and sexy as are strappy sandals, pumps, and high boots. Oxfords and cowboy boots are regarded as masculine. Asexual shoes such as nurses' shoes and career pumps may be relatively comfortable, but they are also deeply unfashionable. Young and casual shoes include flip-flops and clogs.

Tom Ford spoke for many when he said, "It's hard not to be sexy in a pair of high heels." High heels have been fetishized as early as the 1780s, and they continue to play a significant role in sexual fantasies. In 1930s Paris the Diana Slip Company was a manufacturer and purveyor of clothing and footwear for sexual fetishists and sex workers. By the 1970s fetish shoes and boots had begun to influence fashionable footwear. Fashion photographers like Helmut Newton also emphasized images of the powerfully sexual "phallic

Shoes: Yellow silk
damask, blue silk
France, early eighteenth
century

woman." By the 1990s high fashion increasingly referenced the fetish aesthetic, which now tends to be interpreted as female empowerment.

Of course, fashion has often played with mixing masculine and feminine signifiers. Bella Freud's 1998 oxfords, for example, draw on a classic masculine prototype but are "feminized" by their high heels and bright-red color. There are also cultural differences in attitudes toward dress and gender. When a Brazilian journalist visited MFIT's exhibition *Shoes: A Lexicon of Style* (1999), she responded to a pair of Birkenstocks with horror: "No Latin woman would wear shoes like those!"

Shoemakers have existed for thousands of years, but shoe designers emerged only at the beginning of the twentieth century. Italian-born André Perugia learned to make shoes from his father before going on to make shoes for Paul Poiret and other Parisian couturiers. Salvatore Ferragamo was apprenticed to a shoemaker before going to Hollywood to design footwear for the stars. Roger Vivier is credited with inventing the stiletto heel in the early 1950s, when he worked with Christian Dior. Manolo Blahník and Christian Louboutin became international celebrities in the 1990s — women still refer proudly to their Manolos, and everyone recognizes Louboutin's iconic red-soled shoes. Today, there are many shoe designers, some famous under their own names and others associated with fashion brands. Architects like Zaha Hadid have also flirted with shoe design.

Whether or not shoes are art, they have been a favorite subject for artists, from Vincent van Gogh to Andy Warhol. Sylvie Fleury's work is especially compelling as it deals with women's desire for high-end footwear, reminding us that our contemporary fascination with shoes, like our growing consumption of them, may be a type of commodity fetishism inherent to the global fashion system, which is itself a conspicuous feature of contemporary capitalism. Yet Fleury's work also implies an emotional, even erotic subtext to this female longing for shoes. If this is sexual fetishism, however, it seems very different from men's footwear desire.

Bob
Ghillie-style pumps: Red
leather, black leather,
black ribbon
USA, *ca.* 1925

Recent studies suggest that, whereas male shoe fetishism is closely related to fantasies of the phallic woman, female desire for shoes may be associated with a pre-Oedipal sense of longing for a lost unity with the mother. In other words, most women probably don't want a closet full of phallic symbols, but, like fetishizing men, they can associate desire with difference.

As curators and conservators know, while historic fashions may be lovely, old and "worn" shoes can be quite unattractive — with dirty fabric or cracked leather, stretched out of shape by the wearer's feet. On the other hand, a shoe in good condition is much easier to display than an item of clothing, which requires a mannequin or dress form. Shoes can stand up on their own. This may be one reason they appeal to us — we can admire them like small, beautiful sculptures.

Shoes can also stand *for* someone, and this is almost certainly a significant reason why shoes are so important to us. Holocaust museums have exhibited piles of shoes that were confiscated from people who were murdered. Their empty forms powerfully evoke the wearers' absence. But even in ordinary life, certain shoes such as baby shoes are lovingly preserved (even bronzed!) because they embody memories. Lightly worn soles on a little pair of shoes from about 1900 prove the wearer was a toddler. Wedding shoes are also often saved as souvenirs of a liminal experience in the individual's life.

Pierre Cardin's shoes in the form of feet not only recall Magritte's famous Surrealist painting *Philosophy in the Bedroom*, they also evoke the little-analyzed relationship between shoes and feet. There is something abject about feet and shoes since they touch the ground and get dirty. In many cultures, people take off their shoes before entering a house or temple, perhaps putting on a special pair of indoor slippers.

Linguistically, the phrase "barefoot and pregnant" evokes female poverty and powerlessness, but there is something nostalgic about a "barefoot boy." Since bare feet are regarded as "natural," then shoes, being "artificial," are associated with civilization and its many discontents. Some new brands of shoes boast that the experience of wearing them is like going barefoot, and part of the appeal of sandals is the extent to which they expose the naked foot.

Shoes' relationship with the body as a whole is also important, most obviously because shoes influence the way we stand and walk. In high heels we move one way and in army boots another. Sneakers are good for movement, but certain kinds of sneakers are especially designed for running. We also identify different parts of the shoe with other aspects of the body, as when we speak of "toe cleavage" or refer to sling-backs as "fuck-me shoes." Even the small size of Cinderella's shoes is an exaggeration of human sexual dimorphism.

Shoes have long been associated with socioeconomic status, as indicated by expressions such as "well-heeled" versus "down-at-the-heels." In eighteenth-century France, where the poor often went barefoot or wore wooden clogs, Chateaubriand used a clothing metaphor to describe the French Revolution: "The men who wore shoes were ready to leave the drawing rooms, and already the clogs were kicking at the door."

Class distinctions in footwear have evolved, but they continue to exist. Until recently wealthy people tended to prefer bespoke shoes, which are custom-made to fit an individual's feet. Today, the majority of shoes, even expensive ones, are ready-to-wear. The quality of materials and workmanship continues to be important, but so are the status of the fashion brand and the, sometimes artificial, "rarity" of the shoe. Exclusivity is especially important with men's sneakers.

When Colleen Hill and I organized *Shoe Obsession* in 2013, there was a growing trend for extremely high heels and even higher prices. "Why Are Designer Shoes So Damn Expensive All of a Sudden?" demanded blogger Jenna Saunders. Of course, there were business reasons for the trend. Fashion companies, which had made a killing with designer handbags, shifted to a lucrative new accessory. (Apart from shoes and handbags, there are no longer many significant accessories. Even hats, once so important, have been largely reduced to their basic functions.) But it was also the case that many women were unfazed by prices that approached or exceeded $1,000 for a pair of shoes, twice what designer shoes had cost just a few years earlier.

Women have long been the primary collectors of shoes. However, if you research "shoe collections" today, you will also find a growing cadre of male "sneaker fiends" — who collect not just any sneakers, but hard-to-find, special-edition sneakers. The role of sneakers as status symbols in men's wardrobes began in the mid-1980s as the shoes became increasingly associated with legendary athletes such as Michael Jordan of Nike Air Jordan fame and rappers like Run-DMC, whose song "My Adidas" became an international hit. By the twenty-first century, major fashion houses from Lanvin to Dior produced sneakers for men and women. Sneaker collaborations with fashion designers, like Raf Simons, and celebrities, like Kanye West, also became popular, especially among men.

As curator Elizabeth Semmelhack observes: "Today sneakers are worn around the world and in many ways could be considered the most democratic form of footwear, yet commodification and branding have transformed some into highly coveted objects of desire

LA PANTOUFLE DE VAIR

Danseur Louis XIV

that are increasingly central to men's fashion." As a result, certain sneakers are associated not only with "athletic prowess" but also with "exclusivity . . . and shifting constructions of masculinity."

Sneakers may have once been thought of as casual wear associated with the young, but because of their strong association with professional sports and urban culture, they are now mostly coded as masculine. Yet women, too, seek the enhanced mobility, comfort, and coolness associated with sneakers. Phoebe Philo's Celine had huge success with its women's sneakers, and Rihanna's fashion house, Fenty, has collaborated with Puma.

Like its fashion collection, the shoe collection at MFIT is primarily modern and contemporary, with an emphasis on designer fashion. Although there are extraordinary Japanese shoes that sit between design and art, the majority of the museum's shoes are European and American, and women's shoes make up 90 percent of the collection. Some specialized shoe museum collections include medieval poulaines and Renaissance chopines, funerary sandals from ancient Egypt, and shoes from around the world. Yet as we continue to build our shoe collection, we tend to focus on our strength, modern footwear, while seeking to fill in the most important lacunae, especially sneakers, which have emerged as probably the most important type of footwear today.

Shoes have long been collected and exhibited in museums, and shoe exhibitions began to be popular in the 1970s, but they have really proliferated in recent years. As one of our museum guards proudly announced, "Miss Val, people just love shoes!" Some people certainly do, but others are more ambivalent, and shoe exhibitions often have ambiguous titles such as *Shoes: Pleasure and Pain* or *Killer Heels*. As the scholar Julia Emberley observed in an essay on the Bata Shoe Museum, shoe collections and exhibitions "throw the boundary between shoe as commodity and shoe as cultural or aesthetic artefact into question."

PREVIOUS
A. E. Marty,
"The fur slipper,"
Gazette du bon ton,
1912–13, #4. The title is
a pun in French on *vair*
(fur) and *verre* (glass).

OPPOSITE
Diana Slip
Thigh-high fetish
boots: Black leather,
118 brass hooks
France, *ca.* 1930

Castell Sageur
Wedge-heeled sandals:
Black suede and leather
France, *ca.* 1954

Whether shoes were first invented by Neanderthals 40,000 years ago or by Homo sapiens about 10,000 years ago, they have been with us for a very long time. Yet except in extreme conditions, such as a very cold climate, shoes are not absolutely necessary. However, once shoes existed, distinctions were made between people with shoes and people without, people with fine shoes and people with plain shoes. Looking back through the history of dress and fashion, it is clear that, with very few exceptions (like warm boots on an icy day or sturdy boots for soldiers), the functionalism of clothing is much less important than what clothes signify.

"Shoes affect our perceptions of others and our perceptions of self," writes Russell W. Belk, whose research indicates that most Americans believe that "their footwear is an extension and expression of themselves." Shoes are thought to express important information about the wearer's age, gender, social status, sexuality, ethnicity, taste, and personality. For adolescents, in particular, "shoes are a key signifier of their identities." Many people even believe that shoes may even be "capable of magically transforming them." According to the "strong elements of magical beliefs in our regard for shoes," people actually believe that not only will shoes change their appearance or athletic capacity, but that their "lives will be changed utterly."

Shoes are valuable to us because we believe that they provide important information about who we are — and who we could be. In the past our identity was essentially limited to our position in society, while today it is more subjectively defined. Shoes have become more important in recent decades, in large part because of developments in the fashion system that have resulted in a greater variety of footwear, which influences how we consume the objects with which we craft our individual identities: Manolos or Nikes? Ballerinas or Birkenstocks? Which shoe are you?

Die Macht und Anziehungskraft von Schuhen

Valerie Steele

SEITDEM *SEX AND THE CITY* Carrie Bradshaws Faible für Luxusschuhe thematisierte, ist die Populärkultur auf die „intime Beziehung von Frauen" zu Schuhen fixiert.[1] 2001 zeigte eine Kreditkartenwerbung der Citibank den Schuhschrank einer Frau, übertitelt mit der Frage: „War es ein Fetisch?" In *Shoe Obsession* (2012), einer der bestbesuchten Ausstellungen des Museums am Fashion Institute of Technology, die über 100 der extremsten, extravagantesten und teuersten Schuhe des 21. Jahrhunderts präsentierte, hörte ich eine Besucherin ausrufen: „Ich bin gestorben und im Schuhhimmel gelandet!

Schuhe faszinieren die Menschen. Wann immer ich über die Sammlung des FIT-Museums mit ihren über 50 000 Kleidungsstücken und Accessoires von den bedeutendsten Designern der Welt spreche, sind es stets die *4 000 Paar Schuhe*, die das größte Aufsehen erregen.

Schuhe spielen in unserer Gesellschaft schon seit Jahrtausenden eine wichtige Rolle, doch in den letzten Jahrzehnten finden sie allem Anschein nach deutlich mehr Beachtung. Auf alle Fälle werden mehr Schuhe *gekauft*: 1995 besaß die Durchschnittsamerikanerin angeblich zwölf Paar Schuhe, der Durchschnittsamerikaner sechs. Heute sollen es bei ihr 27 bis 30 Paar, bei ihm zwölf Paar sein. In Deutschland nannte im Jahr 2017 die Durchschnittsfrau 20,4 Paar Schuhe ihr Eigen, der Durchschnittsmann 10,2. Einige Frauen liegen mit Hunderten Schuhen weit über dem Durchschnitt, vereinzelte Sammlungen gehen gar in die Tausende – wobei die ehemalige First Lady der Philippinen, Imelda Marcos, über ihre berüchtigte Schuhsammlung letztlich einräumte: „Es waren nicht 3 000 Paar. Es waren 1 060."

Das vorliegende Buch präsentiert rund 400 unserer faszinierendsten Schuhe, darunter sowohl historische Fußbekleidung als auch Kreationen zeitgenössischer Schuhdesigner und Modelabels – von Azzedine Alaïa und Roger Vivier bis Manolo Blahník und Vivienne Westwood.

Wir analysieren zum einen die Schuhe der FIT-Sammlung und ergründen zudem, welche Bedeutung Schuhen von der Frühzeit bis heute in der Realität und in der kulturellen Vorstellung beigemessen wird und wurde. „Der Mensch trägt wahrscheinlich schon seit rund 40 000 Jahren Fußbekleidung", so der Evolutionsbiologe Daniel E. Lieberman, „auch wenn einige vermuten, dass der Neandertaler unbeschuht war." Während der Eiszeit in Europa barfuß unterwegs zu sein, erscheine ihm „unvorstellbar", wie er dem *Scientific American* erklärte, doch „womöglich kamen unsere Vettern, die Neandertaler, damit gut zurecht."[2] Die Eiszeit mag Fußbekleidung erforderlich gemacht haben, doch in Ländern wie Indien oder Kenia tragen selbst heute viele Menschen zeit ihres Lebens keine Schuhe. Wissenschaftliche Untersuchungen entdecken sogar Vorteile im Barfußgehen.

Seit der Jungsteinzeit (ca. 10 000–2 000 v. Chr.) tragen jedenfalls Menschen in vielen Teilen der Welt Sandalen und Schuhe aus Stroh, Rinde, Papyrus- und Yukkablättern, Leder, Fell oder Holz. Davon zeugen archäologische Funde, die in Museen auf der ganzen Welt zu finden sind. Das Historische Museum von Armenien beispielsweise beherbergt einen 5 500 Jahre alten Lederschuh, den man in nahezu perfektem Zustand in der armenischen Höhle Areni-1 fand. Noch älter, vielleicht 10 000 Jahre, ist ein im Südwesten der USA entdecktes Paar Sandalen aus geflochtenen Yukkablättern, das sich heute

PREVIOUS
"Long years of depriva-
tion during World
War II brought forth
a yearning for luxury
and fashionable things,"
wrote fashion historian
Gerda Buxbaum of '50s
style. "Women made
a special effort to
dress appropriately for
every occasion; it was
considered imperative
that one's accessories
matched perfectly." 1951.

Platform fetish heels:
Black patent leather
Mexico, 1973–75

in dem privaten Schuhmuseum SONS (Shoes or No Shoes) im belgischen Kruishoutem befindet.

Die über 5 300 Jahre im Eis konservierten Schuhe und Kleider von Ötzi, dem Gletschermann, sind heute im Südtiroler Archäologiemuseum in Bozen zu sehen. Seine mit Heu gepolsterten Schuhe – gefertigt aus Hirschleder (mit der Fellseite nach innen) und einem Schnurgeflecht – dürften nach Ansicht von Experten, die mit Nachbildungen experimentierten, Ötzis Füße sehr effektiv vor Kälte, schroffem Untergrund und den rauen klimatischen Bedingungen der Alpen geschützt haben.

Doch der ursprünglich bezweckte Schutz vor den Elementen sowie die verbesserte Trittfestigkeit sind offensichtlich nicht die einzigen Gründe, weshalb wir Schuhe tragen – und möglicherweise nicht einmal die wichtigsten.

Schuhe waren von jeher meist einer elitären Minderheit vorbehalten. Im Römischen Reich etwa fertigten professionelle Schuhmacher fein verziertes Schuhwerk für Patrizier beiderlei Geschlechts an, während Plebejer schlicht beschuht gingen und Sklaven das Tragen von Schuhen ausdrücklich verboten war. Ähnlich verhielt es sich noch im 18. Jahrhundert auf Haiti, wo die schwarze Bevölkerung in der Mehrzahl als Sklaven lebte. Dort durften selbst befreite Sklaven keine Schuhe tragen. Soldaten im Römischen Reich dagegen trugen bereits genagelte Sandalenstiefel mit schweren Sohlen, die nicht nur das Marschieren in unwegsamem Gelände erleichterten, sondern auch als Waffen dienten.

Da der Schuh als Symbol für Fortbewegung und Reisen galt, wurde der Gott der Reisenden – Hermes bei den Griechen, Merkur bei den Römern – stets mit geflügelten Stiefeln oder Sandalen dargestellt. Doch zu den prestigeträchtigsten Schuhen zählten in allen Kulturen schon immer solche, die die Mobilität *einschränken*. So zeigen bereits Abbildungen aus dem 1. Jahrhundert v. Chr. Aphrodite, die griechische Göttin der Liebe und Schönheit, mit Plateauschuhen, deren Ursprung man in Persien vermutet. Zwar trugen auch Männer mitunter extremes Schuhwerk, im Mittelalter etwa Schnabelschuhe (mit überlangen Spitzen), doch bietet die Geschichte ungleich mehr Beispiele für Damenschuhe, die das Gehen erschweren, vom chinesischen „Lotosschuh" (für gebundene Füße) bis zur venezianischen Chopine (ein sehr hoher Plateauschuh, den Kurtisanen trugen).

Der früheren Annahme, der Ende des 16. Jahrhunderts in Europa aufgekommene hohe Absatz gehe auf die Chopine zurück, hält Elizabeth Semmelhack ein überzeugendes Argument entgegen: „Die Tatsache, dass der Absatz von der männlichen Oberschicht begeistert angenommen wurde, spricht dagegen, ihn als Variante der äußerst geschlechtsspezifischen Chopine anzusehen ... Vielmehr hat der Schuh mit Absatz seinen Ursprung im Nahen Osten, wo er schon seit Jahrhunderten Bestandteil des Reit- und Rüstzeugs von Männern gewesen war." Als Persien und Frankreich sich gegen das Osmanische Reich verbündeten, wurde

Pierre Cardin
(Carlos Peñafiel)
Men's shoes:
Brown leather
France, 1986

FOLLOWING
Known as the "Fragonard
of the Shoe," Roger Vivier
designed for Christian
Dior from the 1940s to
the 1960s. Advertisement
from 1959–60.

der Absatz in Europa schlagartig unter Herren der
Aristokratie beliebt. Auch sie wussten zu schät-
zen, dass er half, „des Reiters Fuß im Steigbügel"
zu halten.[3]

Im frühen 17. Jahrhundert war der Herren-
reitstiefel mit Absatz als neue Mode bereits in der
europäischen Oberschicht etabliert, desgleichen der
Schuh mit Blockabsatz. Als das gewöhnliche Volk
den neuen Absatz zu tragen begann, gingen Reiche
und Adlige zu *hohen* Absätzen über. Am Hof Lud-
wigs XIV. trugen die wichtigsten Herren Schuhe mit
hohen Absätzen. Frauen wie Männer fanden
die neuen, hohen Modelle attraktiv und repräsenta-
tiv. Dazu bemerkt Giorgio Riello: „Im 17. und 18.
Jahrhundert stand der hohe Absatz noch für Reichtum, Macht und hohen Rang in einer hierarchischen
Gesellschaft; sexuelle Konnotationen kamen erst
eingangs des 19. Jahrhunderts hinzu. Hohe Absätze vergrößerten nicht nur die körperliche Statur,
sie waren auch Zeichen einer selbst auferlegten
‚Mobilitätseinschränkung'. Nur Angehörige der
Oberschicht – Männer wie Frauen – konnten Schuhe
tragen, die eindeutig die Unfähigkeit zu gehen
signalisierten."[4]

Herrenschuhe mit hohem Absatz waren anderer Machart als Damenschuhe und wurden von
anderen Schuhmachern gefertigt. Herrenabsätze
waren eckig und robust, Damenabsätze hingegen
meist höher, schmaler und konisch, was zur Folge
hatte, dass man sie mit einem unsicheren Gang
assoziierte. Obschon oft bespöttelt, wurde diese

Gehweise auch als erotisch empfunden. Ein Vers
aus der Mitte des 18. Jahrhunderts empfahl: „Steig
auf französische Absätze, wenn du zum Ball gehst –
diese Mode lässt dich taumeln und zeigt, dass du
zu fallen verstehst." Ein weiterer Effekt des hohen
Damenschuhs war, dass er den Fuß kleiner wirken
ließ, was weit verbreiteten Weiblichkeitsidealen
entsprach, wie sie etwa in Perraults (1695) und der
späteren Grimm'schen Version des Märchens vom
„Aschenputtel" zum Ausdruck kamen.

Die Gleichsetzung von High Heels mit ero-
tischer Weiblichkeit war ein Wendepunkt im
Schuhdesign. Von nun an sollte die Schuhmode
wie auch die Mode insgesamt klar nach Geschlech-
tern getrennte Wege gehen. Als beispielsweise um
1800 die Damenschuhmode von hohen Schuhen zu
flachen Slippern wechselte, kamen bei den Herren
Stiefel im Militärstil auf, gleichsam als Symbole für
die zarte Frau beziehungsweise den starken Mann.
George Sand erinnerte sich in ihrer Autobiografie
an die fragilen französischen Schuhe der 1830er-
Jahre: „Aber auf dem Pariser Pflaster befand ich
mich wie ein Kahn zwischen Eisschollen. Die fei-
nen Schuhe waren in zwei Tagen zerrissen." Bald
begann sie sich wie ein Mann zu kleiden: „Wie sehr
ich mich über die Stiefel freute, vermag ich gar nicht
zu sagen … Mit den kleinen eisenbeschlagenen Absätzen hatte ich einen sicheren Schritt und lief von
einem Ende der Stadt zum anderen."[5]

Im Lauf des 19. und frühen 20. Jahrhunderts
wurden modische Schuhe durch die Industrialisierung

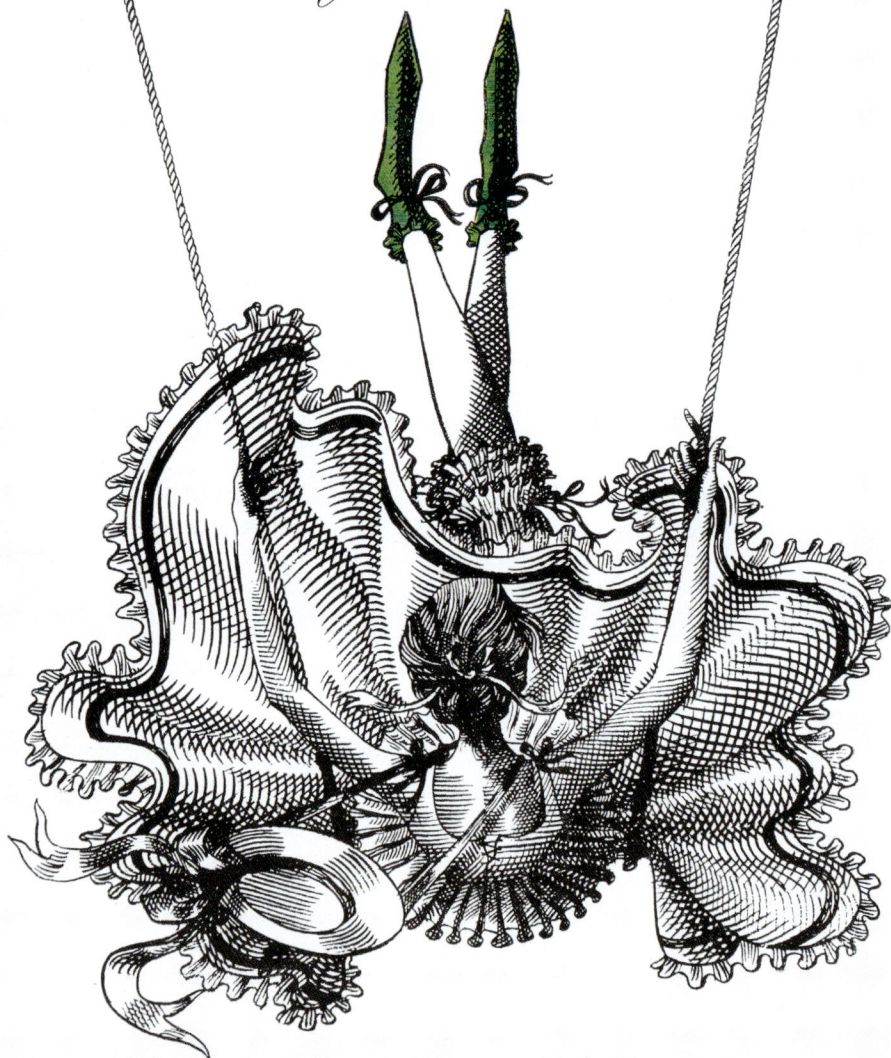

Christian Dior

Souliers créés par

Roger Vivier

En vente à la Boutique : 3o, Avenue Montaigne, Paris - Ély. 93-64

leichter verfügbar, und Frauen gelangten an ein vielfältigeres Angebot von Schuhvarianten – Straßenstiefel und Abendschuhe, hohe Absätze und flache. Auch die Herren erweiterten ihre Garderobe und trugen nun Schuhe und Stiefel mit Schnürung oder seitlicher Knöpfung, ein Trend, der bald auch die Damenschuhmode beeinflusste. Die industrielle Gummiherstellung ermöglichte die Entwicklung von Sportschuhen – einer neuen Kategorie von Fußbekleidung mit Gummisohlen, die Männer wie Frauen zunächst für Sportarten wie Tennis trugen, dann immer öfter auch in anderen Situationen des modernen Lebens.

In unserer heutigen Wahrnehmung hat Fußbekleidung nach wie vor einen deutlichen Geschlechterbezug. Ende des 20. Jahrhunderts durchgeführte Studien zeigen, dass wir dazu neigen, Schuhe als entweder „feminin und sexy", „maskulin", „geschlechtslos und unelegant" oder „jung und leger" zu kategorisieren. High Heels werden klar der Kategorie feminin und sexy zugeordnet, ebenso Riemchensandalen, Pumps und hohe Stiefel. Oxford-Schuhe und Cowboystiefel gelten als maskulin. Geschlechtsneutrale Schuhe wie Schuhe für Pflegepersonal oder Business-Pumps mögen zwar relativ bequem sein, sind aber auch absolut unmodisch. Zur Kategorie jung und leger zählen etwa Flip-Flops und Clogs.[6]

Tom Ford sprach für viele, als er sagte: „Es ist schwer, in High Heels nicht sexy zu sein." Bereits in den 1780er-Jahren zum Fetisch erhoben, spielen High Heels auch heute eine bedeutende Rolle in sexuellen Fantasien. Im Paris der 1930er-Jahre produzierte und verkaufte die Firma Diana Slip Kleidung und Schuhe für Fetischisten und Sexarbeiterinnen. In den 1970er-Jahren nahmen Fetischschuhe und -stiefel bereits merklichen Einfluss auf die Schuhmode. Zudem richteten Modefotografen wie Helmut Newton ihren Fokus auf die sexuell starke, „phallische Frau". In den 1990er-Jahren nahm auch die Couture-Mode immer stärker Bezug auf die Fetischästhetik, die mittlerweile häufig als Ausdruck weiblicher Selbstbestimmung interpretiert wird.

Natürlich hat die Mode schon oft mit dem Vermischen maskuliner und femininer Signifikanten gespielt. So beruhen etwa Bella Freuds Oxford-Pumps von 1998 auf einem klassischen männlichen Prototyp, werden aber durch hohe Absätze und leuchtendes Rot „verweiblicht". In der Auffassung von Kleidung und Geschlecht gibt es auch kulturelle Unterschiede. Die Reaktion einer brasilianischen

Journalistin auf ein Paar Birkenstock-Sandalen, ausgestellt in der MFIT-Schau *Shoes: A Lexicon of Style* (1999), war Entsetzen: „Keine lateinamerikanische Frau würde solche Schuhe tragen!"

Schuhmacher gibt es schon seit Jahrtausenden, doch Schuhdesigner traten erst zu Beginn des 20. Jahrhunderts in Erscheinung. Der gebürtige Italiener André Perugia lernte das Schuhmacherhandwerk von seinem Vater, um anschließend für Paul Poiret und andere Pariser Couturiers Schuhe zu fertigen. Salvatore Ferragamo absolvierte eine Schuhmacherlehre, ehe er nach Hollywood ging, um Schuhe für Filmstars zu entwerfen. Roger Vivier gilt als Erfinder des Stilettoabsatzes, den er in den frühen 1950er-Jahren in seiner Zeit bei Christian Dior entwickelte. Manolo Blahník und Christian Louboutin wurden in den 1990er-Jahren weltberühmt – noch heute sprechen Frauen stolz von ihren Manolos, und das ikonische Rot der Louboutin-Sohle wird von jedermann erkannt. Heutzutage gibt es viele Schuhdesigner, manche von ihnen sind unter eigenem Namen berühmt, manche kooperieren mit Modelabels. Auch Zaha Hadid und andere Architekten haben sich spielerisch mit dem Schuhdesign auseinandergesetzt.

Ob Schuhe nun Kunst sind oder nicht, bei Künstlern von Vincent van Gogh bis Andy Warhol waren sie ein beliebtes Motiv. Besonders fasziniert das Werk von Sylvie Fleury, befasst es sich doch mit dem weiblichen Verlangen nach Luxusschuhen und führt uns vor Augen, dass die Schuhbegeisterung unserer Zeit wie auch der steigende Schuhkonsum eine dem globalen Modesystem immanente Form von Produktfetischismus sein könnte, wobei dieses System seinerseits ein auffälliges Element des Kapitalismus unserer Zeit ist. Doch Fleurys Werk impliziert auch einen emotionalen, ja erotischen Subtext dieser Sehnsucht der Frauen nach Schuhen. Sollte das sexueller Fetischismus sein, so scheint er sich allerdings grundlegend von männlicher Schuhlust zu unterscheiden. Wie jüngere Studien nahelegen, ist der Schuhfetischismus bei Männern eng mit Fantasievorstellungen von der phallischen Frau verknüpft, wohingegen das weibliche Verlangen nach Schuhen mit einem präödipalen Gefühl von Sehnsucht nach einer verlorenen Einheit mit der Mutter zusammenhängen könnte.[7] Mit anderen Worten wollen die meisten Frauen vermutlich keinen Schuhschrank voller Phallussymbole, sondern können – genau wie fetischliebende Männer – Verlangen mit Anderssein in Bezug setzen.

Wie Kuratoren und Konservatoren wissen, können historische Kleider entzückend sein, alte und „abgetragene" Schuhe jedoch ziemlich unansehnlich – mit verschmutztem Oberstoff oder aufgeplatztem, verformtem Leder, das die Füße der Träger ausgeleiert haben. Andererseits lässt sich ein gut erhaltener Schuh wesentlich leichter ausstellen als ein Kleidungsstück, für das eine Schaufenster- oder Schneiderpuppe benötigt wird. Schuhe können von alleine stehen. Das mag ein Grund sein, weshalb sie uns ansprechen – wir können sie bewundern wie kleine, schöne Skulpturen.

Schuhe können auch *für* jemanden stehen, und das ist wohl ein bedeutender Grund, weshalb sie uns so wichtig sind. In Holocaust-Museen sind die zu Haufen aufgetürmten Schuhe der Ermordeten zu sehen. Als leere Behältnisse machen sie die Abwesenheit ihrer Träger eindringlich bewusst. Doch selbst im persönlichen Bereich werden bestimmte Schuhe, Babyschuhe etwa, liebevoll aufbewahrt (sogar bronziert!), weil sie Erinnerungen verkörpern. Ein Paar Schühchen, gefertigt etwa um 1900, beweist durch seine leicht abgenutzten Sohlen, dass es von einem Kleinkind getragen wurde. Auch Hochzeitsschuhe werden häufig aufbewahrt, zur Erinnerung an eine Erfahrung im eigenen Lebenslauf, die einen neuen Lebensabschnitt markiert.

Pierre Cardins Schuhe mit ausgeformten Zehen erinnern nicht nur an Magrittes berühmtes surrealistisches Gemälde *Die Philosophie im Boudoir*, sie thematisieren auch das wenig untersuchte Verhältnis zwischen Schuh und Fuß. Füßen und Schuhen haftet etwas Niedriges an, da sie den Boden berühren und schmutzig werden. In vielen Kulturen zieht man vor Betreten eines Hauses oder Tempels die Schuhe aus und eventuell Pantoffeln an.

Die in der englischen Sprache gängige Redewendung „barefoot and pregnant" (barfuß und schwanger) wird mit weiblicher Armut und Ohnmacht in Verbindung gebracht, denn eine Ehefrau in diesem Zustand wurde Anfang des 20. Jahrhunderts als Garant für eine gefügige, zu Hause bleibende Frau ohne eigenes Einkommen gepriesen. Der „barfüßige Junge" dagegen hat etwas Nostalgisches. Nackte Füße werden als „natürlich" angesehen, „künstliche" Schuhe folglich mit Kultur und sämtlichen Facetten des Unbehagens assoziiert, die sie mit sich bringt. Einige neuere Schuhlabels versprechen vollmundig, ihr Fabrikat zu tragen, fühle sich an wie barfuß zu gehen, und bei Sandalen macht das Maß, in dem sie den Fuß entblößen, einen Teil ihres Reizes aus.

Auch das Verhältnis der Schuhe zum Körper als Ganzem ist von Bedeutung, zuallererst, weil sie die Art, wie wir stehen und gehen, beeinflussen. In High Heels bewegen wir uns auf eine Art, in Militärstiefeln auf eine andere. Turnschuhe eignen sich gut für sportliche Aktivitäten, doch einige Sneaker-Typen sind speziell für den Laufsport gedacht. Zudem ordnen wir die diversen Merkmale eines Schuhs verschiedenen Körperzonen zu, etwa, wenn wir vom „Zehen-Dekolleté" sprechen oder Slingpumps als „Fuck me"-Schuhe bezeichnen. Selbst die geringe Größe von Aschenputtels Schuhen stellt eine Überspitzung des menschlichen Sexualdimorphismus dar.

Schuhe werden seit Langem mit sozioökonomischem Status assoziiert, worauf Redensarten wie „in weiten Schuhen gehen" oder „die Schuhe mit Bast binden" hindeuten. Im Frankreich des 18. Jahrhunderts gingen die Armen oft barfuß oder trugen Holzschuhe, was der Schriftsteller François-René de Chateaubriand in seiner Schilderung der Französischen Revolution als Metapher verwendete: „Die Leute in Schuhen standen auf dem Punkte, den Saal zu verlassen, und schon klopften die Holzschuhe an die Tür."[8]

Statusunterschiede in der Fußbekleidung haben sich weiterentwickelt, doch es gibt sie nach wie vor. Bis vor Kurzem bevorzugten vermögende Schichten meist Maßschuhe, die individuell an den Fuß des Trägers angepasst werden. Heute sind Schuhe größtenteils konfektioniert, selbst im Hochpreissegment. Materialqualität und Verarbeitung sind weiterhin wichtig, aber ebenso der Status des Modelabels und die – mitunter künstlich generierte – „Knappheit" des Schuhs. Besonders wichtig ist Exklusivität bei Herrensneakers.

Als Colleen Hill und ich 2013 *Shoe Obsession* realisierten, ging der Trend gerade zu extrem hohen Absätzen und noch höheren Preisen. „Warum sind Designerschuhe auf einmal so verdammt teuer?", fragte die Bloggerin Jenna Saunders. Natürlich gab es wirtschaftliche Gründe für diesen Trend. Die Modeunternehmen hatten mit Designerhandtaschen ordentlich Kasse gemacht und verlegten sich nun auf ein neues lukratives Accessoire. (Neben Schuhen und Handtaschen gibt es nicht mehr viele Accessoires von Belang. Selbst die früher so wichtigen Hüte sind heute weitgehend auf bloße Funktionalität reduziert.) Tatsache war aber auch, dass Preise von bis zu 1 000 Dollar oder mehr für ein Paar Designerschuhe, also doppelt so viel wie nur wenige Jahre zuvor, viele Frauen unbeeindruckt ließen.[9]

Bella Freud
Oxford pumps: Red faux
alligator, ochre leather
England, 1998

Auch gesammelt wurden Schuhe lange Zeit vorwiegend von Frauen. Wer jedoch heute „Schuhsammlungen" recherchiert, stößt auf einen wachsenden Stamm männlicher „Sneaker-Verrückter" – die nicht einfach beliebige Sneaker sammeln, sondern rare Modelle aus Sondereditionen. Der Aufstieg des Sneakers zum Statussymbol der Herrengarderobe begann Mitte der 1980er-Jahre, als dieser Schuhtyp immer enger mit Sportstars verknüpft wurde, etwa im Fall der Basketball-legende Michael Jordan, der den „Air Jordans" von Nike zu Ruhm verhalf, oder mit Rappern wie Run-DMC, deren Song „My Adidas" ein internationaler Hit wurde. An der Jahrtausendwende produzierten führende Modehäuser von Lanvin bis Dior bereits Sneaker für Damen und Herren. Auch Kooperationen mit Modedesignern wie Raf Simons oder Prominenten wie Kanye West fanden großen Anklang, insbesondere bei Männern.

Die Kuratorin Elizabeth Semmelhack bemerkt: „Sneaker werden heute überall auf der Welt getragen und könnten in vielerlei Hinsicht als demokratischste Form der Fußbekleidung gelten. Doch Kommerzialisierung und Markenbildung haben einige davon in höchst gefragte Objekte der Begierde verwandelt, die in der Männermode eine immer zentralere Rolle spielen." Infolgedessen werden bestimmte Sneaker nicht nur mit „sportlicher Exzellenz" assoziiert, sondern auch mit „Exklusivität ... und im Wandel begriffenen Männlichkeitsmodellen".[10]

Die Turnschuhe von einst mögen als Teil der Freizeitkleidung aller jungen Leute betrachtet worden sein, doch die Sneaker von heute gelten aufgrund ihres starken Bezugs zum Profisport und der urbanen Kultur meist als maskulines Phänomen. Aber auch bei Frauen ist das mit Sneakers verbundene Mehr an Mobilität, Tragekomfort und Coolness gefragt. Phoebe Philos Label Celine landete mit Damensneakers einen Megaerfolg, und Rihannas Modemarke Fenty kooperiert mit Puma.

Genau wie die Modesammlung des MFIT ist auch unsere Schuhsammlung überwiegend modern und zeitgenössisch, wobei Designermode einen Schwerpunkt bildet. Zwar umfasst sie auch außergewöhnliche japanische Stücke, die zwischen Design und Kunst anzusiedeln sind, doch mehrheitlich stammen die Exponate des Museums aus Europa und den USA, wobei Damenschuhe 90 Prozent des Bestandes ausmachen. Die Sammlungen einiger spezialisierter Schuhmuseen umfassen mittelalterliche Poulaines und Renaissance-Chopines, altägyptische Totensandalen und Schuhe aus aller Welt. Wir aber konzentrieren uns beim weiteren Ausbau unserer Sammlung eher auf unsere Stärke – moderne Fußbekleidung – und bemühen uns zugleich, die wichtigsten Lücken zu schließen, speziell bei Sneakers, die sich als wohl wichtigster Typus zeitgenössischer Fußbekleidung entpuppt haben.

Schuhe werden seit Langem gesammelt und in Museen gezeigt. Auch Schuhausstellungen sind seit den 1970er-Jahren verbreitet, kamen jedoch erst in

Birkenstock
Sandal: Taupe
suede, cork
Germany, 1999

FOLLOWING
A model poses in a pair
of two-foot-high (61 cm)
white go-go boots,
ca. 1964.

jüngster Zeit regelrecht in Mode. Wie einer unserer Museumsaufseher stolz vermeldete: „Miss Val, die Leute lieben einfach Schuhe!" Manche Leute tun das gewiss, andere sind eher unentschieden, und oft tragen Schuhausstellungen zweideutige Titel wie *Shoes: Pleasure and Pain* (Schuhe: Lust und Schmerz) oder *Killer Heels* (Mörderabsätze). In ihrem Aufsatz über das Bata-Schuhmuseum in Toronto merkte die Wissenschaftlerin Julia Emberley an, dass Schuhsammlungen und -ausstellungen „die Frage der Grenze zwischen Schuhen als Ware und Schuhen als kulturellem oder ästhetischem Artefakt aufwerfen"[11].

Ob sie vor 40 000 Jahren bei den Neandertalern entstanden oder vor rund 10 000 Jahren beim Homo sapiens, Schuhe begleiten uns seit sehr langer Zeit. Unbedingt notwendig sind sie jedoch nicht, sieht man von extremen Bedingungen wie etwa sehr kaltem Klima ab. Sobald es sie aber gab, unterschied man zwischen Menschen mit und ohne Schuhen, Menschen mit feinem und Menschen mit einfachem Schuhwerk. Wie der Rückblick auf die Entwicklungsgeschichte von Kleidung und Mode verdeutlicht, ist die Funktionalität bei Kleidung (abgesehen von sehr wenigen Ausnahmen wie warmen Winterschuhen oder robusten Stiefel für Soldaten) wesentlich weniger wichtig als das, was sie aussagt.

„Schuhe beeinflussen unsere Fremdwahrnehmung und unsere Selbstwahrnehmung", schreibt Russell W. Belk. Seinen Studien zufolge glauben die meisten Amerikaner, dass „ihre Fußbekleidung eine Erweiterung und ein Ausdruck ihrer selbst ist". Schuhe vermitteln, so die Ansicht, wichtige Informationen über Alter, Geschlecht, sozialen Status, Sexualität, Ethnizität, Geschmack und Persönlichkeit ihres Trägers. Insbesondere für Jugendliche „sind Schuhe ein elementarer Ausdruck der eigenen Identität". Viele Menschen halten es sogar für möglich, dass Schuhe sie „auf wundersame Weise verwandeln können". Entsprechend den „starken Anteilen, die der magische Glaube bei unserer Sicht auf Schuhe hat", glauben Menschen nicht nur, dass Schuhe ihre Erscheinung oder ihre Sportlichkeit verändern werden, sondern sogar, dass sie ihr „Leben von Grund auf verändern"[12].

Schuhe haben für uns einen Wert, weil wir glauben, dass sie wichtige Informationen darüber liefern, wer wir sind – und wer wir sein könnten. In der Vergangenheit war die Identität des Einzelnen im Wesentlichen auf seine gesellschaftliche Stellung beschränkt, während sie heute subjektiver definiert wird. Dass Schuhe seit einigen Jahrzehnten an Bedeutung gewinnen, liegt hauptsächlich an Entwicklungen im Modesystem, die in einer größeren Vielfalt an Schuhtypen resultierten, und diese Vielfalt beeinflusst uns im Konsum der Objekte, mit denen wir unsere individuelle Identität modellieren: Manolo oder Nike? Ballerina oder Birkenstock? Welcher Schuh sind Sie?

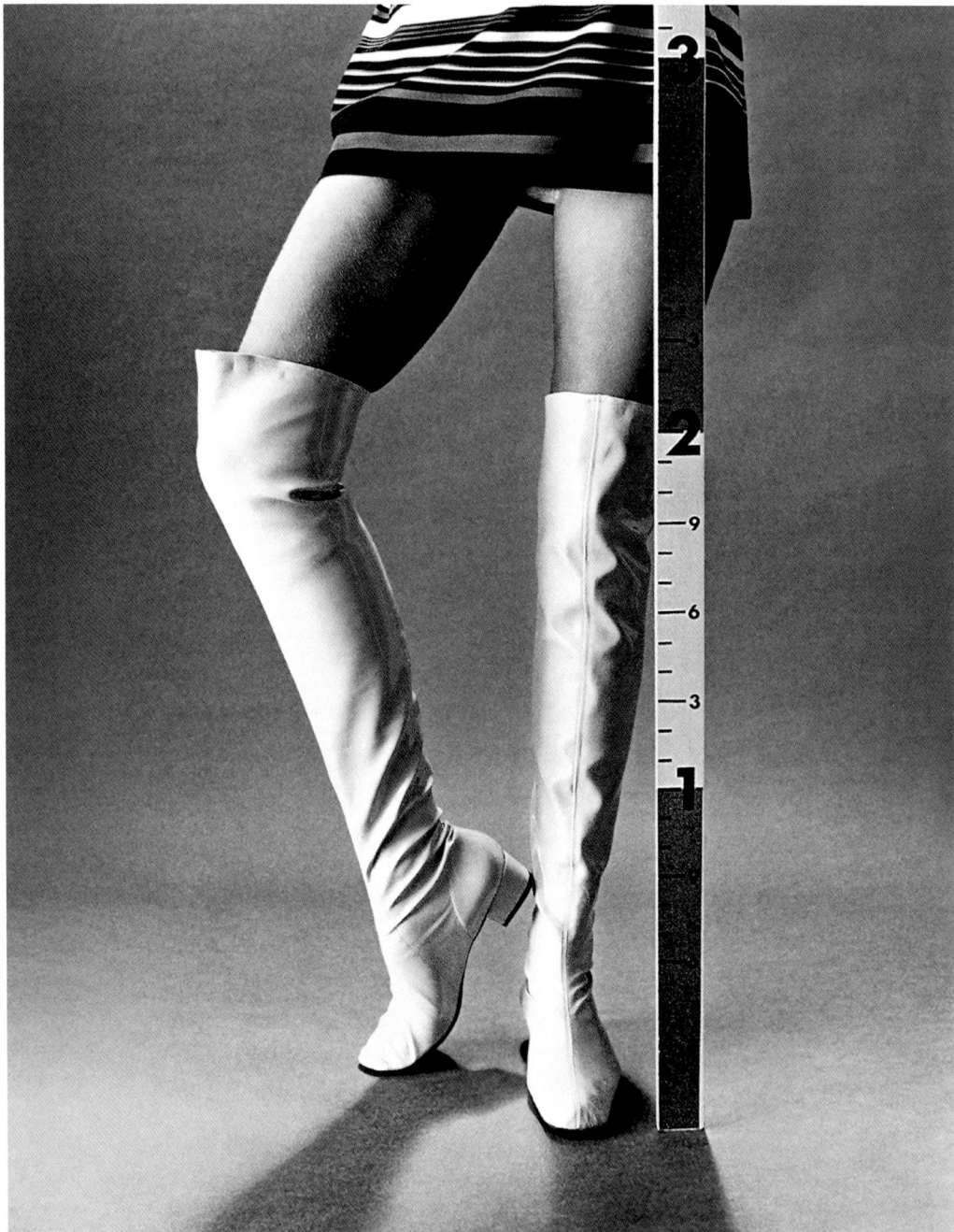

Le pouvoir d'attraction des chaussures

Valerie Steele

DEPUIS QU'ON A VU LE personnage de Carrie Bradshaw collectionner les chaussures de luxe dans la série *Sex and the City*, la culture populaire est obsédée par la « relation intime des femmes » avec les souliers[1]. « Était-ce une obsession ? » interrogeait en 2001 la légende d'une publicité pour la carte Citibank AAdvantage montrant la photo d'une collection de chaussures pour dame. Lors de « Shoe Obsession (2013) », l'une des expositions les plus visitées du musée du Fashion Institute of Technology (FIT) présentant plus d'une centaine de paires parmi les plus extrêmes, extravagantes et onéreuses du XXIᵉ siècle, j'ai entendu une visiteuse s'exclamer : « Je dois être morte, car me voilà au paradis des chaussures ! »

Les gens sont fascinés par les chaussures. Dès que je parle de la collection du musée du FIT, qui comprend plus de 50 000 vêtements et accessoires des plus grands créateurs de mode internationaux, c'est toujours le chiffre des *4 000 paires de chaussures* qui suscite le plus d'enthousiasme.

Les chaussures jouent un rôle important dans la société humaine depuis des millénaires, mais l'intérêt qu'elles inspirent semble s'être considérablement accru au cours des dernières décennies. Évidemment, les gens en achètent davantage : en 1995, on estimait que l'Américaine moyenne possédait douze paires de chaussures contre six pour l'Américain moyen. Aujourd'hui, la femme américaine en posséderait entre vingt-sept et trente contre douze pour ces messieurs. Certaines femmes surpassent largement cette moyenne et possèdent des centaines de paires, quelques plus rares collections se chiffrant en milliers, bien que l'ex-Première dame des Philippines Imelda Marcos ait fini par admettre que sa tristement célèbre collection comptait « non pas 3 000, mais 1 060 paires de chaussures ».

Le livre que vous tenez entre les mains présente quelque 400 paires de chaussures parmi les plus remarquables de la collection du musée du FIT, entre pièces historiques et modèles contemporains de créateurs de chaussures et de mode, d'Azzedine Alaïa à Roger Vivier en passant par Manolo Blahník et Vivienne Westwood.

Avant de les présenter plus en détail, nous nous pencherons sur l'importance accordée aux chaussures depuis la préhistoire, dans la vie quotidienne, comme dans l'imaginaire culturel. Selon le paléoanthropologue Daniel E. Lieberman, « les gens portent des chaussures depuis probablement 40 000 ans, bien que certains pensent que les Néandertaliens marchaient pieds nus ». Il semble « inimaginable » qu'ils aient pu marcher sans chaussures en Europe pendant la période glaciaire, a-t-il ainsi expliqué au magazine *Scientific American*, mais « nos cousins, les Néandertaliens, le supportaient peut-être sans problème »[2]. Si la période glaciaire imposait probablement de se protéger les pieds, aujourd'hui, dans des pays comme l'Inde et le Kenya, beaucoup de gens vivent pieds nus... ce qui, selon certaines études scientifiques, est bénéfique pour la santé.

Toujours est-il qu'au Néolithique (10 000 à 2 000 av. J.-C.), les habitants de nombreuses régions du globe portaient des sandales et des chaussures en paille, en écorce, en feuille de papyrus ou de yucca, en cuir, en fourrure ou en bois. Les musées du monde entier exposent des chaussures mises au jour sur les sites archéologiques. Le musée d'Histoire de l'Arménie possède la chaussure Areni-1, un soulier en cuir vieux de 5 500 ans trouvé dans un état quasi

Chanel
"Miami Vice"
pumps: Black satin,
plastic, metal
France, cruise 2009

intact dans une grotte du pays, et le musée privé SONS (Shoes or No Shoes) de Kruishoutem, en Belgique, conserve dans ses collections une paire de sandales en feuilles de yucca tressées encore plus ancienne : découverte dans le sud-ouest des États-Unis, elle aurait été fabriquée il y a 10 000 ans.

Préservés dans un glacier pendant 5 300 ans, les mocassins et les vêtements d'Ötzi, l'homme des glaces, sont aujourd'hui exposés au musée Archéologique du Haut-Adige à Bolzano, en Italie. D'après les experts qui ont travaillé sur leur reconstitution, les chaussures – faites de cuir de cerf (fourrure côté intérieur), d'un maillage en corde et garnies d'herbes séchées – étaient assez efficaces pour garder les pieds au chaud tout en les protégeant du terrain accidenté et des conditions climatiques extrêmes des Alpes.

Cependant, une plus grande mobilité et la protection contre les intempéries – ce pour quoi les chaussures ont été inventées à l'origine – ne sont évidemment pas les seules raisons d'en porter. Et peut-être même pas les raisons les plus importantes.

Pendant la majeure partie de l'histoire récente de l'humanité, les chaussures sont restées l'apanage d'une élite minoritaire. Sous l'Empire romain, par exemple, les cordonniers professionnels créaient des souliers décorés avec raffinement pour les patriciens des deux sexes, tandis que les plébéiens portaient des modèles basiques. Quant aux esclaves, il leur était formellement interdit d'en porter.

Au XVIIIᵉ siècle en Haïti, où la majorité de la population noire était réduite en esclavage, les Noirs affranchis n'avaient pas non plus le droit de porter de chaussures. Les soldats romains portaient des sandales lacées aux épaisses semelles cloutées qui facilitaient la marche sur les terrains difficiles, mais leur servaient également d'armes.

Comme les chaussures étaient symboliquement associées au mouvement et au voyage, Hermès-Mercure, le dieu gréco-romain des voyageurs, était toujours représenté chaussé de bottes ou de sandales ailées, mais dans toutes les cultures, les souliers qui *réduisent* la mobilité comptaient pourtant parmi les plus prestigieux. Dès le premier siècle avant notre ère, Aphrodite, déesse grecque de l'amour et de la beauté, était représentée avec des chaussures à semelles compensées, un style probablement originaire de Perse. Bien que les hommes aient parfois porté des modèles extravagants, par exemple les poulaines de l'époque médiévale (de très longues chaussures pointues), l'histoire fournit de nombreux autres exemples de souliers féminins qui entravaient la marche, des minuscules chaussures chinoises (pour pieds bandés) aux chopines vénitiennes (modèles à très hautes semelles compensées portés par les courtisanes).

On a longtemps pensé que les talons hauts, qui ont fait leur apparition en Europe à la fin du XVIᵉ siècle, venaient des chopines. Or, ainsi que l'avance de façon pertinente Elizabeth Semmelhack, « la rapide adoption du talon par les hommes de

Christian Louboutin
"Lady Peep" pumps:
Red python snakeskin
France, 2012

FOLLOWING
In an homage to
Michelangelo's *The
Creation of Adam*,
a cherub reaches from
the heavens to touch
the golden heel of a
Jourdan pump. 1980s.

haut rang indique qu'il ne s'agissait pas d'une variante de la chopine, alors très genrée [...]. En réalité, le talon trouve son origine au Proche-Orient, où les hommes en portaient depuis des siècles avec les tenues équestres et militaires ». Quand la Perse et la France se sont alliées contre l'Empire ottoman, les talons sont soudain devenus à la mode chez les hommes de l'aristocratie européenne, notamment parce qu'ils permettaient de maintenir « les pieds du cavalier dans les étriers[3] »

Au début du XVIIe siècle, les Européens de la haute société arboraient des bottes cavalières à talons et des souliers à talons bottiers. Quand le reste de la population a commencé à s'approprier ce nouveau talon, les riches et les aristocrates ont alors adopté les talons *hauts*. À la cour de Louis XIV, les hommes les plus importants étaient juchés sur de hauts talons de couleur rouge. Les femmes, comme les hommes, trouvaient ces nouveaux talons beaux et prestigieux. « Aux XVIIe et XVIIIe siècles, les talons hauts étaient synonymes de richesse, de pouvoir et de supériorité au sein d'une société hiérarchisée ; ils ne possédaient pas encore les connotations sexuelles qu'ils allaient avoir au début du XIXe siècle », observe Giorgio Riello. « Les talons hauts permettaient non seulement de se grandir physiquement, mais ils étaient aussi le signe d'une "mobilité contrainte" volontaire. Seuls les membres des classes supérieures, hommes et femmes confondus, pouvaient porter des souliers qui symbolisaient clairement l'incapacité de marcher[4]. »

Les hommes et les femmes portaient différents types de chaussures à talons hauts qui n'étaient pas fabriqués par les mêmes cordonniers. Les talons masculins étaient carrés et robustes, tandis que ceux des femmes avaient tendance à être plus hauts, plus étroits et fuselés. Ces derniers ont donc fini par être associés à la démarche instable qui, bien que souvent moquée, était aussi considérée comme érotique, comme l'illustre ce poème du milieu du XVIIIe siècle : « Monte sur des talons français pour aller au bal, / C'est la mode de chanceler et de montrer que tu peux tomber. » Sur les femmes, les talons hauts créaient également l'illusion d'un pied plus petit correspondant aux canons de beauté de l'époque comme l'exprime, par exemple, le conte de fées *Cendrillon* (1695) de Charles Perrault.

L'association des talons hauts avec la féminité érotique a marqué un tournant dans l'histoire de la cordonnerie. Comme la mode en général, les souliers masculins et féminins allaient dorénavant emprunter des chemins différents aux distinctions de genre très nettes. En 1800, par exemple, quand la mode pour femme est passée des talons hauts aux chaussons plats, les hommes étaient de plus en plus nombreux à adopter les bottes d'inspiration militaire, les premiers symbolisant la délicatesse et les secondes, le pouvoir. Dans son autobiographie, George Sand évoque la fragilité des chaussures françaises des années 1830 : « Sur le pavé de Paris, j'étais comme un bateau sur la glace. Les fines chaussures craquaient en deux jours. » C'est alors qu'elle a commencé à s'habiller comme un homme : « Je ne peux pas dire quel plaisir me firent mes bottes [...]. Avec ces petits talons ferrés, j'étais solide sur le trottoir. Je voltigeais d'un bout de Paris à l'autre[5]. »

Tout au long du XIXe siècle et au début du XXe siècle, l'industrialisation a démocratisé les chaussures à la mode et les femmes ont eu accès à un plus large choix de modèles à talons hauts et plats, des bottes de marche aux chaussures de soirée. Les hommes aussi ont diversifié leur vestiaire de souliers, adoptant des chaussures et bottes lacées et boutonnées sur le côté qui devaient rapidement influencer les modèles pour femme. La vulcanisation du caoutchouc a permis de créer les « tennis » : une nouvelle catégorie de souliers à semelles en caoutchouc portés par les hommes et les femmes, d'abord pour la pratique de sports comme le tennis, puis progressivement pour d'autres activités de la vie moderne.

Aujourd'hui, les chaussures sont toujours perçues comme très genrées. Des recherches menées à la fin du XXe siècle indiquent que les gens ont tendance à les classer dans des catégories telles que « féminines et sexy », « masculines », « pas sexy et vieux jeu » ou « jeunes et décontractées ». Les talons hauts sont résolument vus comme féminins et sexy, à l'instar des sandales à lanières, des escarpins et des bottes hautes, tandis que les richelieus et les santiags sont considérés comme masculins. Les modèles « pas sexy », comme les chaussures d'infirmière et les ballerines, sont sans doute très confortables, mais tout sauf à la mode. Les claquettes et les sabots sont en revanche actuellement considérés comme jeunes et décontractés[6].

Tom Ford s'est fait l'expression de la majorité en affirmant qu'il est « difficile de ne pas être sexy en talons hauts ». Fétichisés depuis les années 1780, les talons hauts continuent à jouer un rôle important dans les fantasmes sexuels. Dans les années 1930, l'entreprise parisienne Diana Slip fabriquait et vendait des vêtements et des chaussures pour fétichistes et prostituées. Dans les années 1970, les souliers et bottes de fétichisme ont commencé à exercer une influence sur la mode. Des photographes tels Helmut Newton ont aussi mis en avant l'image d'une « femme phallique » sexuellement puissante. Dans les années 1990, la mode de luxe utilisait de plus en plus l'esthétique fétichiste, que l'on tend aujourd'hui à interpréter comme une expression du pouvoir féminin.

Évidemment, la mode s'est souvent amusée à mélanger les signifiants masculins et féminins. Par exemple, les richelieus Bella Freud de 1998 s'inspirent d'un prototype masculin classique, mais sont féminisées par des talons hauts et une couleur rouge vif. Il existe aussi des différences culturelles en termes d'habillement et de genre. « Aucune Latina ne porterait ce genre de chaussures ! » s'est exclamée une journaliste brésilienne horrifiée par une paire de Birkenstock pendant la visite de l'exposition « Shoes : A Lexicon of Style » (1999) au MFIT.

Si le métier de cordonnier existe depuis des millénaires, celui de créateur de chaussures n'est né qu'au début du XXe siècle. D'origine italienne, André Perugia a appris à faire des chaussures auprès de son père avant d'en créer pour Paul Poiret et d'autres couturiers parisiens. Salvatore Ferragamo a été l'apprenti d'un cordonnier avant de partir chausser les stars d'Hollywood. On dit que Roger Vivier a inventé le talon aiguille au début des années 1950 quand il travaillait pour Christian Dior. Manolo Blahník et Christian Louboutin sont devenus des célébrités internationales dans les années 1990 : les femmes sont toujours aussi fières de leurs « Manolos » et tout le monde connaît les semelles rouges emblématiques de Louboutin. On compte aujourd'hui de nombreux créateurs de chaussures, qu'ils soient célèbres sous leur propre nom ou associés à des marques de mode. Des architectes comme Zaha Hadid ont aussi flirté avec la création de chaussures.

Que les chaussures soient ou non des œuvres d'art, elles demeurent un sujet de prédilection pour les artistes, de Vincent Van Gogh à Andy Warhol. L'œuvre de Sylvie Fleury est particulièrement captivante en ceci qu'elle s'intéresse au désir des femmes pour les chaussures de luxe, nous rappelant que notre fascination contemporaine pour ces objets et la consommation croissante que nous en faisons relèvent peut-être d'une sorte de fétichisme matérialiste inhérent au système mondial de la mode, qui est lui-même inhérent au capitalisme contemporain. Pourtant, le travail de Sylvie Fleury implique aussi un sous-texte psychologique, voire érotique au sujet de ce désir féminin pour les chaussures. Même en supposant qu'il s'agisse d'un fétichisme sexuel, il serait très différent de ce qui attire les hommes vers les chaussures. De récentes études suggèrent que si le fétichisme masculin est étroitement associé à des fantasmes de femmes phalliques, le désir de chaussures des femmes pourrait être lié à la nostalgie de l'unité préœdipienne perdue avec la mère[7]. Autrement dit, la plupart des femmes ne rêvent probablement pas d'un placard rempli de symboles phalliques, mais à l'instar des hommes fétichistes, elles peuvent associer le désir à la différence.

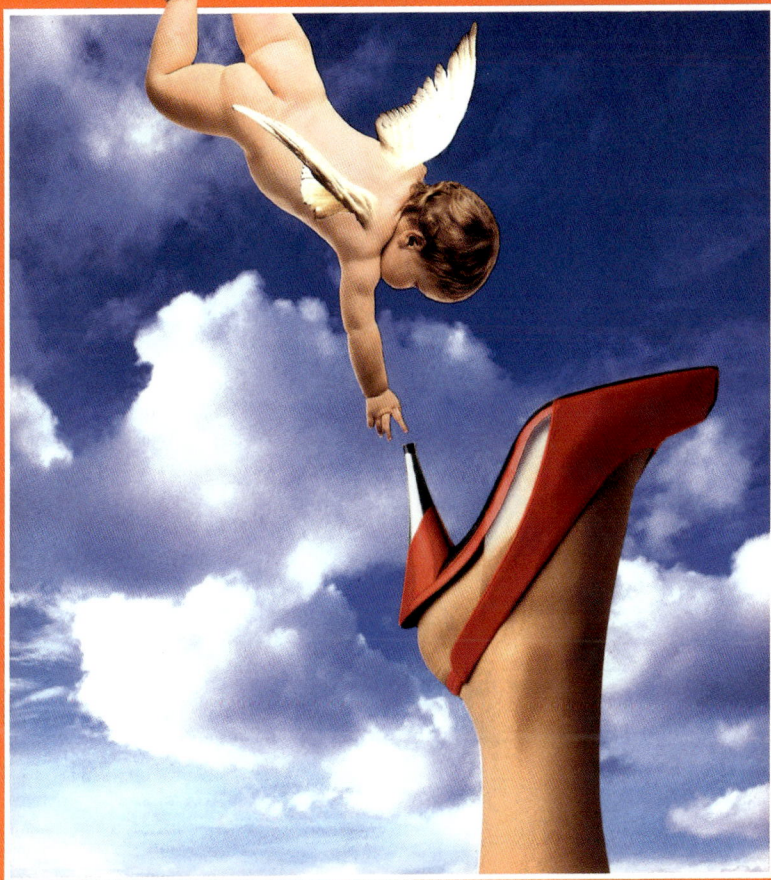

CHARLES JOURDAN
Paris

Fenty X Puma
Sneakers: Pink polyester
satin, rubber
Germany, 2017

Comme le savent les commissaires d'exposition et les conservateurs, aussi charmants que soient les vêtements historiques, les vieilles chaussures « usées » peuvent être assez laides, qu'elles aient été déformées par les pieds de leurs propriétaires, leur tissu sali ou leur cuir craquelé. En revanche, une chaussure en bon état est beaucoup plus facile à exposer qu'un vêtement, qui nécessitera toujours un mannequin ou un buste de tailleur. Les chaussures tiennent debout sans support. C'est peut-être l'une des raisons pour lesquelles elles nous attirent : on peut les admirer comme de sublimes petites sculptures.

Les chaussures peuvent aussi *représenter* quelqu'un et cela explique sans doute en partie pourquoi nous leur accordons une telle importance. Les différents musées de l'Holocauste exposent des piles de souliers confisqués aux victimes des camps de concentration. Leurs formes vides évoquent de façon poignante l'absence de leurs propriétaires. Dans la vie ordinaire aussi, on conserve certains souliers avec amour, par exemple les chaussures de bébé (parfois même sous une couche de bronze !), parce qu'ils symbolisent des souvenirs. Des semelles à peine usées sur une petite paire de chaussures datant des environs de 1900 prouvent qu'elle appartenait à un bambin. Les chaussures de mariage sont aussi souvent conservées comme souvenir d'un événement qui a marqué la vie d'un individu.

Les chaussures Pierre Cardin en forme de pied font écho au célèbre tableau surréaliste *Le Modèle*

rouge de Magritte tout en évoquant la relation rarement étudiée entre les souliers et les pieds. Les pieds et les chaussures sont souvent perçus comme répugnants parce qu'ils sont en contact avec le sol et se salissent. Dans de nombreuses cultures, les gens se déchaussent avant d'entrer dans une maison ou un temple, parfois pour enfiler une paire de chaussons d'intérieur.

Sur le plan linguistique, l'expression anglaise *barefoot and pregnant*, ou littéralement « pieds nus et enceinte », évoque la faiblesse et la vulnérabilité des femmes, alors qu'il y a quelque chose de nostalgique chez un « garçon aux pieds nus ». Les pieds nus étant considérés comme « naturels » et les chaussures comme « artificielles », celles-ci sont associées à la civilisation et à ses nombreux maux. Certaines nouvelles marques affirment que leurs chaussures donnent le sentiment de marcher pieds nus. L'attrait des sandales est en partie dû au fait qu'elles dénudent plus ou moins le pied.

Les chaussures font lien avec le corps, notamment parce qu'elles influencent notre posture et notre démarche. On ne se déplace pas de la même manière en talons hauts et dans des brodequins militaires. Si les tennis offrent une bonne mobilité, certaines sont spécifiquement conçues pour la course. Nous associons par ailleurs certaines parties de la chaussure à certains aspects du corps, par exemple quand on parle de « décolleté de pied » ou lorsque les anglophones qualifient de *fuck-me shoes* les chaussures ouvertes sur l'arrière du talon. Même

Brother Vellies
"Stell" mules: linen,
leather, and wood
USA, spring 2020

FOLLOWING
Grace Jones poses in
Manolo Blahník sling-
back heels, a zippered
motorcycle jacket, and
leather gloves for her
role as May Day in the
1985 James Bond film,
A View to a Kill.

la petite taille des souliers de Cendrillon est une exagération du dimorphisme sexuel humain.

Les chaussures sont depuis longtemps un marqueur social comme l'illustrent les expressions « talon rouge » ou « va-nu-pieds ». Dans la France du XVIIIᵉ siècle, à une époque où les pauvres marchaient souvent pieds nus ou en sabots de bois, Chateaubriand a utilisé une métaphore vestimentaire pour décrire la Révolution française : « Les gens à souliers étaient prêts à sortir des salons, et déjà les sabots heurtaient à la porte[8]. »

Les distinctions de classe associées aux chaussures ont certes évolué, mais elles subsistent. Jusqu'à une période récente, les riches se faisaient faire des souliers sur mesure. Aujourd'hui, la majorité des chaussures, même les plus chères, sont fabriquées en série. Pour les distinguer, la qualité des matières et le savoir-faire sont toujours des critères importants, tout comme le statut de la marque et la « rareté », parfois artificielle, du modèle. L'exclusivité revêt une importance particulière dans le domaine des sneakers pour homme.

Quand Colleen Hill et moi avons organisé l'exposition « Shoe Obsession » en 2013, la tendance était aux talons extrêmement hauts et à des prix toujours plus élevés. « Pourquoi les chaussures de créateurs sont-elles soudain devenues si chères ? » s'interrogeait la blogueuse Jenna Saunders. Cette tendance avait bien sûr une visée commerciale. Après avoir fait fortune avec les sacs à main, les créateurs de mode se sont tournés vers un nouvel accessoire lucratif.

(Les chaussures et les sacs à main sont les derniers accessoires importants : même les chapeaux, autrefois incontournables, sont largement réduits à leur fonction de base.) De nombreuses femmes étaient prêtes à débourser des sommes avoisinant ou surpassant les 1 000 dollars pour une seule paire de chaussures de créateur, soit un prix deux fois supérieur à ceux pratiqués quelques années plus tôt[9].

Ce sont principalement les femmes qui collectionnent les chaussures, mais si vous lancez aujourd'hui une recherche avec les mots-clés « collections de chaussures », vous découvrirez aussi un petit groupe croissant composé d'hommes « obsédés de sneakers » qui ne collectionnent pas n'importe quel modèle, mais uniquement les éditions limitées difficiles à trouver. Le rôle des sneakers en tant que marqueur social dans le vestiaire masculin remonte au milieu des années 1980, quand elles ont commencé à être de plus en plus associées à des sportifs aussi légendaires que Michael Jordan avec la Nike Air Jordan et à des rappeurs comme Run DMC, dont la chanson « My Adidas » a été un tube mondial. Au début du XXIᵉ siècle, les grandes Maisons de mode, de Lanvin à Dior, ont produit des sneakers pour homme et pour femme. Les collaborations des marques de baskets avec des créateurs de mode, par exemple Raf Simons, et des célébrités, dont Kanye West, ont aussi remporté beaucoup de succès, notamment auprès des hommes.

« Aujourd'hui, les sneakers sont portées dans le monde entier et peuvent être considérées comme les chaussures les plus démocratiques à de nombreux égards, mais la marchandisation et le *branding* ont imposé certains modèles comme des objets de désir très convoités occupant une place toujours plus centrale dans la mode masculine », remarque la conservatrice Elizabeth Semmelhack. Certaines sneakers sont donc non seulement associées à « l'exploit sportif », mais aussi à « l'exclusivité [...] et les constructions changeantes de la masculinité »[10].

Auparavant considérées comme des chaussures décontractées associées à la jeunesse, les sneakers sont désormais surtout genrées comme masculines, car relevant des sports professionnels et de la culture urbaine. Et pourtant, les femmes recherchent aussi le supplément de mobilité, de confort et de « coolitude » offert par les baskets. Sous la direction de Phoebe Philo, la Maison Celine a remporté un immense succès avec ses sneakers pour femme, et Fenty, la marque de mode de Rihanna, a collaboré avec Puma.

Principalement moderne et contemporaine, la collection de chaussures du MFIT, tout comme sa collection de mode, fait la part belle aux créateurs. Malgré la présence de modèles japonais extraordinaires, à mi-chemin entre art et design, la majorité des chaussures du musée provient d'Europe et des États-Unis. Les modèles pour femme représentent 90 % de la collection. Les collections de certains musées spécialisés comprennent des poulaines médiévales, des chopines de la Renaissance, des sandales funéraires d'Égypte ancienne et des souliers venus du monde entier. Pour notre part, si nous enrichissons sans cesse notre collection permanente, nous avons tendance à nous concentrer sur notre force - les souliers modernes - tout en cherchant à combler nos lacunes, notamment dans le domaine des sneakers qui sont probablement en passe de devenir les chaussures les plus importantes de notre époque.

Les chaussures figurent dans les collections des musées depuis longtemps. Quant aux expositions de chaussures, si elles drainent le grand public depuis les années 1970, elles prolifèrent depuis quelques années. « Miss Val, les gens adorent les chaussures, tout simplement ! » a un jour fièrement proclamé l'un des gardiens de notre musée. C'est assurément le cas de certaines personnes, mais d'autres sont plus partagées à l'instar des expositions aux titres parfois ambigus comme « Shoes : Pleasure and Pain » (« Chaussures : plaisir et souffrance ») ou « Killer Heels » (« Talons tueurs »). Comme l'a noté la spécialiste Julia Emberley dans un essai sur le Bata Shoe Museum, les collections et les expositions de chaussures « remettent en question la frontière entre la chaussure en tant marchandise et en tant qu'*artefact* culturel ou esthétique[11] ».

Que les chaussures aient été inventées par l'homme de Néandertal il y a 40 000 ans ou par *Homo sapiens* il y a environ 10 000 ans, elles nous accompagnent depuis très longtemps, et ce, alors même qu'elles ne nous sont pas absolument indispensables en dehors de conditions extrêmes telles qu'un climat très froid. Dès leur invention, des distinctions se sont néanmoins opérées entre ceux qui en portaient et ceux qui n'en portaient pas, entre les personnes chaussées de beaux souliers et celles portant des chaussures simples. En remontant l'histoire du vêtement et de la mode, il apparaît clairement que le fonctionnalisme des vêtements est beaucoup moins important que leur signification, du moins à de très rares exceptions près (comme des bottes bien chaudes par une journée glaciale ou des brodequins robustes pour les soldats).

« Les chaussures modifient notre perception des autres et de nous-mêmes », écrit Russell W. Belk, dont les recherches révèlent que la plupart des Américains estiment que « leurs chaussures sont une extension et une expression d'eux-mêmes ». Les chaussures donnent des informations précieuses sur l'âge, le genre, le statut social, la sexualité, l'origine ethnique, le goût et la personnalité de leur propriétaire. Chez les adolescents, « elles sont un signifiant clé de l'identité ». De nombreuses personnes croient même que les chaussures « peuvent les transformer comme par magie ». Selon de « solides éléments liés à des croyances magiques dans notre vision des chaussures », les gens croient vraiment que les chaussures vont non seulement modifier leur apparence ou leurs capacités sportives, mais aussi « totalement transformer leur vie »[12].

Nous accordons de la valeur aux chaussures parce que nous croyons qu'elles fournissent des informations importantes sur ce que nous sommes - et pourrions être. Autrefois, notre identité se limitait essentiellement à notre position sociale, alors qu'elle est aujourd'hui définie de façon plus subjective. Si les chaussures revêtent toujours plus d'importance depuis ces dernières décennies, c'est en grande partie dû au développement du système de la mode qui a engendré un plus grand choix de chaussures, influençant ainsi notre façon de consommer les objets avec lesquels nous façonnons nos identités individuelles. Alors, vous êtes plutôt Manolo ou Nike ? Ballerines ou Birkenstock ? Quelle chaussure êtes-vous ?

Alaïa

AZZEDINE ALAÏA'S BODY-CONSCIOUS AESTHETIC HELPED define the look of 1980s fashion with powerful and sexy suits, dramatic, clinging gowns, and luxurious and glamorous details such as enigmatic hoods or matching gloves. He brought the same refined sensuality to his shoe design. Known for sculptural pieces marked by meticulous draping and tailoring, as well as his distinctive use of materials, Alaïa frequently used leathers, skins, and embellishments, such as corset-lacing and metal eyelets and studs, in both his clothing and his footwear. His strappy sandals suggestively exposed the wearer's foot, and the curved lines and balanced proportions of his platforms and boots show the same emphasis and celebration of the female form as the curved seaming and close fit of his clothing.

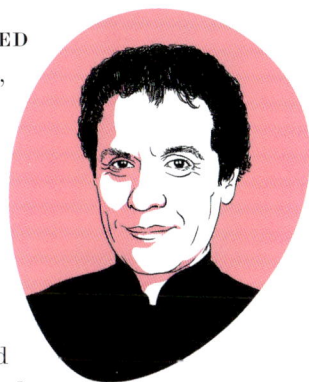

Azzedine Alaïa (1940–2017)

Born in Tunisia in 1940, Alaïa studied at the Tunis Institute of Fine Arts and moved to Paris in 1957. After working for brands such as Christian Dior and Guy Laroche, he opened his own house in 1979 and quickly established his aesthetic: sexy "second skin" clothes that enhanced the natural curves of a woman's body. Conscious of creating a unified silhouette, Alaïa designed shoes that worked together with his clothing, most notably in his fall 1991 collection, which featured head-to-toe leopard looks, including leopard-print platform boots. His wedges were perennial favorites — a "best seller" according to *Women's Wear Daily* — and he redesigned them in multiple fabrications.

Alaïa was an independent designer who worked on his own schedule and focused on the craftsmanship of fashion. In 2000 he partnered with Prada, which helped expand his business, especially in footwear. This collaboration on leather goods continued after he split with the larger company in 2007. Although Azzedine Alaïa died in 2017, his company continues to craft fashions and accessories that memorialize his rigor and refinement. —*E.W.*

PREVIOUS
Alaïa
Sandal: Black, red,
and pink suede, metal
grommets and studs
France, 2012

Supermodel Naomi
Campbell in a form-fitting
ensemble featuring a
leather punched corset,
wedge heels, and bodysuit.
Peter Lindbergh, 1992.

AZZEDINE ALAÏAS KÖRPERBETONTE ÄSTHETIK
zählte zu den maßgeblichen Einflüssen auf den Look
der 1980er-Jahre. Seine Mode prägten sexy Power-
kostüme, hautenge, dramatische Roben und gla-
mouröse Luxusdetails wie geheimnisvoll wirkende
Kapuzen oder zum Look passende Handschuhe.
Ebenso sinnlich und raffiniert waren auch seine
Schuhdesigns. Berühmt für skulpturale Kleider mit
akkuraten Drapierungen und Schnitten sowie sein
Faible für bestimmte Materialien, griff Alaïa auch
im Schuhdesign häufig auf Leder, Fell und Verzierungen wie Korsettschnüre oder Metallnieten und
-ösen zurück. Bei ihm entblößten Riemchensandalen den Fuß der Trägerin verheißungsvoll, feierten
Plateauschuhe und Stiefel mit kurvigen Linien und
ausbalancierten Proportionen die weibliche Form
ebenso wie die kurvenbetonte Taillierung und enge
Passform seiner Kleider.

Alaïa, geboren 1940 in Tunesien, studierte
an der Kunstakadamie in Tunis und zog 1957 nach
Paris. Dort arbeitete er zunächst für Marken wie
Christian Dior und Guy Laroche, ehe er 1979 sein
eigenes Couture-Haus eröffnete und schnell seine
ästhetische Linie etablierte: sexy Kleider, die wie
eine „zweite Haut" saßen und die natürlichen Run-
dungen des weiblichen Körpers hervorhoben. Um
die Silhouette wie aus einem Guss wirken zu lassen,
stimmte Alaïa seine Schuhdesigns auf die Kleider
ab, vor allem in seiner Herbstkollektion 1991, als
er zum Leopardenlook von Kopf bis Fuß Plateau-
stiefeletten mit Leopardenprint präsentierte. Sein
Lieblingsdesign und laut *Women's Wear Daily*
Alaïa-„Bestseller" waren Wedges, Schuhe mit Keil-
absätzen, die er in verschiedensten Ausführungen
immer wieder neu interpretierte.

Alaïa war ein unabhängiger Designer, der
nach seinen eigenen Vorstellungen arbeitete und
sich auf die Schneiderkunst konzentrierte. Seine
Partnerschaft mit Prada im Jahr 2000 förderte die
Expansion seines Unternehmens, insbesondere der
Schuhsparte. Diese Zusammenarbeit im Lederwa-
rensegment setzte sich auch nach der Trennung von
dem großen Partner im Jahr 2007 fort. Azzedine
Alaïa starb 2017, doch das Unternehmen fertigt
weiterhin Kleidung und Accessoires, die seiner Ak-
kuratesse und Raffinesse ein Denkmal setzen. —*E.W.*

L'ESTHÉTIQUE D'AZZEDINE ALAÏA A CONTRIBUÉ à
définir la mode des années 1980 en révélant et en
sublimant le corps de la femme avec des tailleurs
ultra-sexy, de spectaculaires robes moulantes et de
luxueux détails glamour tels que de mystérieuses
capuches ou des gants coordonnés. Le couturier
investissait la même sensualité et le même raffinement dans les chaussures qu'il créait. Réputé pour
ses pièces sculpturales au drapé original et à la
coupe soignée, mais aussi pour son approche particulière des matières, Alaïa utilisait fréquemment
des cuirs, des peaux et des détails décoratifs comme
les lacets de corset, les œillets en métal et les clous,
tant pour ses vêtements que pour ses chaussures.
Ses sandales à lanières dénudaient le pied de façon
suggestive. Tout comme les coutures arrondies et la
coupe ajustée de ses vêtements, les courbes et les
proportions équilibrées de ses souliers compensés
et de ses bottes mettaient en valeur et célébraient
le corps féminin.

Né en 1940 en Tunisie, Alaïa a étudié à l'Ins-
titut supérieur des beaux-arts de Tunis avant de
s'installer à Paris en 1957. Après avoir travaillé pour
des marques comme Christian Dior et Guy Laroche,
il a créé sa propre griffe en 1979 et a rapidement
imposé son esthétique : des vêtements « seconde
peau » sexy qui sublimaient les courbes féminines
naturelles. Conscient de proposer un look intégral, Alaïa concevait des chaussures à porter avec
ses vêtements, en particulier pour sa collection
Automne 1991 faite de looks léopard de la tête aux
pieds, dont des bottes compensées à imprimé léopard. Ses modèles compensés, qualifiés de « *best-
sellers* » par *Women's Wear Daily*, étaient les plus
demandés et il les a déclinés dans de nombreuses
variantes. Alaïa était un créateur indépendant qui
travaillait selon son propre calendrier et s'intéres-
sait avant tout au savoir-faire de la mode. En 2000,
son association avec Prada lui a permis de dévelop-
per son entreprise, notamment dans le domaine des
chaussures, et cette collaboration en maroquinerie
s'est poursuivie après la fin de leur association
en 2007. Après le décès d'Azzedine Alaïa en 2017,
son entreprise a continué à produire des vêtements
et des accessoires qui perpétuent son esthétique
faite de rigueur et de raffinement. —*E.W.*

Alaïa
Bootie: Gray and black
tiger-print calf hair
France, *ca.* 1992

Alaïa
Sandals: Snakeskin
and cowrie shells
France, early 1990s

Alaïa
Sandals: Brown
crocodile, snakeskin-
embossed leather
France, 1990s

Alaïa
Wedge-heeled sandals:
Green embossed
leather, cork
France, 2006

Alaïa
Ankle boot:
Leopard-print calf hair
France, fall 1991

Balenciaga

THE HOUSE OF BALENCIAGA REVOLUTIONIZED womenswear during the postwar period and "laid the foundations of modernity," said French designer and Balenciaga protégé Emanuel Ungaro. Spanish-born Cristóbal Balenciaga, known as "The Master" of haute couture, founded the label in 1937, and his architectural and volumetric designs, which ranged from distinctive sack dresses to cocoon coats, formed silhouettes that remain influential today. Footwear was not a major part of the brand until 1997, when Nicolas Ghesquière took over as head designer and made shoes a central component of the house.

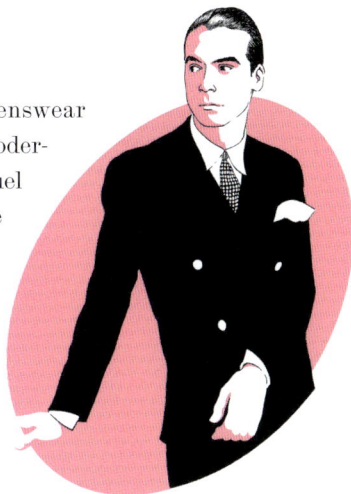

Cristóbal Balenciaga (1895–1972)

Ghesquière's thoughtful studies of Balenciaga's past designs resulted in elegantly crafted clothing and accessories in unexpected silhouettes. His bold designs for each collection were paired with equally audacious and graphic shoes by designer Pierre Hardy. There was a sleek modernism to Ghesquière's and Hardy's work, exemplified by the platform "harness" boots designed for the fall 2006 collection. The boots were paired with sculptural jackets and short, voluminous skirts, and the ensembles were further accessorized with opaque black tights and equestrian-style hats. The effect was long, lean, and thoroughly contemporary. The unique boots became a favorite among fashion editors, and their popularity was heightened by celebrity wearer Mary-Kate Olsen. Georgian-born designer Demna Gvasalia took over as the brand's creative director in 2015. He continued Balenciaga's focus on volume and shape but with a decidedly different aesthetic: fusing the oversized cocoon and "swing" silhouettes that defined Balenciaga's postwar years with unexpectedly quotidian garments such as puffer coats, track suits, and denim jackets. His shoe designs were equally surprising in their combination of references, and his eye-catching "Triple S" sneakers were named for the three different types of rubber soles that were combined to create their recognizably chunky look. As Gvasalia has said of his work, one must "destruct to create." In spring 2025, the brand announced that Gvasalia was leaving Balenciaga. Luxury house veteran Pierpaolo Piccioli stepped in as its newest creative director. —E.M.

Balenciaga
"Triple S" sneakers:
Multicolor leather,
suede, rubber
France, 2018

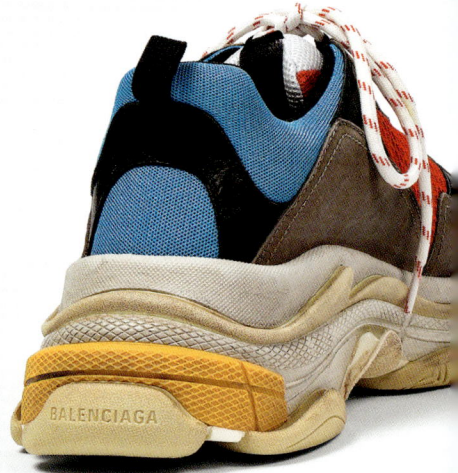

DAS HAUS BALENCIAGA REVOLUTIONIERTE die Damenmode der Nachkriegszeit und „legte das Fundament für die Moderne", so der französische Modeschöpfer und Balenciaga-Protegé Emanuel Ungaro. Der gebürtige Spanier Cristóbal Balenciaga, bekannt als „der Meister" der Haute Couture, gründete sein Modehaus 1937 und schuf Silhouetten, die bis heute wegweisend sind. Das Spektrum seiner geradezu architektonischen und volumetrischen Entwürfe reichte vom charakteristischen Sackkleid bis zum Kokonmantel. Fußbekleidung hatte für die Marke keine größere Bedeutung, bis Nicolas Ghesquière 1997 die kreative Leitung übernahm und Schuhe zu einer zentralen Komponente des Hauses machte.

Ghesquières eingehende Auseinandersetzung mit Balenciagas Entwürfen resultierte in elegant gearbeiteten Kleidern und Accessoires mit überraschenden Silhouetten. Ergänzt wurden seine kühnen Looks für jede Kollektion durch ebenso gewagte, ausdrucksstarke Schuhkreationen des Designers Pierre Hardy. Ghesquières und Hardys Kreationen zeichnete eine moderne Eleganz aus, wie sie am Beispiel des „Harness"-Plateaustiefels aus der Herbstkollektion 2006 erkennbar wird. Die Stiefel wurden mit skulpturalen Jacken und kurzen, voluminösen Röcken kombiniert und als Ensemble abgerundet von blickdichten schwarzen Strumpfhosen und Hüten im Reiterlook. Die resultierende Optik war lang, schlank und vollkommen zeitgemäß. Der unverwechselbare Stiefel wurde zu einem Liebling der Moderedaktionen und gewann durch Mary-Kate Olsen als prominenter Trägerin zusätzlich an Popularität. 2015 übernahm der gebürtige Georgier Demna Gvasalia die kreative Leitung des Hauses. Er führte Balenciagas auf Volumen und Form konzentrierte Linie fort, jedoch in einer entschieden anderen Ästhetik: Die Oversize-Silhouetten der Kokon- und ausgestellten Kurzmäntel, die Balenciagas Stil der Nachkriegsjahre prägten, verband er mit verblüffend alltäglichen Kleidungsstücken wie Daunenmänteln, Trainingsanzügen und Jeansjacken. Auch bei seinen Schuhkreationen bezog er sich auf überraschend unterschiedliche Quellen. Seine auffälligen „Triple S"-Sneaker waren nach der Gummisohle aus drei verschiedenen Lagen benannt, die kombiniert einen klobigen Look von hohem Wiedererkennungswert ergaben. Gvasalia selbst sagte über seine Arbeit, man müsse „zerstören, um zu erschaffen". Im Frühjahr 2025 gab die Marke bekannt, dass Gvasalia Balenciaga verlassen würde. Pierpaolo Piccioli, langjähriger Modedesigner im Luxussement, übernahm die Position des neuen Kreativdirektors. —E.M.

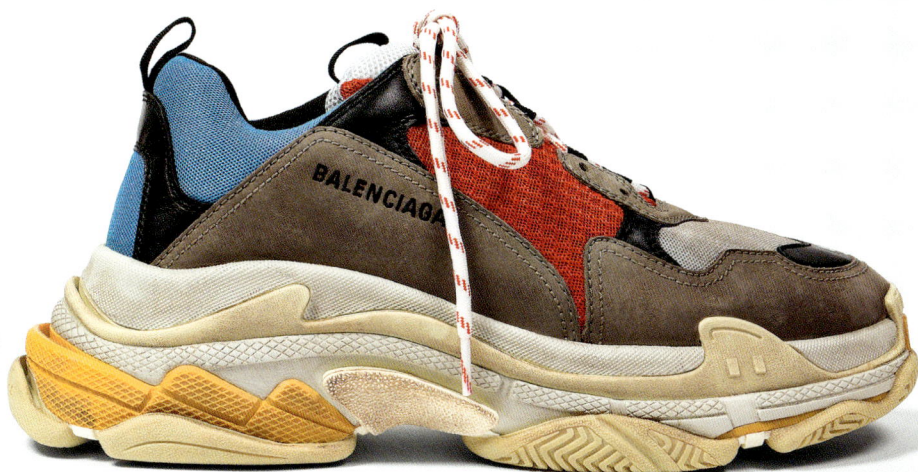

LA MAISON BALENCIAGA A RÉVOLUTIONNÉ la mode féminine de l'après-guerre en « posant les fondations de la modernité », pour reprendre les mots du couturier français Emanuel Ungaro, le protégé de Balenciaga. Réputé comme le « grand maître » de la haute couture, Cristóbal Balenciaga est né en Espagne et a fondé sa Maison en 1937. Ses créations architecturales et volumineuses, de ses robes sacs originales à ses manteaux cocons, composaient des silhouettes qui n'ont aujourd'hui rien perdu de leur influence. Les chaussures ont commencé à occuper une place plus importante en 1997 avec l'arrivée de Nicolas Ghesquière à la direction artistique de la Maison, qui les a établies comme un élément central de la marque.

Grâce à une étude approfondie des archives Balenciaga, Ghesquière a conçu des vêtements et des accessoires élégants donnant vie à des silhouettes inattendues. Dans chaque collection, il associait ses créations audacieuses à des chaussures tout aussi étonnantes et graphiques conçues par Pierre Hardy. La collaboration entre Ghesquière et Hardy avait quelque chose de moderniste et d'épuré, à l'image des bottines compensées à harnais de la collection Automne 2006 : elles étaient portées avec des vestes sculpturales et des minijupes volumineuses, autant d'ensembles accessoirisés de collants noirs opaques et de chapeaux en forme de bombe d'équitation qui dessinaient une silhouette longue, fine et éminemment contemporaine. Ces bottines uniques plébiscitées par les journalistes de mode sont devenues encore plus célèbres une fois vues aux pieds de Mary-Kate Olsen.

Le styliste géorgien Demna Gvasalia a repris la direction artistique de la marque en 2015. Il a perpétué les volumes et les formes typiques de Balenciaga, mais avec une esthétique résolument différente : il a fusionné les silhouettes cocons et « oscillantes » *oversize* qui ont défini le style Balenciaga de l'après-guerre avec des vêtements quotidiens tels que des doudounes longues, des survêtements et des vestes en jean. Ses chaussures surprennent aussi en mélangeant les références. Ses étonnantes sneakers Triple S devaient leur nom à l'association de trois semelles en caoutchouc qui leur donnent cet aspect imposant si caractéristique. Comme le dit lui-même Gvasalia à propos de son travail, il faut « détruire pour créer ». Balenciaga a annoncé le départ de son directeur artistique au printemps 2025. Pierpaolo Piccioli, couturier vétéran des Maisons de luxe, lui a succédé au poste de directeur de la création. —*E.M.*

"Balenciaga was my religion.
Since I'm a believer, for
me there is Balenciaga and
the good Lord."

— HUBERT DE GIVENCHY

Balenciaga
(Pierre Hardy)
"Harness" boot: Brown
leather, brown suede
France, fall 2006

Susan Bennis & Warren Edwards

SUSAN BENNIS AND WARREN EDWARDS began their careers as fashion designers, running a clothing label called Kiss during the early 1970s. In 1972 they took over the Chelsea Cobbler shop that had opened in Manhattan two years prior. Their initial plan was to incorporate their fashion designs with Chelsea Cobbler's shoes, but that plan soon changed when Bennis made her first trip to an Italian shoe factory. She became enamored of footwear design, and stated that "shoes present endless possibilities." She and Edwards started their own footwear label, Susan Bennis & Warren Edwards, that same year. They sold their work in the Chelsea Cobbler store into the late 1970s.

Susan Bennis and
Warren Edwards

In 1980 Bennis and Edwards opened their own store in Manhattan. They immediately introduced an astounding 600 designs. By 1981 *The New York Times* heralded the designers as stars of the shoe world, alongside Manolo Blahník and Maud Frizon. Their shoes were expertly crafted in Italy and never sold wholesale, which resulted in notably high price tags. The designers fully embraced their reputation for extravagance — when asked about the label's prices in a 1980 interview, Edwards stated, "I figure it's like buying a Rolex; once you get over $200, what's the difference?" While the Susan Bennis & Warren Edwards label thrived amid the wealth and excess of the 1980s, its popularity waned during the following decade as new boutiques selling fashionable shoes for lower prices competed with the label's high-priced footwear. The company dissolved in 1997, and Edwards began designing on his own the following year. —*C.H.*

SUSAN BENNIS UND WARREN EDWARDS begannen ihre Karriere als Modedesigner und gründeten Anfang der 1970er-Jahre ein Kleiderlabel namens Kiss. 1972 übernahmen sie das zwei Jahre zuvor eröffnete Chelsea-Cobbler-Geschäft in Manhattan, anfangs mit der Idee, ihre eigenen Kleiderkreationen mit Schuhen von Chelsea Cobbler zu verbinden. Doch dieser Plan änderte sich schnell, als Bennis zum ersten Mal eine italienische Schuhfabrik besuchte, sich ins Schuhdesign verliebte und feststellte: „Schuhe bieten unendlich viele Möglichkeiten." Noch im selben Jahr gründeten sie und Edwards das Schuhlabel Susan Bennis/Warren Edwards, um bis in die späten 70er-Jahre ihre Schuhdesigns im Chelsea-Cobbler-Laden zu verkaufen.

Als sie 1980 ihr eigenes Geschäft in Manhattan eröffneten, gingen sie mit sage und schreibe 600 Modellen an den Start. 1981 rief die *New York Times* die beiden bereits zu Stars der Schuhszene aus, zusammen mit Manolo Blahník und Maud Frizon. Ihre Schuhe wurden in ausgezeichneten italienischen Betrieben gefertigt und niemals über den Großhandel verkauft, was zu beachtlichen Preisen führte. Zu ihrem Ruf, extravagant zu sein, standen die Designer mit voller Überzeugung – in einem Interview auf die Preise des Labels angesprochen, meinte Edwards 1980: „Ich stelle mir vor, es ist, wie eine Rolex zu kaufen; wenn die 200-Dollar-Grenze überschritten ist, macht es doch keinen Unterschied mehr." Prosperierte das Label Susan Bennis/Warren Edwards im Überschwang und Wohlstand der 1980er, so schwand seine Popularität im Folgejahrzehnt, als neue Boutiquen mit modischen Schuhen zu günstigeren Preisen mit ihm konkurrierten. Nachdem das Unternehmen 1997 aufgelöst worden war, arbeitete Edwards ab dem darauffolgenden Jahr solo als Designer weiter. —*C.H.*

SUSAN BENNIS ET WARREN EDWARDS ont débuté leur carrière dans la mode en lançant la marque de vêtements Kiss au début des années 1970. En 1972, ils ont racheté la boutique Chelsea Cobbler qui avait ouvert à Manhattan deux ans plus tôt. Au départ, ils comptaient présenter leurs créations de mode aux côtés des chaussures Chelsea Cobbler, mais ils ont rapidement changé d'avis après que Susan a visité un atelier de chaussures en Italie. Tombée amoureuse des chaussures, elle trouvait que celles-ci offraient « des possibilités créatives illimitées ». La même année, le duo a lancé sa propre marque de chaussures baptisée Susan Bennis & Warren Edwards et a continué à vendre ses créations dans la boutique Chelsea Cobbler jusqu'à la fin des années 1970.

En 1980, ils ont ouvert leur propre boutique à Manhattan avec un choix impressionnant de 600 modèles différents. En 1981, *The New York Times* les a proclamés stars de la chaussure aux côtés de Manolo Blahník et de Maud Frizon. Leurs chaussures étaient fabriquées par des artisans très qualifiés en Italie qui ne vendaient jamais en gros, ce qui se traduisait par des prix particulièrement élevés. Les créateurs assumaient parfaitement leur réputation d'extravagance. « J'imagine que c'est comme acheter une Rolex : au-dessus de 200 dollars, quelle différence cela peut-il faire ? » a répondu Warren Edwards quand on l'a interrogé sur ce qui justifiait de tels prix lors d'une interview en 1980. La marque a prospéré pendant le faste et les excès des années 1980, mais son succès a décliné au cours de la décennie suivante quand de nouvelles boutiques de chaussures tendance moins chères sont venues faire concurrence aux onéreux modèles de la marque. Après la liquidation de l'entreprise en 1997, Warren Edwards a poursuivi une carrière en solo dès l'année suivante. —*C.H.*

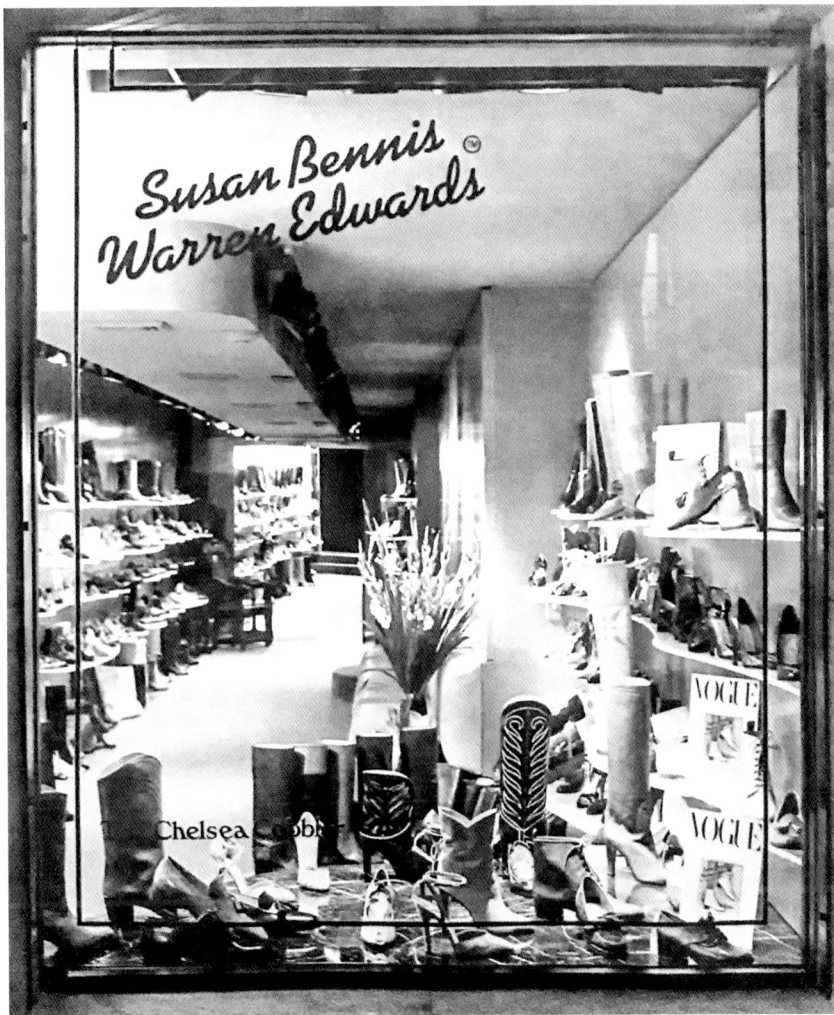

**Susan Bennis &
Warren Edwards**
Mule: Black suede,
silver metallic leather
Couture collection
USA, *ca.* 1979

Susan Bennis and
Warren Edwards' first
store in New York was
described by *The New
York Times* as "one of
the most chic little

boutiques in town —
60 square feet of high-
styled, high-priced men's
and women's shoes."
1980s.

The depiction of a
playful polka dot dress
pattern embellishes a
pair of dancing shoes.
1980s.

**Susan Bennis &
Warren Edwards**
Mules: Green, blue, and
black tartan, faux pearls
USA, *ca.* 1988

**Susan Bennis &
Warren Edwards**
Boots: Black-and-
red leather
Couture collection
USA, *ca.* 1978

Known for their bold
and colorful designs,
Bennis and Edwards
used splashy colors
and comic strip type
to create '80s "Power
Pop" heels.

Manolo Blahník

Manolo Blahník (b. 1942)

NO SHOE DESIGNER TODAY IS as influential and culturally recognizable as Manolo Blahník. While not strictly a character on the pop culture giant *Sex and the City*, the shoe creator's name was so often cited that he has become as synonymous with the show as its cocktail-swilling, fashion-obsessed characters. Sarah Jessica Parker said of the designer: "Manolo makes the perfect heel. There's something about what his heel does for the slightly forward pitch of a woman's body that is really superior. He just makes you look sexier."

Manolo Blahník was born in 1942 in the Canary Islands to a Czech father and Spanish mother. After formal schooling in Switzerland and France, Blahník moved to London in 1969 and soon entered the fashion field. There he met American editor Diana Vreeland and showed her his portfolio of clothing, accessory, and theater sketches. She was especially impressed with his shoe designs and encouraged him to focus on footwear. Over the next decade, Blahník's career took off. He opened his eponymous firm; designed shoes for leading British creators such as Ossie Clark, Jean Muir, and Zandra Rhodes; and sold his footwear in America at Bloomingdale's.

Although Blahník never worked as a shoemaker, he became a dedicated, self-trained technician. In addition to drawing each of his labeled creations, Blahník handcrafts and carves the wooden lasts onto which he molds the uppers and personally oversees the production of his ready-to-wear designs. This singular and painstaking approach has inspired an unrivaled, fanatical following — despite minimal stores worldwide and Blahník's aversion to turning the company into a large corporate engine like similar luxury brands, his shoes fly off the shelves, often overnight. Embracing a range of styles from the curved Louis heel of the eighteenth century to vertiginous stilettos, the Blahník silhouette is always elegant, and his fabric and ornament choices are a balance of lushness and refinement. He dabbled in men's footwear and made platforms during the 1970s but soon abandoned those efforts. Instead, he revived the sleek heeled pump, the shoe that remains his hallmark. —*P.M.*

KEIN SCHUHDESIGNER UNSERER ZEIT KOMMT an Einfluss und medialem Wiedererkennungswert Manolo Blahník gleich. Obwohl er in dem Popkulturphänomen *Sex and the City* keine direkte Rolle spielte, fiel sein Name dort so oft, dass er ebenso zum Synonym für die Serie wurde wie die Cocktails kippenden, modeverrückten Hauptdarstellerinnen der Serie. Sarah Jessica Parker sagte über den Designer: „Manolo macht den perfekten Absatz. Dieser Absatz stellt irgendetwas mit der leichten Vorwärtsneigung des weiblichen Körpers an, das wirklich unerreicht ist. Er lässt dich einfach sexyer aussehen."

Manolo Blahník kam 1942 auf den Kanaren als Sohn einer Spanierin und eines Tschechen zur Welt. Nach seiner Schulzeit in der Schweiz und Frankreich ging Blahník 1969 nach London und betrat bald das Modeparkett. Er lernte die amerikanische Moderedakteurin Diana Vreeland kennen und zeigte ihr sein Portfolio mit Entwürfen für Kleidung, Accessoires und Bühnenbilder. Vreeland war besonders von seinen Schuhdesigns beeindruckt und ermutigte ihn, sich auf Schuhmode zu konzentrieren. In den folgenden zehn Jahren nahm seine Karriere Fahrt auf. Er gründete eine Firma unter seinem Namen, entwarf Schuhe für führende britische Designer wie Ossie Clark, Jean Muir und Zandra Rhodes und vertrieb seine Kreationen über Bloomingdale's auch in Amerika.

Blahník hatte das Schuhmacherhandwerk zwar nicht gelernt, erlangte jedoch als akribischer Autodidakt technische Meisterschaft in seinem Metier. Für jede seiner mit Namen versehenen Kreationen zeichnet Blahník nicht nur eigenhändig den Entwurf, er schnitzt auch die Leisten, formt darauf das Obermaterial und überwacht die Produktion seiner Konfektionsmodelle persönlich. Diese außergewöhnlich akribische Herangehensweise trug ihm eine unvergleichlich enthusiastische Anhängerschaft ein. Trotz weltweit nur weniger Ladengeschäfte und Blahníks Aversion gegen die Umwandlung der Firma in eine große Konzernmaschine, wie es vergleichbare Luxuslabels getan haben, sind seine Schuhe oft über Nacht ausverkauft. Die Blahník-Silhouette ist stets elegant. Stilistisch reicht ihr Spektrum vom geschwungenen Louis-XV-Absatz des 18. Jahrhunderts bis hin zu schwindelerregenden Stilettos, und die gewählten Materialien und Verzierungen halten die Balance zwischen opulent und raffiniert. In den 1970er-Jahren versuchte sich Blahník auch in der Herrenschuhsparte und an Plateauschuhen, gab das jedoch schnell wieder auf und ließ stattdessen den Stöckelschuh wieder aufleben, der bis heute sein Markenzeichen ist. —*P.M.*

MANOLO BLAHNIK
758 MADISON AVENUE • NEW YORK

Le théâtre de m.B.

Andy Warhol drew an advertisement for Blahník's New York Madison Avenue shop in 1979 featuring the designer's iconic pump.

Manolo Blahník
Mules: Ivory silk brocade, burgundy ostrich feathers
England, 1998

AUCUN AUTRE CRÉATEUR DE CHAUSSURES n'est aujourd'hui aussi influent et aussi célèbre que Manolo Blahník. Même s'il ne jouait pas à proprement parler dans *Sex and the City*, son nom y était si souvent cité qu'il est devenu aussi indissociable de cette série culte que ses héroïnes obsédées de mode et de cocktails. « Manolo a créé le talon parfait, proclamait Sarah Jessica Parker. Mieux que tout autre, il incline légèrement le corps de la femme vers l'avant. Son talon vous rend plus sexy, tout simplement. »

Manolo Blahník est né en 1942 dans les îles Canaries d'un père tchèque et d'une mère espagnole. Après des études en Suisse et en France, il s'est installé à Londres en 1969 où il travaille très rapidement dans l'univers de la mode. C'est à cette époque qu'il a rencontré la rédactrice en chef américaine Diana Vreeland, à qui il a présenté son portfolio de dessins de vêtements, d'accessoires et de décors de théâtre. Particulièrement impressionnée par ses chaussures, elle l'a encouragé à poursuivre dans cette voie. La carrière de Manolo Blahník a décollé au cours de la décennie suivante. Il a créé sa griffe éponyme, conçu des chaussures pour de grands créateurs britanniques tels qu'Ossie Clark, Jean Muir et Zandra Rhodes, et vendu ses créations aux États-Unis chez Bloomingdale's.

Sans formation technique en cordonnerie, Manolo Blahník est un autodidacte passionné. Il ne se contente pas de dessiner chaque création de sa marque ; il fabrique et sculpte à la main les formes en bois sur lesquelles il moule les empeignes tout en supervisant personnellement la production de ses chaussures. Cette approche singulière et minutieuse lui a valu une communauté de fans à nulle autre pareille : malgré un très petit nombre de boutiques à travers le monde et son aversion à l'idée de transformer son entreprise en grosse machine commerciale à l'instar de marques de luxe similaires, ses chaussures s'écoulent à toute vitesse, souvent du jour au lendemain. Du talon Louis XV concave du XVIIIᵉ siècle aux vertigineux talons aiguilles, la silhouette Blahník reste toujours élégante. Les choix de tissus et d'ornementation du créateur trouvent le juste équilibre entre opulence et raffinement. Il s'est essayé aux souliers pour homme en créant des modèles compensés dans les années 1970, mais il a vite renoncé, préférant ressusciter l'escarpin à talon avec des lignes épurées, la chaussure qui reste sa marque de fabrique. « On m'a déjà demandé un million de fois pourquoi je ne faisais pas aussi des lunettes, des objets et des chapeaux », a-t-il confié à *Vogue* en 2017. « Les gens ont-ils perdu la tête ? Je n'ai absolument aucune envie de faire ça. Non, je fais des chaussures, et je le fais du mieux possible. » —*P.M.*

OPPOSITE
Manolo Blahník
Pumps: Green,
turquoise, and gray
lizard skin
England, spring 1981

OPPOSITE BELOW
A Bergdorf Goodman
advertisement for the
"Krusostra" sandal,
a jewel-buckle pump in
amber yellow, fuchsia,
and kelly green.
Ca. 1990s.

Manolo Blahník
Evening pumps:
Purple-and-black satin
England, fall 1985

Manolo Blahník
Mules: Pink silk,
glass beads
England, spring 1995

Manolo Blahník
Pump: Navy blue silk
faille, satin, rhinestones
England, *ca.* 1988

Manolo Blahník
Mule: Silver metal-
lic leather
England, spring 1986

Manolo Blahník
Evening sandals:
Red silk satin
England, *ca.* 1988

Manolo Blahník
Boots: Tan and green
leather, rubber
England, *ca.* 1994

Manolo Blahník
Boots: Red, orange, and
burgundy suede, long-
haired pressed shearling
England, 1997

Manolo Blahník
Mules: Leopard print
and gold metallic
silk brocade, faux
pearls, crystals,
beads, rhinestones
England, *ca.* 1998

Manolo Blahník
Ankle strap stilettos:
Black leather
England, 1998

Manolo Blahník
Pumps: Silver metallic
leather, metal,
rhinestones
England, 2003

Manolo Blahník
Pump: Zebra-printed
pony skin
England, 1998

FOLLOWING
Manolo Blahník
Sling-back pumps:
Multicolor lace,
red silk, red leather
England, 2017

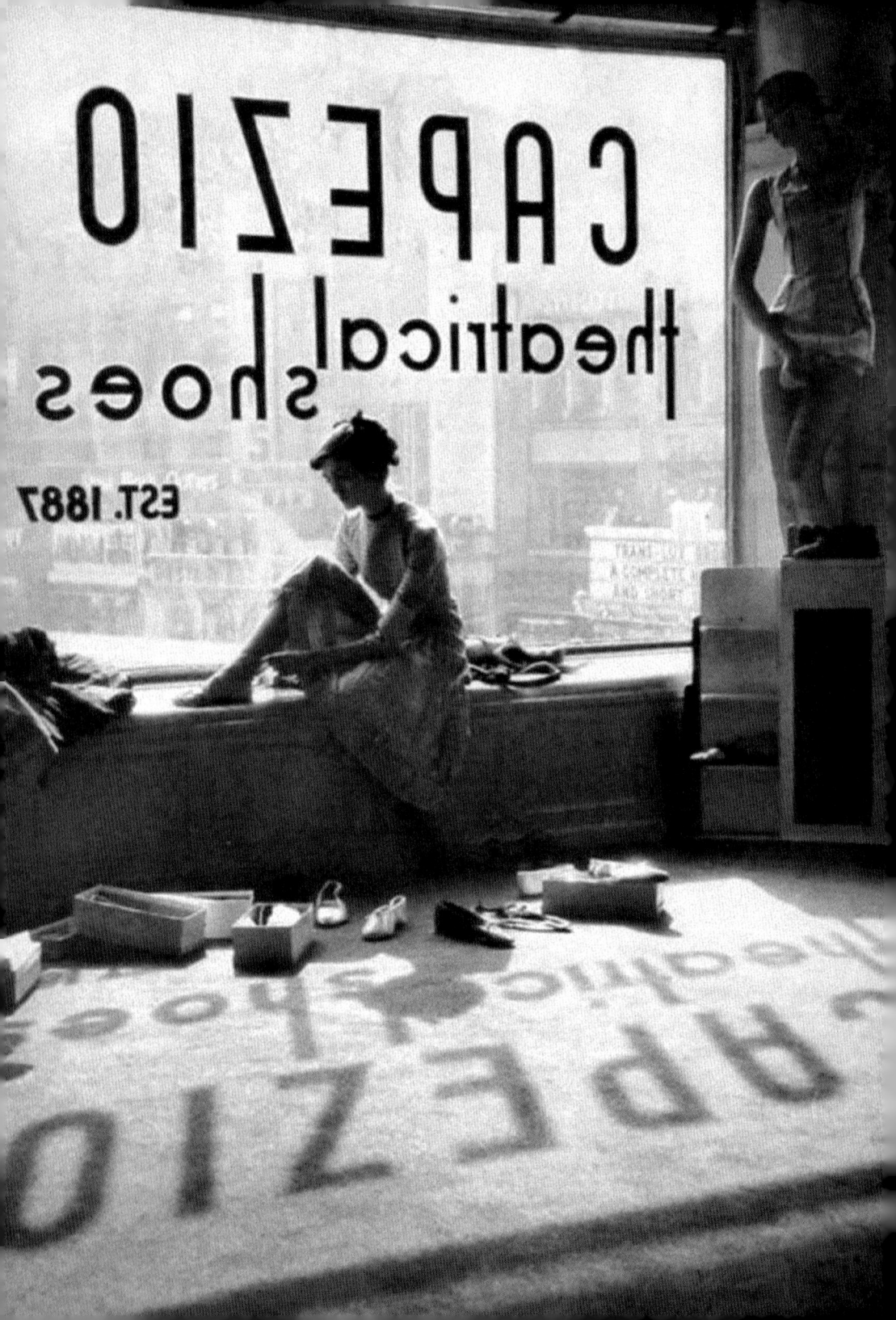

Capezio

THE FLAT-HEELED "BALLERINA" SLIPPER, RADICAL
for its comfort and now ubiquitous as a style worn by
millions, was born from the serendipitous partnership of American fashion designer Claire McCardell
and the ballet footwear creator Salvatore Capezio in
1942. Capezio was founded in 1887, when 17-year-old
Italian émigré Salvatore Capezio opened a shoe repair
shop that specialized in theatrical footwear near the old
Metropolitan Opera House in New York City. Eventually
he began constructing custom-made versions for professional
dancers. By the 1930s the company was producing an array of shoes
for dance disciplines ranging from Broadway to ballet — Bob Fosse, Gene
Kelly, Alicia Alonso, and Fred Astaire are among the many stars that sported the label.

**Salvatore Capezio
(1871–1940)**

Capezio's move from the stage to the sidewalk was thanks to McCardell. During the
1940s and 1950s, McCardell collaborated with Capezio to design street-ready slippers with
fabric uppers that matched her garments. Unable to procure appropriate footwear for one
of her early fashion presentations, McCardell was most likely introduced to the idea of the
ballet slipper by fashion editor Diana Vreeland. During World War II, the United States
imposed restrictions on materials essential to the military effort such as silk, wool, and
leather. One of the very few items that was not rationed happened to be ballet slippers.

Major department stores such as Lord & Taylor and Neiman Marcus were also selling
other versions of Capezio footwear for women and, later, men. By 1949 Capezio shoes were
featured on the cover of *Vogue*, and in 1952 Capezio received the Coty Award, the most
prestigious honor in fashion at the time.

Capezio was also an innovator in the ballet world. Contemporary firms recently began
making pointe shoes in a range of darker skin tones for Black ballerinas. However, it was
during the 1970s that Capezio produced the first brown pointe shoes for ballerinas of the
Dance Theatre of Harlem. —P.M.

DER „BALLERINA"-SCHUH MIT FLACHEM ABSATZ, kompromisslos bequem und heute als ein von Millionen getragener Look allgegenwärtig, entsprang 1942 der glücklichen Verbindung zwischen der amerikanischen Modedesignerin Claire McCardell und dem Ballettschuhmacher Salvatore Capezio. Dessen gleichnamige Firma nahm ihren Anfang 1887, als der damals 17-Jährige, eingewandert aus Italien, in der Nähe des alten Metropolitan-Opernhauses in New York einen auf Bühnenschuhe spezialisierten Schusterladen eröffnete und schließlich auch Maßtanzschuhe für Profitänzer anfertigte. In den 1930er-Jahren stellte seine Firma bereits ein ganzes Sortiment an Schuhen her, das Tänzer vom Broadway bis zum Ballett bediente. Zu den vielen Stars, die sich in Capezios Schuhen zeigten, zählten Bob Fosse, Gene Kelly, Alicia Alonso und Fred Astaire.

Capezios Schritt von der Bühne auf die Straße verdankte sich McCardell. Sie arbeitete während der 1940er- und 50er- Jahre mit der Firma zusammen an der Herstellung straßentauglicher Slipper mit Stoffen als Obermaterial, die auf ihre Kleider abgestimmt waren. Auf die Ballerina-Idee brachte sie höchstwahrscheinlich die Moderedakteurin Diana Vreeland, als McCardell gerade vergebens versuchte, geeignete Schuhe für eine ihrer frühen Modenschauen zu beschaffen. Während des Zweiten Weltkriegs erließ die US-Regierung Handelsbeschränkungen für rüstungsrelevante Materialien wie Seide, Wolle und Leder. Zu den sehr wenigen Produkten, die nicht rationiert waren, zählten Ballettschuhe.

Große Kaufhäuser wie Lord & Taylor oder Neiman Marcus verkauften auch andere Capezio-Damenmodelle, später kamen Herrenschuhe hinzu. 1949 schmückten Capezios die Titelseite der *Vogue*, und 1952 erhielt die Marke den Coty Award, den renommiertesten Modepreis der damaligen Zeit.

Capezio leistete auch Pionierarbeit in der Welt des Balletts. Seit Kurzem produzieren heutige Firmen Spitzentanzschuhe in dunkleren Hauttönen für schwarze Tänzerinnen, doch war es die Firma Capezio, die in den 1970er-Jahren für die Ballerinas des Dance Theatre of Harlem erstmals braune Spitzenschuhe fertigte. —*P.M.*

INSPIRÉE D'UN CHAUSSON DE DANSEUSE, la ballerine extrêmement confortable portée par des millions de femmes est le fruit de la rencontre improbable en 1942 entre la créatrice de mode américaine Claire McCardell et la marque de chaussons de danse Capezio. En 1887, Salvatore Capezio, jeune émigré italien alors âgé de 17 ans, avait ouvert une échoppe de cordonnier à deux pas de l'ancien Metropolitan Opera de New York. D'abord spécialisé dans les chaussures de théâtre, il a ensuite commencé à fabriquer des chaussons sur mesure pour les danseurs professionnels. Dans les années 1930, son entreprise produisait toute une gamme de modèles pour différents types de danse, de la comédie musicale de Broadway au ballet classique. Bob Fosse, Gene Kelly, Alicia Alonso et Fred Astaire comptent parmi les nombreuses stars qui ont porté les créations Capezio.

C'est grâce à Claire McCardell que les chaussons Capezio sont passés de la scène à la ville. Dans les années 1940 et 1950, la créatrice a collaboré avec la marque pour concevoir des chaussons pouvant être portés en extérieur, avec des empeignes assorties à ses créations vestimentaires. C'est très probablement la rédactrice en chef de mode Diana Vreeland qui lui a donné l'idée du chausson de ballerine parce qu'elle ne trouvait pas de chaussures adéquates pour l'une de ses premières présentations de mode. Pendant la Seconde Guerre mondiale, les États-Unis imposaient en effet des restrictions sur les matières premières essentielles à l'effort militaire, dont la soie, la laine et le cuir. Les chaussons de danse figuraient parmi les très rares objets non rationnés.

Les grands magasins comme Lord & Taylor et Neiman Marcus référençaient plusieurs modèles Capezio pour femme, puis pour homme. En 1949, les chaussures Capezio ont fait la couverture de *Vogue*, puis en 1952, la marque a reçu le Coty Award, le prix de mode le plus prestigieux de l'époque.

Capezio a également innové dans le domaine de la danse classique. Si, depuis peu, des entreprises contemporaines fabriquent des chaussons de pointe dans des couleurs chair plus foncées pour les danseuses noires, Capezio les avait devancées dès les années 1970 en créant les premières pointes marron à l'attention des ballerines du Dance Theatre of Harlem. —*P.M.*

PAGE 90
A young woman tries
on a pair of Salvatore
Capezio ballet shoes.
Lisa Larsen, *ca.* 1949.

PREVIOUS
Capezio
Ballet pointe shoes:
Pink satin, ribbons,
cream suede
USA, 1941

**Claire McCardell
(Capezio)**
Ankle boot: Black-and-
beige-striped cotton
twill, elastic
USA, 1945–55

**Claire McCardell
(Capezio)**
Flats: Green velvet
and grosgrain
USA, *ca.* 1955

Capezio, pictured in
his workshop in 1900,
designed high-quality
ballet slippers for
world-renowned dancers,
including Anna Pavlova.

Capezio
Sling-back pump:
Green velvet
USA, *ca.* 1955

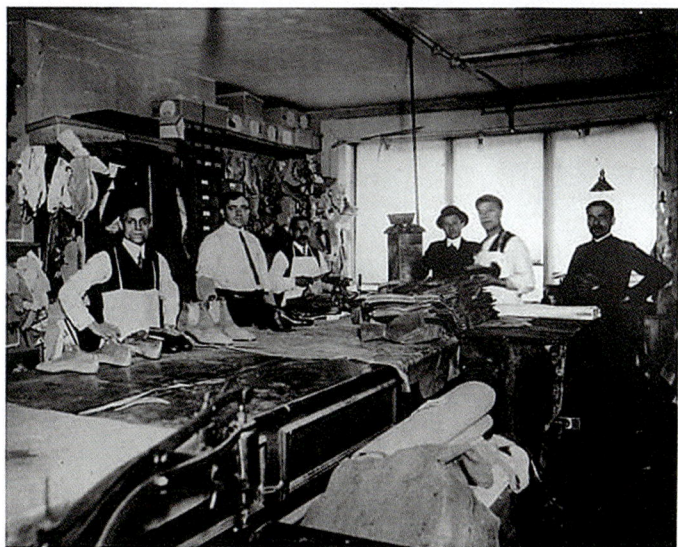

Capezio
Sandal: Aqua, light
green, and beige leather
USA, *ca.* 1970

Capezio
Mules: Light blue leather
USA, *ca.* 1965

"The celebrities and
dance legends who have
championed Capezio
over the years make
for a veritable roll call
of dance royalty."

— GRACE EDWARDS, JOURNALIST

Capezio
Oxfords: Tan and
leopard-print calf
USA, *ca.* 1966

Celine

THE PARIS-BASED COMPANY CELINE WAS a dominant fashion force from 2008 to 2018. Founded in 1945, its recent heyday is credited to Phoebe Philo, who served for a decade as its creative director. Although media-shy, Philo spearheaded a movement with her pragmatic yet luxurious clothing paired with newsworthy "it" accessories, especially cutting-edge shoes. More than any other early twenty-first-century fashion creator, Philo understood what modern women needed. Rather than embrace trends, Celine produced clothes that were practical but never boring. Philo and her team flavored these strong looks with accessories that were novel and directional.

Céline Vipiana (1915–1997)

Although best-selling bags like the "Cabas" and "Trapeze" were innovative, it was Celine's shoes that changed the course of contemporary women's footwear and garnered much press for the brand. Philo is credited with pioneering the "ugly" shoe movement with her luxe slip-on sneakers and fur-lined orthopedic sandals. More sculptural designs included gold and white leather pumps with inverted, triangular heels and brightly colored, blocky platforms.

As is the case with many fashion companies that produce multiple collections each year and a range of accessories, Celine relies on a team of specialized designers. One such creator is Johnny Coca. He worked for Marc Jacobs at Louis Vuitton, Bally, and for Celine during the 1990s when Michael Kors was the design director. Coca, who returned to Celine as the design director of leather goods, shoes, and accessories under Philo, is credited with playing an integral role in the creation of Celine's iconic and inspirational footwear. —P.M.

PREVIOUS
Celine
Pump: Black suede,
blue leather
France, fall 2012

Celine
Pump: Beige patent
leather
France, *ca.* 2010

FOLLOWING
Celine
Pumps: Burgundy
leather
France, fall 2012

DAS 1945 GEGRÜNDETE PARISER UNTERNEHMEN
Celine war von 2008 bis 2018 eine dominierende Ins-
titution in der Modewelt. Zu verdanken war diese
späte Blüte Phoebe Philo, die das Haus ein Jahrzehnt lang als Kreativchefin leitete. Die eigentlich
medienscheue Philo wurde zur Anführerin einer
neuen Bewegung mit Mode, die praktisch, aber
luxuriös war, und von spektakulären „It"-Acces-
soires, insbesondere innovativen Schuhen, ergänzt
wurde. Kein Modeschöpfer des frühen 21. Jahrhunderts verstand besser als Philo, was moderne
Frauen brauchten. Anstatt auf Trends zu setzen,
brachte Celine Kleidung heraus, die zweckmäßig,
jedoch niemals langweilig war. Philo und ihr Team
akzentuierten diese starken Looks mit neuartigen,
richtungsweisenden Accessoires.

Taschen-Bestseller wie „Cabas" und „Trapeze"
waren durchaus innovativ, doch mit der Schuhlinie änderte Celine den Kurs der zeitgenössischen
Damenschuhmode und erntete große mediale
Beachtung. Philo gilt als Wegbereiterin des „Ugly"-
Trends bei Schuhen, mit Slip-on-Sneakers in
Luxusversionen und pelzgefütterten Gesundheits-
sandalen. Zu ihren eher skulpturalen Designs
zählten weiß-goldene Lederpumps mit umge-
kehrtem Dreieckabsatz und Plateauschuhe mit
Blocksohle in intensiven Farben.

Wie viele andere Modeunternehmen, die
alljährlich mehrere Kollektionen samt Accessoire-
Sortiment produzieren, setzt auch Celine beim
Design auf ein Team von Spezialisten. Einer von
ihnen ist Johnny Coca, der zuvor für Marc Jacobs
bei Louis Vuitton, für Bally und bereits in den 90er-
Jahren unter Michael Kors als Chefdesigner für
Celine tätig war. Unter Philo kehrte Coca als Kre-
ativchef für Lederwaren, Schuhe und Accessoires
zurück und gilt als maßgeblich verantwortlich für
die Kultdesigns der wegweisenden Schuhmode
von Celine. —P.M.

DE 2008 À 2018, LA MAISON PARISIENNE Celine a
occupé une place dominante dans la mode. Cette
marque fondée en 1945 doit son apogée à Phoebe
Philo, sa directrice artistique pendant dix ans. Bien
que fuyant les médias, la styliste a insufflé une dyna-
mique avec ses vêtements pratiques et luxueux associés à des « It-accessoires », que les magazines de
mode ont plébiscités, en particulier ses chaussures
avant-gardistes. Mieux que tous les autres créateurs
du début du XXIe siècle, elle a compris ce dont la
femme moderne avait besoin. Au lieu de suivre les
tendances, Celine a produit des vêtements faciles
à porter sans jamais être ennuyeux. Phoebe Philo
et son équipe ont sublimé ces looks forts avec des
accessoires novateurs qui dictaient la tendance.

Les sacs *best-sellers* comme le Cabas et le
Trapèze étaient innovants, mais ce sont surtout
les souliers Celine qui ont fait évoluer le marché
contemporain de la chaussure pour femme et valu
une telle couverture médiatique à la marque. On dit
de Phoebe Philo qu'elle a inventé le mouvement de
la chaussure « moche » en lançant ses sneakers de
luxe et ses sandales orthopédiques doublées de fourrure. Parmi ses modèles plus sculpturaux, on peut
citer les escarpins en cuir doré et blanc aux talons
triangulaires inversés et les escarpins compensés
monolithiques à plateforme de couleur vive.

Comme de nombreuses marques de mode
qui produisent chaque année plusieurs collections
et une gamme d'accessoires, Celine s'appuie sur
une équipe de designers spécialisés, par exemple
Johnny Coca qui a travaillé pour Marc Jacobs chez
Louis Vuitton, pour Bally et pour Celine dans les
années 1990 quand Michael Kors en était le directeur artistique. De retour chez Celine pour diriger
le design de la maroquinerie, des chaussures et des
accessoires sous la houlette de Phoebe Philo, il a
joué un rôle crucial dans la création des chaussures
iconiques et inspirantes de la Maison. —P.M.

Chanel

Gabrielle "Coco" Chanel (1883–1971)

GABRIELLE "COCO" CHANEL, A POWERHOUSE who created couture clothing, jewelry, handbags, and the iconic Chanel No. 5 fragrance, solidified her place in history as one of the most important figures in fashion by introducing post-World War I women to casual yet chic sportswear, with shoes playing an essential part. She opened her first shop in 1913 selling hats and select garments, and by the 1920s she had risen to the forefront of fashion with her androgynous style. While Chanel's 1920s shorter hemlines helped turn fashionable footwear into a necessity, she did not launch her own line of shoes until decades later, in 1957, when she introduced her now-famous two-tone pumps.

According to Raymond Massaro, the shoemaker who helped Chanel create the iconic design, the style was conceived as a way to shorten the appearance of the foot. As he explained to *British Vogue* in 2007, "The black, slightly square toe shortened the foot. The beige melted into the whole and lengthened the leg. It was a very pure design, accentuated by the fineness of the straps." Of course, fashion legend suggests that Mademoiselle Chanel also liked the design because the black toe hid any signs of scuffing, allowing the wearer to lead her active lifestyle without unsightly grime from city streets ruining the look of her shoes. Coco was known to say, "A woman with good shoes is never ugly. They are the last touch of elegance."

The Massaro firm continues to fabricate Chanel shoes today. Of course, the house's range of styles has expanded dramatically. After Karl Lagerfeld took over the house in 1983, shoes became increasingly essential elements of each seasonal ready-to-wear collection. He unveiled highly decorative, elaborate, and ornate footwear in tandem with each collection's theme while also continuing the legacy of Chanel's classic two-tone style in updated versions. —E.M.

DIE POWERFRAU GABRIELLE „COCO" CHANEL kreierte Couture-Mode, Schmuck, Handtaschen und den Kultduft Chanel No. 5. Ihren Platz in der Geschichte als eine der wichtigsten Figuren der Mode festigte sie nach dem Ersten Weltkrieg mit der Einführung legerer und zugleich eleganter Freizeitkleidung für Frauen, bei der Schuhe eine wesentliche Rolle spielten. 1913 eröffnete sie ihre erste Boutique für Hüte und erlesene Kleidung und etablierte sich in den 1920er-Jahren mit ihrem androgynen Look an der Spitze der Couture. Chanels kürzere Saumlängen der 1920er-Jahre waren zwar einer der Gründe, weshalb modisches Schuhwerk zu einer Notwendigkeit wurde, doch ihre eigene Schuhlinie lancierte sie erst 1957 mit Einführung der heute berühmten zweifarbigen Two-Tone-Pumps.

Der Schuh sollte den Fuß kürzer wirken lassen, so Raymond Massaro, der Chanel bei der Entwicklung des berühmten Designs als Schuhmacher zur Hand ging. Der britischen *Vogue* erklärte er 2007: „Die schwarze, leicht eckige Kappe verkürzte den Fuß. Das Beige verschmolz nahtlos mit dem Ganzen und verlängerte das Bein. Es war ein sehr klares Design, akzentuiert durch die Feinheit der Riemchen." Natürlich gibt es in der Modewelt auch die Legende, dass Mademoiselle Chanel das Design deshalb mochte, weil die schwarze Kappe jegliche Spur von Abnutzung kaschierte und so der Trägerin erlaubte, ein aktives Leben zu führen, ohne die Optik ihrer Schuhe durch unansehnlichen Straßenschmutz zu ruinieren. Chanel selbst sagte bekanntlich: „Eine Frau mit guten Schuhen ist niemals hässlich. Sie sind das i-Tüpfelchen der Eleganz."

Noch heute werden Chanel-Schuhe von Massaros Firma gefertigt, wobei die stilistische Bandbreite sich natürlich erheblich erweitert hat. Unter Karl Lagerfeld, der Chanel 1983 übernahm, wurden Schuhe ein immer wichtigerer Bestandteil jeder neuen Prêt-à-porter-Kollektion. Er präsentierte hoch dekorative, aufwendig gearbeitete und verzierte Schuhe, die auf das jeweilige Kollektionsthema abgestimmt waren, führte aber mit zeitgemäßen Versionen des klassischen Two-Tone-Pumps auch Chanels Vermächtnis fort. —*E.M.*

CRÉATRICE DE HAUTE COUTURE, de bijoux, de sacs à main et de l'emblématique parfum Chanel N°. 5, Gabrielle « Coco » Chanel a gagné sa place au panthéon de la mode après la Première Guerre mondiale en proposant aux femmes un *sportswear* à la fois chic et décontracté où les chaussures jouaient un rôle important. Après avoir vendu quelques vêtements dans sa boutique de chapeaux ouverte en 1913, elle s'est hissée à la pointe de la mode dans les années 1920 grâce à son style androgyne. Les jupes et robes Chanel plus courtes des années 1920 ont imposé les chaussures comme des accessoires de mode indispensables, mais la Maison n'a proposé sa propre collection de souliers que des décennies plus tard lorsqu'elle a lancé ses célèbres escarpins bicolores en 1957.

D'après Raymond Massaro, le cordonnier qui a aidé Coco Chanel à créer ce modèle iconique, cet escarpin était conçu pour créer l'illusion d'un pied plus petit. « Le bout noir légèrement carré raccourcissait le pied », a-t-il expliqué dans l'édition britannique de *Vogue* en 2007. « Le beige se fondait dans l'ensemble et allongeait la jambe. Cette création très épurée était accentuée par la finesse des brides. » La légende dit que Mademoiselle Chanel appréciait également ce modèle parce que le bout noir dissimulait les taches, permettant ainsi aux femmes d'adopter un mode de vie actif sans que la saleté des rues de la ville vienne gâcher l'élégance de leurs souliers. « Une femme bien chaussée n'est jamais laide : ses chaussures lui apportent l'ultime touche d'élégance », disait Coco Chanel.

L'entreprise de Raymond Massaro continue aujourd'hui de fabriquer les chaussures Chanel, dont l'offre s'est évidemment considérablement étoffée. Quand Karl Lagerfeld a repris la direction artistique en 1983, il a accordé une place de plus en plus importante aux souliers dans les collections de prêt-à-porter proposées chaque saison. Il présentait des modèles très décoratifs, complexes et richement ornés inspirés du thème de chaque collection tout en revisitant l'héritage de l'escarpin bicolore Chanel classique à travers de nouvelles versions. —*E.M.*

CHANEL
BOUTIQUE

Chanel
Flats: Black satin,
yellow grosgrain
France, *ca.* 1985

Chanel
Pumps: Red-and-
black satin
France, *ca.* 1984

Chanel
Boots: Bronze metallic leather, patent leather, black resin
France, 2010

Chanel
Ankle boots: Off-white-and-gold brocade, resin
France, cruise 2013

Chanel
Sling-back pumps: Black satin, gold metallic net, gold tone resin
France, *ca.* 2015

FOLLOWING
Chanel
Sneakers: Gold metallic leather, white rubber
France, cruise 2013

The Chelsea Cobbler

RICHARD SMITH AND AMANDA WILKINS opened the first Chelsea Cobbler boutique in London in 1967. They initially focused on custom-made shoes, and some of their earliest work involved making footwear to match the ensembles featured in fashion magazines. Soon, Chelsea Cobbler became especially known for its ultra-fashionable boots. *Vogue* sang the company's praises in a 1968 column when it declared that Chelsea Cobbler made "*the* boot everyone orders to give proportion to the mini." The label also designed men's footwear. As the styles were made to order, customers expected to wait eight to 12 weeks for their delivery.

Richard Smith, Amanda Wilkins, and George Macfarlane

The label expanded to the United States in 1970, opening a boutique in Manhattan that was initially run by Wilkins. Although the fashion press regularly commented on the high prices of Chelsea Cobbler footwear, its prestige continued to grow as American celebrities such as Lauren Bacall, Diana Ross, and Carly Simon became clients. The brand also maintained its success in Britain. In 1973 it opened a division at Harrods, situated in the store's youth-oriented "Way In" department, which sold readymade footwear. By 1978 Chelsea Cobbler had grown to include several freestanding boutiques in London. The following year, the brand was subsumed by British manufacturer Rayne, and its presence slowly declined during the 1980s. A relaunch of the label in 2009 was unsuccessful. —*C.H.*

The Chelsea Cobbler
Boots: Multicolor
tapestry-woven silk
England, *ca.* 1971

The Chelsea Cobbler
Platform pump:
Black, red-orange,
and green suede
England, *ca.* 1968

The Chelsea Cobbler
Boots: Burgundy suede
and snakeskin
England, *ca.* 1970

RICHARD SMITH UND AMANDA WILKINS eröffneten ihre erste Chelsea-Cobbler-Boutique 1967 in London. Anfangs konzentrierten sie sich auf Maßschuhe, und einige ihrer frühesten Kreationen waren passend zu den in Modemagazinen vorgestellten Ensembles entworfen. Bald wurde Chelsea Cobbler speziell für ultramodische Stiefel bekannt. Die *Vogue* stimmte 1968 in einer Kolumne ein Loblied auf die Firma an, als sie verkündete, Chelsea Cobbler mache „*den* Stiefel, den jede Frau bestellt, um dem Mini Proportion zu geben". Auch Herrenschuhe zählten zum Sortiment des Labels. Da die Modelle auf Bestellung gefertigt wurden, war mit Lieferzeiten von acht bis zwölf Wochen zu rechnen.

1970 expandierte die Firma in die USA und eröffnete eine Boutique in Manhattan, die anfangs von Wilkins geführt wurde. Obwohl sich die Modepresse regelmäßig über die hohen Preise des Labels ausließ, gewann Chelsea Cobbler weiter an Prestige, denn es zog prominente Kundinnen wie Lauren Bacall, Diana Ross und Carly Simon an. Auch in England hielt der Erfolg der Firma an. Bei Harrods eröffnete sie 1973 in der auf junge Mode ausgerichteten Abteilung „Way In" einen eigenen Verkaufsbereich für Konfektionsschuhe. 1978 war Chelsea Cobbler in London auf mehrere eigenständige Boutiquen angewachsen. Im Jahr darauf wurde das Label von dem britischen Schuhfabrikanten Rayne übernommen, verlor aber im Lauf der 1980er-Jahre allmählich an Präsenz. Ein Relaunch im Jahr 2009 misslang. —*C.H.*

RICHARD SMITH ET AMANDA WILKINS ont ouvert la première boutique Chelsea Cobbler à Londres en 1967. D'abord spécialisée dans la chaussure sur mesure, notamment de modèles assortis aux ensembles présentés dans les magazines de mode, leur marque a vite attiré l'attention, en particulier grâce à leurs bottes ultra-tendance. *Vogue* en a chanté les louanges dans un éditorial de 1968, affirmant que Chelsea Cobbler faisait « *la* botte que toutes les femmes commandent pour équilibrer les proportions de la minijupe ». La marque concevait aussi des souliers pour homme. Les modèles étant fabriqués à la commande, les clients devaient attendre huit à douze semaines pour être livrés.

En 1970, The Chelsea Cobbler s'est implanté aux États-Unis en ouvrant une boutique à Manhattan gérée au départ par Amanda Wilkins. Malgré les commentaires suscités par ses prix élevés dans les magazines de mode, la marque a encore gagné en prestige quand des célébrités américaines telles Lauren Bacall, Diana Ross et Carly Simon sont devenues ses clientes. En 1973, surfant sur sa notoriété au Royaume-Uni, la marque a ouvert un stand de modèles prêts-à-porter au sein du grand magasin Harrods dans l'espace Way In consacré à la jeunesse. En 1978, The Chelsea Cobbler comptait plusieurs boutiques indépendantes à Londres. L'année suivante, la marque a été rachetée par le fabricant britannique Rayne, puis sa présence a lentement décliné pendant les années 1980. En 2009, elle a fait l'objet d'un nouveau lancement qui n'a pas remporté le succès escompté. —*C.H.*

Chloé

FROM ITS INCEPTION THE FRENCH fashion house Chloé
has been associated with relaxed, modern elegance.
In 1952 Gaby Aghion founded this luxury label to
offer young women accessible prêt-à-porter (ready-
to-wear) clothing that broke from the formalities of
the decade's haute couture. Since then the label has
maintained a strong presence among Parisian ready-
to-wear houses, becoming synonymous with youthful
femininity. Chloé has boasted a number of celebrities
among its clientele, from Jackie Kennedy, Grace Kelly, and
Brigitte Bardot to contemporary style icons like Sienna Miller
and Kirsten Dunst. The house has also earned a reputation as a
springboard for some of fashion's greatest talents. Karl Lagerfeld, Martine Sitbon, Stella
McCartney, Phoebe Philo, and Clare Waight Keller have all served as creative directors
for the label.

Gaby Aghion (1921–2014)

Chloé has produced some of the most coveted "it" shoes of the twenty-first century.
Launched in 2008, the "Susanna" ankle boot embodied the free-spirited nature of the label
and became a mainstay of the Chloé style. In 2017, Clare Waight Keller brought a folkloric
sensibility to the house by introducing suede gladiator-style sandals. Since then, Chloé's
creative directors have expanded the label's footwear offerings with their take on the contemporary Chloé style. In 2018, Natacha Ramsay-Levi debuted the "Rylee" ankle boot.
This western-style, lace-up bootie with buckles and cutouts around the ankle emerged
as an "it" shoe. Gabriela Hearst focused on sustainability during her tenure at Chloé and
helped the company to achieve B Corp certification. Her "Nama" sneaker was crafted from
more sustainable, lower-impact materials than Chloé's previous "Sonnie" sneaker. Most
recently, Chemena Kamali was appointed Chloe's creative director, where she continues
the legacy of reimagining the brand's carefree spirit. —M.M.A.

DAS FRANZÖSISCHE MODEHAUS CHLOÉ STEHT seit seinen Anfängen für legere, moderne Eleganz. Gaby Aghion gründete das Luxuslabel 1952, um jungen Frauen ungezwungene Prêt-à-porter-Mode anzubieten, die aus dem starren Korsett der damaligen Haute Couture ausbrach. Seitdem behauptet das Label im Kreis der Pariser Prêt-à-porter-Häuser eine starke Präsenz und ist zum Synonym für jugendlich-feminine Mode geworden. Chloé kann sich einer Reihe prominenter Kundinnen rühmen, von Jackie Kennedy, Grace Kelly und Brigitte Bardot bis hin zu Stilikonen unserer Zeit wie Sienna Miller und Kirsten Dunst. Zudem hat sich das Haus einen Ruf als Sprungbrett für einige der größten Talente der Modebranche erworben. Neben Karl Lagerfeld waren Martine Sitbon, Stella McCartney, Phoebe Philo und Clare Waight Keller allesamt Chefdesignerinnen bei Chloé.

Chloé hat einige der begehrtesten „It"-Schuhe des 21. Jahrhunderts entworfen. Die 2008 lancierte Stiefelette „Susanna" verkörperte den freigeistigen Charakter des Labels und wurde zu einer wichtigen Stütze des Chloé-Stils. Im Jahr 2017 brachte Clare Waight Keller Sinn für Folklore in das Haus, indem sie Sandalen im Gladiatorenstil aus Wildleder entwarf. Seitdem haben die Kreativdirektoren von Chloé das Schuhangebot des Labels mit ihrer Interpretation des zeitgenössischen Chloé-Stils erweitert. Im Jahr 2018 stellte Natacha Ramsay-Levi die Stiefelette „Rylee" vor. Dieser Schnürstiefel im Western-Stil mit Schnallen und Aussparungen um den Knöchel entwickelte sich zum „It"-Schuh. Gabriela Hearst konzentrierte sich während ihrer Zeit bei Chloé auf das Thema Nachhaltigkeit und verhalf dem Unternehmen zu einer B Corp-Zertifizierung. Ihr „Nama"-Sneaker wurde aus nachhaltigeren und umweltfreundlicheren Materialien hergestellt als der vorherige „Sonnie"-Sneaker von Chloé. 2023 wurde Chemena Kamali zur Kreativdirektorin von Chloé ernannt, wo sie die Tradition fortführt und gleichzeitig den für das Haus charakteristischen Geist der Unbeschwertheit neu erfindet. —M.M.A.

LA MAISON DE MODE FRANÇAISE Chloé a toujours symbolisé une élégance moderne et décontractée. Quand Gaby Aghion a fondé sa marque de luxe en 1952, elle voulait proposer un prêt-à-porter abordable pour les jeunes femmes, en alternative au formalisme de la haute couture des années 1950. Incarnation d'une féminité rayonnante de jeunesse, Chloé reste depuis l'une des plus solides marques de prêt-à-porter parisiennes. Elle a toujours revendiqué de nombreuses stars parmi sa clientèle, de Jackie Kennedy, Grace Kelly et Brigitte Bardot à des icônes contemporaines telles Sienna Miller et Kirsten Dunst. La Maison est aussi réputée comme un tremplin professionnel pour de grands talents de la mode : Karl Lagerfeld, Martine Sitbon, Stella McCartney, Phoebe Philo et Clare Waight Keller ont tous officié en tant que directeur ou directrice artistique de la griffe.

Chloé a produit certaines des « It-chaussures » les plus convoitées du XXIᵉ siècle. La bottine Susanna lancée en 2008 symbolisait la liberté d'esprit de la marque et s'est imposée comme un pilier du style Chloé. En 2017, Clare Waight Keller a insufflé une sensibilité folklorique à la Maison en proposant des sandales de gladiateur en daim. Par la suite, les différentes directrices artistiques ont élargi l'offre de chaussures de la marque à travers leurs visions respectives du style Chloé contemporain. En 2018, Natacha Ramsay-Levi a lancé la bottine Rylee à lacets inspirée des santiags : entre ses brides et ses découpes autour de la cheville, elle est devenue l'un des modèles incontournables de l'année. Gabriela Hearst s'est quant à elle focalisée sur le développement durable et a aidé l'entreprise à obtenir la certification B Corp. Sa sneaker Nama a été produite dans des matériaux plus durables et à plus faible impact que le modèle Sonnie qui l'avait précédé. En 2023, Chemena Kamali a été nommée directrice de la création de Chloé, où elle perpétue la tradition tout en réinventant l'esprit d'insouciance caractéristique de la Maison. —*M.M.A.*

PAGE 118 AND BELOW
Chloé
Boots: Brown calfskin
and goatskin, viscose,
rubber, aluminum
France, fall 2018

PAGE 120
Chloé
"Susanna" ankle boot:
Black leather, gold
metal studs
France, 2017

PREVIOUS
Chloé
Sandals: Brown leather,
cork
France, 2017

OPPOSITE
Chloé
"Rylee" boots:
Black calfskin, metal,
cotton, rubber
France, summer 2018

"For me elegance is the opposite of ennui, of conservative chic and obvious style. Elegance must be continuously reinvented, for each woman."

— KARL LAGERFELD

Chloé
Sandals: Pink suede
France, spring 2015

Chloé
"Sonnie" sneaker:
White, green, and red
calfskin, cotton, polyes-
ter, nylon, rubber
France, pre-fall 2018

Jimmy Choo

"**WAIT! WAIT! I LOST MY CHOO!**" cried Sarah Jessica Parker's character, Carrie Bradshaw, in one of the most memorable shoe moments of *Sex and the City*. As Carrie dashed to catch the last ferry from Staten Island to Manhattan, her foot slipped out of one of her sling-back, high-heeled sandals. Although she missed the ferry, fans of the show were treated to a close-up of the lilac silk, feather-trimmed design as she placed it back on her foot. The gesture was accompanied by tinkling music that accented the shoe's delicate, fairy tale–like beauty.

Founded in 1996, the Jimmy Choo label was the brainchild of Choo, a custom shoemaker already known for crafting styles for Princess Diana; Sandra Choi, Choo's niece and the designer for the brand's ready-to-wear styles; and Tamara Mellon, an entrepreneur

Jimmy Choo (b. 1948)

who also helped to shape the Jimmy Choo image. The label quickly made a name for itself in the high-end footwear market, combining glamour and sex appeal with a youthful aesthetic. Jimmy Choo had become a household name by the end of the decade, and its popularity among celebrities continues. The brand's designs feature regularly on the red carpet, and Jennifer Lopez, Michelle Obama, and Reese Witherspoon are just a few of its high-profile clients.

Although Choo and Mellon have left the company, Choi continues to lead the brand in her role as creative director. "Jimmy Choo is that sexy, strappy, stiletto thing — but it can be something else too," says Choi, whose designs have also included glittery, high-topped sneakers and chic, tasseled flats. Choi asserts that the Jimmy Choo client need not present an image of polished perfection, but rather an attitude of self-assurance, and her embrace of her customers' individual styles has proven highly successful. *—C.H.*

PREVIOUS
Jimmy Choo
"Orchid" boot:
Brown leather
England, 2001

Sandra Choi, Choo's
niece, was appointed
creative director in 1996.
Her "Head Over High
Heels" sketch for Jimmy

Choo features a stiletto
in silver-and-black
leather embellished with
a large cut-glass stone on
the toe. 2014.

„HALT! HALT! ICH HABE MEINEN CHOO verloren!",
rief Carrie Bradshaw, verkörpert von Sarah Jessica
Parker, in einem der denkwürdigsten Schuhmomente von *Sex and the City*. Bei ihrem Spurt
in hohen Slingback-Sandaletten, um die letzte
Fähre von Staten Island nach Manhattan zu erwischen, war Carrie mit einem Fuß aus dem Schuh
gerutscht. Die Fähre fuhr ohne sie ab, doch dafür
bekamen die Fans der Serie die federbesetzte Kreation aus fliederfarbener Seide in Nahaufnahme geboten, als sie wieder in den Schuh schlüpfte. Untermalt wurde dieser Moment von leise klimpernden
Klängen, die die märchenhaft zarte Schönheit des
Schuhs betonten.

Das 1996 gegründete Label Jimmy Choo
war eine Idee von Choo, der als Schuhmacher mit
Maßanfertigungen für Prinzessin Diana bereits Bekanntheit erlangt hatte, von Choos Nichte Sandra
Choi, die für die Prêt-à-porter-Linie verantwortlich
zeichnete, und von Tamara Mellon, einer Unternehmerin, die auch das Image der Marke entscheidend
mitprägte. Mit seiner Kombination aus Glamour,
Sexappeal und jugendlicher Ästhetik machte sich
das Label schnell einen Namen im Luxusschuhsegment. Am Ende des Jahrzehnts war Jimmy Choo
ein etablierter Begriff und ist bis heute ein Lieblingslabel der Prominenz. Regelmäßig erscheinen
Choo-Kreationen auf dem roten Teppich und an den
Füßen berühmter Trägerinnen wie Jennifer Lopez,
Michelle Obama und Reese Witherspoon, um nur einige zu nennen.

Choo und Mellon haben die Firma zwar verlassen, doch Choi führt die Marke in ihrer Rolle
als Kreativchefin weiter. „Bei Jimmy Choo denkt
man an sexy Stilettos und Riemchen – aber das
ist nicht alles", sagt Choi, zu deren Looks auch
High-Top-Sneaker mit Glitzerbesatz und elegante
Quastenslipper zählen. Wie sie betont, muss die
Jimmy-Choo-Trägerin kein Bild makelloser Perfektion abgeben, sondern sollte vielmehr eine
selbstbewusste Haltung an den Tag legen. Chois
Konzept, auf den individuellen Stil ihrer Kundinnen einzugehen, hat sich als höchst erfolgreich
erwiesen. —*C.H.*

« ATTENDEZ ! ATTENDEZ ! J'AI PERDU MA CHOO ! »
s'écrie Carrie Bradshaw dans l'une des scènes les
plus mémorables de *Sex and the City*. En courant
pour attraper le dernier ferry de Staten Island à
Manhattan, son pied a glissé et elle a perdu l'une de
ses sandales à talon et à bride. Le personnage interprété par Sarah Jessica Parker a raté le ferry, mais
les fans de la série ont eu droit à un gros plan sur le
soulier en soie lilas orné de plumes dès qu'elle a pu
le remettre à son pied – un geste accompagné d'une
musique de clochettes digne d'un conte de fées pour
souligner la beauté délicate de la sandale.

Créateur réputé pour ses modèles sur mesure
destinés à la princesse Diana, Jimmy Choo a créé
sa marque éponyme en 1996 avec Sandra Choi, sa
nièce et créatrice des souliers « prêts-à-porter » de
la griffe, et Tamara Mellon, une entrepreneuse qui a
aussi contribué à façonner l'image de Jimmy Choo.
La marque a vite trouvé une place de choix sur le
marché des chaussures haut de gamme grâce à son
alliance entre glamour, *sex-appeal* et jeunesse. À la
fin des années 1990, le nom de Jimmy Choo était
connu du grand public et son attrait auprès des
célébrités perdure jusqu'à aujourd'hui. Les créations
de la marque s'affichent régulièrement sur les tapis
rouges. Jennifer Lopez, Michelle Obama et Reese
Witherspoon ne sont que quelques-unes des nombreuses stars clientes de la marque.

Après le départ de Jimmy Choo et Tamara
Mellon, Sandra Choi est restée à la tête de la
marque en tant que directrice artistique. « Jimmy
Choo est synonyme de talons aiguilles sexy, mais ça
ne se limite pas à ça », explique Sandra Choi, dont
les créations incluent aussi de flamboyantes baskets montantes et des ballerines chics à pompons.
Elle insiste sur le fait que la cliente Jimmy Choo
ne cherche pas à donner une image parfaite d'elle-
même, mais plutôt à gagner en assurance. Son
adaptation au style personnel de chaque femme lui
vaut un immense succès. —*C.H.*

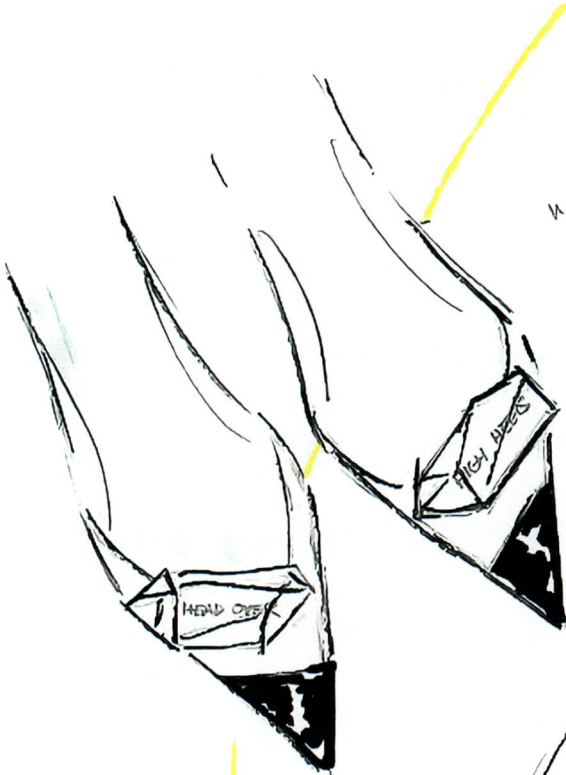

"HEAD OVER HIGH HEELS"

SILVER LINED, SILVER MIRROR LEATHER T/ BLACK PATENT TOES & HEELS W/ LARGE GLASS CUT STONE & HIDDEN QUOTE.

METALLIC / PATENT / GLASS —

HEAD OVER

HIGH HEELS

Sandra Choi For Jimmy Choo —
FEB'2014

"A designer knows he has achieved perfection not when there is nothing left to add, but when there is nothing left to take away."

— JIMMY CHOO

Jimmy Choo
High-heeled mule:
Silver leather, glitter
England, 2019

Choo's "Trapeze" heels
evoke aerial acrobat-
ics in green and gold.
Sandra Choi, 2015.

Jimmy Choo
Sandals: Lavender suede
and feathers
England, 2000
(remade 2021)

Comme des Garçons

Rei Kawakubo (b. 1942)

FEW FASHION LABELS EMBODY a boundary-breaking aesthetic quite like Rei Kawakubo's Comme des Garçons. The Japanese designer has garnered international acclaim for her avant-garde designs, which embrace abstraction and continually challenge fashion's norms. Comme des Garçons — French for "like some boys" — was established in Tokyo in 1968. The label did not receive international recognition until 1981, following the debut of Kawakubo's collection in Paris. Although her deconstructed garments, in asymmetric cuts and austere colors, were initially met with criticism from the French fashion press, not long after Kawakubo would assemble a fashion empire, which included diffusion lines, fragrances, and footwear.

Over the years, Comme des Garçons has produced unique interpretations of classic and obscure footwear. Early shoe designs featuring distressed, unisex styles reinforced Kawakubo's radical departure from the Eurocentric fashion of the 1980s. Her continued evolution is evident in the revolutionary ideas represented in later footwear designs. A pair of patent leather ballet-style shoes from spring 2005 buck conventional notions of grace and femininity associated with the ballerina, while navy polka dot flip-flops from 2017 broaden our perception of fashion as art. Comme des Garçons was among the first high-fashion labels to engage in sneaker collaborations, effectively blurring the lines between high fashion and casual wear. The label's long-standing collaboration with Nike has earned Comme des Garçons a cult following with sneakerheads around the world. The label has collaborated on countless styles, from Junya Watanabe's Nike Zoom Haven in 1999 to the more recent "Nike Cortez flatform" sneakers — featuring an outrageous striped platform silhouette — which debuted on the Comme des Garçons fall 2018 runway. —M.M.A.

NUR WENIGE MODELABELS VERKÖRPERN eine Ästhetik, die in ähnlichem Maß Grenzen sprengt wie Comme des Garçons von Rei Kawakubo. Die japanische Designerin erntet internationalen Beifall für ihre avantgardistischen Kreationen, die mit Abstraktion spielen und modische Normen unablässig infrage stellen. Comme des Garçons – auf Deutsch „Wie Jungen" – wurde 1968 in Tokio gegründet, doch internationale Anerkennung fand das Label erst 1981, nachdem Kawakubos Kollektion ihre Premiere in Paris hatte. Ihre dekonstruierten Kreationen in asymmetrischen Schnitten und dunklen Farben stießen in der französischen Modepresse zunächst auf Kritik, doch schon bald baute Kawakubo ein Modeimperium auf, zu dem auch Zweitlinien, Düfte und Schuhmode zählten.

Im Lauf der Jahre hat Comme des Garçons klassische und obskure Fußbekleidung auf einzigartige Weise neu interpretiert. Während frühe Unisex-Entwürfe im Used-Look Kawakubos radikale Abkehr von der eurozentrischen Mode der 1980er-Jahre unterstrichen, belegen die revolutionären Ideen, die in ihren späteren Schuhkreationen zum Ausdruck kamen, ihre ständige Weiterentwicklung. So trotzen Lacklederschuhe im Ballettstil aus dem Frühjahr 2005 den mit der Ballerina assoziierten, konventionellen Vorstellungen von Anmut und Weiblichkeit, während marineblaue Flipflops mit Punkten aus dem Jahr 2017 unsere Wahrnehmung von Mode als Kunstform erweitern. Als eines der ersten Haute-Couture-Label begann Comme des Garçons eine Kooperation mit Sportschuh-Herstellern und ließ so die Grenzen zwischen Couture und Streetwear gekonnt verschwimmen. Die langjährige Zusammenarbeit mit Nike trug dem Label unter Sneaker-Fans auf der ganzen Welt Kultstatus ein. Comme des Garçons wirkte an zahllosen Nike-Looks mit, angefangen bei Junya Watanabes „Nike Zoom Haven" aus dem Jahr 1999 bis zu den „Nike Cortez Flatform"-Sneakern mit einer nie dagewesenen gestreiften Plateau-Silhouette, die ihr Debüt im Herbst 2018 auf dem Laufsteg von Comme des Garçons feierten. —M.M.A.

RARES SONT LES MARQUES de mode qui incarnent une esthétique aussi révolutionnaire que Comme des Garçons. Inspirées par l'art abstrait, les créations avant-gardistes de la styliste japonaise Rei Kawakubo remettent toujours en question des règles de la mode et lui ont valu un succès planétaire. Elle a fondé Comme des Garçons en 1968 à Tokyo, mais la griffe n'a eu une reconnaissance internationale qu'en 1981 après une première présentation de sa collection à Paris. Bien que ses vêtements déconstruits aux coupes asymétriques et aux couleurs austères aient d'abord été critiqués par la presse de mode française, la créatrice a rapidement bâti un vaste empire incluant des lignes de diffusion, des parfums et des chaussures.

Au fil des années, Comme des Garçons a proposé des interprétations uniques de souliers classiques ou plus obscurs. Ses premières créations dans ce domaine – des modèles unisexes à l'aspect vieilli – ont encore creusé l'écart radical séparant Rei Kawakubo de la mode eurocentrique des années 1980. L'évolution permanente de la créatrice transparaît de façon évidente dans les idées révolutionnaires qu'elle a exprimées ultérieurement à travers ses chaussures. Au printemps 2005, une paire de ballerines en cuir verni bousculait les notions de grâce et de féminité habituellement associées aux danseuses classiques, tandis que les tongs bleu marine à pois de 2017 élargissaient notre perception de la mode en tant qu'art. Comptant parmi les premières griffes haut de gamme à créer des baskets en collaboration, Comme des Garçons a réussi à brouiller la frontière entre mode de luxe et look décontracté. Sa collaboration de longue date avec Nike a vu la production d'innombrables modèles qui lui ont valu un statut de marque culte auprès des fans de sneakers du monde entier, de la Nike Zoom Haven de Junya Watanabe en 1999 à la plus récente Nike Cortez Platform – avec son extravagante semelle compensée rayée – présentée au défilé Automne 2019 de Comme des Garçons. —*M.M.A.*

PAGE 132
Comme des Garçons
Flats: Pale-pink patent
leather, black elastic
Japan, spring 2005

PAGE 134
Comme des Garçons
Booties: White perfo-
rated leather, rubber
Japan, spring 1998

PREVIOUS
Comme des Garçons
Sneakers: White faux
fur, rubber
Japan, fall 2016

OPPOSITE
Comme des Garçons
Shoes: Black rubber,
tan fibers
Japan, *ca.* 1983

OPPOSITE BELOW
Comme des Garçons
Men's slides: Black glacé
leather, white foam
rubber
Japan, 1984–85

Comme des Garçons
(Junya Watanabe)
Pumps: Purple-and-gold
silk brocade
Japan, spring 1997

Comme des Garçons
Pumps: Red vinyl
Japan, fall 1998

Nike
(Comme des Garçons)
"Cortez" sneakers:
Black leather, black-and-
white rubber, nylon
USA, spring 2019

Comme des Garçons
Flip-flop sandals:
Blue-and-white rubber
Japan, 2017

Courrèges

André Courrèges (1923–2016)

ANDRÉ COURRÈGES, KNOWN AS THE Space Age Couturier, was among the most influential and innovative fashion designers of the mid-to-late 1960s. He and a handful of other French couturiers such as Paco Rabanne and Pierre Cardin embraced futuristic design at a time when the world was rapt with the US and Russia's race to moon — an aesthetic move that was a dramatic break from French haute couture. Their creations were the Parisian answer to the emergence of a powerful, global youth culture, for which accessories played an integral part.

Born in 1923 in the French Pyrenees, Courrèges studied engineering before serving as a pilot in the French Air Force during World War II. He approached fashion through his desire to liberate the female body, and his technical background informed his modern designs. He trained under Cristóbal Balenciaga, working in the established designer's atelier from 1950 until he opened his own house in 1961. Courrèges's groundbreaking mid-'60s silhouettes included trousers for women and the miniskirt — both paired with flat shoes, which encouraged freedom of movement and changed the proportion of the fashionable figure. His flat white-leather boots were not only among his most famous space age designs but one of the most popular looks of the period. Rebranded as go-go boots and further immortalized in pop culture by Nancy Sinatra in "These Boots Are Made for Walkin'," they were frequently copied by lower-priced manufacturers in France and internationally.

Courrèges continued to design youthful, playful styles throughout his career. His bright-orange loafers with attached bells are an example of his experimental and lighthearted designs. Yves Saint Laurent described the designer's impact on fashion culture, stating in 1966: "Things have never been the same since Courrèges had his explosion . . . It was a necessary and healthy happening in the fashion world." —*E.W.*

PAGE 140
A model wears a patterned swimsuit and open-toe flats, 1965.

The designer with model Linda Mestre and others at Orly Airport, in Paris, in 1967, before departing for Los Angeles to present a new line.

ANDRÉ COURRÈGES, BEKANNT ALS SCHÖPFER des Weltraumlooks, war einer der einflussreichsten und innovativsten Modedesigner der mittleren und späten 1960er-Jahre. In einem ästhetischen Schritt, der einen dramatischen Bruch mit Frankreichs Haute Couture darstellte, setzten er und eine Handvoll anderer französischer Couturiers wie Paco Rabanne und Pierre Cardin auf futuristisches Design – zu einer Zeit, da die Welt gebannt den sowjetisch-amerikanischen Wettlauf ins All verfolgte. Es waren ihre Kreationen, mit denen Paris auf das Aufkommen einer weltweiten, mächtigen Jugendkultur reagierte, für die Accessoires eine wesentliche Rolle spielte.

Der 1923 in den französischen Pyrenäen geborene Courrèges studierte zunächst Ingenieurwissenschaften und diente im Zweiten Weltkrieg als Pilot bei der französischen Luftwaffe. Der Mode wandte er sich mit dem Wunsch zu, den weiblichen Körper zu befreien, und sein technischer Hintergrund bildete die Basis seiner modernen Designs. Ab 1950 erlernte er das Handwerk im Atelier des renommierten Modeschöpfers Cristóbal Balenciaga, ehe er 1961 sein eigenes Haus eröffnete. Zu den wegweisenden Silhouetten, die Courrèges Mitte der 1960er-Jahre schuf, zählten Hosen für Frauen und der Minirock – beides gepaart mit fußfreundlich flachen Schuhen, die die Proportionen der modischen Figur veränderten. Seine weißen Lederstiefel mit flachem Absatz zählten nicht nur zu seinen berühmtesten Weltraumdesigns, sondern auch zu den beliebtesten Looks der Zeit. In „Go-go-Stiefel" umgetauft und durch Nancy Sinatras „These Boots Are Made for Walkin'" zusätzlich in der Popkultur verewigt, wurden sie von preisgünstigeren Modefirmen in Frankreich und aller Welt vielfach kopiert.

Courrèges kreierte seine gesamte Karriere lang jugendlich verspielte Looks. Ein Beispiel für sein experimentelles, unbeschwertes Design bieten die Loafer in leuchtendem Orange mit applizierten Glöckchen. Yves Saint Laurent sagte 1966 über André Courrèges' Einfluss auf die Modekultur: „Seit der Explosion von Courrèges ist nichts mehr, wie es war ... Das war für die Modewelt notwendig und gesund." —E.W.

PARIS MATCH

N° 957 / 12 AOUT 1967 / 1,20 F

MODE: LE COURT A GAGNÉ Exclusif : les mannequins de Courrèges dans leur présentation-ballet. (Voir à l'intérieur.)

Pictured on a 1968 *Paris Match* cover, Courrèges' bold geometric designs defined French fashion in the 1960s.

Courrèges
Loafer: Orange leather, brass bell
France, spring 1969

FOLLOWING
Courrèges
Boots: White kid leather and plastic sunglasses
France, 1964

RÉPUTÉ COMME LE COUTURIER DU *SPACE AGE*, André Courrèges a été l'un des créateurs de mode les plus influents et innovants de la seconde moitié des années 1960. Pendant que le monde entier se passionnait pour la course à la Lune opposant les États-Unis et la Russie, lui et quelques couturiers français, tels Paco Rabanne et Pierre Cardin, lançaient une mode futuriste dont l'esthétique tranchait radicalement avec la haute couture de l'époque. Leurs créations étaient la réponse de Paris à la puissante culture de la jeunesse qui déferlait sur le monde et pour laquelle les accessoires jouaient un rôle important.

Né en 1923 dans les Pyrénées, André Courrèges a fait des études de génie civil avant de servir en tant que pilote dans l'armée de l'air pendant la Seconde Guerre mondiale. Il s'est tourné vers la mode pour libérer le corps de la femme, et ses créations modernes témoignent de ses connaissances techniques. Il s'est formé auprès de Cristóbal Balenciaga et a travaillé dans l'atelier du célèbre couturier de 1950 à 1961, année où il a ouvert sa propre Maison. Les looks Courrèges révolutionnaires du milieu des années 1960 incluaient des pantalons pour femme et des minijupes – tous deux portés avec des chaussures plates qui offraient plus de liberté de mouvement tout en modifiant les proportions de la silhouette à la mode. Les bottes plates en cuir blanc restent l'une des créations *Space Age* les plus célèbres de Courrèges, mais aussi l'un des modèles les plus populaires de l'époque. Renommées *go-go boots* par les Anglo-Saxons et immortalisées dans la *pop culture* par Nancy Sinatra avec la chanson « These Boots Are Made for Walkin' », elles ont souvent été copiées par des fabricants bon marché français et étrangers.

André Courrèges a continué à créer une mode jeune et ludique tout au long de sa carrière. Ses mocassins orange vif à clochettes illustrent bien son style expérimental et léger. En 1966, Yves Saint Laurent a décrit l'impact du couturier sur la culture de la mode en ces termes : « Les choses n'ont plus jamais été les mêmes après l'explosion provoquée par André Courrèges… une explosion nécessaire et saine pour le monde de la mode. » —*E.W.*

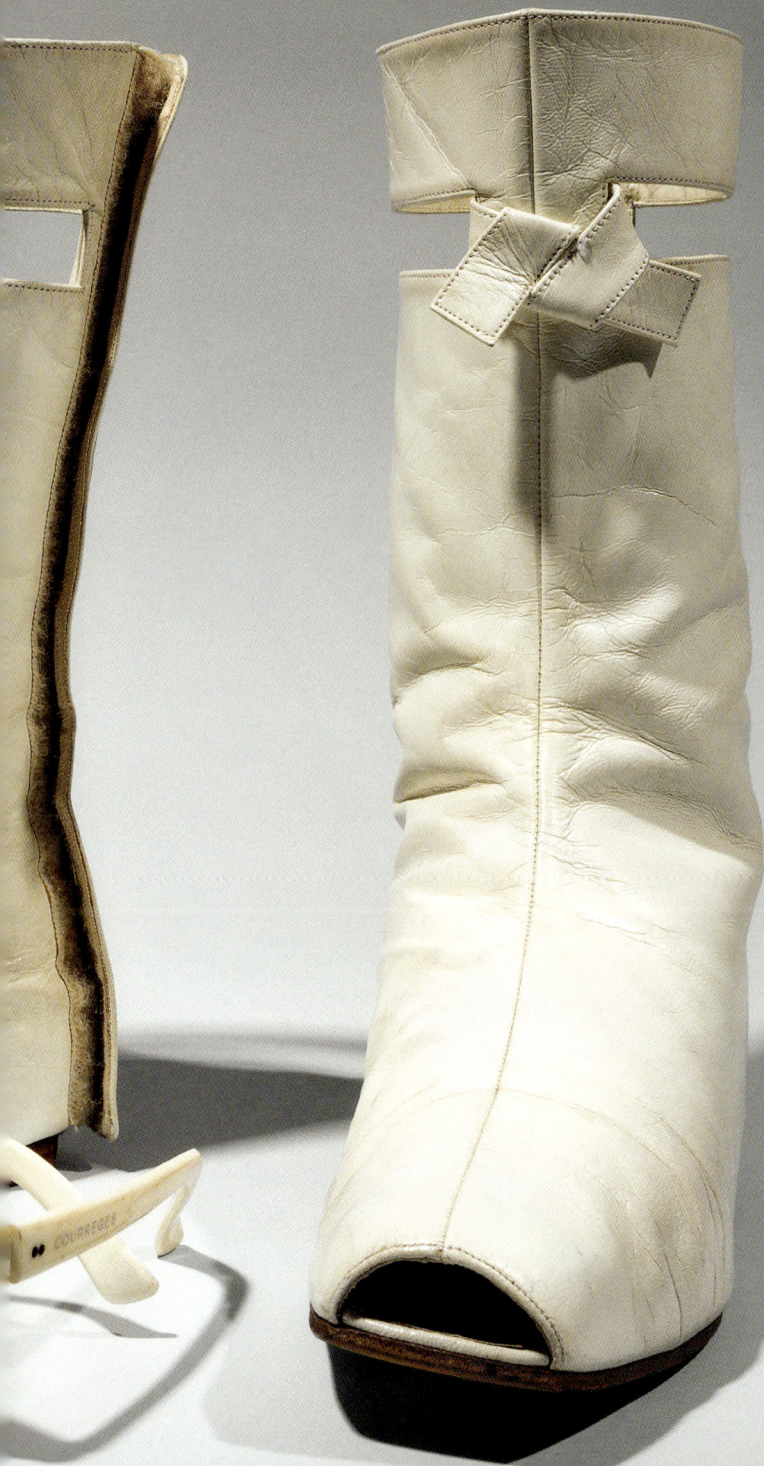

Patrick Cox

Patrick Cox (b. 1963)

THE BRITISH-CANADIAN DESIGNER PATRICK COX is the mastermind behind the cult "Wannabe" moccasin loafer, dubbed by *British GQ* as "the most desirable shoe" of the 1990s, rendered in countless variations, and sold in the hundreds of thousands since the design's inception. His creations can be tongue-in-cheek and provocative, while others are elegant, sophisticated, and seductive.

Born in Edmonton, Canada, in 1963, Patrick Cox has called many countries home, and lived in Canada, various countries in Africa, and England as a child due to the peripatetic nature of his father's career as a linguist. Although Cox trained to be a veterinarian, his immersion in club culture introduced him to alternative fashion scenes that transformed his career path. He created his first shoe at age 19 for Toronto designer Loucas Kleanthous, who encouraged him to study design at Cordwainers Technical College in London. While still a student, Cox created shoes for Vivienne Westwood's 1984 *Clint Eastwood* collection and went on to design for BodyMap and John Galliano, producing the shoes himself. Cox became known for his idiosyncratic styles that riffed on traditional silhouettes, adding unexpected fabrications and details — one of his most popular early designs was a 1984 customization of Dr. Martens boots that revealed the steel toe construction. He opened his first shop in London in 1991, and by the end of the decade his business had expanded internationally.

Cox draws inspiration from a multitude of references, from music (Gene Simmons and Pat Benatar inspired his 1997 red silk dragon-embroidered pumps) to British culture to art. Sharp graphic colors and black and white are favored motifs, as seen in his "Mondrian" Mary Janes and "Roll-Tongue" spectators, designed for John Galliano. The latter was so popular that it appeared on a British talk show three times in one week, worn by Boy George, Elton John, and a member of the band Wet Wet Wet. —*E.W.*

PATRICK COX IST DER KREATIVE Kopf hinter dem Kult-Loafer „Wannabe", einem in zahllosen Variationen abgewandelten Mokassin, der sich seit Einführung des Designs hunderttausendfach verkaufte und von der britischen *GQ* als „begehrenswertester Schuh" der 1990er-Jahre bezeichnet wurde. Die Kreationen des Anglokanadiers können ebenso gut witzig und provokativ sein wie elegant, mondän und verführerisch.

Der 1963 im kanadischen Edmonton geborene Cox nannte schon viele Länder sein Zuhause, verbrachte er doch seine Kindheit in Kanada, England und verschiedenen Ländern Afrikas, da sein Vater als Sprachforscher beruflich viel unterwegs war. Cox' Laufbahn begann mit einer Ausbildung zum Tierarzt, doch seine Kursrichtung änderte sich, als er in die Klubkultur eintauchte und die alternative Modeszene kennenlernte. Seinen ersten Schuh entwarf er mit 19 für den in Toronto ansässigen Modeschöpfer Loucas Kleanthous, der ihn zu einem Designstudium am Cordwainers Technical College in London ermutigte. Noch während des Studiums kreierte Cox Schuhe für Vivienne Westwoods Kollektion *Clint Eastwood* von 1984, anschließend auch in eigener Fertigung für BodyMap und John Galliano. Cox wurde bekannt für einen eigenwilligen Stil, der traditionelle Silhouetten spielerisch um überraschende Einfälle und Details ergänzte. Zu den beliebtesten Entwürfen seiner Anfangszeit zählt ein Dr.-Martens-Sondermodell mit freigelegter Stahlkappenkonstruktion. 1991 öffnete sein erstes Ladengeschäft in London, und gegen Ende des Jahrzehnts war sein Label international vertreten.

Inspiration schöpft Cox aus verschiedensten Quellen, von der Musik (für seine roten Seidenpumps mit Drachenapplikation aus dem Jahr 1997 standen Gene Simmons und Pat Benatar Pate) über britische Kultur bis hin zur Kunst. Er bevorzugt klare, grafische Farben und Schwarz-Weiß, zu sehen etwa bei seinen „Mondrian"-Spangenschuhen oder bei dem für John Galliano entworfenen Budapester-Herrenschuh „Roll Tongue". Letzterer war so erfolgreich, dass er in einer englischen Talkshow innerhalb einer Woche dreimal zu sehen war: an den Füßen von Boy George, Elton John und einem Bandmitglied von Wet Wet Wet. —*E.W.*

PREVIOUS

Patrick Cox
"Mondrian" Mary Jane:
White, blue, red, and
black leather
England, spring 1995

Patrick Cox
"Roll-Tongue" shoe:
Black-and-white leather
England, 1987

Patrick Cox
Pump: Embroidered
red silk crepe
England, 1997

CRÉATEUR ANGLO-CANADIEN, PATRICK COX est l'inventeur du Wannabe, un mocassin culte qualifié de « soulier le plus désirable » des années 1990 dans l'édition britannique de *GQ*, décliné dans d'innombrables variantes et écoulé à des centaines de milliers d'exemplaires depuis son lancement. Si certaines créations de Patrick Cox sont ironiques et provocatrices, d'autres séduisent par leur élégance et leur sophistication.

Né en 1963 à Edmonton au Canada, Patrick Cox a vécu dans de nombreux pays entre l'Afrique, le Canada et l'Angleterre, la carrière de son père linguiste amenant sa famille à déménager régulièrement. Bien qu'il ait suivi des études de vétérinaire, son immersion dans la culture club lui a donné accès à des milieux alternatifs de la mode qui ont suscité un changement de vocation. Il a créé son premier soulier à l'âge de 19 ans pour Loucas Kleanthous, un créateur de Toronto qui l'a incité à s'inscrire au Cordwainers Technical College de Londres. Patrick Cox a créé des chaussures pour la collection Clint Eastwood de Vivienne Westwood en 1984 alors qu'il était encore étudiant, puis pour BodyMap et John Galliano en fabriquant lui-même les souliers. Il s'est distingué grâce à ses modèles singuliers librement inspirés de silhouettes traditionnelles auxquelles il ajoutait des fabrications et des détails inattendus : en 1984, l'un de ses premiers modèles à succès était une bottine Dr. Martens customisée révélant la construction du bout en acier. Après l'ouverture d'une première boutique à Londres en 1991, son entreprise était présente dans le monde entier à la fin de la décennie.

Patrick Cox s'inspire d'une multitude de références, qu'il s'agisse de musique (en 1997, Gene Simmons et Pat Benatar lui ont inspiré des escarpins en soie rouge brodés d'un dragon), de culture britannique ou d'art. Les couleurs graphiques soutenues ainsi que le noir et blanc comptent parmi ses thèmes de prédilection, à l'image de ses babies Mondrian ou des *spectators* Roll-Tongue conçus pour John Galliano. Ces derniers remportaient un tel succès qu'on les a vus trois fois en une semaine dans le même *talk-show* anglais : aux pieds de Boy George, d'Elton John et d'un membre du groupe Wet Wet Wet. —*E.W.*

Delman

HERMAN DELMAN IS REMEMBERED AS one of the most influential figures in the New York footwear industry. A native of Portland, Oregon, he was born in 1895, the son of dedicated shoe retailers. The timing of Delman's career was fortuitous. By the time he opened his first boutique in New York City in 1919, fashionable hemlines had risen above the ankle. His shoes became increasingly visible, stylistically varied, and were made for every occasion both public and private. Delman was actively designing at this time but did not limit his efforts to the creation of new shoe styles. What elevated his products and solidified his influence was the focus on quality (both custom and ready-made), his brilliance at promoting the brand, and his ability to spot and hire highly innovative talents. He was one of the first designers to harness the power of celebrity as a selling tool, using film stars in his advertisements, and with the same savvy, understood the power of label recognition by having his name appear on each of his shoes, unusual for the time.

**Herman Delman
(1895–1955)**

Delman's shoes were made with unique materials that ranged from exotic animal skins to synthetics and plastics. The shoes were known for their comfort, fit, and, as Delman himself noted, "so much handwork in them that they will defy the copyist." The shoes were also cleverly promoted, from the Cinderella logo on the label to licensing agreements with leading retailers. In 1933 Delman entered into an exclusive agreement with Saks Fifth Avenue, and in 1936 he formed a decades-long partnership with Bergdorf Goodman. He sustained the company's reputation by hiring stellar talents such as Beth Levine, Kenneth Jay Lane, and Roger Vivier. The latter worked for Delman on and off, from the 1930s to the 1990s, including the period Vivier designed for the house of Dior.

Although Delman died in 1955 and his company has been bought and sold numerous times since, the firm continues to this day, more than 100 years after its creation. —*P.M.*

HERMAN DELMAN GILT BIS HEUTE als eine der einflussreichsten Größen der New Yorker Schuhmodebranche. 1895 als Sohn passionierter Schuhhändler in Portland, Oregon, geboren, begann Delman seine Laufbahn zu einem günstigen Zeitpunkt. Als er 1919 seine erste Boutique in New York eröffnete, hatten die Rocksäume es bereits über den Knöchel geschafft. Solchermaßen besser sichtbar, wurden seine Schuhe stilistisch vielfältiger und dem Anlass entsprechend gefertigt, sei er gesellschaftlich oder privat. Delman war zu dieser Zeit ein aktiver Designer, beschränkte seine Bemühungen aber nicht auf neue Schuhstile. Was seine Produkte auszeichnete und seinen Einfluss festigte, waren sein Qualitätsanspruch (bei Maßschuhen wie bei Konfektionsware), sein Vermarktungsgenie und seine Fähigkeit, innovative Ausnahmetalente zu entdecken und zu engagieren. Als einer der ersten Designer, die Prominenz als mächtiges Verkaufsinstrument zu nutzen wussten, engagierte Delman Filmstars für seine Werbeanzeigen. Auch begriff er die Macht des Wiedererkennungswerts einer Marke und ließ alle Schuhe mit seinem Namenszug versehen, was damals noch unüblich war.

Gefertigt aus außergewöhnlichen Materialien, von exotischen Tierhäuten über Kunstleder bis Plastik, waren Delmans Schuhe bekannt für hohen Tragekomfort und gute Passform. Zudem steckte, wie er selbst erklärte, „so viel Handarbeit in ihnen, dass sie sich nicht kopieren lassen". Auch der Vertrieb der Schuhe wurde klug gefördert, angefangen mit dem Cinderella-Logo im Label bis hin zu Lizenzverträgen mit führenden Einzelhändlern. So schloss Delman 1933 einen Exklusivvertrag mit Saks Fifth Avenue ab und besiegelte im Jahr 1936 eine jahrzehntelange Partnerschaft mit Bergdorf Goodman. Durch die Verpflichtung von Stardesignern wie Beth Levine, Kenneth Jay Lane und Roger Vivier wusste er das Markenprestige zu wahren. Vivier arbeitete von den 1930ern bis in die 1990er sporadisch für Delman, auch während seines Engagements bei Dior.

Seit Delmans Tod 1955 wechselte sein Unternehmen mehrmals den Eigentümer, doch es besteht noch heute, über 100 Jahre nach seiner Gründung. —P.M.

PREVIOUS
Evening sandal:
Hand-painted black
patent leather
USA, *ca.* 1954

Delman
Evening sandals: Blue
silk satin, rhinestones
USA, *ca.* 1936

Gold kidskin sandal
worn by Queen
Elizabeth II for her
coronation in 1953.
Designed by Roger
Vivier for Delman, the
style features a garnet-
studded medallion
inspired by the rose
window of Chartres
Cathedral in France.

Le Carrosse de la Reine (State Coach) (4 tonnes) date de 1762 et a eu 6 couronnements. Les panneaux peints par Cipriani représentaient les victoires anglaises pendant la guerre de 7 ans.

La deuxième Couronne de la Reine (Imperial State Crown) (1 kg, 940) est en argent, sertie de 2,783 diamants, 277 perles, 11 émeraudes et 5 rubis. Les deux arches symbolisent l'Empire.

Le Soulier de la Reine « » : une sandale de chevreau or, cloutée de rubis. La rubis, que les rois portent en bague le jour du Couronnement, est la règne de mariage avec le pays. La sandale d'Elisabeth est française. Elle a été créée à Mougins (A.-M.) par Roger Vivier, modéliste de Delman en Amérique, et exécutée à Londres. « N'oubliez pas avoit dit la Reine Mary à sa petite-fille, que le jour du Couronnement vous resterez 5 heures debout, que vous ne devez ni trébucher, ni hésiter sur vos pieds afin d'éviter la chute de la Couronne. Chaussez-vous confortablement. » La peinture d'Elisabeth est un petit « II ».

HERMAN DELMAN RESTE À TOUT jamais l'un des créateurs de chaussures les plus influents qu'ait connu New York. Originaire de Portland dans l'Oregon (États-Unis), il est né en 1895 dans une famille de vendeurs de chaussures passionnés. Sa carrière a bénéficié d'un *timing* providentiel : quand il a ouvert sa première boutique à New York en 1919, l'ourlet des jupes avait raccourci, remontant la longueur à la mode au-dessus de la cheville. Ses chaussures devenaient donc de plus en plus visibles. De styles variés, elles étaient adaptées à toutes sortes d'occasions publiques ou privées. La priorité que Delman accordait à la qualité (tant pour les modèles sur mesure que prêts-à-porter), son génie publicitaire ainsi que sa capacité à repérer et embaucher des talents particulièrement novateurs ont fait le succès de ses produits et consolidé son influence. Il est l'un des premiers créateurs à avoir exploité le pouvoir de la célébrité en tant qu'outil commercial en utilisant des stars de cinéma dans ses publicités. C'est avec la même intuition qu'il a pris conscience du puissant attrait des marques en inscrivant son nom sur chacune de ses chaussures, chose inhabituelle à l'époque.

Les chaussures Delman étaient fabriquées dans des matières uniques, qu'il s'agisse de peaux d'animaux exotiques, de tissus synthétiques ou de plastique. Elles étaient réputées pour leur confort, leur coupe et, comme l'a lui-même observé Herman Delman, « une somme de travail manuel si impressionnante qu'elles sont un défi aux imitateurs ». Les modèles bénéficiaient également d'une promotion ingénieuse, entre le logo représentant Cendrillon sur l'étiquette et les accords de licence avec de grands détaillants. En 1933, Herman Delman a signé un accord exclusif avec Saks Fifth Avenue, puis, en 1936, il a conclu un partenariat de plusieurs décennies avec Bergdorf Goodman. Il entretenait la réputation de l'entreprise en embauchant des créateurs aussi doués que Beth Levine, Kenneth Jay Lane et Roger Vivier. Ce dernier a travaillé pour Delman par intermittence entre les années 1930 et les années 1990, y compris pendant la période où il créait pour Dior.

Après le décès d'Herman Delman en 1955 et les rachats successifs de l'entreprise, la marque existe toujours aujourd'hui, plus d'un siècle après sa création. —*P.M.*

THE BEST SHOES YOU CAN BUY ARE THE BEST BUY!

Advertised in 1943 as both "the best shoe" and "the best buy," Delman shoes were renowned for fine craftsmanship.

Delman
Sling-back pumps:
Red satin
USA, *ca.* 1952

Christian Dior
(**Delman**)
Evening pumps: Red silk brocade, metallic bead embroidery
France, *ca.* 1959

FOLLOWING
Delman
Wedges: Cream satin, gold metal
USA, *ca.* 1940

Delman
Wedges: Blue silk crepe,
silver metallic kid
USA, *ca.* 1940

Delman
Sandal: Green, red,
blue, white suede
USA, *ca.* 1939

Delman
Wedges: Black crepe,
gold hobnail studs,
gold rhinestone buckle
USA, *ca.* 1940

"Not since Cinderella's
slipper has such footwear
magic been worked as
in the exquisite designs
of…Herman Delman."

— *ATLANTA DAILY WORLD*

Delman
Pumps: Olive suede and
glacé leather
USA, 1940–42

Delman
Sling-back pumps:
Brown lizard
USA, *ca.* 1950

By the late 1930s,
American-born Delman
was known for smart
footwear, like these 1938
wedge shoes.

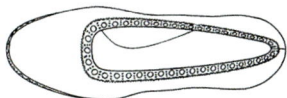

Fig. 1.

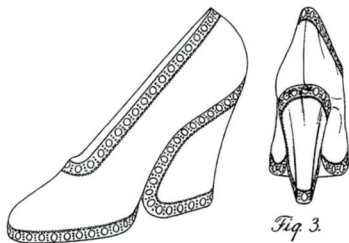

Fig. 2.   Fig. 3.

INVENTOR
Herman B. Delman
BY
Frank H. Ashley
ATTORNEY

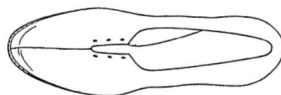

Fig. 1.

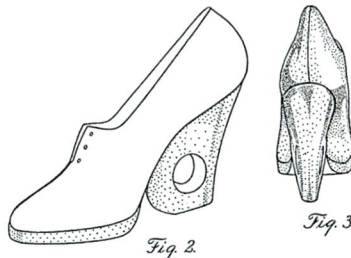

Fig. 2.   Fig. 3.

INVENTOR
Herman B. Delman
BY
Frank H. Ashley
ATTORNEY

Dolce & Gabbana

DOMENICO DOLCE AND STEFANO GABBANA have built their fashion house on sexy, sensuous designs reverential to Italian craftsmanship. Their first collection, debuting in Milan in the early 1980s, veered from the popular, sharply tailored trends of the time to focus on more romantic and feminine styles. The duo is deeply inspired by their Italian roots and archetypes of Italian women. However, their look quickly attracted customers internationally, and they became a staple of Milan fashion. The signature D&G aesthetic is no different in their shoe design: rich materials such as leathers and skins, silks, and whimsical details adorn classic shapes, from luxurious appliqué patchwork on sneakers to delicate butterflies and leopard print on sandals. Their women's shoes, designed with cutouts and bold colors and embellishments, especially convey the sex appeal for which the company is known.

Stefano Gabbana (b. 1962) and
Domenico Dolce (b. 1958)

Dolce, born in 1958 in Sicily, was exposed to fashion and clothing construction early through his father who worked as a tailor. Gabbana was born outside Milan in 1962 and went on to study graphic design before beginning his career in fashion. The two met while working in the fashion industry in Milan and have collaborated ever since, producing their earliest collection at a Dolce family factory in Sicily. They quickly established their design philosophy as unapologetically sexy and also became known for courting controversy through provocative designs and advertisements. —*E.W.*

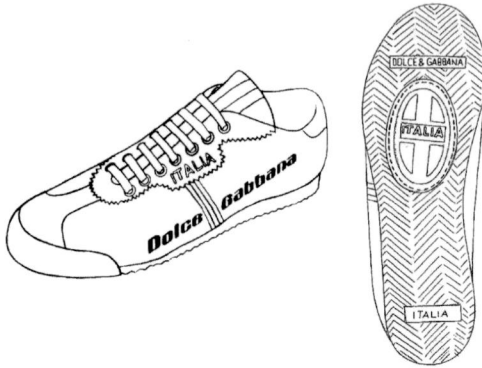

PREVIOUS
Dolce & Gabbana
Sandal: Faux leopard
fur, black silk crepe
Italy, spring 1998

A 2006 patent for
Italian-made sneakers.

DOMENICO DOLCE UND STEFANO GABBANA begründeten ihr Modehaus mit sexy, sinnlichen Designs, die der italienischen Handwerkskunst huldigten. Ihre erste Kollektion, die sie Anfang der 1980er-Jahre in Mailand präsentierten, wandte sich vom damaligen Trend der messerscharfen Schnitte ab und verfolgte eine romantischere, femininere Richtung. Wesentliche Inspiration bezieht das Designerduo aus seinen italienischen Wurzeln und den archetypischen Italienerinnen. Bald jedoch lockte ihr Look auch internationale Kundschaft an und machte die beiden zu einer festen Größe der Mailänder Modeszene. Genauso zeigt sich die D&G-Markenästhetik in ihren Schuhdesigns: Wertige Materialien wie Leder, Fell oder Seide und neckische Details schmücken klassische Silhouetten, von Sneakern mit opulenten Patchwork-Applikationen bis hin zu Sandaletten mit zarten Schmetterlingen und Leo-Print. Speziell ihre Damensandaletten, verziert und in gewagten Farben, vermitteln jenen Sexappeal, für den die Marke bekannt ist.

Der Sizilianer Dolce, geboren 1958, kam als Sohn eines Schneiders schon früh mit Mode und Schnittherstellung in Berührung. Gabbana, Jahrgang 1962, stammt aus der Nähe von Mailand und studierte zunächst Grafikdesign, ehe er das Modeparkett betrat. Die beiden lernten sich in Mailand kennen und produzierten ihre erste Kollektion in einer Fabrik der Dolces auf Sizilien. Seitdem ein Team, definierten sie ihre Designphilosophie bald als unverblümt sexy und schürten mit provokanten Designs und Werbeanzeigen Kontroversen, die ihnen zusätzliche Bekanntheit eintrugen. —E.W.

DOMENICO DOLCE ET STEFANO GABBANA ont bâti leur Maison de mode grâce à des créations sexy et sensuelles, respectueuses du savoir-faire italien. Leur première collection, présentée à Milan au début des années 1980, s'éloignait de la tendance aux lignes acérées en proposant des modèles plus romantiques et féminins. Bien que le duo soit profondément inspiré par ses racines et les archétypes de la femme italienne, les collections ont rapidement séduit la clientèle internationale, la marque s'imposant alors comme un pilier de la mode milanaise. Son esthétique signature reste la même pour les chaussures : elle habille des formes classiques de matières aussi somptueuses que les cuirs, les peaux et les soies, ainsi que de détails fantaisistes tels qu'un patchwork appliqué sur des sneakers, ou un délicat papillon et un imprimé léopard sur des sandales. Conçus avec des découpes, des couleurs audacieuses et des ornementations, les modèles pour femme incarnent particulièrement bien le *sex-appeal* qui a fait la réputation de Dolce & Gabbana.

Né en 1958 en Sicile, Domenico Dolce a découvert la mode et la couture dès son plus jeune âge auprès de son père qui était tailleur. Stefano Gabbana, né en 1962 dans la région de Milan, a, lui, fait des études de graphisme avant de se lancer dans le secteur. Depuis leur rencontre dans le milieu de la mode milanaise et la production de leur première collection dans une usine de la famille Dolce en Sicile, ils n'ont jamais cessé de collaborer. Ils ont rapidement établi leur philosophie créative à travers un style sexy décomplexé, mais aussi à travers leurs créations et leurs publicités provocantes qui flirtent bien souvent avec la controverse. —E.W.

Dolce & Gabbana
Men's sneakers:
Brown-and-red leather,
snakeskin
Italy, spring 1995

Dolce & Gabbana
Mule: Leopard-print
pony skin, clear vinyl,
pink sequins, pink and
green passementerie
Italy, spring 2005

David Evins

DAVID EVINS WAS KNOWN AS the "King of Pumps" and the "Dean of American Shoe Designers." While today's footwear creators are often as famous as clothing designers, this was a less common phenomenon when Evins secured a contract with I. Miller to produce shoes under his own label in 1941. By the end of that decade, his works were so well respected and influential that he earned a coveted Coty Award. Throughout the mid-twentieth century, Evins designed high-quality footwear, from ready-made to custom-crafted, that was created in his Manhattan-based factory.

David Evins (1906–1991)

Born David Levin in 1907, he was raised in London and came of age in Brooklyn, New York. He studied illustration at the Pratt Institute and had a short-lived career sketching for *Vogue* and *Harper's Bazaar*. Soon after, he became a shoe patternmaker for McGee Patterns, Inc. It was there that Evins learned the craft of shoemaking and established vital industry contacts. By the onset of World War II, Evins was creating classic, understated, and superbly crafted footwear with subtle yet innovative and distinctive ornamentation. These elegant and comfortable shoes become popular with well-to-do women throughout the United States, as well as with such world-recognized figures as Princess Grace of Monaco, First Ladies Mamie Eisenhower and Nancy Reagan, and the Duchess of Windsor (who dubbed Evins "a genius"). He also collaborated with leading American designers such as Norman Norell and James Galanos, as well as the venerated French leather house Hermès.

The most famous of Evins's designs, however, were far flashier. Movie stars Ava Gardner ironically wore his shoes in *The Barefoot Contessa*, Marilyn Monroe in the iconic subway grate scene in *The Seven Year Itch*, and Elizabeth Taylor donned his specially made and richly ornamented clogs and platform sandals in *Cleopatra*. —*P.M.*

On the set of Billy
Wilder's 1955 film *The
Seven Year Itch*, Marilyn
Monroe poses for the
infamous subway scene
in a pleated white halter

dress and a pair of
David Evins sling-back
heels. His classic designs
were ubiquitous among
Hollywood stars.

DAVID EVINS WAR ALS KÖNIG der Pumps und
Doyen der amerikanischen Schuhdesigner bekannt.
Während heutige Schuhdesigner oft so berühmt wie
Modeschöpfer sind, war dieses Phänomen noch die
Ausnahme, als Evins ab 1941 mit der Schuhhan-
delskette I. Miller kooperierte, um Schuhe unter
eigenem Label produzieren zu können. Am Ende
des Jahrzehnts waren seine Kreationen bereits
so renommiert und bedeutend, dass ihm der
begehrte Coty Award verliehen wurde. Zur Mitte
des 20. Jahrhunderts und in der Folgezeit entwarf
Evins hochwertige Konfektions- und Maßschuhe,
die in seiner New Yorker Fabrik in Manhattan
gefertigt wurden.

Evins, 1907 als David Levin geboren, wuchs
in London auf. Als junger Erwachsener lebte er in
Brooklyn und studierte am dortigen Pratt Institute
Illustration. Nach kurzen Engagements als Mode-
zeichner bei *Vogue* und *Harper's Bazaar* trat er bald
eine Stelle als Mustermacher für Schuhe bei McGee
Patterns an. Dort erlernte Evins das Schuhmacherhandwerk und knüpfte wichtige Branchenkontakte.
Bei Beginn des Zweiten Weltkriegs schuf Evins
bereits exquisit gearbeitete, klassisch-schlichte
Schuhe mit Verzierungen, die zwar dezent, aber innovativ und unverwechselbar waren. Diese elegante,
bequeme Fußbekleidung fand landesweit Beifall
unter betuchten Amerikanerinnen, aber auch bei
weltbekannten Kundinnen wie Fürstin Gracia
Patricia von Monaco, den First Ladies Mamie
Eisenhower und Nancy Reagan sowie der Herzogin
von Windsor (die Evins als „Genie" bezeichnete).
Er arbeitete auch mit führenden US-Designern
wie Norman Norell und James Galanos oder dem
hoch angesehenen Lederwarenhersteller Hermès in
Frankreich zusammen.

Doch Evins' berühmteste Kreationen waren
weitaus glamouröser, wurden sie doch von Filmstars getragen. Etwa von Ava Gardner in - Ironie
des Titels - *Die barfüßige Gräfin*, von Marilyn
Monroe über dem U-Bahn-Schacht in der Kultszene
aus *Das verflixte siebente Jahr*, oder von Elizabeth
Taylor, die in der Titelrolle von *Cleopatra* in eigens
für diesen Film gefertigte, reich verzierte Holzpan-
toletten und Plateausandalen schlüpfte. *—P.M.*

DAVID EVINS ÉTAIT CONSIDÉRÉ COMME le roi de
l'escarpin et le doyen des chausseurs américains.
Si les créateurs de chaussures sont aujourd'hui
souvent aussi célèbres que les créateurs de mode,
c'était un phénomène moins courant en 1941 quand
David Evins a signé un contrat avec I. Miller pour
produire des souliers sous sa propre griffe. À la fin
de la décennie, ses créations étaient si respectées
et leur influence telle qu'elles lui ont valu un prestigieux Coty Award. Tout au long des années 1950,
ses chaussures de qualité supérieure, sur mesure ou
en prêt-à-porter, étaient fabriquées dans son usine
de Manhattan.

Né David Levin en 1907, il a d'abord grandi à
Londres avant de partir vivre à Brooklyn avec sa
famille quand il était adolescent. Il a étudié le des-
sin au Pratt Institute, brièvement travaillé comme
illustrateur pour *Vogue* et *Harper's Bazaar*, puis
est devenu modéliste de chaussures chez McGee
Patterns, Inc., une expérience qui l'a formé à l'art de
la cordonnerie tout en lui permettant de nouer
de précieux contacts avec les fabricants. Lorsque
la Seconde Guerre mondiale a éclaté, David Evins
créait des chaussures classiques, sobres et de superbe
facture, décorées de détails subtils, mais néanmoins
innovants et originaux. Ces modèles élégants et
confortables remportaient un immense succès auprès
des femmes aisées à travers tous les États-Unis, mais
aussi auprès de célébrités mondiales, telles la princesse Grace de Monaco, les Premières dames Mamie
Eisenhower et Nancy Reagan, ainsi que la duchesse
de Windsor (qui qualifiait David Evins de « génie »).
Evins a aussi collaboré avec de grands créateurs de
mode américains, dont Norman Norell et James
Galanos, ainsi qu'avec la célèbre Maison de maroquinerie française Hermès.

Les créations les plus célèbres d'Evins, celles
qu'on découvrait aux pieds des stars de cinéma,
étaient beaucoup plus extravagantes. Ava Gardner
a porté ses chaussures dans *La Comtesse aux pieds
nus*, et Marilyn Monroe dans l'emblématique scène
de la bouche de métro de *Sept ans de réflexion*. Dans
Cléopâtre, Elizabeth Taylor était chaussée de sabots
et de sandales compensées richement ornés qu'Evins
avait spécialement créés sur mesure pour elle. *—P.M.*

David Evins
Pump: Purple velvet,
ribbon
USA, *ca.* 1970

David Evins
Ankle boots:
Multicolored printed
leather
USA, 1970

David Evins
Sling-back pump:
Metallic silk brocade,
leather
USA, 1955

**Oscar de la Renta
(David Evins)**
Wedge: Lurex fabric,
rhinestone buckle
USA, *ca.* 1973–74

David Evins
Sandal: Gold-tone
rouleau, gilded wood,
black faceted stones
USA, 1961

David Evins
Sandals: Ivory patent
leather, wood
USA, 1960

David Evins
Sandal: Ivory calfskin,
metal tassel, patent
leather
USA, *ca.* 1972

Fenton Footwear

FENTON FOOTWEAR WAS ESTABLISHED IN 1924 with the opening of Manhattan's storied Saks Fifth Avenue department store, which helped establish its eponymous avenue as the city's shopping mecca. Founded by Horace Saks and Bernard Gimbel, already well-established retailers in the city, Saks was designed to be a "dream store" offering high-quality men's and women's fashions. Fenton Footwear was the exclusive women's shoes label produced by Saks, and was sold

Horace Saks (1882–1925) and Bernard Gimbel (1885–1966)

on the fourth floor, the largest women's shoe department in New York at the time. Much like the copies of French couture offered by American department stores, Fenton was advertised as luxury and style at a reduced price. Their democratic approach to design emphasized expanded sizing and widths.

During the 1920s, as hemlines rose, shoes became a newly important fashion accessory, and Fenton emphasized its elegant silhouettes, made on a custom-designed "high-arched" last, and trendy fabrications in the latest colors. From 1924 through the 1960s, Fenton Footwear exemplified the fashionable shoe styles consumed by the American public with heavy influences from respected shoe designers such as André Perugia and Roger Vivier. Sumptuous materials such as brocade and metallic leathers were popular for evening shoes during the 1920s and 1930s, while open-toed sandals and platform soles became fashionable in the 1940s. Thin stiletto heels on dainty embellished silk pumps show the influence of French couture during the 1950s and early 1960s. —*E.W.*

FENTON FOOTWEAR NAHM SEINEN ANFANG 1924 mit der Eröffnung von Saks Fifth Avenue, jenem sagenumwobenen Kaufhaus in Manhattan, dem der namensgebende Straßenzug seinen Aufstieg zum Einkaufsmekka der Stadt mitverdankt. Gegründet von Horace Saks und Bernard Gimbel, zwei bereits etablierten New Yorker Einzelhändlern, war Saks als „Traumgeschäft" für hochwertige Herren- und Damenmode konzipiert. Fenton Footwear war Saks' hauseigene Damenschuhmarke und wurde exklusiv im vierten Stock verkauft, der damals größten Damenschuhabteilung in New York. Ähnlich wie die von amerikanischen Kaufhäusern angebotenen Kopien französischer Couture-Mode wurden auch Fenton-Schuhe als stilvoller Luxus zum vergünstigten Preis beworben. Zu ihrem demokratischen Designansatz gehörte auch eine breitere Auswahl an Größen und Weiten.

Als während der 1920er-Jahre die Röcke kürzer wurden, gelangten Schuhe als modische Accessoires zu neuer Bedeutung. Fenton setzte auf elegante Silhouetten, die auf „aufgewölbten" Maßleisten gefertigt wurden, sowie modische Ausführungen in Trendfarben. Von 1924 bis Ende der 1960er-Jahre verkörperte Schuhmode von Fenton Footwear beispielhaft den Geschmack der amerikanischen Konsumenten, wobei die Ästhetik stark von renommierten Schuhdesignern wie André Perugia und Roger Vivier geprägt war. So waren in den 1920er- und 30er-Jahren für Abendschuhe luxuriöse Materialien wie Brokat und Metallicleder beliebt, in den 40ern kamen zehenfreie Sandalen und Plateausohlen in Mode, und der Einfluss der französischen Couture kam in den 1950er- und frühen 60er-Jahren an exquisiten Seidenpumps mit Verzierungen und dünnem Stilettoabsatz zum Tragen. —E.W.

L'ENTREPRISE FENTON FOOTWEAR a été créée en 1924 lors de l'ouverture du légendaire grand magasin Saks Fifth Avenue de Manhattan qui a contribué à établir la Cinquième Avenue comme la Mecque du shopping new-yorkais. Ses fondateurs Horace Saks et Bernard Gimbel, des commerçants déjà bien établis, avaient imaginé Saks comme un « magasin de rêve » vendant de la mode masculine et féminine de qualité supérieure. Marque exclusive de Saks, Fenton Footwear était proposée au quatrième étage, alors le plus grand espace de vente de chaussures pour dame de New York. À l'image des copies de modèles haute couture français proposées par les grands magasins américains, Fenton se présentait comme un moyen d'accéder au luxe et à l'élégance à moindre coût. Cette approche démocratique mettait aussi en avant un plus vaste choix de tailles et de largeurs.

La longueur des jupes ayant raccourci pendant les années 1920, les chaussures étaient devenues le nouvel accessoire de mode incontournable. Fenton utilisait les couleurs au goût du jour pour mettre en valeur ses élégantes silhouettes fabriquées sur une forme « très arquée » conçue sur mesure, ainsi que ses modèles plus tendance. De 1924 jusqu'aux années 1960, la marque a répondu aux désirs de mode du public américain avec des chaussures fortement inspirées par des créateurs aussi respectés qu'André Perugia et Roger Vivier. Dans les années 1920 et 1930, les matières somptueuses comme le brocart et les cuirs métallisés remportaient beaucoup de succès sur les chaussures de soirée, tandis que, dans les années 1940, la mode était aux sandales à bout ouvert et aux semelles compensées. Quant aux escarpins en soie délicatement décorés à talons aiguilles, ils illustraient l'influence de la haute couture française pendant les années 1950 et au début de la décennie suivante. —E.W.

Fenton Footwear
Platform sandals:
Blue-and-brown suede
USA, 1940s

FOLLOWING
Fenton Footwear
Sling-back pumps:
Red satin, gold metallic
embroidery, rhinestones
USA, ca. 1962

Salvatore Ferragamo

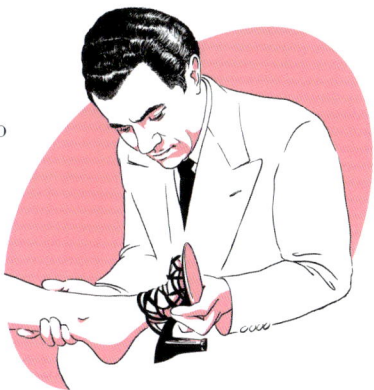

SALVATORE FERRAGAMO, BILLED AS THE "Shoemaker to the Stars" for his one-of-a-kind-designs for Hollywood actresses, was born in the town of Bonito near Naples, Italy, in 1898. After apprenticing with shoemakers when he was as young as nine, he immigrated to the United States at the age of 16, settling in California. Having found success in the United States, Ferragamo returned to Italy in 1927 and established the Ferragamo Company in Florence. In 1938 he purchased the city's Palazzo Spini Feroni palace for his company headquarters. It was also during the 1930s that Ferragamo began to use

Salvatore Ferragamo (1898–1960)

specialized materials for his footwear, such as a lace produced in convents in Tuscany. When leather came to be rationed during World War II, he adapted his designs to include heels made from cork or wood and began to experiment with new materials such as cellophane, fish skin, canvas, Bakelite, and plastic resins — artistic innovation born out of deprivation. One of his best-known works, the "Invisibile" sandal from 1947, was made with nylon thread used for fishing line. The inspiration came to him as he watched fishermen on the Arno River in Florence.

Ferragamo devoted much of his life and work to the anatomical study of the foot, particularly the plantar arch, and how it bears the weight of the body. His interest in well-fitted shoes resulted in a range of shoe widths, with particular emphasis on sizes for narrow feet. Following his death in 1960, the Ferragamo family expanded the brand to a full fashion house that includes men's shoes, clothing, and handbags. While first courting his wife, Wanda, who would go on to preside over the company for more than 50 years, Ferragamo slyly asked her to model a pair of his shoes for a fitting. "I had never worn anything so comfortable," she said. "I thought I could fly." —*M.M.*

FORTNUM & MASON

present

Ferragamo
OF FLORENCE

"MANILLA"

"MANILLA"   An exquisite whole cut Court, in natural
Manilla Hemp delicately embroidered in pastel blue.
High slender heel covered in fine blue Kid to
match. In A & B American fittings . . £9.19.6

"SPARTIA" Presenting the high fashion note expressed in backless Sandal
of delicate straps that grip foot perfectly, ensuring excellent fit. In
American fittings A, B & C £10.19.6

"VIETTA"   Suede Court designed by Ferragamo and made in
England, featuring the open front and slender high heel.
In black, white or mushroom Suede or in Patent
Leather. Also with medium heel in black or white
AA, B & C fittings £7.7.0

"NATIA"   Similar to above in a Sandal bar
shoe with medium heel. In black or
white Suede, also Patent Leather.
AA, B & C fittings . £7.7.0

"SPARTIA"

"VIETTA"

"NATIA"

FORTNUM
& MASON

181 PICCADILLY, LONDON, WI   REGENT 8040

SALVATORE FERRAGAMO WURDE FÜR SEINE unvergleichlichen Kreationen für Hollywoodschauspielerinnen als „Schuhmacher der Stars" tituliert. Geboren 1898 im italienischen Städtchen Bonito nahe Neapel, ging er bereits im Alter von neun Jahren bei Schuhmachern in die Lehre und wanderte mit 16 nach Amerika aus, um sich in Kalifornien niederzulassen. Nach erfolgreichen Arbeitsjahren in den USA kehrte er 1927 in seine Heimat zurück, gründete in Florenz sein eigenes Unternehmen und erwarb 1938 den Palazzo Spini Feroni als Firmenhauptsitz. In den 1930ern begann Ferragamo auch, eigens für seine Schuhkreationen gefertigte Materialien zu verwenden, beispielsweise handgeklöppelte Spitze aus toskanischen Klöstern. Als während des Zweiten Weltkriegs Leder rationiert war, änderte er seine Designs so ab, dass auch Absätze aus Kork oder Holz dazu passten. Zudem begann er mit neuen Materialien zu experimentieren, etwa mit Cellophan, Fischhaut, Segeltuch, Bakelit und Kunstharz – künstlerische Innovationen, die aus der Not

entstanden. Für eines seiner bekanntesten Modelle, die „unsichtbare" Sandale Invisible aus dem Jahr 1947, verwendete er Angelschnur aus Nylon. Die Idee dazu kam ihm, als er Fischer auf dem Arno in Florenz beobachtete.

Ferragamo verwandte viel Zeit und Arbeit auf anatomische Studien des Fußes, insbesondere des tiefen Fußsohlenbogens, und untersuchte, wie der Fuß das Gewicht des Körpers trägt. Sein Bemühen um gute Passform resultierte in einer Reihe unterschiedlicher Schuhweiten, speziell auch für schmale Füße. Als Ferragamo 1960 starb, wurde die Marke von seiner Familie zu einem Modehaus mit Komplettsortiment einschließlich Herrenschuhen, Kleidung und Handtaschen ausgebaut und über 50 Jahre lang von seiner Frau Wanda geleitet. Als Ferragamo ihr einst den Hof machte, bat er sie listig, ihm zur Passprobe eines seiner Schuhmodelle vorzuführen. „Ich hatte noch nie etwas derart Bequemes an", sagte sie. „Ich dachte, ich kann fliegen." —*M.M.*

SURNOMMÉ « LE BOTTIER DES STARS » en raison de ses créations uniques destinées aux actrices hollywoodiennes, Salvatore Ferragamo est né en 1898 dans la ville de Bonito près de Naples en Italie. Après un apprentissage en cordonnerie commencé à l'âge de 9 ans, il a émigré en Californie, aux États-Unis, après son seizième anniversaire. Couronné de succès en Amérique, il est revenu en Italie en 1927 pour fonder l'entreprise Ferragamo à Florence. En 1938, il a acheté le *palazzo* florentin Spini Feroni pour y installer son siège social. C'est aussi pendant les années 1930 qu'il a commencé à utiliser des matières spéciales sur ses chaussures, dont une dentelle confectionnée dans des couvents de Toscane. Quand le cuir a été rationné pendant la Seconde Guerre mondiale, il s'est adapté en créant des talons en liège ou en bois ; il a aussi expérimenté de nouveaux matériaux, tels que la cellophane, la peau de poisson, la toile, la bakélite et les résines plastiques - autant d'innovations artistiques nées des pénuries de matières premières. L'une de ses plus célèbres créations, la sandale Invisibile de 1947, était fabriquée avec du fil de pêche en nylon, une inspiration qui lui était venue en regardant travailler des pêcheurs sur le fleuve Arno à Florence.

Salvatore Ferragamo a consacré une grande partie de sa vie et de son travail à l'étude anatomique du pied, en particulier de la voûte plantaire, et à la manière dont il supporte le poids du corps. Comme il tenait à ce que ses chaussures soient parfaitement ajustées, il les proposait dans un choix de plusieurs largeurs, notamment dans des tailles adaptées aux pieds étroits. Après sa mort en 1960, la famille Ferragamo a transformé la marque en Maison de mode à part entière en produisant des souliers pour homme, des vêtements et des sacs à main. À l'époque où il faisait la cour à sa future épouse Wanda, qui allait présider l'entreprise pendant plus de cinquante ans, Salvatore Ferragamo lui avait timidement demandé de jouer les mannequins en portant l'une de ses paires de chaussures pour un essayage. « Je n'avais jamais rien porté d'aussi confortable, a-t-elle confié. J'ai cru que j'allais m'envoler. » — M.M.

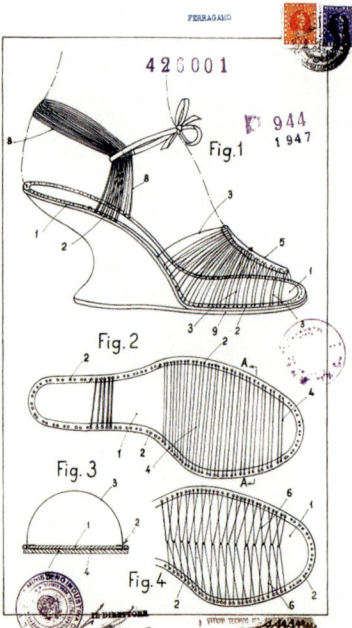

Salvatore Ferragamo
Stiletto pump: Purple velvet, kid gold leather
Italy, 1958–59

An innovator in the use of unconventional materials, Ferragamo employed monofilament to create the "Invisibile Sandal," designed so that the foot floats on the "F-heel." 1940s.

Salvatore Ferragamo
Wedge-heeled evening sandal: Gold metallic leather, cream satin
Italy, 1947

"That has been my life's work: striving to learn to make shoes that always fit, and the refusal to put my name to any that do not fit. Therefore please look behind the story of the small, barefoot, unlettered boy who became a famous shoemaker, and seek the pleasure you will obtain from walking well."

—SALVATORE FERRAGAMO

Salvatore Ferragamo
Pumps: Multicolored
needle lace, black leather
Italy, *ca.* 1950

Salvatore Ferragamo
Espadrille sandals:
Blue-gray raffia, natural
plaited cord
Italy, *ca.* 1950

Salvatore Ferragamo
Evening pumps: Black
silk satin, seed beads
Italy, 1950s

Salvatore Ferragamo
"Vinci" sandal:
Black suede, metal,
gold leather
Italy, 2017

Peter Fox

Peter Fox

EIGHTEENTH-CENTURY FLAIR FOUND A HOME in the then artist's mecca of Soho when Peter Fox Shoes opened its doors in 1982. Founded by husband and wife duo Peter and Linda Fox, the label was a family affair, right down to what *The New York Times* described as its "shoe-box-sized shop" run by their daughter, Tanya. The Foxes met in Vancouver at Peter Fox's first shoe shop, started with fellow designer John Fluevog in 1970. Peter Fox and Fluevog sold vintage styles and avant-garde, glam rock–inspired footwear until parting ways amicably in 1980.

From the outset, Peter Fox Shoes made an impression; fashion writers at *The Times* and *Vogue* pointed readers to the small shop for unique styles that were ahead of the current fashions. The Foxes designed the shoes: Linda focusing on colors and details, while Peter created the lasts. The limited runs — only 18 of each style were produced at first, replaced by new models as they sold out — were made in Italy. During the 1980s, the brand became known for looking to history for inspiration, reviving styles such as the granny boot, eighteenth-century court shoes, and platforms, while updating the familiar shapes and details. A pair of late-1980s two-tone spectator pumps, for example, recall shoe styles of the 1930s and 1940s but feature a distinctive curved heel shape. This penchant for history and modernizing classics made Peter Fox Shoes popular with brides and costume designers for theater and film. Linda and Peter Fox ran Peter Fox Shoes until 2007 when the designers retired. —*E.W.*

Peter Fox
Platform pump:
Black suede
USA, 1989

Peter Fox
Pumps: Pale green satin
USA, 1989

ALS PETER FOX SHOES 1982 seine Pforten öffnete, zog in New Yorks damaligem Künstlermekka Soho das Flair des 18. Jahrhunderts ein. Das laut *New York Times* „schuhkartongroße Geschäft" wurde von Tanya geführt, der Tochter von Peter und Linda Fox, die ihr gemeinsames Label als Familienunternehmen betrieben. Kennengelernt hatte sich das spätere Ehepaar in Peter Fox' erstem Schuhgeschäft, das er 1970 zusammen mit Designpartner John Fluevog im kanadischen Vancouver eröffnet hatte. Bis zur freundschaftlichen Trennung 1980 verkauften die beiden dort Vintage-Designs und avantgardistische, vom Glamrock inspirierte Schuhmode.

Peter Fox Shoes sorgte von Anfang an für Aufsehen; Moderedakteure der *Times* und der *Vogue* empfahlen ihrer Leserschaft den kleinen Laden für ausgefallene Schuhmode, die ihrer Zeit voraus war. Entworfen wurden die Schuhe in Teamarbeit: Linda konzentrierte sich auf Farben und Details, Peter gestaltete die Leisten. Die Endfertigung erfolgte in Italien, und waren die limitierten Serien ausverkauft – anfangs wurden nur 18 Stück pro Modell produziert –, wurden sie durch neue Designs ersetzt. Im Lauf der 1980er-Jahre wurde die Marke für historisierende Looks bekannt, etwa durch Neuauflagen der viktorianischen Schnürstiefel, Pumps im Stil des 18. Jahrhunderts oder Plateauschuhe, wobei vertraute Formen und Details zeitgemäß aufgefrischt wurden. So erinnern beispielsweise zweifarbige Spectator-Pumps an die Mode der 1930er- und 40er-Jahre, weisen jedoch eine markant gewölbte Absatzform auf. Dieses Faible für historische Moden und die Neuinterpretation von Klassikern machte die Marke Peter Fox Shoes beliebt bei Bräuten und Kostümdesignern für Bühne und Film. Linda und Peter Fox führten das Label weiter, bis sie sich 2007 zur Ruhe setzten. —*E.W.*

QUAND LA BOUTIQUE PETER FOX SHOES a ouvert ses portes en 1982 à Soho, le style du XVIIIe siècle a trouvé une place dans ce qui était alors le quartier artistique de New York. Créée par Peter et Linda Fox, un couple marié, la marque était une véritable affaire familiale puisque c'est leur fille Tanya qui gérait ce que *The New York Times* a qualifié de magasin « à peine plus grand qu'une boîte à chaussures ». Les Fox s'étaient rencontrés à Vancouver dans la première boutique de chaussures que Peter avait ouverte avec son confrère créateur John Fluevog en 1970 pour vendre des modèles vintage et avant-gardistes d'inspiration *glam rock* jusqu'à leur séparation en bons termes en 1980.

Peter Fox Shoes a fait forte impression dès sa création. Les journalistes de mode du *Times* et de *Vogue* orientaient vers cette petite boutique les lectrices souhaitant s'offrir des créations uniques ayant une longueur d'avance sur les tendances du moment. Les Fox créaient eux-mêmes leurs chaussures : Linda travaillait sur les couleurs et les détails, tandis que Peter fabriquait les formes. Leurs éditions limitées étaient fabriquées en Italie – au départ, chaque modèle n'était produit qu'à 18 exemplaires, puis remplacé par des nouveautés une fois le stock épuisé. Dans les années 1980, la marque s'est inspirée de modèles historiques et a revisité la bottine victorienne, l'escarpin du XVIIIe siècle ou ces chaussures à semelles compensées en remettant leurs formes familières et leurs détails au goût du jour. Par exemple, une paire d'escarpins *spectator* bicolores de la fin des années 1980 rappelait les modèles des années 1930 et 1940, mais présentait une forme de talon aux courbes insolites. Ce penchant pour l'histoire et la modernisation des classiques a fait le succès de Peter Fox Shoes auprès des futures mariées, mais aussi des créateurs de costumes de théâtre et de cinéma. Linda et Peter Fox ont dirigé Peter Fox Shoes jusqu'à leur retraite en 2007. —*E.W.*

"If you're looking for Cinderella-
worthy bridal footwear — or
something suited for a royal
audience — this is the place."

— *NEW YORK* MAGAZINE

FOX & FLUEVOG BOOTS & SHOES LTD.
221 carrall street, gastown, vancouver 4, b.c.   688-4710

Style 1891
Last. 85

Style 3825
Last 67

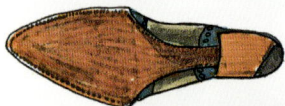

Style 809
Last 85

Style 1268
Last. 85

Gentlemen's Footgear
8481 Sunset Blvd
Los Angeles
California 90069.
Attn. Mr Patrick Martinet

also at #2 powell street, vancouver, b.c.   and 1005 broad street, victoria, b.c.
688-1919   385-4743

Before launching his own
brand in the mid-1980s,
Peter Fox collaborated
with fellow designer
John Fluevog. The duo
were known in the 1970s
for chunky, leather,
genderless designs.

Peter Fox
Ankle boots:
Brown leather, tan suede
USA, 1989

Peter Fox
Spectator pumps:
Brown-and-white leather
USA, *ca.* 1987

Maud Frizon

PARIS NATIVE MAUD FRIZON BEGAN her career as a high-fashion model during the 1960s, where she was required to provide her own shoes for runway shows and photoshoots. Displeased with the footwear produced by other designers, she left modeling in 1969 and began to design her own shoe line. A decade later, she started a joint business with her husband, Luigi de Marco, and opened a small shop on Rue des Saints-Pères in Paris. Her debut collection of just three styles was an immediate success, with a zipper-less boot being the biggest seller. Each pair of shoes was carefully cut and finished by hand.

Maud Frizon (b. 1941)

As a female shoe designer, Frizon was able to test all of her creations to ensure their comfort. Frizon believed that "Working women can buy interesting, feminine shoes that are flat or low-heeled. They don't have to be sneakers." During the 1980s, at the height of her success, she created just under 100 styles for women and 60 for men per year. In addition to her namesake brand, she also designed shoes for fashion designers such as Azzedine Alaïa, Claude Montana, and Sonia Rykiel, and her shoes have been worn and collected by Brigitte Bardot, Cher, Catherine Deneuve, and Donna Summer. Her signature cone heel was most recently revived as part of Saint Laurent's fall 2017 collection by Anthony Vaccarello. The brand's current motto states, "Be Maud Frizon, take an avant-garde step." —*M.M.*

PREVIOUS
Maud Frizon
Boot: Black suede
France, 1977–78

Maud Frizon
Pump: Bronze
metallic leather
France, *ca.* 1982

Maud Frizon
Spectator pumps:
Black-and-white leather
France, *ca.* 1978

ALS DIE GEBÜRTIGE PARISERIN MAUD FRIZON in den 1960er-Jahren ihre Laufbahn als Couture-Model begann, musste sie zu Modenschauen und Foto-shootings ihre Schuhe selbst mitbringen. Aus Unzu-friedenheit mit den verfügbaren Schuhdesigns gab sie das Modeln 1969 auf, um ihre eigene Schuhlinie zu entwerfen. Ein Jahrzehnt später gründete sie gemeinsam mit ihrem Ehemann Luigi de Marco eine eigene Firma und eröffnete ein kleines Laden-geschäft in der Pariser Rue des Saints-Pères. Ver-kaufsschlager ihrer Debütkollektion, die gerade einmal drei Modelle umfasste und auf Anhieb erfolg-reich war, war ein Stiefel ohne Reißverschluss. Jeder Schuh wurde in sorgfältiger Handarbeit gefertigt.

Als Frau konnte Frizon die Tragbarkeit jeder ihrer Kreationen persönlich überprüfen. Und sie war überzeugt: „Berufstätige Frauen können inter-essante, feminine Schuhe kaufen, die flach sind oder einen niedrigen Absatz haben. Es müssen keine Sneaker sein." Auf dem Höhepunkt ihres Erfolgs in den 1980er-Jahren kreierte sie alljährlich knapp 100 Schuhdesigns für Damen und 60 für Herren. Hinzu kamen Entwürfe für Modeschöpfer wie Azzedine Alaïa, Claude Montana und Sonia Rykiel. Getra-gen und gesammelt wurden ihre Kreationen von Stars wie Brigitte Bardot, Cher, Catherine Deneuve und Donna Summer. Ihr unverkennbarer Cone-Absatz erlebte vor Kurzem ein Revival in Anthony Vaccarellos Herbstkollektion 2017 für Yves Saint Laurent. Das aktuelle Labelmotto lautet: „Sei Maud Frizon, sei einen Schritt voraus." —*M.M.*

NÉE À PARIS, MAUD FRIZON a débuté sa carrière en tant que mannequin de haute couture dans les années 1960, une époque où elle devait porter ses propres chaussures lors des défilés et des séances photo. Insatisfaite des souliers disponibles sur le marché, elle a abandonné le mannequinat et créé sa propre marque de chaussures en 1969. Dix ans plus tard, elle s'est associée à son mari Luigi de Marco pour fonder une entreprise et ouvrir une petite boutique dans la rue des Saints-Pères à Paris. Sa première collection composée de seulement trois modèles a remporté un succès immédiat, la botte sans fermeture à glissière s'imposant comme son *best-seller*. Chaque paire de chaussures était soigneusement coupée et finie à la main.

En tant que femme, Maud Frizon pouvait tester elle-même ses propres créations pour s'assurer de leur confort. « Plutôt que des baskets, les femmes actives peuvent acheter des souliers féminins intéressants avec un talon plat ou un petit talon », estimait-elle. À l'apogée de sa réussite dans les années 1980, elle créait un peu moins de 100 modèles pour femme et 60 modèles pour homme par an. En dehors de sa griffe éponyme, elle a aussi travaillé pour des créateurs de mode tels Azzedine Alaïa, Claude Montana et Sonia Rykiel. Brigitte Bardot, Cher, Catherine Deneuve et Donna Summer ont porté et collectionné ses créations. Anthony Vaccarello a récemment ressuscité son talon conique signature pour la collection Automne 2017 d'Yves Saint Laurent. « Soyez Maud Frizon, faites un pas dans l'avant-garde », proclame l'actuel slogan de la marque. —*M.M.*

"I have a perfect foot.
I'm obsessed with shoes;
it's a sickness that's
never been cured."

— MAUD FRIZON

Maud Frizon
Oxfords: Pale blue suede
France, 1995

Maud Frizon
Pumps: Black suede
France, *ca.* 1988

Maud Frizon
Sling-back pumps:
Black satin, white
pendant pearls
France, *ca.* 1988

Romeo Gigli

WHEN ROMEO GIGLI BEGAN SHOWING his collections in Milan in the early 1980s, the look was so different from the overtly sexual and power-dressing styles of his contemporaries that other Italian designers thought he made "sad" clothes. However, the fashion press and customers recognized the beauty and value of his outsider perspective, which combined minimalist sportswear in soft shapes with rich materials and thoughtful details. Although Gigli's clothing design was undeniably modern in its layers, oversized silhouettes, and ease, it also made strong

Romeo Gigli (b. 1949)

allusions to history and various cultures. His shoes are meticulously linked to his clothing design in material, form, and feeling to create a unified overall style that conveys Gigli's distinctly romantic artisanship.

Gigli was born in Castel Bolognese, Italy, in 1949 to a father who worked as an antique book dealer. An upbringing surrounded by books and antiques, art, and furniture gave him a deep appreciation for references that explored history and geography. As a child he obtained his clothing from tailors and shoemakers, who allowed him to pick out his own materials. These experiences gave him a knowledge and appreciation for fabrics, later evident in his designs. Gigli studied architecture in Florence and traveled and collected widely before entering the fashion industry. He designed menswear and womenswear in New York during the late 1970s and opened his own house in Italy in 1983.

Gigli's shoes were revolutionary departures from the styles en vogue in the '80s and '90s: He crafted flat, soft shoes, recalling medieval shapes and ballet slippers, at a time when very high heels ruled on Italian runways. The heels he *did* create were of medium height and incorporated romantic details — curvilinear Baroque cutwork or delicate rosebuds and vines. Gigli even revived the elevated chopine silhouette, lending a Renaissance spirit to his spring 1998 collection. —*E.W.*

PREVIOUS
Historical influences
and innovative shapes
earned Gigli the title of
Italy's "poet designer."
Shoes by Gigli in an edi-
torial for *Marie Claire*
Japan, 1988.

Romeo Gigli
Pump: Brown suede
Italy, 1989–90

Romeo Gigli
Shoes: Gold metallic silk
Italy, 1989

ALS ROMEO GIGLI IN DEN frühen 1980er-Jahren seine ersten Kollektionen in Mailand präsentierte, bildete sein Look einen solchen Kontrast zum Power-Dressing-Stil und den unverblümt sexy Designs seiner Zeitgenossen, dass andere italienische Designer seine Kleider als „traurig" empfanden. Modepresse und Kundschaft jedoch erkannten Schönheit und Qualität seiner Außenseiterästhetik, die minimalistische Sportswear in weichen Schnitten mit hochwertigen Materialien und durchdachten Details kombinierte. Mit legeren Lagenlooks und Oversized-Silhouetten war Giglis Kleidermode unstrittig modern, es gab aber auch starke Bezüge zur Geschichte und zu anderen Kulturen. Seine Schuhdesigns sind in Material, Form und Ausstrahlung genau auf seine Kleidermode abgestimmt, um einen einheitlichen Gesamtlook zu erzielen, der Giglis ausnehmend romantische Handwerkskunst zum Ausdruck bringt.

Gigli, geboren 1949 im italienischen Castel Bolognese, wuchs als Sohn eines Antiquars inmitten von Büchern, Kunst und Antiquitäten auf. So entwickelte er ein ausgeprägtes Faible für Bezüge zur Geschichte und zu anderen Kulturen. Als Kind ließen ihn die Schneider und Schuhmacher, die seine Garderobe anfertigten, die Materialien selbst aussuchen. Diese Erfahrung vermittelte ihm das Fachwissen und die Wertschätzung für Stoffe, die sich später in seinen Designs zeigte. Gigli studierte zunächst Architektur in Florenz und begann auf ausgedehnten Reisen mit dem Sammeln, bevor er in die Modebranche einstieg. In den späten 1970er-Jahren arbeitete er als Designer für Herren- und Damenmode in New York. 1983 folgte die Gründung seines eigenen Unternehmens in Italien.

Giglis Schuhdesigns stellten eine revolutionäre Abkehr von den Modetrends der 1980er- und 90er-Jahre dar: Zu einer Zeit, als auf italienischen Laufstegen extrem hohe Absätze dominierten, fertigte er flache, weiche Schuhe in Formen, die an Mittelalter und Ballett erinnerten. *Wenn* er aber Absätze kreierte, so waren diese halbhoch und wiesen romantische Details auf – durchbrochene Schnörkelmuster im Barockstil oder zarte Rosenknospen und Ranken. Sogar die erhöhte Chopine-Silhouette ließ Gigli wieder aufleben und hauchte seiner Frühjahrskollektion 1998 damit Renaissanceflair ein. —*E.W.*

QUAND ROMEO GIGLI A COMMENCÉ à défiler à Milan au début des années 1980, son look était si éloigné du *power dressing* ouvertement sexy de ses contemporains que les autres créateurs italiens qualifiaient sa mode de « triste ». En revanche, la presse spécialisée et les clientes ont su apprécier la beauté et la valeur de son approche d'*outsider* qui associait un *sportswear* minimaliste aux formes douces avec des matières somptueuses et des détails réfléchis. Malgré la modernité indéniable des superpositions, des silhouettes *oversize* et du confort qui distinguait son style, Gigli faisait aussi beaucoup référence à l'histoire et à différentes cultures. Minutieusement assorties à ses vêtements en termes de matière, de forme et de style, ses chaussures composent un look intégral unifié qui reflète le savoir-faire artisanal particulièrement romantique du créateur.

Romeo Gigli est né en 1949 à Castel Bolognese en Italie. Comme son père vendait des livres anciens, il a passé son enfance au milieu de toutes sortes d'ouvrages, d'antiquités, d'œuvres d'art et de meubles qui lui ont permis de s'imprégner profondément de ces références historiques et géographiques.

Enfant, il s'habillait chez des tailleurs et des chausseurs qui le laissaient sélectionner les matières de son choix. Grâce à ces expériences, il a acquis une connaissance et une appréciation des tissus qui allaient transparaître de façon évidente dans ses futures créations. Gigli a étudié l'architecture à Florence, puis a voyagé et amassé une vaste collection de tissus et d'objets avant de se lancer dans la mode. Dans les années 1970, il a créé des lignes pour homme et pour femme à New York, puis a ouvert sa propre Maison en Italie en 1983.

Par rapport aux modèles à la mode dans les années 1980 et 1990, ses souliers étaient révolutionnaires : ses chaussures plates et souples évoquaient des formes médiévales et des chaussons de danse à une époque où les talons vertigineux dominaient les podiums italiens. Il a aussi créé des talons de hauteur intermédiaire et intégré des détails romantiques sur ses créations, par exemple des découpes curvilignes d'inspiration baroque ou des branches ornées de délicats boutons de rose. Il a même ressuscité la chopine surélevée pour conférer un esprit Renaissance à sa collection Printemps 1998. —*E.W.*

"The silhouette of my women was soft. At the beginning it was always flat shoes, too, only flats; I love them because they make women walk gently."

— ROMEO GIGLI

Romeo Gigli
Platform shoes:
Yellow silk faille
Italy, spring 1998

Romeo Gigli
Sandals: Red cotton,
red-and-green silk
Italy, spring 1998

Romeo Gigli
Bootie: Gray suede,
gray satin
Italy, 1989

Givenchy

THE ELEGANT AND ARISTOCRATIC Hubert James Marcel Taffin de Givenchy founded his namesake haute couture house, Givenchy, now known as one of the most venerated in fashion, in 1952. Born in Beauvais, France in 1927, he was the younger son of the Marquis of Givenchy. During his long career, which lasted until his retirement in 1995, the couturier dressed countless stylish women, most famously the actress Audrey Hepburn, who wore his designs in real life and on screen in films such as *Sabrina* and *Breakfast at Tiffany's*. On the advice of his mentor Cristóbal Balenciaga, Givenchy expanded and diversified his business during the 1960s and 1970s. Along with his successful perfumes, he created a range of accessories, including shoes.

Hubert de Givenchy
(1927–2018)

Givenchy would hire a string of high-profile artistic directors of womenswear in the coming years: John Galliano, Alexander McQueen, Riccardo Tisci, and, most recently, Clare Waight Keller, the first woman to hold that position. Tisci embraced a dark, sensual, and romantic aesthetic, bearing no connection to Hepburn's ladylike look. (It has been reported that Tisci, when a candidate for the position, was the only interviewee who did not mention the actress, which helped him cinch the job.) Broadening the house's chromatic palette, his ornately gothic gowns were rendered in "delicate oxblood and putty-colored gauze." At the same time, he created more vibrant prints of flora and fauna. The accessories designed to accompany his clothes likewise embraced the new edgy side of haute couture. —*P.M.*

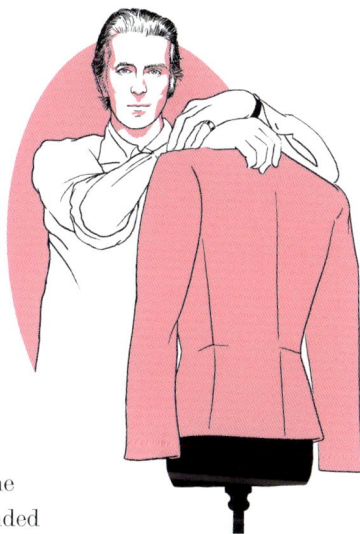

Now,
try
and go
unnoticed.

CHAUSSURES GIVENCHY

PREVIOUS
Founded in 1952,
Givenchy's haute couture
fashion house came to
define the essence of
chic.

An advertisement for
crystal-studded heels.
"Now, try and go
unnoticed." *Vogue*, 1978.

Givenchy
Evening sandals: Bronze
leather, rhinestones
France, 1978

DAS COUTURE-HAUS GIVENCHY, HEUTE als eine der namhaftesten Adressen der Modebranche bekannt, wurde 1952 von Hubert James Marcel Taffin de Givenchy gegründet. Der elegante Aristokrat, 1927 im französischen Beauvais als jüngerer Sohn des Marquis de Givenchy geboren, kleidete im Lauf seiner langen Karriere zahllose Frauen von Welt ein, ehe er sich 1995 zur Ruhe setzte. Berühmteste Trägerin seiner Couture-Mode war die Schauspielerin Audrey Hepburn, die privat wie auf der Leinwand Givenchy trug, etwa in den Filmen *Sabrina* und *Frühstück bei Tiffany*. In den 1960er- und 70er-Jahren erweiterte und diversifizierte Givenchy auf Anraten seines Mentors Cristóbal Balenciaga sein Unternehmen. Neben seinen erfolgreichen Düften kreierte er nun auch eine Auswahl an Accessoires einschließlich Schuhen.

In den folgenden Jahren engagierte das Haus Givenchy für seine Damenmode eine Reihe namhafter Chefdesigner: John Galliano, Alexander McQueen, Riccardo Tisci und zuletzt mit Clare Waight Keller auch die erste Frau in dieser Position. Tisci wandte sich einer dunklen, sinnlich romantischen Ästhetik zu, die nichts mit dem damenhaften Hepburn-Look gemein hatte. (Dass Tisci, wie es heißt, im Bewerbungsgespräch als einziger Kandidat nicht auf die Schauspielerin zu sprechen kam, soll ihm entscheidende Pluspunkte eingetragen haben.) Mit prächtigen gotischen Roben, ausgeführt in „delikatem Ochsenblutrot und kalkweißer Gaze", erweiterte er die Farbpalette des Hauses. Auf der anderen Seite kreierte er lebhaftere Prints mit Motiven aus Flora und Fauna. Ergänzt wurden seine Kreationen durch Accessoires, die diese neue, gewagte Seite der Haute Couture in gleicher Weise feierten. —*P.M.*

C'EST EN 1952 QUE L'ÉLÉGANT aristocrate Hubert James Marcel Taffin de Givenchy a fondé sa Maison de haute couture éponyme, aujourd'hui l'une des plus respectées. Né en 1927 à Beauvais en France, il était le plus jeune fils du marquis de Givenchy. Au cours d'une longue carrière qui a duré jusqu'à sa retraite en 1995, le couturier a habillé d'innombrables élégantes, en particulier l'actrice Audrey Hepburn qui portait ses créations à la ville comme à l'écran, notamment dans les films *Sabrina* et *Diamants sur canapé*. Dans les années 1960 et 1970, Givenchy a diversifié ses activités sur les conseils de son mentor Cristóbal Balenciaga et a créé, outre ses parfums à succès, une ligne d'accessoires incluant des chaussures.

Dans les années suivant le départ d'Hubert de Givenchy, la Maison a fait appel à une série de célèbres créateurs pour femme : John Galliano, Alexander McQueen, Riccardo Tisci et, depuis, peu, Clare Waight Keller, première femme à occuper le poste de directrice artistique. Riccardo Tisci a adopté une esthétique sombre, sensuelle et romantique qui n'avait plus aucun rapport avec le look distingué d'Audrey Hepburn (on dit qu'il aurait décroché le poste parce qu'il était le seul candidat à ne pas avoir mentionné l'actrice pendant son entretien). Ses robes gothiques richement ornées étaient coupées dans « une délicate gaze aux couleurs sang de bœuf et mastic » qui venait élargir la palette chromatique de la Maison. Parallèlement, il a créé des imprimés plus vibrants inspirés de la faune et de la flore. Les accessoires conçus pour accompagner ses vêtements reflétaient aussi cette nouvelle approche plus pointue de la haute couture. —*P.M.*

Givenchy
Mules: Pink and
lavender suede
France, 1979

Givenchy
Boot: Black kangaroo
leather and patent
python
France, spring 2018

Givenchy
Sandals: Beige
leather, metal
France, spring 2009

Givenchy
Boots: Black leather
France, spring 2011

Alberto Guardiani

"IT IS FROM THE HEEL that the last, the shoe's shape, is made but it is also from the heel that the shoe's magic blossoms," said designer Alberto Guardiani, for whom heels are a central focus. The Guardiani footwear factory was founded in 1947 in Montegranaro, Italy, by brothers Luigi and Dino Guardiani, who initially specialized in men's footwear. In 1972 Dino's son Alberto took over the family business and expanded its offerings into luxury fashion shoes for men and women. His "Lipstick Heel" has been made in several iterations since its initial release in 2010. The playful shoes have an interchangeable lipstick-shaped heel in various shades that encourages wearers to mix and match and uniquely engage with the design.

Alberto Guardiani (b. 1952)

In 2012 Guardiani and the British style magazine *i-D* staged an international competition to create a new style for the brand. The winner was the "Flutterby" shoe, from multidisciplinary designer Lady San Pedro, which was released in 2013. The painstakingly hand-painted heels, cast from metal shaped like butterfly wings, won out of more than 800 entries from 50 countries. Guardiani has since designed and produced sandals and boots with the "Flutterby" heel for his seasonal collections. —*M.M.*

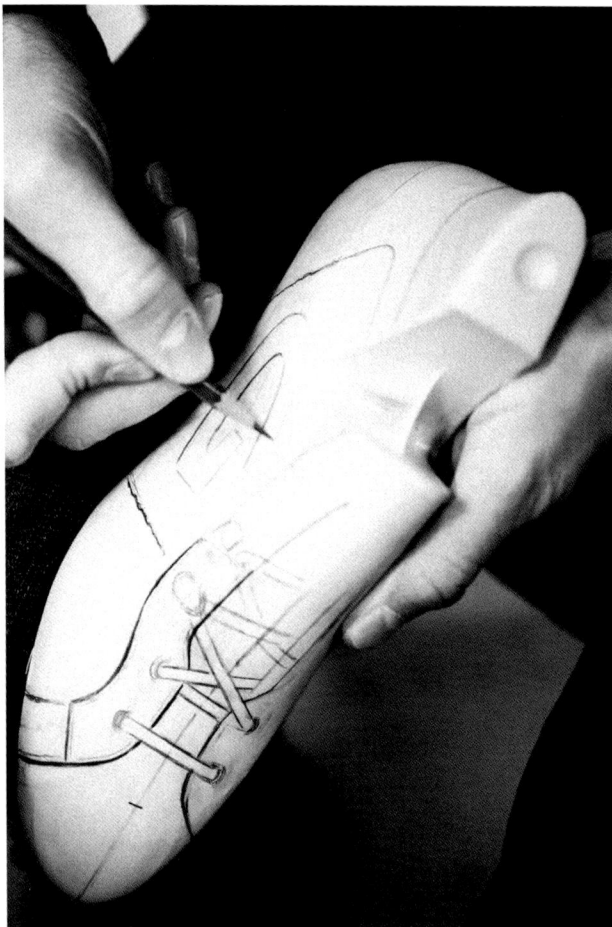

PREVIOUS
Alberto Guardiani
"Lipstick Heel" pump:
Patent leather, plastic
Italy, spring 2013

Hand-painted lasts are
crafted with precision
for Guardiani's sports
shoe. *Ca.* 2007.

Alberto Guardiani
"Flutterby" pumps: Red
suede, painted cast metal
Italy, spring 2013

„AUS DEM ABSATZ ERGIBT sich der Leisten, die Form eines Schuhs, doch auch der Zauber des Schuhs erwächst aus dem Absatz", so Alberto Guardiani, für dessen Entwürfe Absätze eine zentrale Rolle spielen. Die Guardiani-Schuhfabrik wurde 1947 im italienischen Montegranaro von den Brüdern Luigi und Dino Guardiani gegründet. 1972 übernahm Dinos Sohn Alberto den Familienbetrieb und erweiterte das anfangs auf Herrenschuhe spezialisierte Sortiment um Luxuslinien für Damen und Herren. Sein „Lipstick Heel" wurde seit seiner Einführung 2010 mehrfach neu aufgelegt. Er verfügt über einen Wechselabsatz in Lippenstift-Form, der in verschiedenen Farbtönen verfügbar

ist, nach Lust und Laune kombiniert werden kann und die Trägerin auf einzigartige Weise in das Design einbindet.

2012 rief Guardini gemeinsam mit dem britischen Modemagazin *i-D* einen internationalen Wettbewerb aus, um einen neuen Stil für seine Marke zu finden. Unter 800 Einsendungen aus 50 Ländern gewann ein Entwurf der vielseitigen Designerin Lady San Pedro: das Modell „Flutterby" mit Absätzen aus Gussmetall in Form von Schmetterlingsflügeln, die aufwendig von Hand bemalt werden. Seit Markteinführung des Modells 2013 produziert Guardini für seine Saisonkollektionen Sandalen und Stiefel mit „Flutterby"-Absatz. —*M.M.*

« C'EST À PARTIR DU talon que la forme est fabriquée, mais c'est aussi grâce à lui que la magie de la chaussure opère », a déclaré Alberto Guardiani, un créateur particulièrement intéressé par les talons. En 1947, les frères Luigi et Dino Guardiani avaient ouvert l'usine Guardiani à Montegranaro en Italie pour produire initialement des souliers pour homme. Alberto, le fils de Dino, a repris l'entreprise familiale en 1972 avant d'élargir son offre aux chaussures de luxe pour homme et pour femme. Son modèle Lipstick Heel a été décliné sous plusieurs variantes depuis son lancement en 2010. Cet escarpin ludique présente un talon interchangeable en forme de rouge à lèvres de différentes couleurs qui encourage les femmes à l'assortir à leur tenue et à interagir de façon unique avec leurs chaussures.

En 2012, Guardiani et le magazine de mode britannique *i-D* ont organisé un concours international en vue de créer un nouveau modèle pour la marque. La designeure multidisciplinaire Lady San Pedro a remporté le concours grâce aux escarpins Flutterby, lancés en 2013. Avec leurs talons moulés dans des ailes de papillon en métal et minutieusement peints à la main, ils se sont distingués parmi plus de 800 candidatures venues de 50 pays. Depuis, Guardiani conçoit et produit des sandales et des bottes avec le talon Flutterby pour ses collections. —*M.M.*

Gucci

THE GLOBAL LUXURY POWERHOUSE WE know today bears little resemblance to the modest, family-owned leather goods store founded in 1920s Florence by Guccio Gucci. The company initially specialized in leather travel and equestrian goods such as steam trunks and saddles, and eventually expanded into printed canvas suitcases and accessories in the 1930s. Gucci's first major success with footwear came in 1953 with the launch of its signature leather loafer. Modeled after Indigenous American moccasins, the men's shoe featured a distinctive gold-tone metal buckle in the shape of a horse bit,

Guccio Gucci (1881–1953)

an homage to Gucci's equestrian legacy. The loafers were purposely relaxed and casual, which made them popular among the jet set of the '60s and '70s — and they still hold their position today as a status symbol with a fevered following.

In spite of its history of success, disputes within the Gucci family, as well as over-expansion, brought the company to the brink of bankruptcy in the 1980s. In the next decade, Tom Ford, then a little-known designer at Perry Ellis, was hired to head Gucci's womenswear design and reincarnated the brand as a premier fashion house. During his tenure, Ford paid tribute to the company's jet set, Studio 54 heritage and infused the vintage styles with modern glamour and potent '70s sex appeal. After Ford's departure in 2004, Italian-born Frida Giannini took over as creative director. She had started as an accessories designer, and shoes became an important part of her vision for Gucci, which continued to revel in a sexy, '70s-infused glamour. Alessandro Michele headed Gucci from 2015 to 2022. Like Giannini, Michele began his career at Gucci in accessory design. Under his direction, the house's aesthetic was radically transformed into a celebration of romantic, eclectic, gender-fluid design. Accessories, particularly shoes, were key to the new Gucci sensibility, and Michele reimagined signature products, including the horse-bit loafers, which he adapted into colorful slides. "To do the wrong things in the right way is complicated," Michele said. "But that is my idea of beautiful." —*E.M.*

PREVIOUS AND LEFT
Gucci
Sling-back pumps:
Black crocodile skin,
metal, rhinestones
Italy, spring 1998

Gucci
Sling-back pumps: Red
alligator skin, multicolor
floral-print silk, metal
Italy, *ca.* 1988

DER WELTKONZERN FÜR LUXUSGÜTER, den man heute kennt, hat wenig Ähnlichkeit mit dem bescheidenen Florentiner Lederwarengeschäft, das in den 1920er-Jahren von Guccio Gucci gegründet wurde. Der Familienbetrieb, anfangs auf Reise- und Reitzubehör aus Leder wie Schiffskoffer und Sättel spezialisiert, erweiterte sein Sortiment in den 1930er-Jahren um Koffer aus bedrucktem Segeltuch und Accessoires. Den ersten großen Erfolg im Schuhsektor feierte die Firma, als sie 1953 ihren klassischen Lederslipper auf den Markt brachte. Markantes Detail dieses nach dem Vorbild indianischer Mokassins gestalteten Herrenschuhs war eine goldfarbene Spange in Form einer Trense, eine Hommage an Guccis Wurzeln als Sattlerei. Der bewusst sportlich-leger gestaltete Gucci-Loafer war beim Jetset der 1960er- und 70er-Jahre beliebt – und wurde zum Statussymbol, das bis heute Fans in Entzücken versetzt.

Trotz seiner Erfolgsgeschichte geriet das Unternehmen aufgrund innerfamiliärer Streitigkeiten und Überexpansion in den 1980er-Jahren an den Rand des Bankrotts. Mit der Verpflichtung von Tom Ford, einem damals kaum bekannten Designer

bei Perry Ellis, erfuhr die Marke Gucci im folgenden Jahrzehnt ihre Wiedergeburt als führendes Modehaus. Als neuer Chefdesigner der Damenlinie zollte Ford dem einstigen Studio-54-Jetset-Image der Marke Tribut, indem er den klassischen Looks modernen Glamour und starken 1970er-Jahre-Sexappeal einflößte. Nach seinem Abschied 2004 übernahm die Italienerin Frida Giannini, zuvor für Accessoires zuständig, die kreative Leitung. Schuhe wurden ein wichtiger Teil ihrer Vision für Gucci, das weiterhin auf sexy Glamourlooks im Stil der 1970er setzte. Von 2015 bis 2022 wurde das Haus von Alessandro Michele geführt, der genau wie Giannini als Designer für Accessoires bei Gucci begann. Unter seiner Leitung wandelte sich die Markenästhetik radikal und huldigt heute einer romantischen, eklektischen Mode mit fließenden Geschlechtergrenzen. Accessoires und insbesondere Schuhe sind der Schlüssel zu dieser neuen Sensibilität, für die Michele Gucci-Klassiker überdenkt und beispielsweise den Slipper mit Trensenspange in farbenfrohe Schlappen übersetzt. „Das Falsche auf richtige Weise zu tun, ist kompliziert", sagte Michele. „Aber genau das finde ich schön." —*E.M.*

LA GRANDE MARQUE DE LUXE mondiale que nous connaissons aujourd'hui n'a plus grand-chose à voir avec la modeste entreprise familiale de maroquinerie fondée par Guccio Gucci dans les années 1920 à Florence. Spécialisée à ses débuts dans la bagagerie en cuir et l'équipement équestre, notamment les malles de voyage et les selles, elle s'est diversifiée dans les années 1930 en proposant des valises et des accessoires en toile imprimée. Côté chaussures, Gucci a connu son premier grand succès en 1953 en lançant son mocassin en cuir signature. Ce modèle pour homme inspiré des mocassins amérindiens présentait une étonnante boucle en métal doré en forme de mors à cheval qui rendait hommage à l'héritage équestre de la Maison. Il affichait un style délibérément décontracté et informel qui a assuré son succès auprès de la jet-set des années 1960 et 1970 – et reste aujourd'hui un symbole de statut social plébiscité par ses fervents admirateurs.

Malgré une histoire jalonnée de succès, l'entreprise a frôlé la faillite dans les années 1980 à cause d'une expansion démesurée et de différends au sein de la famille Gucci. Au cours de la décennie suivante, Tom Ford, un créateur alors quasiment inconnu qui travaillait chez Perry Ellis, a été recruté comme directeur artistique des collections pour femme et a réimposé Gucci comme une Maison de premier plan. Il a rendu hommage à l'héritage jet-set et Studio 54 de la griffe en insufflant un glamour moderne et un puissant *sex-appeal* typiquement *seventies* aux modèles vintage. L'Italienne Frida Giannini lui a succédé après son départ en 2004. Comme elle avait débuté en tant que créatrice d'accessoires, les chaussures ont occupé une place importante dans sa vision pour Gucci, toujours marquée par un glamour sexy inspiré des années 1970. Alessandro Michele a ensuite été directeur de la création de Gucci de 2015 à 2022. À l'instar de Frida Giannini, il a débuté sa carrière chez Gucci en tant que créateur d'accessoires. Sous sa direction, l'esthétique de la Maison a été radicalement transformée en célébrant une mode romantique et éclectique au genre fluide. Les accessoires, en particulier les chaussures, ont joué un rôle clé dans la nouvelle sensibilité Gucci. Michele a réinterprété des produits signature, par exemple les mocassins à mors qu'il a transformés en mules colorées. « Il est compliqué de bien faire ce qu'il ne faut pas faire, mais telle est ma vision de la beauté », a-t-il déclaré. —E.M.

"It's quite certain that when Guccio Gucci started out, he never dreamed that his small luggage company would grow to one carrying such cultural significance. But since Gucci was founded in Florence in 1921, the company has built a catalog of genuinely iconic trademarks. The interlocking GG logo; the bar-and-bit belt buckle; the bamboo-handle handbag; the omnipresent loafer—all of them have helped the brand penetrate mainstream culture like no other Italian label in history."

— *VOGUE*

Gucci
Pumps: Red patent
leather
Italy, spring 1998

Gucci
Men's loafers: Multicolor
silk jacquard, blue
grosgrain
Italy, spring 2016

Gucci
Men's loafers: Blue
molded rubber, white
rubber, metal
Italy, 2014

Gucci
Sling-back pump: White
and red beads, black
leather, blue resin
Italy, spring 1999

Gucci
Pump: Green leather
Italy, spring 2016

Gucci
Men's slides: Blue
silk brocade, multi-
color beads
Italy, spring 2017

Gucci
Slides: Multicolor
printed canvas, red
leather, metal
Italy, spring 2016

Pierre Hardy

PIERRE HARDY'S SHOES ARE RENOWNED for their bold, graphic aesthetic. The French designer, who launched his eponymous label in 1999, is known for his experimental style predicated on an interest in geometric shape, color, and movement. Born in Paris in 1956, Hardy trained as both a designer and dancer, eventually earning a teaching degree in plastic arts from École Normale Supérieure in Cachan, France. Early in his career, Hardy drew illustrations for *Vanity Fair Italia* and *Vogue Homme* and joined a contemporary ballet company. "My years as a dancer left me with a real understanding of movement and the intricacies of the foot," Hardy said. "I work within a scale that's extremely precise, and I've always appreciated the sense of strictness that demands."

Pierre Hardy (b. 1956)

Hardy's illustrations caught the attention of the team at Dior, and in 1987 he was hired to design the house's shoe collections. From Dior he moved to Hermès in 1990 to create footwear for the storied legacy brand, and in 2001 he began designing the house's fine jewelry collection. He continues to create both lines for Hermès alongside his own brand.

From 2001 to 2013, Hardy also had an ongoing collaboration with his close friend Nicolas Ghesquière, who was then the head designer of Balenciaga. Hardy would create the shoes for each Balenciaga collection, but rather than design the footwear as exact references after seeing Ghesquière's clothes, Hardy described their relationship as a dialogue. They would discuss form, color, textures, and volume, and then Hardy would synthesize these elements into unique designs. "In the end, shoes are simply a vehicle," Hardy said. "I try to make a strong contrast between the ankle, leg, and the body. I try to find the right moment where a woman can stand — and catch her at just her limit." —*E.M.*

Pierre Hardy
Sandal: Multicolor
painted leather, metal
France, summer 2015

Pierre Hardy
Pump: Printed cowhide,
orange suede
France, fall 2013

PIERRE HARDYS SCHUHKREATIONEN SIND FÜR ihre kühne, klare Ästhetik berühmt. Der französische Designer gründete sein nach ihm benanntes Label 1999 und wurde für einen experimentellen Stil bekannt, der auf seinem Interesse an geometrischen Formen, Farben und Bewegung basiert. Hardy, geboren 1956 in Paris, absolvierte neben einer Ausbildung als Tänzer auch ein Designstudium und machte an der École Normale Supérieure in Cachan einen Abschluss als Lehrer für Bildhauerei. Zu Beginn seiner Karriere zeichnete er Illustrationen für die italienische *Vanity Fair* und *Vogue Homme* und gehörte einem Contemporary-Dance-Ensemble an. „Meine Jahre als Tänzer haben mir ein echtes Verständnis von Bewegung und den komplexen Feinheiten des Fußes vermittelt", sagte Hardy. „Der Maßstab, in dem ich arbeite, ist extrem präzise, was einen Sinn für Genauigkeit erfordert, den ich schon immer geschätzt habe."

Nachdem seine Illustrationen die Aufmerksamkeit des Kreativteams bei Dior geweckt hatten, wurde Hardy 1987 als Designer für die Schuhkollektionen des Hauses verpflichtet. Von dort wechselte er 1990 zu Hermès, um für die geschichtsträchtige Marke Schuhe zu entwerfen, ehe er 2001 auch die Schmuckkollektion übernahm. Bis heute führt er neben seinem eigenen Label beide Linien für Hermès weiter.

Von 2001 bis 2013 arbeitete Hardy auch mit seinem engen Freund Nicolas Ghesquière zusammen, der damals Chefdesigner bei Balenciaga war. Hardy kreierte die Schuhe für jede Balenciaga-Kollektion, allerdings nicht in exakter Abstimmung auf die Kleider, die er zu sehen bekam. Vielmehr entstanden sie, wie er sagt, aus dem Dialog mit Ghesquière, wobei Form, Farbe, Texturen und Volumen besprochen wurden. Aus diesen Elementen formte Hardy anschließend seine einzigartigen Designs. „Schuhe sind letztlich einfach ein Fortbewegungsmittel", sagt Hardy. „Ich versuche, einen starken Kontrast zwischen Knöchel, Bein und Körper zu erzeugen. Ich versuche, den richtigen Punkt zu finden, an dem eine Frau stehen kann – und sie in dem Moment zu erwischen, wenn sie gerade noch steht." —*E.M.*

LES SOULIERS DE PIERRE HARDY sont réputés pour leur esthétique graphique audacieuse. Ce créateur français qui a lancé sa marque éponyme en 1999 affiche un style expérimental né de son intérêt pour les formes géométriques, la couleur et le mouvement. Né en 1956 à Paris, il a suivi une formation de dessinateur et de danseur avant d'obtenir une agrégation d'arts plastiques à l'École normale supérieure de Cachan. Il a débuté sa carrière comme illustrateur pour l'édition italienne de *Vanity Fair* et *Vogue Homme* tout en intégrant une compagnie de danse contemporaine. « Mes années de danseur m'ont offert une véritable compréhension du mouvement et des complexités du pied, dit-il. Je travaille à une échelle extrêmement précise et j'ai toujours aimé la rigueur que cela exige. »

Les illustrations de Pierre Hardy ont attiré l'attention de l'équipe Dior, qui l'a recruté en 1987 pour dessiner les collections de chaussures de la Maison. Il a ensuite rejoint Hermès en 1990 pour créer les souliers de la marque mythique, puis sa collection de joaillerie à partir de 2001. Outre sa propre marque, il continue aujourd'hui à créer ces deux lignes pour Hermès.

De 2001 à 2013, il a également collaboré de manière continue avec Nicolas Ghesquière, un ami proche alors directeur artistique de Balenciaga. Au lieu de concevoir les chaussures comme des références exactes aux vêtements de Ghesquière, il créait les souliers de chaque collection Balenciaga en dialogue avec lui. Ils discutaient des formes, des couleurs, des textures et des volumes, puis Hardy synthétisait ces éléments dans des créations uniques. « En fin de compte, les souliers ne sont que des véhicules, explique-t-il. Je cherche à accentuer le contraste entre la cheville, la jambe et le corps. J'essaye de trouver le bon équilibre où la femme peut tenir debout – tout en la saisissant juste à sa limite. » —*E.M.*

"Taking inspiration from geometry and everyday objects, his pieces can be fun and surprising and almost mathematical in their purity: the epitome of modern luxury."

— KATE FINNIGAN, *TELEGRAPH*

Pierre Hardy
Booties: Multicolor
metallic leather, suede
France, winter 2008

Pierre Hardy
Ankle boots: Black
suede, silver-and-gray
leather, metal
France, winter 2015

Pierre Hardy
Wedge sandals: Blue
suede, silver leather
France, winter 2015

FOLLOWING
Pierre Hardy
Pumps: Off-white linen,
black leather, silver-and-
copper-tone plastic
France, summer 2015

Charles Jourdan

SHOEMAKER CHARLES JOURDAN BUILT HIS first factory in the French town of Romans-sur-Isère in 1921, in the early days of shoes' meteoric rise to the forefront of fashion. As skirt hems rose, bright colors and luxurious materials began to replace the more conservative footwear bent of the early 1900s. Jourdan, already known for quality women's shoes, launched the fashion-forward Séducta ready-to-wear line. His 1928 national advertising campaign for the line in high-end fashion magazines was the first for a shoe designer. Although his business suffered along with many others during the Depression and World War II, Jourdan, aided by his three sons, thrived in the postwar period, opening boutiques in Paris, London, and Munich.

Charles Jourdan (1883–1976)

Charles Jourdan became known for its limited range of chic styles, available in many colors. In 1954 the company signed an exclusive contract with Christian Dior and would go on to produce shoes for Pierre Cardin, Yves Saint Laurent, and Balmain, among other brands. Charles Jourdan also collaborated with designers Roger Vivier, André Perugia, Patrick Cox, and Christian Louboutin. Perugia worked with Charles Jourdan between 1962–1965 and gave his entire personal archive to the company, which re-released some of his most notable designs.

The 1960s and '70s were a time of rapid expansion for the company as it further established its commercial foothold, opening new boutiques and attracting large investors. The company pioneered new art-driven advertisements, hiring such photographers as Guy Bourdin to create ads that did not center on the staged product but rather on humorous, sexy, and surrealist scenes–often featuring disembodied legs strutting their stuff in Jourdan's designs. From 1947 to 1981, the company was led by the founder's youngest son, Roland Jourdan, and focused on fashion-forward silhouettes in eye-catching colors and fabrications. Their shoes are time capsules of transforming trends of the past decades — from the 1960s Mary Jane to the pump and mule styles of the 1970s and 1980s and the resurgence of the ballet flat. *–E.W.*

DER SCHUHMACHER CHARLES JOURDAN errichtete seine erste Fabrik 1921 im französischen Romans-sur-Isère, als der kometenhafte Aufstieg der Fußbekleidung als essenzieller Teil der Mode begann. Mit den kürzer werdenden Röcken wichen bei den Schuhen die eher konservativen Tendenzen zu Beginn des Jahrhunderts allmählich leuchtenden Farben und edlen Materialien. Jourdan war bereits für hochwertige Damenschuhe bekannt, als er die modisch progressive Konfektionslinie Séducta einführte. Die landesweite Werbekampagne, die er 1928 dafür in Premium-Modezeitschriften lancierte, war die Erste ihrer Art. Zwar brachten Weltwirtschaftskrise und Zweiter Weltkrieg sein Unternehmen ebenso in Bedrängnis wie viele andere auch, doch in der Nachkriegszeit prosperierte das Haus. Mit der Unterstützung seiner drei Söhne eröffnete Jourdan Boutiquen in Paris, London und München.

Charles Jourdan wurde bekannt für ein limitiertes Sortiment an eleganten Modellen, die in vielen Farben erhältlich waren. 1954 unterzeichnete die Firma einen Exklusivvertrag mit Christian Dior, um in der Folgezeit auch für Marken wie Pierre Cardin, Yves Saint Laurent und Balmain Schuhe zu fertigen. Darüber hinaus kooperierte Charles Jourdan mit den Modeschöpfern Roger Vivier, André Perugia, Patrick Cox und Christian Louboutin. Perugia, der von 1962 bis 1965 für Jourdan arbeitete, überließ dem Haus sein komplettes persönliches Archiv, was Jourdan erlaubte, einige von Perugias bedeutendsten Designs neu aufzulegen.

Die 1960er- und 70er-Jahre waren für die Firma eine Zeit rasanten Wachstums, in der sie ihre kommerzielle Basis weiter festigte, neue Boutiquen eröffnete und große Investoren anlockte. Als Wegbereiter einer neuen, künstlerischen Form von Werbung engagierte das Unternehmen Fotografen wie Guy Bourdin für Anzeigen, die nicht das eigentliche Produkt in den Mittelpunkt stellten, sondern Szenen zeigten, die witzig, sexy und surrealistisch waren – oft nur körperlose Beine in all ihrer Pracht und beschuht von Jourdan. Von 1947 bis 1981 leitete Charles' jüngster Sohn Roland Jourdan das Unternehmen, das sich nun auf modische Silhouetten in markanten Farben und Ausführungen konzentrierte. Jourdan-Schuhe sind Zeitkapseln der sich wandelnden Trends der vergangenen Jahrzehnte – von den Mary Janes der 1960er-Jahre über Pumps und Pantoletten der 1970er und 80er bis hin zu den wieder auferstandenen Ballerinas. —E.W.

CHARLES JOURDAN A CONSTRUIT SA première usine dans la ville française de Romans-sur-Isère en 1921, une époque où les chaussures débutaient leur ascension spectaculaire au titre d'accessoires de mode. Depuis que la longueur des jupes avait raccourci, elles arboraient des couleurs vives et des matières luxueuses qui commençaient à supplanter le style plus conservateur du début du XXᵉ siècle. Déjà connu pour ses modèles féminins de qualité supérieure, Jourdan a lancé Séducta, une collection de chaussures de prêt-à-porter au style visionnaire. La campagne publicitaire nationale dont elle a fait l'objet en 1928 dans les magazines de mode de luxe était la toute première jamais publiée par un chausseur. Bien que son entreprise ait souffert comme beaucoup d'autres pendant la crise de 1929 et la Seconde Guerre mondiale, Jourdan et ses trois fils l'ont fait prospérer pendant l'après-guerre en ouvrant des boutiques à Paris, Londres et Munich.

Charles Jourdan est devenu célèbre pour son offre limitée de modèles chics proposés dans de nombreuses couleurs différentes. En 1954, l'entreprise a signé un accord exclusif avec Christian Dior, puis a produit des chaussures pour Pierre Cardin, Yves Saint Laurent et Balmain, entre autres. La marque a aussi collaboré avec les créateurs de chaussures Roger Vivier, André Perugia, Patrick Cox et Christian Louboutin. Perugia, qui a travaillé avec Charles Jourdan de 1962 à 1965, a offert toutes ses archives personnelles à l'entreprise, qui a relancé certains de ses modèles les plus remarquables.

Les années 1960 et 1970 ont marqué une période d'expansion rapide pour l'entreprise qui a continué à consolider sa présence commerciale en ouvrant de nouvelles boutiques et en attirant d'importants investisseurs. Elle a inventé un nouveau type de publicité plus artistique en faisant appel à des photographes tels que Guy Bourdin pour créer des visuels qui n'étaient pas focalisés sur le produit, mais misaient sur des scènes humoristiques, sexy et surréalistes – souvent avec des jambes désincarnées paradant en chaussures Jourdan. Roland Jourdan, le plus jeune fils du fondateur, a dirigé l'entreprise de 1947 à 1981 en proposant des créations tendance aux couleurs et aux fabrications accrocheuses. Les modèles de la marque sont de véritables capsules temporelles qui transforment les tendances des décennies passées, des babies des *sixties* au renouveau de la ballerine en passant par les escarpins et les mules des années 1970 et 1980. —E.W.

CHARLES JOURDAN

10 - 10 a OLD BOND STREET, LONDON W. 1.

HYDE PARK 0871 - 1768

"MARBRE" Expresso CROCODILE - Eyelash (illusion) heel. 29,5 Gns. ● "HAND-BAG" Expresso CROCODILE
beautiful quality. 75 Gns. ● "BESANÇON" Black CALF - vamp in ebony KID - High straight. 6,5 Gns. ●
"HOSSEGOR" Black glazed BABY CALF - vamp in porto coloured KID . High straight black calf heel. 6,5 Gns.

PAGE 240
Charles Jourdan
Sling-back pump:
Black suede, silver
metallic leather
France, *ca.* 1979

PREVIOUS
Jourdan's innovative
shoe designs rose to
fame in the 1950s. A
London advertisement
features pointed-toe,
high-heeled shoes. 1960s.

Charles Jourdan
Ankle boots: Red glacé
leather, faux fur
France, *ca.* 1975

Charles Jourdan
Pumps: Black suede,
bronze metallic leather
France, *ca.* 1979

Charles Jourdan
Mary Jane:
Purple suede, metal
France, *ca.* 1966

"When I looked at the [Charles Jourdan] archive I thought, 'Oh my god, this is the entire history of footwear in one room.'"

— PATRICK COX

Charles Jourdan
Sandals: Black,
red, green, and
blue patent leather
France, *ca.* 1979

Charles Jourdan
(Copy of an André
Perugia design)
Sandal: Red, gray, and
black leather, metal
France, 1984

"Charles Jourdan created high quality ready-to-wear shoes that could be afforded by many women. He gave a touch of French chic to millions of feet!"

— CAROLINE COX, FASHION HISTORIAN

Charles Jourdan
Mules: Leopard-print vinyl, black patent leather
France, *ca.* 1980

Charles Jourdan
Flats: Green leather, peach satin
France, *ca.* 1982

Charles Jourdan
Sling-back pumps: Red patent leather
France, *ca.* 1986

Stephane Kélian

Stephane Kéloglanian (b. 1942)

DURING THE 1980S, SOME OF the most prominent and innovative fashion designers in Paris collaborated with Stephane Kélian. The company was founded in 1960 by three brothers, Georges, Gerard, and Stephane Kéloglanian, sons of an Armenian dyer who'd fled Turkey for France. Originally a men's shoe brand, their women's line was launched in 1978 and named after the youngest brother.

The late 1970s was a pivotal time in French fashion history. Ready-to-wear had exploded, and fashion was absorbing influences from conceptual Japanese designers to subcultural movements like punk. Newcomers such as Thierry Mugler, Claude Montana, and Jean Paul Gaultier responded with sexually charged, flamboyant, and cutting-edge designs. Their looks called for a new kind of shoe that was sculptural, colorful, and eye-catching. Stephane Kélian's shoes not only graced the runways; they were often featured in leading fashion magazines in editorials that became increasingly sexual.

At the height of its popularity and profitability in the 1980s, Stephane Kélian employed nearly 100 people, including upward of 50 artisans whose only job was to braid leather, one of the firm's hallmark features. Kélian also produced the footwear line of Maud Frizon and expanded into the American market with designer Jean-Michel Cazabat serving as its Stateside president until 1995. It was during the 1990s that Martine Sitbon collaborated with Stephane Kélian, just as she opened her eponymous boutique. Although thoroughly restructured, the firm still exists. —*P.M.*

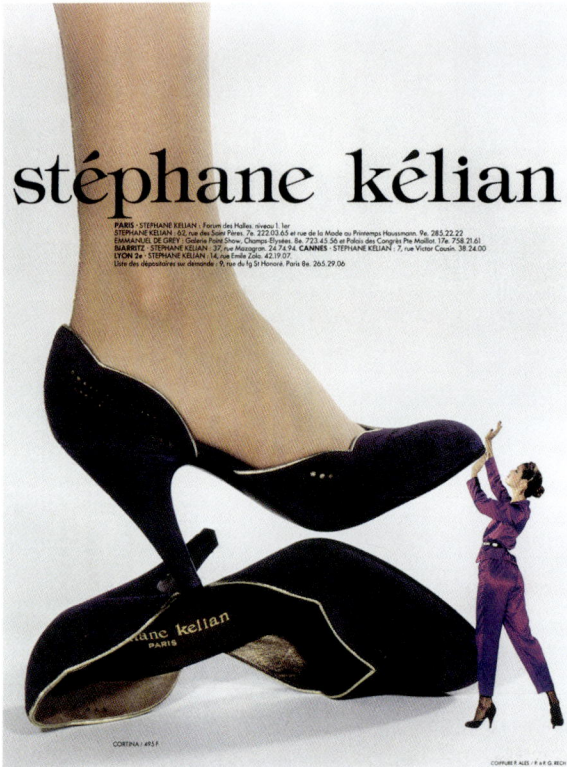

stéphane kélian

PARIS · STEPHANE KÉLIAN : Forum des Halles, niveau 1. 1er
STEPHANE KÉLIAN : 62, rue des Saint Pères. 7e. 222.03.65 et rue de la Mode au Printemps Haussmann. 9e. 285.22.22
EMMANUEL DE GREY : Galerie Point Show, Champs-Elysées. 8e. 723.45.56 et Palais des Congrès Pte Maillot. 17e. 758.21.61
BIARRITZ · STEPHANE KÉLIAN : 37, rue Mazagran. 24.74.94. CANNES · STEPHANE KÉLIAN : 7, rue Victor Cousin. 38.24.00
LYON 2e · STEPHANE KÉLIAN : 14, rue Emile Zola. 42.19.07.
Liste des dépositaires sur demande : 9, rue du fg St Honoré. Paris 8e. 265.29.06

CORTINA / 495 F.

COIFFURE F. ALES / P.s/F. G. RECH

STEPHANE KÉLIAN KOOPERIERTE IN DEN 1980er-Jahren mit einigen der prominentesten und innovativsten Modeschöpfer in Paris. Gegründet wurde das Unternehmen 1960 von den Brüdern Georges, Gerard und Stephane Kéloglanian, den Söhnen eines aus der Türkei nach Frankreich geflohenen armenischen Färbers. Die ursprünglich auf Herrenschuhe spezialisierte Marke lancierte ihre nach dem jüngsten der Brüder benannte Damenlinie 1978.

Die späten 1970er-Jahre markierten eine historische Zeitenwende in der französischen Mode. Der Prêt-à-porter-Sektor war explosionsartig angewachsen, und die Mode absorbierte Einflüsse von japanischem Konzeptdesign bis hin zu subkulturellen Strömungen wie dem Punk. Newcomer wie Thierry Mugler, Claude Montana und Jean Paul Gaultier reagierten mit sexuell aufgeladenen, extravaganten und avantgardistischen Designs. Ihre Looks verlangten nach einer neuen Art Schuh, der

skulptural, farbenfroh und auffällig war. Schuhe von Stephane Kélian zierten nicht nur Laufstege, sondern auch die zunehmend sexualisierten Bildstrecken führender Modemagazine.

Auf dem Höhepunkt seiner Popularität und Profitabilität in den 1980er-Jahren beschäftigte Stephane Kélian fast 100 Mitarbeiter, darunter über 50 Handwerker, deren einzige Aufgabe im Flechten von Leder bestand, einer der Spezialitäten des Hauses. Kélian fertigte auch die Schuhlinie von Maud Frizon und expandierte auf den amerikanischen Markt, für den Jean-Michel Cazabat als Designer und US-Geschäftsführer bis 1995 verantwortlich zeichnete. In den 1990er-Jahren begann Martine Sitbon ihre Zusammenarbeit mit Stephane Kélian, als sie unter eigenem Namen ihre Boutique eröffnete. Trotz grundlegender Umstrukturierungen existiert die Firma bis heute. —P.M.

DANS LES ANNÉES 1980, STEPHANE KÉLIAN a collaboré avec certains des plus importants et des plus innovants créateurs de mode parisiens. Fondée en 1960 par les trois frères Georges, Gérard et Stéphane Kéloglanian, fils d'un teinturier arménien qui avait fui la Turquie pour la France, la marque a d'abord proposé des souliers pour homme avant de lancer sa collection pour femme en 1978 sous le nom du benjamin de la fratrie.

La fin des années 1970 a marqué un tournant dans l'histoire de la mode française. Le prêt-à-porter explosait et la mode absorbait toutes sortes d'influences, du style conceptuel des créateurs japonais aux mouvements *underground* comme le punk. De nouveaux venus tels Thierry Mugler, Claude Montana et Jean Paul Gaultier proposaient des créations sexuellement chargées, flamboyantes et avant-gardistes qui exigeaient une nouvelle chaussure sculpturale, colorée et accrocheuse. Si les créations Stephane Kélian arpentaient les podiums des défilés, on les retrouvait aussi régulièrement dans les séries de mode toujours plus sexualisées publiées par les magazines.

À l'apogée de sa notoriété et de sa rentabilité dans les années 1980, l'entreprise Stephane Kélian employait une centaine de personnes, dont plus de cinquante artisans dédiés uniquement au tressage du cuir, l'une des signatures de la marque. Stephane Kélian a aussi produit la collection de chaussures de Maud Frizon et s'est exporté sur le marché américain, le créateur Jean-Michel Cazabat officiant comme président de la marque aux États-Unis jusqu'en 1995. C'est pendant les années 1990 que Martine Sitbon a collaboré avec Stephane Kélian, juste au moment où elle ouvrait sa boutique éponyme. Bien que l'entreprise ait été entièrement restructurée, elle est toujours en activité aujourd'hui. —*P.M.*

"With their long, pointy toes and thick inward-slanting heels, [Kélian's shoes] look like a cross between a Western boot and something a wicked witch would wear."

— CARRIE DONOVAN, *THE NEW YORK TIMES*

**Jean Paul Gaultier
(Stephane Kélian)**
Men's shoes: Black-and-
brown leather
France, 1988–91

**Martine Sitbon
(Stephane Kélian)**
T-Straps: Black
patent leather
France, 1995

**Jean Paul Gaultier
(Stephane Kélian)**
Men's shoe: Black
hair calf
France, 1988

Nicholas Kirkwood

FOOTWEAR DESIGNER NICHOLAS KIRKWOOD'S BOLD
creations are unabashedly statement shoes. Their sculptural
aesthetic fuses unlikely materials with theatrical yet sexy silhouettes. Kirkwood uses the latest technological innovations
like laser-cutting and 3D-printing to achieve a unique dyna-
mism in his work. This eye toward the future led *ELLE*
magazine to hail that he has "the hand of a sculptor
and the mind of an inventor."

Kirkwood attended Central Saint Martins as
an art student, and after graduating began working
with milliner Philip Treacy in his London shop, assist-
ing with sales, mingling with prestigious clientele, and
learning the craft of accessory design. This inspired him to
enroll in a footwear design course at Cordwainers Technical
College in 2001. Four years later he launched his eponymous
label with his first women's shoe collection. His work was quickly recognized by *Vogue*, and
the designer was lauded for his ability to balance inspiration from the past with his ideas
for something new.

Nicholas Kirkwood (b. 1980)

Kirkwood has since garnered a cultlike following for his exceedingly individualistic
shoes. High-profile runway collaborations with labels such as Rodarte, Fendi, and Erdem
have helped to increase his global reputation, and he has opened a fleet of stand-alone
stores worldwide. Heels have always been a particular focal point of the designer's work,
whether notched, sculpted, or crafted with unusual and creatively reimagined materials
such as metal hex nuts or electrical wire. While Kirkwood's designs are undeniably graphic
and sculptural, he is quick to point out that his aesthetic is not about a cold, pure modernism. As he once put it, "There is a femininity that brings a certain humanness and warmth
to it." His work is ultimately about both form and fun. —*E.M.*

Nicholas Kirkwood
Sandals: White
leather, snakeskin, and
patent leather
England, spring 2012

Rodarte
(**Nicholas Kirkwood**)
Thigh-high boots:
Gray leather
USA, spring 2009

DIE VERWEGENEN KREATIONEN DES Schuh-designers Nicholas Kirkwood sind ungenierte Statements. Ihre skulpturale Ästhetik vereint unerwartete Materialien mit Silhouetten, die theatralisch und zugleich sexy sind. Kirkwood bedient sich innovativer Technologien wie Laserschnitt und 3-D-Druck, die seinem Werk eine einzigartige Dynamik verleihen. Dieser zukunftsorientierte Ansatz ließ die Zeitschrift *ELLE* jubeln, er habe „die Hand eines Bildhauers und den Kopf eines Erfinders".

Nach einem Kunststudium am Central Saint Martins College begann Kirkwood, als Verkaufs-assistent in der Boutique des Londoner Modisten Philip Treacy zu arbeiten, wo er sich unter die prominente Kundschaft mischte und das Handwerk des Accessoire-Designs erlernte. Davon inspiriert, belegte er 2001 einen Schuhdesignkurs am Cordwainers Technical College. Vier Jahre später brachte er seine erste Damenschuhkollektion unter eigenem Namen heraus. Schnell fand seine Arbeit den Beifall der *Vogue*, die Kirkwoods Fähigkeit pries, die Balance zwischen Inspirationen aus der Vergangenheit und eigenen Ideen für Neues zu finden.

Seither hat Kirkwood mit seinen ungemein individualistischen Schuhkreationen eine eingeschworene Fangemeinde um sich geschart. Viel beachtete Laufstegkooperationen mit Labels wie Rodarte, Fendi und Erdem trugen dazu bei, seine internationale Bekanntheit zu steigern. Zudem eröffnete er rund um den Globus zahlreiche Einzelgeschäfte. Beim Design gilt sein besonderes Augenmerk von jeher dem Absatz, sei er gekerbt, speziell geformt oder aus ungewöhnlichen, schöpferisch neu gedachten Materialien wie Metallmuttern oder Stromkabeln gefertigt. Seine Designs sind unbestreitbar bildhaft und skulptural, dennoch legt er Wert auf die Feststellung, dass es bei seiner Ästhetik nicht um einen kalten, reinen Modernismus geht: „Sie hat etwas Feminines, das ihr eine gewisse Menschlichkeit und Wärme verleiht." Letzten Endes geht es bei seiner Arbeit gleichermaßen um Form und Vergnügen. —*E.M.*

LES AUDACIEUSES CHAUSSURES DE Nicholas Kirkwood sont d'une extravagance totalement décomplexée. Leur esthétique sculpturale allie des matières improbables avec des silhouettes théâtrales, mais néanmoins sexy. Kirkwood utilise des innovations technologiques de pointe comme la découpe au laser et l'impression 3D pour conférer un dynamisme unique à ses créations. Son œil visionnaire a incité le magazine *ELLE* à écrire qu'il possède « une main de sculpteur et un esprit d'inventeur ».

Après ses études artistiques à Central Saint Martins et l'obtention de son diplôme, Kirkwood a travaillé aux côtés du chapelier Philip Treacy dans sa boutique de Londres, où il l'a assisté en tant que vendeur, a fait connaissance avec une clientèle prestigieuse et s'est formé à la création d'accessoires. Cette expérience l'a poussé à suivre un cursus en création de chaussures au Cordwainers Technical College en 2001. Quatre ans plus tard, il a lancé sa griffe éponyme avec une première collection pour femme. Son travail a vite été repéré par *Vogue*, qui a salué sa capacité à trouver le juste équilibre entre inspirations historiques et idées novatrices.

Depuis, ses chaussures absolument uniques en leur genre l'ont imposé comme un créateur culte. Ses collaborations médiatisées avec des marques telles Rodarte, Fendi et Erdem ont contribué à sa réputation internationale et lui ont permis d'ouvrir un réseau de boutiques indépendantes dans le monde entier. Kirkwood a toujours accordé une importance particulière aux talons, qu'ils soient entaillés, sculptés ou construits dans des matériaux insolites détournés avec ingéniosité, par exemple des écrous hexagonaux ou du fil électrique. Bien que ses créations soient indéniablement graphiques et sculpturales, il insiste toujours sur le fait que son esthétique ne relève pas d'un modernisme pur et froid : « Elle a une certaine féminité qui apporte une touche d'humanité et de chaleur. » En fin de compte, son travail repose autant sur la forme que sur le fun. —*E.M.*

Nicholas Kirkwood
Sandal: Gold leather,
metal chain,
electrical wire
England, spring 2009

Rodarte
(**Nicholas Kirkwood**)
Wedges: White-and-
blue printed leather,
resin, vinyl, suede
USA, spring 2011

Nicholas Kirkwood
Wedges: Black, off-
white, and rose gold
leather, suede
England, spring 2013

Nicholas Kirkwood
Sling-back pumps: Black
patent leather, elastic,
purple reptile skin
England, fall 2010

Nicholas Kirkwood
"Aqua Neon Swirl"
pumps: Multicolor
silk, leather
England, spring 2013

FOLLOWING
Rodarte
(Nicholas Kirkwood)
Sandal boots: Black
leather and metal
USA, spring 2010

"I think women have a connection to shoes in a different way to clothing because it physically changes the shape of your body. It makes you taller, arches your back, and makes your feel more confident."

— NICHOLAS KIRKWOOD

Tokio Kumagai

A GENERATION OF JAPANESE-BORN ARTISTS and designers who came of age in the 1960s and 1970s had a wide-sweeping global impact. Among them was shoe and fashion designer Tokio Kumagai. Born in Sendai, Japan, in 1947, he graduated from the Bunka Fukuso Gakuin, the Japanese college of fashion design, in 1970. And like his compatriots Issey Miyake and Kenzo Takada, Kumagai moved to Paris. For the next decade, Kumagai worked as a fashion designer in France for Yves Saint Laurent and Jean-Charles de Castelbajac, designed shoes for Pierre d'Alby, and collaborated with Cerutti and Issey Miyake. Elio Fiorucci became aware of Kumagai's work and invited him to collaborate on his newly founded fashion label, where Kumagai designed gold-and silver sneakers. Around the same time, he began experimenting with hand-painting footwear. Within two years, Kumagai opened his own company and boutiques in Paris and became known for his witty and surrealist ornamented footwear.

Tokio Kumagai
(1947–1987)

Kumagai openly acknowledged the influence of art movements ranging from surrealism to abstract expressionism, as well as the works of Salvador Dalí, Wassily Kandinsky, Piet Mondrian, and Jackson Pollock. Kumagai's shoes ranged from his decidedly playful "cat-and-mouse" designs to "eye" and "mask" ornamented shoes. He pushed the surrealist envelope further with his 1982 trompe-l'œil series entitled *Shoes to Eat*, or *Taberu Kutsu* in Japanese, which was inspired by cast-resin faux entrées seen in the windows of many Japanese restaurants.

The shoe designer was not limited to the creation of conceptual artist shoes. He made an array of footwear that was both practical and fashionable, such as his lace-up ballerina flats. Kumagai died in 1987 at 40. Despite his short career, his unique footwear resides in museum collections around the world. —*P.M.*

EINE GENERATION JAPANISCHER KÜNSTLER und Designer, die ihre Karrieren in den 1960er- und 70er-Jahren starteten, erlangte weltweit bleibende Geltung. Zu ihnen zählte der Schuh- und Modedesigner Tokio Kumagai. Geboren 1947 in Sendai, zog er nach einem Studium an der japanischen Modeakademie Bunka Fukuso Gakuin 1970 nach Paris, so wie auch seine Landsleute Issey Miyake und Kenzo Takada. In den folgenden zehn Jahren arbeitete er als Modedesigner für Yves Saint Laurent und Jean-Charles de Castelbajac, entwarf Schuhe für Pierre d'Alby und kooperierte mit Cerutti und Issey Miyake. Elio Fiorucci, auf Kumagais Arbeit aufmerksam geworden, lud ihn zur Zusammenarbeit unter seinem neu gegründeten Modelabel ein, für das Kumagai Sneaker in Gold und Silber entwarf. Etwa zur gleichen Zeit begann er, mit Handbemalungen zu experimentieren. Binnen zwei Jahren gründete er seine eigene Firma, eröffnete Boutiquen in Paris und machte sich mit witzigen, surrealistisch verzierten Schuhkreationen einen Namen.

Zu Kumagais erklärten Einflüssen gehörte Kunst vom Surrealismus bis zum abstrakten Expressionismus, darunter die Werke von Salvador Dalí, Wassily Kandinsky, Piet Mondrian und Jackson Pollock. Zu seinen Designs zählten etwa der ausnehmend verspielte „Katz-und-Maus"-Look oder als „Auge" und „Maske" ornamentierte Schuhe. Noch weiter auf die Spitze trieb er den Surrealismus mit seiner 1982 präsentierten Trompe-l'oeil-Kollektion *Shoes to Eat*, japanisch: *Taberu Kutsu*, zu der ihn die Lebensmittelattrappen aus Gießharz inspirierten, mit denen viele japanische Restaurants ihre Schaufenster dekorierten.

Sein Schuhdesign war nicht auf Konzeptkunst beschränkt. Eine ganze Reihe seiner Kreationen, wie etwa seine Schnürballerinas, war praktisch und modisch zugleich. Kumagai starb 1987 mit 40 Jahren. Trotz dieser nur kurzen Karriere sind seine einzigartigen Schuhdesigns in Museumssammlungen rund um die Welt zu finden. —*P.M.*

LE CRÉATEUR DE MODE ET de chaussures Tokio Kumagai appartenait à la génération d'artistes et de créatifs japonais devenus adultes dans les années 1960 et 1970 et dont le travail a exercé une influence mondiale. Né en 1947 à Sendai au Japon, il a obtenu son diplôme de l'école supérieure de mode Bunka Fukuso Gakuin en 1970, puis s'est installé à Paris à l'instar de ses compatriotes Issey Miyake et Kenzo Takada. Pendant la décennie suivante, Kumagai a travaillé en France comme créateur de mode pour Yves Saint Laurent et Jean-Charles de Castelbajac, a conçu des chaussures pour Pierre d'Alby et a travaillé avec Cerutti et Issey Miyake. Quand Elio Fiorucci a découvert son travail, il lui a proposé de collaborer au lancement de sa nouvelle marque de mode, pour laquelle Kumagai a conçu des sneakers dorées et argentées. C'est à la même époque qu'il a commencé à peindre ses chaussures à la main. En l'espace de deux ans, il a créé sa propre entreprise, ouvert des boutiques à Paris et s'est fait connaître pour ses créations aux décors surréalistes pleins d'esprit.

Kumagai admettait ouvertement s'inspirer de mouvements artistiques tels que le surréalisme et l'expressionnisme abstrait, ainsi que des œuvres de Salvador Dalí, Vassily Kandinsky, Piet Mondrian et Jackson Pollock. Il a créé des souliers résolument ludiques dont le bout était décoré d'un museau de chat ou de souris, d'un œil ou d'un masque. En 1982, il a encore creusé cette influence surréaliste dans sa collection en trompe-l'œil *Taberu Kutsu*, une expression japonaise signifiant « chaussures à manger », inspirée par les faux hors-d'œuvre en résine moulée qui sont exposés dans les vitrines de nombreux restaurants japonais.

Tokio Kumagai ne se contentait pas de créer des chaussures d'art conceptuel. Il a aussi conçu de nombreux modèles aussi tendance que pratiques, à l'image de ses ballerines à lacets. Il est décédé en 1987 à l'âge de 40 ans. Malgré la brièveté de sa carrière, ses créations uniques font désormais partie des collections de nombreux musées à travers le monde. —*P.M.*

Tokio Kumagai
Men's boots: Black-
and-white giraffe-
printed calfskin
Japan, 1981–84

Tokio Kumagai
Sling-back pump: Black
patent leather, black
suede, gold metallic
leather
Japan, 1985–86

Tokio Kumagai
Flats: Printed pony skin
France, *ca.* 1997

"Inspired by surrealism, abstract art and expressionist styles, and artists such as Kandinsky, Pollock and Mondrian, Kumagai handpainted his shoes in a manner reminiscent of a particular artist's style. He often altered the structure of the shoe to accommodate his painting."

— FASHION MODEL DIRECTORY

Masaya Kushino

MASAYA KUSHINO'S OTHERWORLDLY CREATIONS HAVE established him as one of Japan's most imaginative footwear designers. Exemplifying a decidedly artistic vision, his unique shoes blur the lines between footwear and sculpture. Not one to follow seasonal trends, Kushino prefers to focus on the aesthetic quality of his work to produce timeless designs often inspired by nature. His fantastical footwear has incorporated feathered wings, talons, antlers, faux horns, and flowers into its designs. "I'm borrowing power from nature and redesigning it, interpreting it through my own filter. That's my role as an artist," Kushino has said.

Masaya Kushino (b. 1982)

    Based in Kyoto, Kushino works with local artisans to produce designs that make use of traditional Japanese materials and craftsmanship in novel ways not typically associated with shoe making. Meticulously crafted, these shoes may take up to six months to complete. For Kushino, his designs are a form of visual storytelling. His "Lung-ta" shoe, Tibetan for "wind horse," was inspired by the French equestrian theater company Zingaro. The shoe, which features a long blond "ponytail" cascading from the heel, was crafted from *Shiro-nameshi*, a traditional white leather that is produced in Himeji, a city in the Kansai region of Japan, and was used for samurai armor. According to Kushino, the shoe represents a hybrid of cultures as it also incorporates antique lace from France. Kushino's unique approach to shoe design has led him to collaborate with the Japanese fashion house Somarta for its fall/winter 2010–11 collection, and his shoes have garnered the admiration of style icon Lady Gaga. —*M.M.A.*

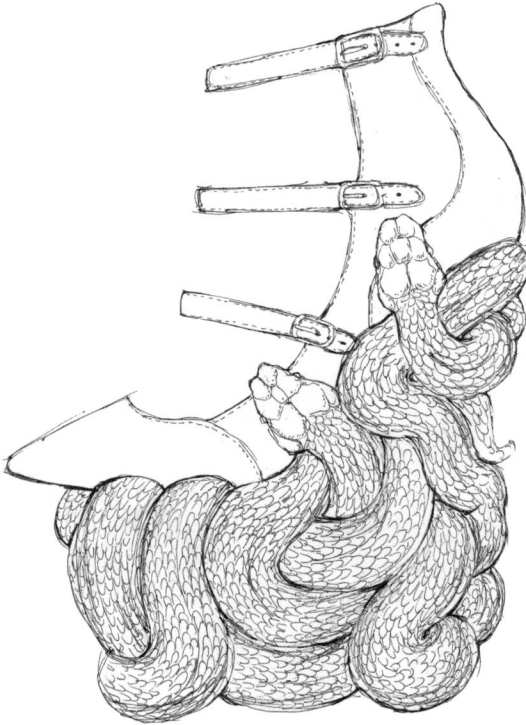

PREVIOUS
Masaya Kushino
"Ceryneian Hind" boot:
Black cowhide leather,
lamb fur, stingray,
resin, metal
Japan, 2010

Kushino's baroque 2020
sketch features a buckle-
fastened stiletto envel-
oped by two intertwining
snake embellishments.

Masaya Kushino
"Lung-ta" (Wind Horse)
shoes: Nude leather, gold
Leavers lace, lacquered
Japanese cypress wood,
blond human hair
Japan, 2008

MIT WELTENTRÜCKTEN KREATIONEN HAT Masaya Kushino sich als einer der einfallsreichsten Schuhdesigner Japans etabliert. Seine einzigartigen Designs sind Ausdruck einer dezidiert künstlerischen Vision und lassen die Grenzen zwischen Schuh und Skulptur verschwimmen. Anstatt saisonalen Trends zu folgen, zieht Kushino es vor, sich auf die ästhetische Qualität seiner Arbeit zu konzentrieren, um zeitlose, oft von der Natur inspirierte Designs zu kreieren. So kommen bei seinen fantastischen Entwürfen etwa gefiederte Flügel, Krallen, Geweihe, Hornimitate und Blumen zum Einsatz. „Ich leihe mir die Kraft der Natur und gestalte sie um, indem ich sie durch meinen eigenen Filter interpretiere. Das ist meine Rolle als Künstler", so Kushino.

Der in Kioto ansässige Kushino arbeitet mit heimischen Handwerkern zusammen, um Entwürfe zu realisieren, bei denen traditionelle japanische Materialien und Handwerkskünste so zum Einsatz kommen, wie man es üblicherweise nicht mit der Schuhmacherei in Verbindung bringt. Die akribische Fertigung dieser Schuhe kann bis zu sechs Monate in Anspruch nehmen. Für Kushino stellen seine Kreationen eine Form des visuellen Erzählens dar. Zu seinem Entwurf „Lung-ta", tibetisch für „Windpferd", inspirierte ihn das französische Pferdetheater Zingaro. Der Schuh mit langem blondem „Pferdeschwanz", der von der Hinterkappe zu Boden fließt, wurde aus *Shiro-nameshi* gefertigt, einem traditionell für Samurai-Rüstungen verwendeten weißen Leder, das in der Stadt Himeji in der Region Kansai hergestellt wird. Als weiteres Obermaterial diente alte französische Spitze, weshalb Kushino den Schuh als Hybrid der Kulturen versteht. Sein einzigartiger Designansatz führte zu einer Zusammenarbeit an der Herbst-/Winterkollektion 2010/2011 des japanischen Modehauses Somarta. Zu den Verehrerinnen seiner Kreationen zählt die Stilikone Lady Gaga. —*M.M.A.*

LES ÉTRANGES CRÉATIONS DE MASAYA KUSHINO font de lui l'un des designers de souliers les plus originaux du Japon. Issues de sa vision résolument artistique, elles brouillent la frontière entre sculpture et création de chaussures. N'étant pas du genre à suivre les tendances saisonnières, Kushino préfère se concentrer sur la qualité esthétique de son travail pour produire des créations intemporelles souvent inspirées de la nature. Ses chaussures fantasmagoriques intègrent des ailes en plumes, des pattes d'oiseau, des bois de cerf, de fausses cornes et des fleurs. « J'emprunte son pouvoir à la nature afin de la réinventer, de la réinterpréter à travers mon propre filtre, dit-il. C'est mon rôle en tant qu'artiste. »

Basé à Kyoto, Masaya Kushino travaille avec des artisans locaux pour produire ses créations. Celles-ci utilisent des matériaux et des savoir-faire japonais traditionnels de façon inédite en ceci qu'ils sont rarement associés à la création de souliers. Leur minutieuse fabrication peut prendre jusqu'à six mois. Il considère ses créations comme une forme de narration visuelle. Sa chaussure Lung-ta, un terme tibétain signifiant « cheval du vent », lui a été inspirée par la compagnie de théâtre équestre française Zingaro. Avec une longue « queue-de-cheval » blonde tombant en cascade depuis le sommet du talon, elle a été fabriquée en *Shiro-nameshi*, un cuir blanc traditionnel produit à Himeji, une ville de la région du Kansai au Japon, qui servait à créer l'armure des samouraïs. Kushino considère ce soulier comme un hybride culturel, car il intègre aussi de la dentelle française ancienne. Son approche unique l'a amené à collaborer avec la Maison de mode japonaise Somarta sur sa collection Automne/Hiver 2010-2011. Ses créations sont aussi particulièrement prisées par l'icône de la mode Lady Gaga. —*M.M.A.*

Christian Lacroix

NO LATE TWENTIETH-CENTURY DESIGNER exemplified the idea of haute couture opulence more than Christian Lacroix. After studying art history and museum studies at the University of Montpellier and the Sorbonne with an eye toward becoming a fashion curator, Lacroix accepted his first major post at the House of Patou, where his signature style gained international notice. In 1987 he opened his eponymous house with backing from fashion executive Bernard Arnault.

Lacroix unveiled his debut haute couture collection for the 1987 autumn-winter season. A "radiant, opulent, virtuosic homage" to his roots, the 60-piece collection was infused with Mediterranean influences such as "traditional Arlesian outfits" and "the toreador's cape." As Lacroix noted, "it was a departure from the minimalistic look of the influential Japanese designers en vogue at that time." In a sea of black, his clothes were crafted in "blood red, fuchsia pink, and bright yellow." Within two years, both ready-to-wear and accessories collections (jewelry, handbags, shoes, and more) were launched, and several international boutiques opened. Despite support from the fashion community and an ardent client base, the house was never profitable and shuttered in 2009.

Christian Lacroix (b. 1951)

For more than 20 years, Lacroix's devotion to craftsmanship and his brilliance as a colorist and draper could be seen in his theatrical, historizing creations. Leading magazines featured the hallmark Lacroix look from head to toe: "le pouf" (or puffball) dresses were topped with cabbage rose hats and balanced with satin pumps ornamented with stripes and oversized ribbons and bows. For all their baroque opulence, Lacroix preferred heeled shoes and sandals with silhouettes that were always elegant and refined. *—P.M.*

Christian Lacroix
Pump: Pink silk satin,
ivory shirred silk
France, 2000

KEIN DESIGNER DES AUSKLINGENDEN 20. Jahrhunderts zeigte anschaulicher als Christian Lacroix, wie opulente Haute Couture aussieht. Mit dem Ziel, Modekurator zu werden, studierte Lacroix zunächst Kunstgeschichte und Museumswissenschaften an der Universität von Montpellier und der Sorbonne in Paris, ehe er seinen ersten bedeutenden Posten im Haus Patou annahm, wo sein unverkennbarer Stil internationale Beachtung fand. Mit Unterstützung des Modeunternehmers Bernard Arnault eröffnete er 1987 sein eigenes Haus.

Zur Herbst-/Wintersaison 1987 präsentierte Lacroix seine erste Haute-Couture-Schau. Die 60-teilige Kollektion, eine „glanzvolle, opulente, virtuose Hommage" an seine Herkunft, war von mediterranen Einflüssen geprägt, etwa von der „traditionellen Kleidung aus Arles" oder dem „Torero-Cape". „Es war eine Abkehr vom minimalistischen Look der damals so einflussreichen japanischen Designer", wie Lacroix erklärte. In einem Meer aus Schwarz tauchten seine Kleider in „Blutrot, Fuchsia und leuchtendem Gelb" auf. Binnen zwei Jahren wurden sowohl Prêt-à-porter- als auch Accessoire-Kollektionen (Schmuck, Handtaschen, Schuhe und mehr) eingeführt und weltweit mehrere Boutiquen eröffnet. Doch trotz des Rückhalts in der Modegemeinde und seiner getreuen Stammkundschaft war das Haus nie profitabel und schloss 2009 seine Pforten.

Über 20 Jahre kam Lacroix' Hingabe an die Handwerkskunst und seine Brillanz als Kolorist und Stoffkünstler in seinen theatralischen, historisierenden Kreationen zum Ausdruck. Führende Modemagazine präsentierten den typischen Lacroix-Look von Kopf bis Fuß: Kleider mit „Le pouf", einem Ballonrock, gekrönt von einem Hut mit Gartenrose und abgerundet durch Satinpumps, die mit Streifen und überdimensionierten Bändern und Schleifen verziert waren. Lacroix bevorzugte Schuhe und Sandalen mit Absatz, deren Silhouetten – bei all seiner sonstigen barocken Opulenz – stets von raffinierter Eleganz waren. —P.M.

AUCUN AUTRE CRÉATEUR DE LA fin du XXᵉ siècle n'a mieux incarné l'opulence en haute couture que Christian Lacroix. Après une formation en histoire de l'art suivie d'études muséales à l'université de Montpellier et à la Sorbonne en vue de devenir créateur de mode, Lacroix a occupé son premier poste important chez Patou, où son style signature a vite attiré l'attention de la presse internationale. Il a ensuite ouvert sa Maison éponyme en 1987 grâce à un financement du magnat de la mode Bernard Arnault.

Christian Lacroix a présenté sa première collection de haute couture pour la saison Automne/ Hiver 1987. « Hommage éclatant, opulent et virtuose » à ses racines, cette collection de soixante pièces était imprégnée d'influences méditerranéennes, telles que les « costumes arlésiens traditionnels » et la « cape de toréador ». Comme le couturier l'a lui-même observé, « ce style tranchait avec le look minimaliste des influents créateurs japonais en vogue à cette époque ». Au milieu d'un océan de noir, ses vêtements affichaient des couleurs « rouge sang, rose fuchsia et jaune vif ». En l'espace de deux ans, il a lancé une collection de prêt-à-porter et une ligne d'accessoires (bijoux, sacs à main et chaussures, entre autres), et ouvert plusieurs boutiques à l'étranger. Malgré le soutien du monde de la mode et une clientèle fervente, la Maison n'a jamais été rentable et a dû fermer ses portes en 2009.

Pendant plus de vingt ans, Christian Lacroix a exprimé sa dévotion au savoir-faire ainsi que son génie de la couleur et du drapé dans des créations théâtrales d'inspiration historique. Les plus grands magazines mettaient en avant son look signature de pied en cap : ses robes « pouf » se portaient avec des chapeaux parés de roses centfeuilles et des escarpins en satin rayé ou ornés de gros nœuds en ruban. C'est pour leur opulence baroque que Lacroix privilégiait les chaussures et les sandales à talons à la silhouette toujours élégante et raffinée. —P.M.

"There was no darkness or sobriety in Lacroix's world, as fizzy and effervescent as champagne. It was an exercise in extreme fantasy and make-believe, in the seductive power of fashion as a dream."

— ALEXANDER FURY, FASHION WRITER

Christian Lacroix
Pumps: Black-and-
pink satin
France, 2004

Christian Lacroix
Pumps: Red silk
satin, silver metallic
leather, Velcro
France, spring 2003

Christian Lacroix
Mules: Yellow, brown,
blue-violet striped
silk taffeta
France, spring 1998

Lanvin

JEANNE LANVIN FOUNDED MAISON LANVIN in 1889, now one of the oldest fashion houses in operation. Before setting up her millinery business at 18, Lanvin worked as a dressmaker's errand girl. By 1909 she entered the couture business. Her daughter, Marguerite Marie-Blanche, would serve as the inspiration for many of her youthful designs. According to fashion historian Caroline Milbank, Lanvin was an early proponent of *le costume complet* and presented her clothes with matching hats and shoes.

Jeanne Lanvin (1867–1946)

With the appointment of Alber Elbaz as creative director in 2001, Lanvin was transformed into one of the most coveted labels of the early twenty-first century. Of his time at the label, Elbaz explained, "I feel like an acrobat balancing between two worlds: the past and present." During Elbaz's tenure, accessories became a greater part of the Lanvin aesthetic than ever before. The brand's shoes — whether chunky-heeled sandals, spike heels, or chic sneakers — were statement making and allowed fans to tap into the heritage of the brand. Under the creative leadership of Bruno Sialelli, imaginative footwear included knee-high boots printed with an etching depicting the legend of Saint George taming and slaying a dragon. The powerful design of the iconic tale positioned footwear at the forefront of Sialelli's vision for Lanvin. In 2024, Peter Copping succeeded Sialelli as the new artistic director of the brand. —*M.M.*

DAS 1889 VON JEANNE LANVIN gegründete Maison Lanvin ist eines der ältesten noch heute bestehenden Couture-Häuser. Lanvin hatte als Gehilfin eines Damenschneiders begonnen, mit 18 ihr eigenes Hutgeschäft eröffnet und war 1909 bereits ins Couture-Geschäft eingestiegen. Zu ihren jugendlichen Designs ließ sie sich häufig von ihrer Tochter Marguerite Marie-Blanche inspirieren. Der Modehistorikerin Caroline Milbank zufolge war Lanvin eine frühe Befürworterin des *costume complet* und präsentierte ihre Kleider mit den passenden Hüten und Schuhen.

Mit der Ernennung von Alber Elbaz zum Kreativdirektor im Jahr 2001 wurde Lanvin zu einem der begehrtesten Labels des frühen 21. Jahrhunderts. Über seine Zeit bei dem Label erklärte Elbaz: „Ich fühle mich wie ein Akrobat, der zwischen zwei Welten balanciert: der Vergangenheit und der Gegenwart." Während Elbaz' Amtszeit bei Lanvin wurden Accessoires wichtiger als je zuvor. Die Schuhe der Marke – ob Sandaletten mit klobigen Absätzen, Stöckelschuhe oder schicke Sneaker – setzten Akzente und ermöglichten es den Fans, ihren Stil zu betonen und gleichzeitig auf das Erbe der Marke zuzugreifen. Unter der kreativen Leitung von Bruno Sialelli entstanden fantasievolle Schuhe, darunter kniehohe Stiefel, die mit einer Radierung bedruckt sind, die die Legende vom Heiligen Georg darstellt, der einen Drachen besiegt. Diese kraftvolle Kreation der ikonischen Geschichte setzte Schuhe in den Vordergrund von Sialellis Ästhetik für Lanvin. Im Jahr 2024 trat Peter Copping seine Nachfolge als neuer künstlerischer Leiter an. —*M.M.*

EN 1889, JEANNE LANVIN a fondé la Maison Lanvin, aujourd'hui l'une des plus anciennes encore en activité. Avant d'ouvrir sa propre boutique de chapeaux à l'âge de 18 ans, elle avait travaillé comme livreuse pour une couturière. C'est en 1909 qu'elle a commencé à créer des vêtements, sa fille Marguerite Marie-Blanche lui inspirant de nombreux modèles pour enfant. Selon l'historienne de la mode Caroline Milbank, Jeanne Lanvin a été l'une des premières à proposer « le costume complet » en présentant ses créations avec des chapeaux et des souliers assortis.

Quand Alber Elbaz a été nommé directeur de la création en 2001, il a transformé Lanvin en l'une des marques les plus désirables du début du XXIᵉ siècle. « J'avais l'impression d'être un acrobate en équilibre entre deux mondes : le passé et le présent », dit-il à propos de cette expérience. Sous la direction d'Elbaz, les accessoires ont pris plus d'importance que jamais dans l'esthétique de la Maison. Qu'il s'agisse de sandales à talons épais, de modèles à talons aiguilles ou de baskets chics, les chaussures Lanvin permettaient aux fans d'affirmer leur style tout en accédant à l'héritage de la marque. Sous la direction artistique de Bruno Sialelli, des souliers pleins d'imagination ont vu le jour, notamment des bottes hautes imprimées d'une eau-forte qui illustre la légende de saint Georges terrassant le dragon. Cette création fascinante inspirée d'un récit emblématique a imposé les chaussures au premier plan de l'esthétique de Sialelli pour Lanvin. En 2024, Peter Copping lui a succédé au poste de directeur artistique. —*M.M.*

Lanvin
Sandal: Black leather,
gold metal
France, summer 2011

Lanvin
Sandals: Dark teal
patent leather, brass
France, summer 2008

LaValle

Dominick LaValle (1892–1952)

ESTABLISHED AROUND 1915, NEW YORK-BASED shoe company LaValle and LoPresti specialized in making adaptations of Parisian shoes for an American clientele, who preferred more simplified and practical designs than their European peers. By 1929 the company was known simply as LaValle. Although little is known about LaValle today, the company was consistently a fashion press darling. Its silhouettes were always in step with fashion trends, while the designers' choices of high-quality materials and embellishments were striking, exemplified by choices such as bright purple suede or colorfully printed leather.

In 1936 LaValle introduced its Val-Ars line, which was overseen by company president Dominick LaValle's son, Placido. Val-Ars shoes were made using simplified construction techniques, allowing for their lower retail prices. While LaValle's hand-turned shoes could cost upward of $57 in 1936 (more than $1,100 in 2025), the most expensive Val-Ars styles sold for just $14.50. In 1940 the label introduced yet another economical line, LaValle, Jrs. *Women's Wear Daily* reported that this was the first time a high-end shoemaker had produced a line of lower-priced shoes in his own factory, which helped to lower overhead costs. Despite the company's efforts to appeal to a wider clientele through more accessible options, LaValle went into bankruptcy in the mid-1950s and soon disappeared from the pages of fashion magazines. —*C.H.*

PREVIOUS
LaValle
Pump: Brown suede,
brown snakeskin
USA, *ca.* 1940

LaValle
Pump: Purple suede,
gold metal studs
USA, *ca.* 1940

DIE UM 1915 GEGRÜNDETE New Yorker Schuh-manufaktur LaValle and LoPresti, die ab 1929 nur noch unter dem Namen LaValle firmierte, war auf Adaptionen der Pariser Schuhmode für eine ame-rikanische Klientel spezialisiert, die schlichtere, praktischere Designs bevorzugte als Europäerin-nen. Zwar weiß man heute nur noch wenig über LaValle, doch war die Marke ein Liebling der damaligen Modepresse. Ihre Silhouetten waren stets auf dem neuesten Stand der Mode, doch her-vorstechend waren die von den Designern gewähl-ten hochwertigen Materialien und Verzierungen, etwa Veloursleder in leuchtendem Violett oder far-benfroh bedrucktes Leder.

1936 führte LaValle seine Val-Ars-Linie ein, die der Sohn des Firmenchefs Dominick LaValle, Placido, beaufsichtigte. Val-Ars-Schuhe wurden mit vereinfachten Konstruktionstechniken produ-ziert, wodurch sie zu günstigeren Preisen verkauft werden konnten. Waren von Hand gefertigte La-Valle-Schuhe 1936 nicht unter 57 Dollar zu haben (was 2025 mehr als 1 100 Dollar entspräche), kos-teten die teuersten Val-Ars-Modelle gerade einmal 14,50 Dollar. 1940 lancierte das Label mit LaValle, Jrs eine weitere preisgünstige Linie. Damit hatte laut *Women's Wear Daily* erstmals ein Luxusschuh-hersteller eine preiswertere Schuhlinie im eigenen Betrieb produziert, was die Fixkosten senken half. Trotz aller Bemühungen des Unternehmens, mit er-schwinglicheren Angeboten eine breitere Klientel anzusprechen, meldete LaValle Mitte der 1950er-Jahre Konkurs an und war bald von den Seiten der Modemagazine verschwunden. *—C.H.*

CRÉÉ VERS 1915, LE chausseur new-yorkais LaValle and LoPresti se spécialisait dans l'adaptation des créations parisiennes à l'attention d'une clien-tèle américaine en quête de modèles plus simples et plus pratiques que ceux prisés des Européens. En 1929, l'entreprise a raccourci son nom pour devenir LaValle. Bien qu'on dispose de peu d'in-formations sur la marque, c'était l'une des préfé-rées des magazines de mode. Ses modèles étaient toujours en phase avec les tendances. Surtout, ils créaient la surprise grâce aux choix des créateurs en termes de matières et de détails décoratifs de qualité supérieure, par exemple, le daim vio-let vif ou le cuir imprimé de plusieurs couleurs.

En 1936, LaValle a lancé Val-Ars, une collec-tion supervisée par Placido, le fils du président de l'entreprise, Dominick LaValle. Les chaussures Val-Ars étaient fabriquées à l'aide de techniques simplifiées qui permettaient de les proposer à des prix inférieurs. Alors que les modèles LaValle faits main pouvaient coûter plus de 57 dollars en 1936 (soit l'équivalent de plus de 1 100 dollars en 2025), les modèles Val-Ars les plus chers n'excédaient pas 14,50 dollars. En 1940, la marque a lancé une autre ligne de diffusion baptisée LaValle, Jrs. Selon *Women's Wear Daily*, c'était la première fois qu'un chausseur de luxe produisait une ligne de souliers moins chers dans sa propre usine pour réduire les coûts. Malgré les efforts déployés par l'entreprise pour élargir sa clientèle à l'aide d'options plus abordables, LaValle a fait faillite au milieu des années 1950 et a rapidement disparu des pages des magazines de mode. *—C.H.*

LaValle
Pumps: Red, white,
and blue leather,
gold metal studs
USA, *ca.* 1940

Val-Ars (LaValle)
Evening shoes:
Black crepe, silver
metallic leather
USA, *ca.* 1935

LaValle
Pumps: Printed
black leather
USA, *ca.* 1940

Beth and Herbert Levine

BETH AND HERBERT LEVINE WERE the most playful of American mid-century shoe manufacturers. Born in 1914, Elizabeth "Beth" Katz moved to New York at the height of the Depression, where she secured a job as a foot model, then soon moved from stylist to head designer at the leading American shoe firm I. Miller. In 1944 she met Herbert Levine when she applied for a design position with the Brooklyn-based shoe manufacturer Andrew Geller. Three months later, the two were married. By 1948 they formed their own company, Herbert Levine, Inc., where Beth designed and Herbert ran the business.

Self-taught, Beth became one of the mid-century's leading avant-garde shoemakers. She blended sex appeal with practicality, wit with innovation. Examples include her 1959 "Kabuki" shoe made with brocaded fabric uppers and golden, curved wooden platforms. During the 1960s, Beth crafted

Beth Levine (1914–2006) and Herbert Levine (1916–1991)

tongue-in-cheek designs that often incorporated the latest, new age materials such as her 1961 "Cinderella" made of clear plastic. In 1957, on a dare from the legendary retailer Stanley Marcus, Beth debuted perhaps her most experimental and theoretical design, the topless "No-Shoe." The topless, heeled sole was wearable thanks to adhesive pads, a conceptual product decades ahead of its time.

The Levines also pioneered ideas that are now footwear mainstays, such as the fashionable boot. In the early 1950s, such boots did not sell well because they were marketed as protective or work wear. But the Levines persevered. By the end of that decade and into the 1960s, their fashionable boots were so popular that they created a new label, Beth's Bootery. Other labels followed, such as Tony the Shoemaker, as well as collaborations with many top American fashion designers. —P.M.

In a 1969 extraterrestrial-
inspired advertise-
ment for Colt 45 malt
liquor, models pose in
futuristic silver boots
by Levine. "Take off
on a completely unique
experience."

BETH UND HERBERT LEVINE FERTIGTEN die ver-
spielteste Schuhmode im Amerika der 1950er- und
60er-Jahre an. Die 1914 geborene Elizabeth „Beth"
Katz zog auf dem Höhepunkt der Weltwirtschaftskrise nach New York, wo sie zunächst Arbeit als
Fußmodel fand, um bald zur Stylistin und schließlich Chefdesignerin des führenden US-Schuhunter-
nehmens I. Miller aufzusteigen. Als sie sich 1944 bei
dem Brooklyner Schuhfabrikanten Andrew Geller
als Designerin bewarb, lernte sie Herbert Levine
kennen. Drei Monate später waren die beiden ver-
heiratet und gründeten 1948 ihr eigenes Unternehmen, Herbert Levine, Inc., wo Beth das Design und
Herbert die Geschäfte übernahm.

Zur Mitte des 20. Jahrhunderts hatte die
Autodidaktin Beth sich an vorderster Front der
Schuhdesigner-Avantgarde etabliert. Ihre Kreatio-
nen verbanden Sexappeal und Tragbarkeit, Witz
und Innovation, beispielsweise ihr „Kabuki"- Pla-
teauschuh von 1959, dessen Obermaterial aus
Brokat bestand und der geschwungene, goldfarbene
Holzsohlen hatte. In den 1960er-Jahren kreierte
Beth ironische Designs, die häufig mit den neuesten Materialien der Zeit spielten, etwa 1961 der
„Cinderella"-Schuh aus durchsichtigem Plastik.
Angespornt von Kaufhauskönig Stanley Marcus
präsentierte Beth 1957 ihr vielleicht experimentells-
tes und konzeptionellstes Design, den „No-Shoe".
Dieser „Nichtschuh", der bloß aus Sohle und Absatz bestand, war dank Haftpads zwar tragbar, als
konzeptuelles Produkt seiner Zeit jedoch um Jahrzehnte voraus.

Die Levines brachen auch Ideen Bahn, die
heute fester Bestandteil der Schuhmode sind, etwa
dem modischen Stiefel. Anfang der 50er-Jahre
verkauften sich solche Stiefel nicht gut, da sie als
Schutz- oder Arbeitsschuhe vermarktet wurden.
Doch die Levines ließen nicht locker. Ab Ende des
Jahrzehnts bis in die 1960er-Jahre waren ihre modischen Stiefel so beliebt, dass sie ein eigenes Label
bekamen, Beth's Bootery. Es folgten weitere Label,
etwa Tony the Shoemaker, und Kooperationen mit
vielen amerikanischen Topdesignern. —P.M.

BETH ET HERBERT LEVINE ONT CRÉÉ les chaussures les plus ludiques qu'on pouvait trouver aux
États-Unis dans les années 1950. Née en 1914,
Elizabeth « Beth » Katz s'est installée à New York
pendant la crise de 1929. Elle y a décroché un emploi
de mannequin de pied avant de devenir styliste, puis
créatrice en chef chez le grand chausseur américain
I. Miller. Elle a rencontré Herbert Levine en 1944 en
postulant pour un poste de créatrice chez Andrew
Geller, un fabricant de chaussures basé à Brooklyn,
et ils se sont mariés trois mois plus tard. En 1948,
ils ont fondé la société Herbert Levine, Inc. : Beth
créait les modèles et Herbert dirigeait l'entreprise.

Autodidacte, Beth est devenue l'une des créatrices de chaussures les plus avant-gardistes des
années 1950. Elle savait conjuguer *sex-appeal* et sens
pratique, traits d'esprit et innovation, à l'image du
soulier Kabuki de 1959 avec son empeigne en bro-
card et sa plateforme arrondie en bois doré. Dans
les années 1960, elle a créé des modèles teintés
d'une pointe d'humour, souvent avec des matériaux
issus des dernières innovations de l'époque, comme
l'illustre l'escarpin Cinderella de 1961 en vinyle
translucide. En 1957, sur un défi lancé par le légendaire détaillant Stanley Marcus, elle a conçu ce qui
reste peut-être sa création la plus expérimentale et
la plus théorique : la No-Shoe. Ce modèle « topless »
à talon pouvait se porter grâce aux coussinets adhé-
sifs placés sur la semelle : un produit conceptuel qui
avait des décennies d'avance sur son temps.

Les Levine ont aussi fait figure de pionniers en
lançant des idées aujourd'hui incontournables dans
le monde de la chaussure, par exemple en rendant la
botte tendance. Au début des années 1950, les bottes
se vendaient mal, car elles étaient promues comme
des chaussures de protection ou de travail, mais les
Levine ont persévéré. À la fin de la décennie et pendant les années 1960, leurs bottes remportaient un
tel succès qu'ils ont créé une nouvelle marque baptisée Beth's Bootery. D'autres ont suivi, notamment
Tony the Shoemaker, ainsi que des collaborations
avec de grands créateurs de mode américains. —P.M.

Take off on a completely unique experience.

Look for the spaceship display wherever
Colt 45 Malt Liquor is sold. Then put a couple of
extra six packs in cold storage.
It's out of this world.

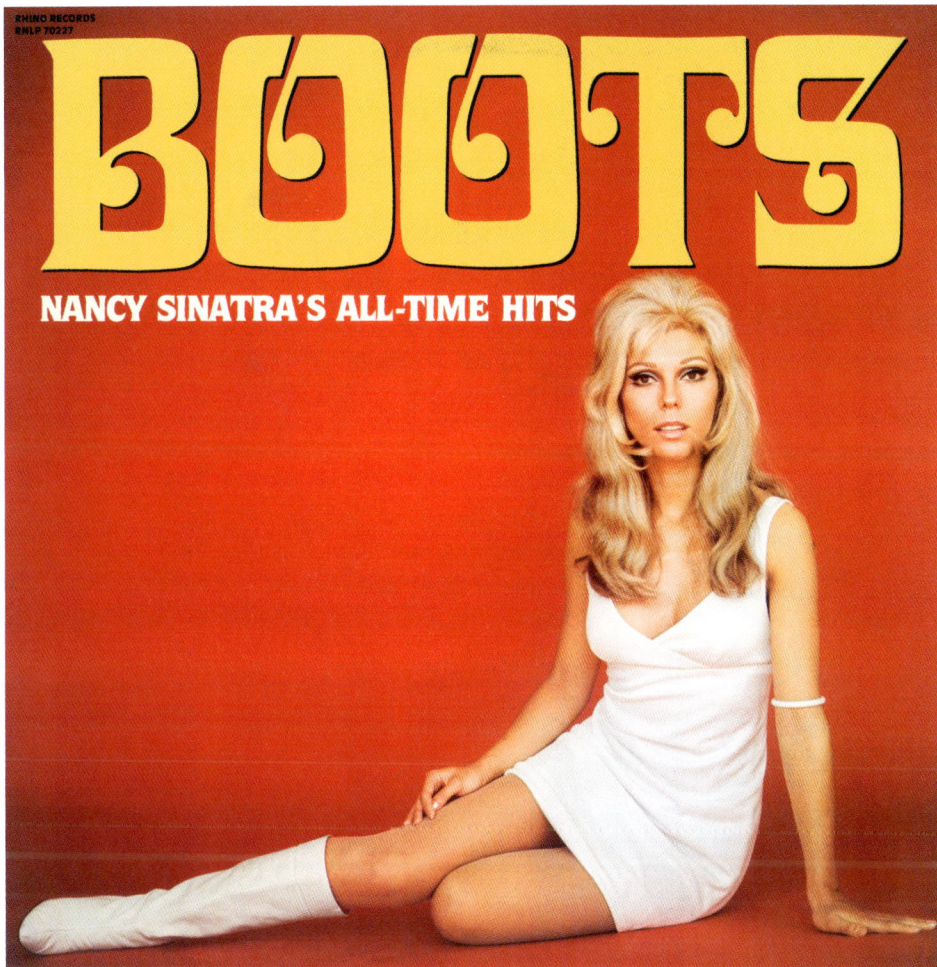

BOOTS

NANCY SINATRA'S ALL-TIME HITS

RHINO RECORDS
RNLP 70227

**Tony the Shoemaker
(Beth and
Herbert Levine)**
Boot: Multicolor
printed rayon challis,
gold-tone metal
USA, *ca.* 1970

American singer Nancy
Sinatra poses in a pair of
white vinyl go-go boots
to promote her 1966
song "These Boots Are
Made for Walkin'."

"Before Manolo Blahník, there was the
cutting-edge shoe designer Beth Levine...
Stockinged boots that extended into a
wrapped bodysuit, slides lined in Astroturf,
and driving pumps in the forms of cars —
all were part of her rich vocabulary."

— ANDRÉ LEON TALLEY, EDITOR

**Beth and
Herbert Levine**
Sandals: Tan leather
USA, 1958

**Beth and
Herbert Levine**
Topless "no-shoe" sandals: Black satin, double-stick adhesive pads
USA, *ca.* 1958

**Beth and
Herbert Levine**
Sling-back pump:
Printed beige velvet
USA, *ca.* 1962

FOLLOWING
**Beth and
Herbert Levine**
"Kabuki" pumps:
Black satin, wood
USA, *ca.* 1965

**Beth and
Herbert Levine**
Pumps: Pink-and-blue
striped raw silk
USA, 1959

**Beth and
Herbert Levine**
Pumps: Silk satin,
rhinestones
USA, *ca.* 1956

**Beth and
Herbert Levine**
Sandal: Clear vinyl, lucite
USA, *ca.* 1965

**Beth and
Herbert Levine**
Pumps: Black suede,
multicolored leather
appliqués
USA, 1958–59

Christian Louboutin

"IN A WORLD OF ENDLESS hyperbole, it's difficult to overstate the aura of Christian Louboutin," fashion writer Bridget Foley wrote of "one of the great gods of fashion." The signature red soles of his beautifully crafted and often provocatively sexy shoes have been immortalized in popular culture as the ultimate fashion status symbol. "Louboutin took a part of the shoe that had previously been ignored and made it not only visually interesting but commercially useful," said curator Elizabeth Semmelhack.

Louboutin was born in 1963 in Paris and started sketching at an early age. He began his first design job at Charles Jourdan in 1981, where he met Roger Vivier, eventu-

Christian Louboutin (b. 1963)

ally going on to work in his atelier. After freelancing for fashion companies such as Chanel, Yves Saint Laurent, and Maud Frizon, Louboutin partnered with his childhood friends Bruno Chamberland and Henri Seydoux to found his own company and Paris boutique in 1992. A meticulous designer, Louboutin's process involves sketching and producing 400 samples in his Italian factory, which are then narrowed to a collection of 120–140 styles, each made with the finest materials and embellishments.

Although he designs a variety of shapes from boots and sneakers to flats and wedges, the high stiletto heel is the jewel of the Christian Louboutin brand. The famous red sole first appeared in 1994 on his "Pensée" high heel bar pump and quickly became his calling card. Louboutin's popularity expanded worldwide, and he has opened boutiques on five continents. On the importance of shoes, he declared, "The woman carries the clothes, but the shoe carries the woman. The shoe carries the character, a big part of the attitude...this is where the sexuality comes. It's just on your foot, but it diffuses something all over your body." —E.W.

PREVIOUS
Rodarte
(Christian Louboutin)
"Isanami" pumps:
Metallic pink leather,
rhinestones, metal
spikes and studs
France, fall 2008

Christian Louboutin
Boot: Red silk satin,
black passementerie
France, fall 1997

Christian Louboutin
"Pensee" pumps: Pale
purple silk crepe, suede
France, 1994–95

„DIE WELT IST VOLLER ÜBERTREIBUNGEN, aber die Strahlkraft von Christian Louboutin kann kaum zu hoch gepriesen werden", so die Moderedakteurin Bridget Foley, die ihn „einen der großen Götter der Mode" nennt. Seine wundervoll gearbeiteten Schuhe, deren Markenzeichen die rote Sohle ist und die oft aufreizend sexy sind, gingen als ultimatives Statussymbol der Mode in die Populärkultur ein. „Louboutin nahm einen bis dahin unbeachteten Teil des Schuhs und machte ihn nicht nur optisch interessant, sondern auch kommerziell wertvoll", so die Kuratorin Elizabeth Semmelhack.

Geboren 1964 in Paris, begann Louboutin schon in jungen Jahren zu zeichnen. Bei Charles Jourdan trat er 1981 seine erste Stellung als Designer an und lernte dort Roger Vivier kennen, in dessen Atelier er schließlich arbeitete. Nach einer Zeit als freier Mitarbeiter bei Modeunternehmen wie Chanel, Yves Saint Laurent und Maud Frizon eröffnete Louboutin 1992 zusammen mit seinen Jugendfreunden Bruno Chamberland und Henri Seydoux eine eigene Firma und eine Boutique in Paris. Als akribischer Designer lässt Louboutin für jede Kollektion 400 handgezeichnete Entwürfe in seiner Fabrik in Italien realisieren, von denen anschließend 120 bis 140 Modelle ausgewählt und unter Verwendung feinster Materialien und Verzierungen produziert werden.

Obwohl sein Designspektrum Silhouetten von Stiefeln bis zu Sneakern und vom flachen bis zum Keilabsatz umfasst, ist der hohe Stiletto das Juwel der Marke Christian Louboutin. Die berühmte rote Sohle feierte ihre Premiere 1994 mit dem hochhackigen Riemchenpumps „Pensée" und wurde schnell zu seiner Visitenkarte. Heute genießt Louboutin weltweite Popularität und betreibt auf allen Kontinenten Boutiquen. Über die Bedeutung von Schuhen sagte er: „Die Frau trägt die Kleider, doch der Schuh trägt die Frau. Der Schuh trägt die Persönlichkeit, einen großen Teil der Haltung ... genau da kommt die Sexualität ins Spiel. Er ist nur am Fuß, aber er beeinflusst den ganzen Körper." —E.W.

« DIFFICILE D'EXAGÉRER L'AURA de Christian Louboutin dans un monde qui use et abuse de l'hyperbole », a écrit la journaliste de mode Bridget Foley à propos de « l'un des plus grands dieux de la mode ». La culture populaire a immortalisé les semelles rouges de ses superbes chaussures souvent sexy et provocantes comme l'ultime signature de mode. « Louboutin a utilisé une partie de la chaussure qui était auparavant ignorée et l'a rendue visuellement intéressante, mais aussi commercialement utile », explique la conservatrice Elizabeth Semmelhack.

Né à Paris en 1963, Christian Louboutin a commencé à dessiner à un âge précoce. Il a décroché son premier emploi dans la mode en 1981 chez Charles Jourdan. C'est là qu'il a rencontré Roger Vivier, dans l'atelier duquel il a ensuite travaillé. Après des missions en free-lance pour des Maisons telles que Chanel, Yves Saint Laurent et Maud Frizon, il s'est associé avec ses amis d'enfance Bruno Chamberland et Henri Seydoux en 1992 pour créer sa propre entreprise et ouvrir une boutique à Paris.

Le processus de ce créateur méticuleux repose sur des esquisses et la production de 400 prototypes dans son usine en Italie, qui sont ensuite réduits à une collection de 120 à 140 modèles, chacun fabriqué dans les meilleures matières et avec les plus beaux détails décoratifs.

Bien que Christian Louboutin crée toute une variété de formes, des bottes aux sneakers en passant par des modèles plats et à semelles compensées, l'escarpin à talon aiguille reste le fleuron de sa griffe. La fameuse semelle rouge qui a fait son apparition en 1994 sur Pensée, un escarpin à bride et talon haut, s'est rapidement imposée comme sa carte de visite. Le succès de Louboutin est devenu international quand il a ouvert des boutiques sur les cinq continents. « La femme porte les vêtements, mais la chaussure porte la femme », a-t-il déclaré au sujet de l'importance des chaussures. « La chaussure porte le personnage et une grande partie de son attitude... c'est là que la sexualité entre en jeu. Bien qu'elle n'habille que le pied, la chaussure a un effet sur tout le corps. » —E.W.

"Louboutin's aesthetic is part Marie Antoinette and part the Mummers...Beyond adornment, what draws the eye to the Louboutin foot is its silhouette."

— LAUREN COLLINS, *THE NEW YORKER*

Christian Louboutin
"Deena" pumps: Dark
red satin and silk chiffon
France, fall 2006

Christian Louboutin
"Lainey" mules: Gilt
crochet, tan pony skin
France, spring 1999

Christian Louboutin
T-strap pump: Deep red
silk satin, suede
France, *ca.* 1998

Christian Louboutin
"Love" flats: Black
suede, camel patent
leather
France, fall 1991

Christian Louboutin
"Plumetita" pump:
Brown silk crepe,
feathers
France, fall 1997

Christian Louboutin
"Snake-Fourré" pumps:
Black suede, fur
France, fall 2005

Christian Louboutin
"China Queen" wedge:
Black pony skin,
engraved metal
France, fall 2002

Christian Louboutin
Wedge-heeled sandal:
Red linen, sequins
France, *ca.* 2005

"Red is fire, blood, love, and passion. It carries a symbolism that you don't get with other shades."

— CHRISTIAN LOUBOUTIN

**Rodarte
(Christian Louboutin)**
Sandals: Black leather,
zipper tape
France, spring 2008

Christian Louboutin
Pumps: Gray suede,
metal studs
France, fall 2007

Christian Louboutin
"Moulamax" ankle
boots: Printed sequins,
grosgrain piping
France, 2018

"There's the promise of something wicked in Christian's shoes. They're a little dangerous, and there's a sense of teetering on the precipice between avoiding dreary conventional good taste and tumbling into something far more outrageous."

— HAMISH BOWLES, FASHION EDITOR

A glimpse of the signature red-lacquered sole instantly identifies a shoe as a Louboutin — in a 2018 sketch by the designer.

Christian Louboutin "Fetish Ballerine" pumps: Black patent leather, cotton grosgrain trim France, 2014

Louis Vuitton

THE NAME LOUIS VUITTON IS synonymous with French
luxury. The historic company began as a luggage shop in
Paris during the nineteenth century but has since expanded
exponentially into a major fashion conglomerate. Founded
in 1854 by a young Frenchman, the brand specialized in
producing steamer trunks for elite travelers for nearly
150 years before launching its first women's ready-to-wear
and footwear lines in 1996. The trunks were renowned both
for their construction, using innovative materials like coated
canvas, as well as their stylish colors, including a shade called
"Trianon grey."

Louis Vuitton
(1821–1892)

When Louis Vuitton tapped young American designer
Marc Jacobs to design its inaugural women's collections in 1996, he
first looked back to this storied heritage for inspiration. As he explained,
"When I saw the first trunk in Trianon grey canvas, I said to myself,
'That's how Louis Vuitton got started and that's how we, too, are going to start, with greys
and whites.'" But he quickly moved to develop a high-impact aesthetic for the house that
fused luxurious materials with a range of historical and contemporary references, from
1980s graffiti to 1940s film noir. He also instilled the brand with celebrity status through
collaborations and advertisements that brought the elite brand into the mainstream spotlight. Shoes were key to the expansion of the Louis Vuitton brand into fashion and would
act as an extension of Jacobs's seasonal themes.

French designer Nicolas Ghesquière succeeded Jacobs in 2013. Shoes remain a crucial
product line for the house under Ghesquière's leadership, but the house's aesthetic has
evolved into a more sculptural, geometric, and modernist approach in both footwear and
ready-to-wear. —*E.M.*

U.S. Patent   Oct. 30, 2018   Sheet 1 of 7   US D831,938 S

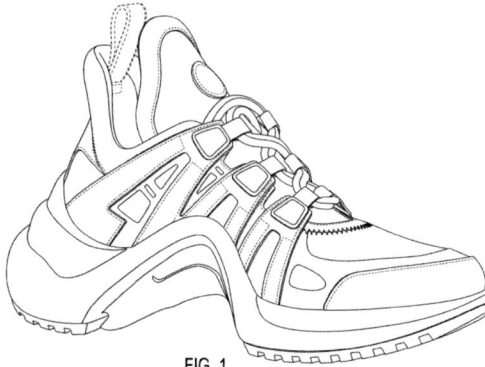

FIG. 1

PREVIOUS
Louis Vuitton
Boot: Brown
monogram canvas
France, 2017

A 2017 patent for
sneakers by Nicolas
Ghesquière for the
French house, where he
became creative director
in 2013. "Louis Vuitton
has always incarnated
for me the symbol of
ultimate luxury, innova-
tion, and exploration,"
he said.

**Louis Vuitton
(Nicolas Ghesquière)**
"Archlight" sneakers:
Silver leather, black
leather, gray mesh,
white rubber
France, spring 2018

DER NAME LOUIS VUITTON IST ein Synonym für französischen Luxus. Das geschichtsträchtige Unternehmen nahm im 19. Jahrhundert als Geschäft für Reisegepäck in Paris seinen Anfang, wuchs jedoch exponentiell zu einem der führenden Modekonzerne an. 1854 von einem jungen Franzosen gegründet, blieb die Marke fast 150 Jahre lang auf die Herstellung von Überseekoffern für betuchte Reisende spezialisiert, ehe 1996 ihre erste Prêt-à-porter- und Schuhlinie für Damen erschien. Die Koffer wurden nicht nur ihrer Verarbeitung wegen geschätzt, bei der innovative Materialien wie beschichtetes Segeltuch Verwendung fanden, sondern auch für ihre eleganten Farben wie etwa Trianon-Grau.

Als Louis Vuitton 1996 Marc Jacobs als Designer für die erste Damenkollektion engagierte, warf der junge Amerikaner zur Inspiration als Erstes einen Blick zurück auf diese ruhmreiche Vergangenheit. Er selbst erklärte: „Als ich den ersten Segeltuchkoffer in Trianon-Grau sah, sagte ich mir: ‚Damit hat bei Louis Vuitton alles angefangen,

und genau damit werden auch wir anfangen, mit einer Farbpalette in Grau und Weiß.'" Im nächsten Schritt entwickelte er jedoch schnell eine kraftvolle Ästhetik für das Haus, die edle Materialien mit unterschiedlichsten historischen und aktuellen Bezügen verband, von den Graffitis der 1980er-Jahre bis zum Film noir der 1940er. Zudem verhalf er der Marke durch Kooperationen und Werbekampagnen, die das Nobellabel ins Scheinwerferlicht der breiten Öffentlichkeit rückten, zu Glamourstatus. Schuhe waren für den Einstieg der Marke Louis Vuitton in die Mode von entscheidender Bedeutung und fungierten als Erweiterungen von Jacobs' saisonalen Kollektionsthemen.

2013 trat der französische Designer Nicolas Ghesquière Jacobs' Nachfolge an. Schuhe bleiben unter seiner Leitung ein Kernsegment der Marke, doch die Ästhetik des Hauses hat sich weiterentwickelt und zeigt sich nun in der Schuhmode wie im Prêt-à-porter-Bereich eher skulptural, geometrisch und modernistisch. —E.M.

LE NOM LOUIS VUITTON EST synonyme de luxe à la française. La Maison historique qui a vu le jour dans un magasin de bagages à Paris au XIXᵉ siècle a connu une croissance exponentielle au point de devenir une véritable multinationale de la mode. Cette marque fondée en 1854 par un jeune Français s'est spécialisée dans la fabrication de malles de voyage destinées aux voyageurs fortunés pendant près de cent cinquante ans, puis a lancé ses premières collections de prêt-à-porter et de souliers pour femme en 1996. Ses malles étaient à la fois réputées pour leur fabrication, qui utilisait des matériaux innovants comme la toile enduite, et pour leurs couleurs élégantes, dont le fameux « gris Trianon ».

Quand la Maison a fait appel au jeune créateur américain Marc Jacobs pour concevoir ses premières collections pour femme en 1996, celui-ci a d'abord puisé l'inspiration dans son héritage historique : « Quand j'ai vu la première malle en toile gris Trianon, je me suis dit : "C'est ainsi que Louis Vuitton a commencé et nous allons faire de même, avec des gris et des blancs." » Il a toutefois rapidement développé une esthétique accrocheuse qui fusionnait des matières luxueuses avec toutes sortes de références historiques et contemporaines, des graffitis des années 1980 aux films noirs des années 1940. Il a aussi insufflé une aura de célébrité à cette marque d'élite grâce à des collaborations et des publicités qui l'ont fait connaître au grand public. Les souliers ont joué un rôle clé dans l'expansion de Louis Vuitton sur le marché de la mode et reflétaient les thèmes choisis chaque saison par Marc Jacobs.

Le créateur français Nicolas Ghesquière lui a succédé en 2013. Sous sa direction, les souliers revêtent toujours une importance cruciale pour la Maison, mais son esthétique a évolué vers une approche plus sculpturale, plus géométrique et plus moderniste, tant pour les chaussures que pour le prêt-à-porter. —E.M.

"Louis Vuitton has always incarnated for me the symbol of ultimate luxury, innovation, and exploration."

— NICOLAS GHESQUIÈRE

Louis Vuitton
"Archlight" sneaker
boots: Brown leather,
gold tone rubber, mono-
gram canvas
France, cruise 2019

Louis Vuitton
Pumps: Off-white-and-
gold satin brocade, fox
fur, beads, resin
France, fall 2012

Maison Martin Margiela

MARTIN MARGIELA PIONEERED AND POPULARIZED the deconstructed aesthetic in fashion, known in France as "la mode Destroy." For two decades beginning in 1989, the Belgian designer crafted an array of cutting-edge looks. Best known for taking garments apart and reassembling them so their interior structures and seams were exposed, Margiela was also among the first to reject the logo-mania that swept fashion in the 1990s.

Martin Margiela (b. 1957)

Of all the accessories Margiela designed, none was as popular, enduring, and emblematic as his cloven-footed "Tabi" boot. Its inspiration came, in part, from the medieval Japanese sock known as the *tabi* that divides the foot's large toe from the other four toes and is worn with the *geta* (traditional thong sandals). Margiela's interest in Japan arose after he saw the early 1980s presentations of Rei Kawakubo and Yohji Yamamoto. According to Margiela, the boot's silhouette also had menswear roots: "British, 1900s, masculine shoe styles on feminine lasts, with high heels that looked chunky seen from the side and quite narrow seen from the back. The chosen leather, assembly and finishing were as those used in traditional footwear for men." The first women to wear the "Tabi" shoe were fellow Belgians designer Ann Demeulemeester and fashion professor Linda Loppa.

From his debut 1989 collection, Margiela's "Tabi" was continually presented on the runway because he had "no budget for a new form." Although the look varied — from paint-splattered to "topless" versions that had to be taped to the foot — their popularity increased and remained constant even after his departure from his own company. The "Tabi" was even a key element of the collection produced in collaboration with the mass market, fast fashion company H&M in 2012. —*P.M.*

MARTIN MARGIELA BRACHTE MIT „La Mode Destroy" die Ästhetik der Dekonstruktion in die Mode und machte sie populär. Ab 1989 schuf der belgische Designer zwei Jahrzehnte lang eine Vielzahl avantgardistischer Looks und wurde vor allem dafür bekannt, Kleidungsstücke auseinanderzunehmen und neu zusammensetzen, um Innenkonstruktion und Säume sichtbar zu machen. Margiela zählte auch zu den Ersten, die sich dem Markenwahn widersetzten, der in den 1990er-Jahren die Mode befiel.

Von allen Accessoires, die Margiela kreierte, war keines so erfolgreich, langlebig und emblematisch wie der hufartige „Tabi"-Stiefel. Die Inspiration dazu stammte zum Teil vom japanischen *Tabi*, einer Socke mit separatem großen Zeh, die seit dem Mittelalter zur Geta, der traditionellen Zehensandale, getragen wird. Margielas Interesse für Japan wurde in den frühen 1980ern durch die Schauen von Rei Kawakubo und Yohji Yamamoto geweckt. Als weiteren Einfluss auf die Silhouette seines Stiefels nennt Margiela die Männermode: „Britische, maskuline Schuhformen des 20. Jahrhunderts auf femininen Leisten, mit hohen Absätzen, die von der Seite klobig wirkten und von hinten betrachtet eher schmal. Das verwendete Leder, der Aufbau und das Finish waren so wie bei traditionellen Herrenschuhen." Als Erste trugen den „Tabi" zwei Belgierinnen, die Designerin Ann Demeulemeester und die Modedozentin Linda Loppa.

Von seiner Debütkollektion 1989 an brachte Margiela den „Tabi" immer wieder auf den Laufsteg, da er „kein Budget für eine neue Form" hatte. Auch wenn der Look variierte – von farbbespritzt bis „oben ohne", einer Version, die mit Klebeband am Fuß fixiert wurde –, stieg seine Popularität weiter und blieb auch nach Margielas Ausscheiden aus dem eigenen Unternehmen ungebrochen. Selbst in der 2012 für den Massenmarkt produzierten Kooperationskollektion mit dem Billiganbieter H&M war der „Tabi" ein Schlüsselelement. —*P.M.*

MARTIN MARGIELA A INVENTÉ et démocratisé une esthétique de la déconstruction communément qualifiée de « mode destroy ». À partir de 1989 et pendant vingt ans, le créateur belge a proposé un large éventail de looks avant-gardistes. Surtout connu pour ses vêtements déconstruits puis réassemblés de façon à en exposer les structures internes et les coutures, Margiela comptait aussi parmi les premiers à rejeter la logomania qui a déferlé sur la mode dans les années 1990.

De tous les accessoires créés par Margiela, aucun n'est aussi emblématique et couronné d'un succès aussi durable que sa bottine Tabi à bout fendu. Ce modèle lui a été en partie inspiré par la chaussette médiévale japonaise appelée *tabi* qui sépare le gros orteil des quatre autres et se porte avec des *geta* (tongs traditionnelles). Margiela a commencé à s'intéresser au Japon après avoir vu les premiers défilés de Rei Kawakubo et Yohji Yamamoto au début des années 1980. Selon lui, la silhouette de la Tabi trouve aussi des origines dans la mode pour homme, en l'occurrence dans « des modèles de souliers masculins anglais des années 1900 créés sur des formes féminines, avec des talons hauts qui paraissaient gros de profil et assez étroits de dos : le cuir choisi, l'assemblage et la finition sont les mêmes que ceux utilisés en cordonnerie traditionnelle pour homme ». La créatrice Ann Demeulemeester et la professeure de mode Linda Loppa, toutes deux Belges, ont été les premières femmes à porter la Tabi.

Depuis la première collection de 1989, la Tabi a toujours été présente aux défilés Margiela parce que le créateur « n'avait pas le budget pour concevoir une nouvelle forme ». Bien qu'il en ait proposé différentes versions, des modèles avec taches de peinture aux variantes « topless » à coller sous le pied, le succès de la Tabi n'a fait que s'accroître et ne s'est jamais démenti, même après que Martin Margiela a quitté sa propre entreprise. Elle a même été un élément clé de la collection produite en collaboration avec la grande marque de *fast-fashion* H&M en 2012. —*P.M.*

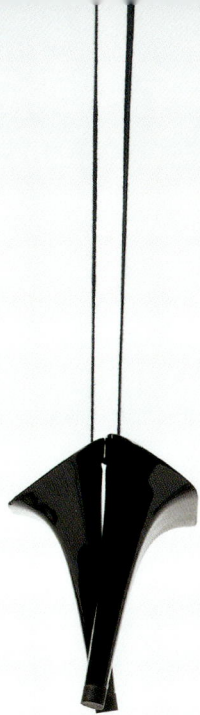

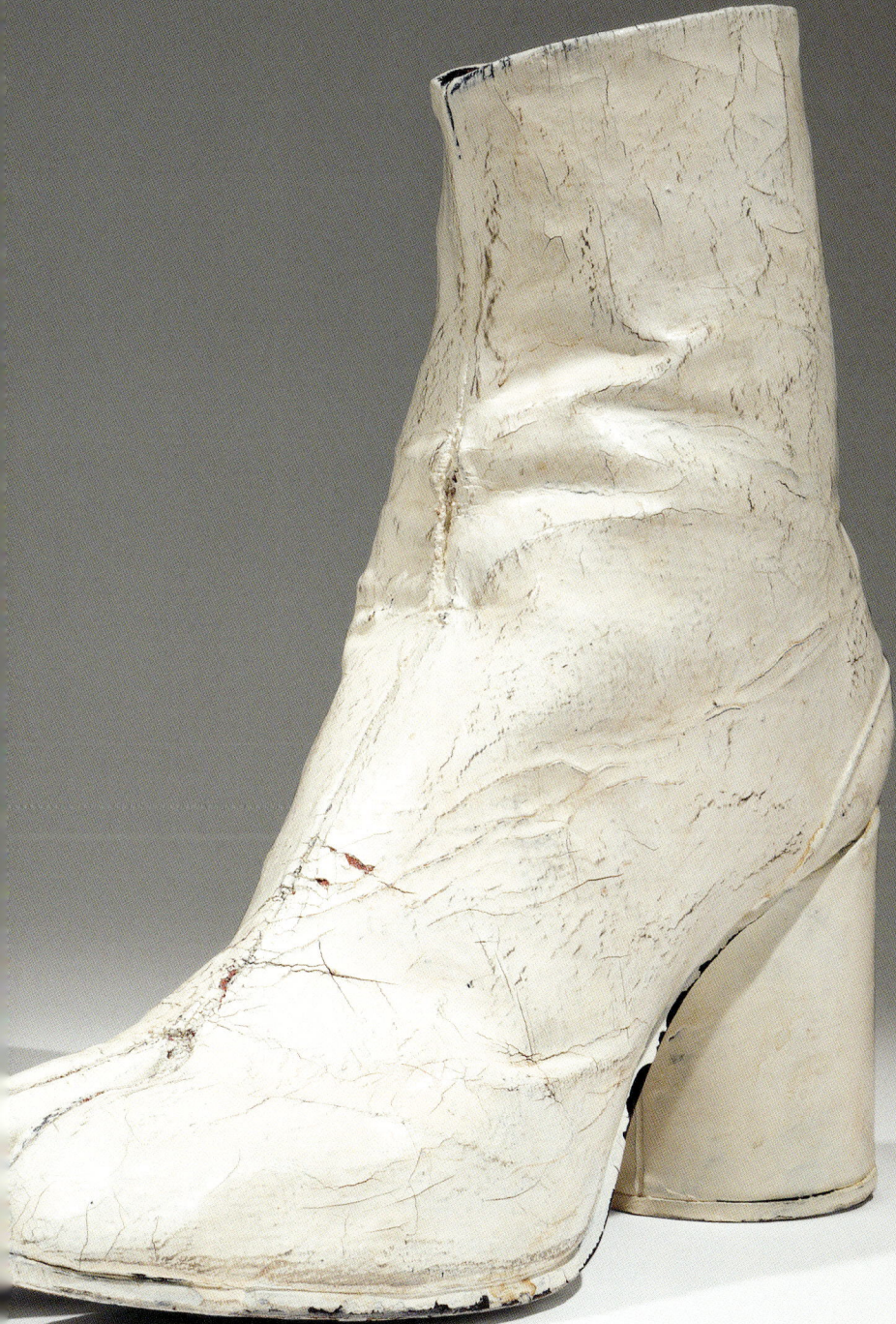

Alexander McQueen

ALEXANDER McQUEEN CREATED SOME OF the most visually arresting designs in the recent history of fashion. To McQueen beauty was entirely determined by individual perception, and it could be found in the most unassuming places. His provocative collections explored "dark subjects through lavish design and beauty."

A graduate of Central Saint Martins College of Art and Design, McQueen showed his first eponymous collection in 1993. He was appointed head designer at the French haute couture house Givenchy only three years later. Although his tenure was short, McQueen infused Givenchy with his darkly romantic aesthetic. In 2001 McQueen sold a share of his business to Gucci Group, ultimately transforming his label into a luxury fashion house.

Alexander McQueen
(1969–2010)

Through his designs, Alexander McQueen aimed to empower women, and footwear formed an integral part of McQueen's imaginative silhouettes. "My shoes form the foundation of the look, and the way a woman walks in [them] exudes power," he said. His designs included savage boots with a horn-shaped heel, biomorphic pumps, and men's boots laser-engraved with galleons and other classic nautical imagery. Collaborating with the sneaker company Puma, McQueen also created conceptual sneakers inspired by human anatomy. McQueen's footwear provoked visceral responses like the garments he created. His spring 2010 "Armadillo" shoe explored an entirely new silhouette in footwear and is arguably one of his most revolutionary creations.

After McQueen's untimely death in 2010, subsequent creative directors, including his longtime associate Sarah Burton and Seán McGirr, an experienced designer formerly of JW Anderson, Dries Van Noten, and Burberry, continued to explore the imaginative footwear designs that have become a signature of the McQueen brand. —*M.M.A.*

**Givenchy
(Alexander McQueen)**
Boot: Black leather,
orange lizard skin
France, spring 1998

Alexander McQueen
Boot: Black leather,
plastic
England, spring 2003

ALEXANDER MCQUEEN SCHUF EINIGE DER atemberaubendsten Looks der jüngeren Modegeschichte. Für ihn lag Schönheit ausschließlich im Auge des Betrachters und war selbst an den schlichtesten Orten zu finden. Seine provokanten Kollektionen erkundeten „dunkle Sujets durch verschwenderisches Design und Schönheit".

Nach Abschluss seines Studiums am Central Saint Martins College of Art and Design präsentierte McQueen 1993 die erste Kollektion unter eigenem Namen. Nur drei Jahre später wurde er zum Chefdesigner von Givenchy ernannt und durchdrang das französische Couture-Haus in der Kürze seines Engagements mit seiner dunklen, romantischen Ästhetik. Mit dem Verkauf von Unternehmensanteilen an die Gucci-Gruppe im Jahr 2001 wandelte McQueen seine eigene Marke endgültig zum Luxuslabel.

Alexander McQueens Kreationen zielten darauf ab, Frauen Macht zu verleihen, und Schuhe waren ein ganz wesentlicher Bestandteil seiner fantasievollen Silhouetten. „Meine Schuhe bilden das Fundament des Looks, und die Art, wie eine Frau [in ihnen] geht, strahlt Stärke aus", wie er erklärte. Zu seinen Kreationen zählten barbarisch wirkende Stiefel mit Absatz in Hornform, biomorphe Pumps und Herrenstiefeletten mit lasergravierten Bildmotiven wie Galeonen und anderen klassischen nautischen Motiven. In Kooperation mit dem Sportartikelhersteller Puma konzipierte McQueen zudem ein Sneaker-Design, das von der menschlichen Anatomie inspiriert war. Wie die von ihm entworfenen Kleider lösten auch McQueens Schuhkreationen emotionale Reaktionen aus. Sein im Frühjahr 2010 vorgestelltes Modell „Armadillo" (Gürteltier) zeigt eine völlig neue Schuhsilhouette und zählt zu seinen wohl revolutionärsten Designs.

Nach McQueens frühem Tod im Jahr 2010 setzten nachfolgende Kreativdirektoren, darunter seine langjährige Mitarbeiterin Sarah Burton und Seán McGirr, ein erfahrener Designer, der zuvor für JW Anderson, Dries Van Noten und Burberry tätig war, die Entwicklung fantasievoller Schuhdesigns fort, die zu einem Markenzeichen von McQueen geworden sind. —*M.M.A.*

ON DOIT À ALEXANDER MCQUEEN certaines des créations les plus visuellement saisissantes de l'histoire récente de la mode. À ses yeux, la beauté n'était qu'une question de perception personnelle et pouvait se trouver dans les choses les plus simples. Ses collections provocatrices exploraient « des thèmes sombres à travers l'opulence et la beauté ».

Diplômé en mode de Central Saint Martins, McQueen a présenté sa première collection éponyme en 1993. À peine trois ans plus tard, il était nommé directeur artistique de Givenchy. Bien qu'il ait passé peu de temps dans la Maison de haute couture française, il lui a insufflé son esthétique romantique et sombre. En 2001, il a vendu une part de son entreprise au groupe Gucci pour transformer sa marque en Maison de luxe.

Alexander McQueen cherchait à libérer la femme à travers ses créations. Ses chaussures jouaient un rôle important dans ses looks débordant d'imagination. « Mes chaussures représentent la base de la silhouette et donnent aux femmes une démarche qui rayonne de puissance », disait-il. Il a notamment créé des bottes dotées d'un talon en forme de corne, des escarpins biomorphiques ainsi que des bottes pour homme gravées au laser de galions et d'autres motifs nautiques classiques. À l'occasion d'une collaboration avec le fabricant de baskets Puma, McQueen a aussi créé des sneakers conceptuelles inspirées de l'anatomie humaine. Les souliers de McQueen suscitaient des réactions aussi viscérales que ses vêtements. Sa chaussure Armadillo du Printemps 2010 explorait une toute nouvelle silhouette et peut sans conteste être considérée comme l'une de ses créations les plus révolutionnaires.

Après le décès précoce d'Alexander McQueen en 2010, ses successeurs à la direction de la création, dont son associée de longue date Sarah Burton et le couturier expérimenté Seán McGirr, qui avait travaillé chez JW Anderson, Dries Van Noten et Burberry, ont continué à décliner l'inventivité caractéristique des chaussures qui sont devenues une signature de la marque McQueen. —*M.M.A.*

Alexander McQueen
Men's boots: Dark gray-
brown tooled leather
England, 2003

Alexander McQueen
T-strap pumps:
Crackled gold leather
England, 2011

FOLLOWING
Alexander McQueen
X Puma
Sneakers: Black leather
USA, spring 2008

"When it comes to rebellion through designer clothes, no one has mastered the trick better than Alexander McQueen, fashion's closest thing to a rock star."

— AMY SPINDLER, *THE NEW YORK TIMES*

Charlotte Olympia

CHARLOTTE OLYMPIA DELLAL LAUNCHED HER brand in 2008 after training in technical craftsmanship at Cordwainers Technical College and graduating from the London College of Fashion. Her designs are known for their whimsical and feminine aesthetic and vibrant colors, in addition to retro styling that is reminiscent of old Hollywood glamour. The designer's signature pieces include "Dolly" pumps, which combine a thick platform with a high stiletto heel, and her charming "Kitty" flats, which feature an embroidered cat's face and ears. Once a devoted wearer of stiletto heels, Dellal began designing flats shortly after launching her brand. She was pregnant with her first child and recognized the need for shoes that were both chic and functional. All Charlotte Olympia products are handcrafted in Italy, and each shoe is finished with a distinctive gold spider's web on the sole. Fittingly, the brand's motto is "Dress from the Feet Up."

Charlotte Olympia Dellal (b. 1981)

For the brand's tenth anniversary in 2018, it launched a limited re-edition of 10 of its most memorable shoes and accessories, including the playful "I Scream" platforms with a tall heel shaped like an ice cream cone. That same year, Charlotte Olympia produced a limited-edition collaboration with Zaha Hadid Design, a division of the renowned architect's design studio led by Woody Yao and Maha Kutay. The resulting platform wedge shoes evoke the fluid forms that characterized Hadid's work. *—M.M.*

BEVOR CHARLOTTE OLYMPIA DELLAL 2008 ihr gleichnamiges Label gründete, absolvierte sie eine handwerklich-technische Fachausbildung am Cordwainers Technical College und ein Modestudium am London College of Fashion. Ihre Kreationen sind für eine feminin-verspielte Ästhetik und lebhafte Farben bekannt, wobei Retro-Anklänge vergangenen Hollywood-Glamour in Erinnerung rufen. Zu ihren charakteristischen Looks zählen die „Dolly"-Pumps, die dicke Plateausohlen mit einem hohem Stilettoabsatz kombinieren, oder der reizende flache „Kitty"-Slipper mit aufgesticktem Katzenkonterfei inklusive Ohren. Ursprünglich begeisterte Stilettoträgerin, begann Dellal schon bald nach dem Start ihrer Marke, flache Schuhe zu entwerfen, da sie zum ersten Mal schwanger war und die Notwendigkeit für modisches und zugleich zweckmäßiges Schuhwerk erkannte. Sämtliche Charlotte-Olympia-Produkte werden in Italien handgefertigt und jeder Schuh mit einem markanten goldenen Spinnennetz auf der Sohle vollendet. Passenderweise heißt das Markenmotto „Dress from the Feet Up" („Fang beim Anziehen mit den Füßen an").

Zu seinem zehnjährigen Bestehen im Jahr 2018 brachte das Label zehn seiner markantesten Schuhe und Accessoires in limitierter Neuauflage heraus, so etwa den kuriosen „I Scream"-Plateauschuh mit hohem Absatz in Eistütenoptik. Im selben Jahr und ebenfalls in limitierter Stückzahl präsentierte Charlotte Olympia das Ergebnis einer Kooperation mit Zaha Hadid Design, dem Designbüro der berühmten Architektin unter Leitung von Woody Yao und Maha Kutay: einen Plateauschuh mit Keilabsatz, dessen fluide Formen an Hadids unverkennbaren Stil erinnern. —M.M.

CHARLOTTE OLYMPIA DELLAL A LANCÉ sa marque éponyme en 2008 après avoir suivi une formation technique au Cordwainers Technical College et obtenu un diplôme du London College of Fashion. Ses créations sont réputées pour leur esthétique féminine pleine de fantaisie, leurs couleurs éclatantes et leur coupe rétro rappelant le glamour de l'ancien Hollywood. Les pièces signature de la créatrice incluent les escarpins Dolly à plateforme épaisse et talon aiguille vertigineux, ou encore les charmantes ballerines Kitty brodées d'un museau et d'oreilles de chat. Cette ancienne fan de talons aiguilles a commencé à concevoir des modèles plats peu de temps après le lancement de sa marque : comme elle attendait son premier enfant, elle avait besoin de chaussures à la fois chics et pratiques. Tous les produits Charlotte Olympia sont fabriqués à la main en Italie, et chaque chaussure est signée d'une toile d'araignée de couleur or sur la semelle. Le slogan de la marque, « Dress from the Feet Up », ne manque pas d'à-propos.

Pour son dixième anniversaire en 2018, la marque a lancé une réédition limitée de dix modèles de chaussures et d'accessoires qui ont marqué les esprits, notamment les fantasques escarpins compensés I Scream perchés sur leur haut talon en forme de cornet de glace. La même année, Charlotte Olympia a produit une édition limitée en collaboration avec le département Zaha Hadid Design du studio de la célèbre architecte dirigé par Woody Yao et Maha Kutay : il s'agit d'un modèle à semelle compensée dont les formes fluides rappellent le travail de Zaha Hadid. —M.M.

Rick Owens

DESIGNER RICK OWENS HAS CARVED out a cultlike following for his distinctively dark yet glamorous clothing. "I see myself balancing out a world that can be kind of very strict in its aesthetics," Owens said. "There have to be people like me that have other suggestions." His collections fuse sportswear elements like sneakers, leggings, and jersey knits with lush materials, from cashmere to leather, in unique and futuristic silhouettes. Almost always black or greige, his designs challenge the boundaries of fashion — divisions between menswear and womenswear, high and low, formal and casual. Each look is a full ensemble from head to toe, with shoes providing crucial punctuation for his gothic style.

Born in California in 1962, Owens did not gain wide recognition until the early 2000s when he was in his 40s. He began his career in Los Angeles as a pattern cutter for a company that made illegal copies of designer clothes. He started his own womenswear line in 1994, but his big break came when Kate Moss was photographed in one of his leather jackets for French *Vogue* in April 2001. He hosted his first runway show at the spring 2002 New York Fashion Week. Not long after, he relocated his business to Paris, where he continues to show today.

Rick Owens (b. 1962)

Shoes became a major component of Owens' business in 2006 with the launch of his first sneaker. Dubbed the "Dustulator Dunk," it was a chunky black-and-white high-top designed with exaggerated proportions — an ode to Owens' love of California skater culture. Since 2006 Owens has launched an army of other sneaker styles, including ones in collaboration with Adidas, and shoes have become increasingly expressive components of each collection. His boots and heels echo the chunky and towering silhouettes of his sneakers and further emphasize his reverence for goth and punk subcultures. —*E.M.*

RICK OWENS 346

PREVIOUS

Rick Owens
"Kiss" thigh-high
boots: Red leather,
rubber, metal
France, fall 2019

Rick Owens
Thigh-high boot: Brown-
and-black leather, faux
Russian broadtail velvet
France, fall 2011

DER DESIGNER RICK OWENS hat mit ausgesprochen düsterer und zugleich glamouröser Mode bei seiner Fangemeinde Kultstatus erlangt. „Ich empfinde meine Arbeit als das Ausbalancieren einer Welt, die in ihrer Ästhetik doch sehr streng sein kann", sagte Owens. „Es muss Leute wie mich geben, die etwas anderes vorschlagen." In seinen Kollektionen verschmelzen Sportswear-Elemente wie Sneaker, Leggings und Strickjersey mit edlen Materialien wie Kaschmir und Leder zu einzigartig futuristischen Silhouetten. Seine fast immer in Schwarz oder Graubeige gehaltenen Designs stellen die Grenzen der Mode infrage – die Einteilung in Herren- und Damenbekleidung, in Couture und Konfektion, in formell und leger. Er entwirft jeden seiner Gothic-Looks als Komplettensemble von Kopf bis Fuß und setzt mit Schuhen entscheidende Akzente.

Owens, geboren 1962 in Kalifornien, fand erst in seinen 40ern, zu Beginn des neuen Jahrtausends, breite Anerkennung. Er startete seine Karriere als Zuschneider bei einer Firma in Los Angeles, die gefälschte Designerkleidung produzierte. 1994 lancierte er seine eigene Damenlinie, doch seine große Stunde kam im April 2001, als die französische *Vogue* Kate Moss in einer Lederjacken zeigte. Seine erste Modenschau war bei der New Yorker Fashion Week im Frühjahr 2002. Bald darauf siedelte er mit seinem Unternehmen nach Paris um, wo er seine Kollektionen seither zeigt.

Mit der Vorstellung seines ersten Sneakers 2006 wurden Schuhe zu einer Kernkomponente der Marke. Der „Dustulator Dunk" war ein klobiger Schwarz-Weiß-High-Top mit übertriebenen Proportionen – Owens' Liebeserklärung an die kalifornische Skaterkultur. Seither hat Owens einen ganzen Katalog an Sneaker-Looks kreiert, einige davon in Kooperation mit Adidas. Seither sind Schuhe zu immer ausdrucksstärkeren Bestandteilen seiner Modeschauen geworden. Stiefel und High Heels greifen die klobigen, turmhohen Silhouetten seiner Sneaker auf und zeigen noch deutlicher, wie sehr er die Gothic- und Punk-Subkultur schätzt. —*E.M.*

PARTICULIÈREMENT SOMBRE, MAIS NÉANMOINS glamour, la mode de Rick Owens lui vaut un statut de créateur culte. « Je me vois comme quelqu'un qui apporte de l'équilibre à un monde dont l'esthétique peut être très stricte, dit-il. Il faut qu'il y ait des gens comme moi pour proposer autre chose. » Ses collections fusionnent des éléments issus du *sportswear* tels que baskets, leggings et maille de jersey avec des matières luxueuses comme le cachemire ou le cuir dans des silhouettes futuristes uniques. Presque toujours de couleur noire ou grège, ses créations repoussent les frontières de la mode en remettant en question les différences entre vêtements pour homme et pour femme, mode haut de gamme et bas de gamme, élégance et décontraction. Chaque silhouette est un look intégral de la tête aux pieds, les chaussures apportant une touche cruciale pour le style gothique du créateur.

Né en 1962 en Californie, Rick Owens n'a connu la notoriété qu'au début des années 2000 après avoir atteint la quarantaine. Il a débuté sa carrière à Los Angeles en tant que modéliste dans une entreprise qui copiait illégalement des vêtements de créateurs. Il a lancé sa propre griffe pour femme en 1994, mais c'est en avril 2001 que sa carrière a réellement décollé quand l'édition française de *Vogue* a photographié Kate Moss dans l'une de ses vestes en cuir. Il a présenté son premier défilé au printemps 2002 pendant la Fashion Week de New York. Peu de temps après, il a déménagé son entreprise à Paris, où il continue aujourd'hui de présenter ses collections.

Les chaussures sont devenues un composant majeur de l'activité de Rick Owens lorsqu'il a présenté sa première sneaker en 2006 : baptisé Dustulator Dunk, c'était une imposante basket aux proportions exagérées qui exprimait sa passion pour la culture californienne du skate. Depuis, il a lancé de nombreux autres modèles de sneakers, dont certains en collaboration avec Adidas. Ses chaussures reflètent de plus en plus les thèmes abordés dans chaque collection. Ses bottes et ses talons font écho à la silhouette imposante de ses baskets tout en mettant encore plus en valeur son intérêt pour les mouvements gothiques et punk. —*E.M.*

Rick Owens
Thigh-high boots:
Green leather, rubber
France, fall 2016

Rick Owens
"Geobasket" sneaker:
Black-and-white
leather, rubber
France, 2019

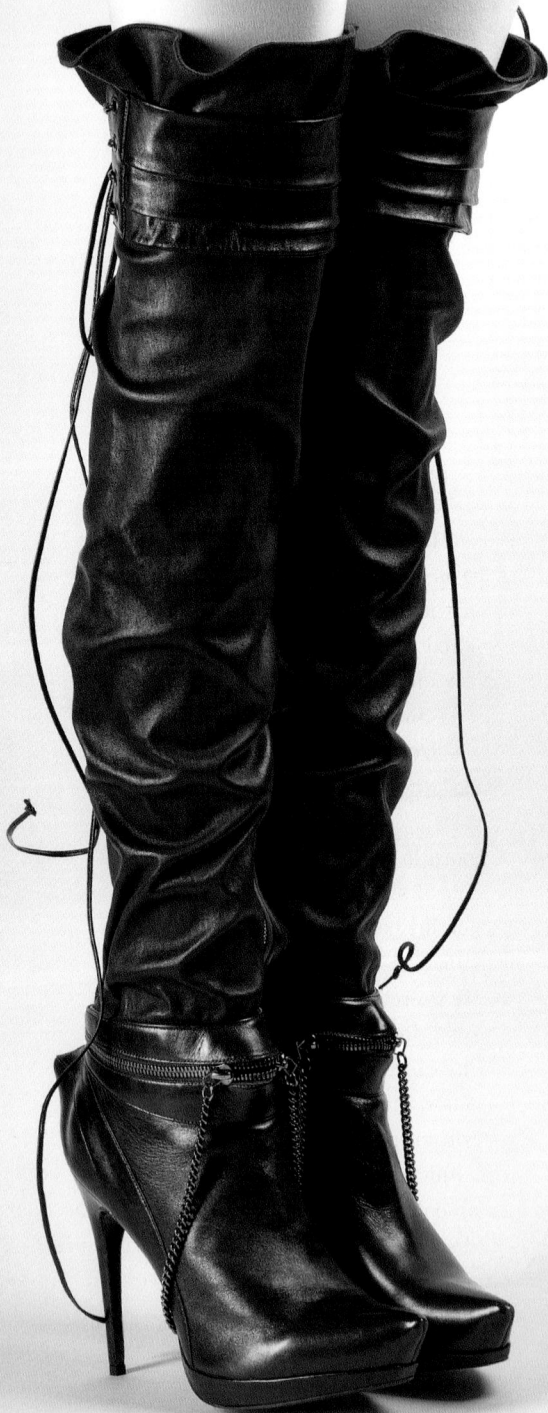

Cesare Paciotti

DUBBED BY *VOGUE* **AS THE** "king of evening altitude," shoe designer Cesare Paciotti is known for his vertiginous stilettos made for a night out on the town. His sexy, provocative shoe designs — often embellished with hardware, straps, and jewels — have earned him worldwide recognition. In keeping with the nightlife culture he cites as inspiration, Paciotti's shoes have a seductive glam-rock style. Describing his typical footwear customer, Paciotti remarked, "She's not much of a wife. She's much more the mistress."

Cesare Paciotti was born in Civitanova Marche, a seaside town in Italy with a long history of shoemaking. He was introduced to the art of shoemaking when his parents started a business in classic handmade men's shoes in 1948. Paciotti designed his first men's shoe collection in 1980. Shortly thereafter, he began designing women's shoes for Italy's most prestigious fashion houses, including Versace, Romeo Gigli, Roberto Cavalli, and Dolce & Gabbana. He launched his

Cesare Paciotti
(b. 1958)

collection in the 1990s, where he began showcasing his trademark stilettos. Eschewing conventional still-life photography, Paciotti was among the first shoe designers to use advertising campaigns in which his shoes were worn by live models.

In 2008 Paciotti began collaborating with the New York–based label Ohne Titel, creating skyscraping boots and sensual booties to complement the sharp-edged, body-conscious fashion designs of Flora Gill and Alexa Adams. Referring to this collaboration, Paciotti remarked, "Just as their creations aim to enhance a modern woman's form while paying attention to the fine details, I strive to glamorize and empower a woman through shoes which are a perfect complement to her clothes." —*M.M.A.*

DER SCHUHDESIGNER CESARE PACIOTTI, von der *Vogue* als „König abendlicher Höhen" tituliert, ist für schwindelerregend hohe Stilettos bekannt, die für den Abendauftritt geschaffen sind. Sexy und aufreizend, oft mit Beschlägen, Riemchen und Schmucksteinen verziert, finden seine Kreationen weltweit Beachtung. Ihr verführerischer Glamrockappeal passt zur Kultur des Nachtlebens, die Paciotti als seine Inspirationsquelle nennt. Über die typische Käuferin seiner Schuhe sagte Paciotti: „Als Ehefrau macht sie nicht viel her. Sie ist viel eher die Geliebte."

Cesare Paciotti kam in Civitanova Marche zur Welt, einer Stadt an der Adriaküste mit langer Schuhmachertradition. Er selbst wurde in die Kunst dieses Handwerks eingeführt, nachdem seine Eltern 1948 ein Geschäft für handgefertigte klassische Herrenschuhe eröffneten. Seine erste Herrenkollektion entwarf Paciotti 1980, um bereits wenig später für die renommiertesten Modehäuser Italiens, darunter Versace, Romeo Gigli, Roberto Cavalli und Dolce & Gabbana, auch Damenschuhe zu kreieren. In den 1990er-Jahren etablierte er seine eigene Linie und präsentierte erstmals seine unverkennbaren Stilettos. Für seine Werbekampagnen verzichtete Paciotti als einer der ersten Schuhdesigner auf konventionelle Produktfotografie und zeigte seine Schuhe an den Füßen echter Models.

2008 begann Paciottis Zusammenarbeit mit dem New Yorker Modelabel Ohne Titel. Die scharfkantigen, figurbetonten Kreationen von Flora Gill und Alexa Adams komplettierte er mit verwegen hohen Stiefeln und sinnlichen Booties. Paciotti bemerkte über diese Kooperation: „So wie sie mit ihren Designs einer modernen Frau optimale Gestalt geben wollen und zugleich auf feine Details achten, versuche ich, einer Frau Glamour und Stärke zu verleihen, durch Schuhe, die diese Kleidung perfekt ergänzen." —*M.M.A.*

QUALIFIÉ DE « ROI DES nuits en altitude » par *Vogue*, le créateur de chaussures Cesare Paciotti est réputé pour ses talons aiguilles vertigineux destinés aux soirées en ville. Ses modèles sexy et provocants, souvent décorés de détails métalliques, de brides et de bijoux, lui ont valu une reconnaissance internationale. Leur style *glam rock* séduisant est le reflet de la vie nocturne que Paciotti cite comme source d'inspiration. Il décrit sa cliente typique dans les termes suivants : « Elle n'a rien d'une épouse, et tout d'une maîtresse. »

Cesare Paciotti est né à Civitanova Marche, une ville côtière d'Italie revendiquant une longue tradition en cordonnerie, un art qu'il a découvert quand ses parents ont créé une entreprise de souliers masculins classiques faits main en 1948. Il a dessiné sa première collection de chaussures pour homme en 1980. Peu de temps après, il a conçu des modèles pour femme à l'attention des plus prestigieuses Maisons de mode italiennes, dont Versace, Romeo Gigli, Roberto Cavalli et Dolce & Gabbana. Dans les années 1990, il a lancé sa collection éponyme et a commencé à introduire ses talons aiguilles caractéristiques. Évitant la photographie de nature morte traditionnelle, Paciotti a été l'un des premiers créateurs de chaussures à présenter ses modèles sur de vrais mannequins dans ses campagnes publicitaires.

En 2008, il a entamé une collaboration avec la marque new-yorkaise Ohne Titel : il crée des bottes d'une hauteur vertigineuse et des bottines sensuelles pour compléter les vêtements moulants aux lignes acérées de Flora Gill et Alexa Adams. « Tout comme leurs créations cherchent à sublimer les formes de la femme moderne en prêtant attention aux moindres détails, je m'efforce de lui donner du glamour et du pouvoir avec des chaussures qui complètent parfaitement sa tenue », a-t-il expliqué à propos de cette collaboration. —*M.M.A.*

"There are brands...that have become part of Italian collective imagination, helping to shape tastes and aesthetics that have marked eras and decades. In Italy and abroad, Cesare Paciotti – and its iconic dagger – was a cultural phenomenon, a high-sounding name that immediately evokes an idea of over-the-top... and infinitely glamorous luxury."

— *NSS MAGAZINE*

Ohne Titel
(Cesare Paciotti)
Ankle boots:
Gray leather, metal
Italy, fall 2009

Ohne Titel
(Cesare Paciotti)
Wedges: Red leather,
metal
Italy, fall 2007

Cesare Paciotti
Mules: Pale grey leather
Italy, spring 1998

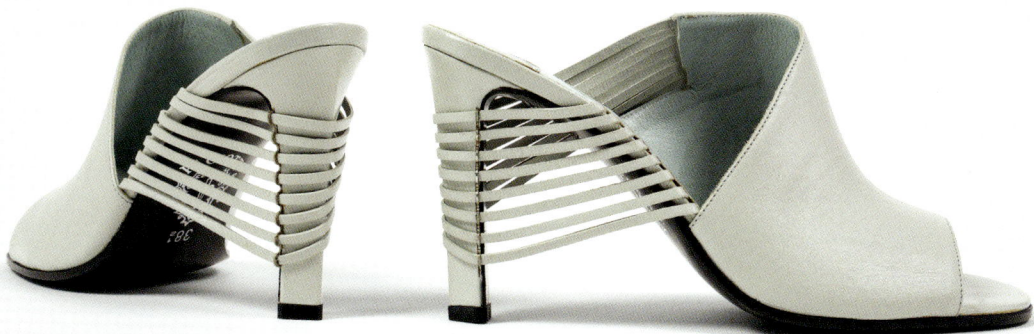

Pelican Footwear

JOE BASCETTA AND CAROLE REIDFORD founded their custom-made shoes company, Pelican Footwear, in 1972 — a particular favorite of the glam rock set, specializing in sky-high, showstopping platforms for men and women. The duo designed, manufactured, and sold their shoes from their loft on the Bowery in New York City, which doubled as their living quarters. The inspiration for their first design — a pair of wedge heels adorned with palm trees — was taken from a pair of hand-carved "souvenir shoes" made in the Philippines during the 1940s.

The designers could not afford to make lasts for their shoes. Instead, they traced the feet of their friends, averaging the measurements to form three basic sizes (called one, two, and three). The uppers were sized similarly. Reidford described the process as "trial and error" but noted that they were able to fit nearly every client using their simplified sizing system. As she further explained, "We wanted to make shoes that were lightweight, strong, beautiful, comfortable, and that could be cleaned with a damp cloth."

Joseph Bascetta and
Carole Reidford Bascetta

Although Pelican Footwear was a small label with very little staff, they boasted an impressive clientele. David Bowie owned several pairs of the brand's colorful shoes, including the palm tree wedges. David Johansen, vocalist for the band New York Dolls, wore a pair of studded Pelican mules on the cover of the band's first album, released in 1973. In a 1972 issue of *Vogue*, Andy Warhol starlet Cyrinda Foxe (who would later marry Johansen) was said to "literally live in her red platform shoes" by Pelican. Although the short-lived company closed during the mid-1970s, it has reached cult status among shoe collectors and glam rock aficionados. —*C.H.*

PREVIOUS
Pelican Footwear
Platform sandal:
Painted polyurethane,
green synthetic satin
USA, 1971–74

OPPOSITE
Lead vocalist David
Johansen shows off stud-
ded Pelican Footwear
mules on the cover of the
New York Dolls' 1973
debut album.

FOLLOWING
Pelican Footwear
Platform sandals:
Painted polyurethane,
red satin
USA, 1972

DAS 1972 VON JOE BASCETTA und Carole Reidford gegründete Label Pelican Footwear, spezialisiert auf Maßschuhe, war ein besonderer Liebling der Glamrockszene, in der man die himmelhohen Plateaus mit Hingucker-Effekt für Herren und Damen schätzte. Als Atelier, Werkstatt und Verkaufsraum für ihre Modelle diente den beiden Designern ein Loft in der New Yorker Bowery, das zugleich ihre Wohnung war. Die Inspiration zu ihrem ersten Design – Plateausandalen mit palmenverziertem Keilabsatz – lieferte ihnen ein Paar handgeschnitzte Holzschuhe, ein Souvenir von den Philippinen aus den 1940er-Jahren.

Mangels Geld für die Anfertigung eigener Leisten zeichneten die beiden Designer die Fußumrisse ihrer Freunde nach und ermittelten aus den Maßen drei Durchschnittsgrundgrößen (eins, zwei und drei genannt). Für das Obermaterial galt eine ähnliche Einteilung. Reidford beschrieb ihr Vorgehen als „Versuch und Irrtum", betonte aber, dass sie mit ihrem vereinfachten Größensystem fast jedem Kundenfuß gerecht wurden. Weiter erläuterte sie: „Wir wollten Schuhe machen, die leicht, stabil, schön und bequem waren und sich mit einem feuchten Tuch reinigen ließen."

Obwohl Pelican Footwear ein kleines Label mit nur wenigen Mitarbeitern war, konnte es sich eines beeindruckenden Kundenstamms rühmen. David Bowie etwa besaß mehrere Modelle der farbenfrohen Marke, darunter die Palmenplateaus. David Johansen, Sänger der Band New York Dolls, posierte 1973 auf dem ersten Albumcover der Band in Nieten-Mules von Pelican. Über Cyrinda Foxe, Andy Warhol-Starlet und spätere Ehefrau Johansens, stand 1972 in der *Vogue* zu lesen, sie lebe buchstäblich in ihren roten Pelican-Plateaus. Obwohl die Marke nur bis Mitte der 70er-Jahre bestand, genießt sie heute Kultstatus unter Schuhsammlern und Aficionados des Glamrock. —*C.H.*

JOE BASCETTA ET CAROLE REIDFORD ont créé l'entreprise de chaussures sur mesure Pelican Footwear en 1972. Spécialisée dans des créations extravagantes aux semelles compensées vertigineuses pour homme et pour femme, c'était l'une des marques préférées de la scène *glam rock*. Le duo dessinait, fabriquait et vendait ses chaussures dans le loft new-yorkais du Bowery qui lui servait aussi d'appartement. Sa première création, une sandale compensée ornée de palmiers, s'inspirait d'une paire de « chaussures souvenirs » sculptées à la main aux Philippines dans les années 1940.

Les créateurs n'avaient pas les moyens de fabriquer des formes pour leurs souliers. À la place, ils dessinaient le contour des pieds de leurs amis, puis calculaient la moyenne des mesures relevées pour obtenir trois pointures de base (appelées « un », « deux » et « trois »). Ils utilisaient la même méthode pour dimensionner les empeignes. Selon Carole Reidford, ils procédaient « par tâtonnements », mais étaient capables de chausser presque tous leurs clients grâce à ce système de pointures simplifié. « Nous voulions créer des chaussures légères, solides, belles et confortables qui se nettoient facilement avec un chiffon humide », a-t-elle précisé.

Pelican Footwear avait beau n'être qu'une petite marque avec très peu d'employés, sa clientèle avait de quoi impressionner. David Bowie possédait plusieurs paires de souliers colorés de la griffe, notamment le modèle compensé décoré de palmiers. David Johansen, le chanteur des New York Dolls, portait des mules cloutées de Pelican sur la pochette du premier album du groupe sorti en 1973. Dans un numéro de 1972, *Vogue* a écrit que Cyrinda Foxe, starlette d'Andy Warhol (qui devait par la suite épouser Johansen), « vivait littéralement dans ses chaussures rouges à semelles compensées » signées Pelican. Bien que l'entreprise ait fermé ses portes au milieu des années 1970 après une courte existence, elle reste culte aux yeux des collectionneurs de chaussures et des fans de *glam rock*. —*C.H.*

Pelican Footwear
Platform sandals:
Painted polyurethane,
glitter, black syn-
thetic satin
USA, 1972

Pelican Footwear
Men's platform mule:
Painted polyurethane,
glitter, red metallic
leather
USA, 1971–74

Pelican Footwear
Platform sandals:
Painted polyurethane,
black synthetic satin
USA, 1971–74

"Their joyful extra-
vagance is maybe just
what we need."

— ANNA BATTISTA, JOURNALIST

Perugia

RISING TO FAME IN THE 1920S, André Perugia represents one of the earliest examples of the celebrity shoe designer. According to *Vogue*, Perugia was to shoes what Chanel and Vionnet were to fashion. A skilled shoemaker and designer, he created cutting-edge footwear for many celebrities, including entertainers Josephine Baker and Mistinguett and actress Gloria Swanson. Modern for the time, his luxury footwear was heavily influenced by cubism and surrealism. Perugia's time as an airplane factory engineer during World War I sharpened his ability to solve design problems and profoundly influenced his design aesthetic.

André Perugia
(1893–1977)

Having learned technical skills from his father, a shoemaker from Nice, Perugia took over the family business in 1913. His designs drew the attention of couturier Paul Poiret, and in 1922 Perugia moved his business to the Rue du Faubourg Saint-Honoré in Paris. His footwear interested a number of couturiers, and he eventually designed shoes for Elsa Schiaparelli, Jacques Fath, and Hubert de Givenchy. Perugia's last collaboration was with Charles Jourdan, with whom he worked in the 1960s.

Perugia was an eccentric genius with a deep understanding of footwear engineering. Known for his ornamented shoes, he pioneered the use of exotic skins, braided leathers, and lacquered straps. A pair of gold kid evening shoes, which leave the instep unsupported, demonstrate the designer's talent for combining engineering and aesthetics; a pair of brown suede pumps with gold sculpted heels illustrate his modernist sensibilities. Throughout his career, Perugia's drive to explore novel materials, silhouettes, and textures led him to create shoes of striking originality. —*M.M.A.*

PREVIOUS
Perugia
T-strap pumps: Beige leather and suede, polychrome floral appliqué France, 1925

Advertised as a must-have addition to a trendy summer wardrobe, Perugia's "Padova" shoe features vibrant, panchromatic stripes and a wedge heel — shown with a matching pantoufle. Pierre Roy, 1940.

ANDRÉ PERUGIA STIEG IN DEN 1920er-Jahren als einer der Ersten seines Metiers in den Rang eines Stardesigners auf. Nach Ansicht der *Vogue* war Perugia für die Schuhmode, was Chanel und Vionnet für die Couture waren. Als gelernter Schuhmacher und Designer kreierte er innovative Fußbekleidung für viele Prominente wie die Entertainerinnen Josephine Baker und Mistinguett oder die Schauspielerin Gloria Swanson. Luxuriös und für ihre Zeit modern, waren seine Kreationen stark von Kubismus und Surrealismus beeinflusst. Dass Perugia während des Ersten Weltkriegs als Flugingenieur gearbeitet hatte, steigerte seine Fähigkeit, gestalterische Probleme zu lösen, und prägte seine Designästhetik nachhaltig.

Das Handwerk erlernte Perugia von seinem Vater, einem Schuhmacher aus Nizza, und übernahm das Familienunternehmen 1913. Der Couturier Paul Poiret wurde auf seine Entwürfe aufmerksam, und 1922 siedelte Perugia mit seinem Geschäft nach Paris um, in die Rue du Faubourg Saint-Honoré. Seine Designs interessierten eine Reihe von Couturiers, und schließlich kreierte er Schuhe für Elsa Schiaparelli, Jacques Fath und Hubert de Givenchy. Zuletzt arbeitete er in den 1960ern mit Charles Jourdan zusammen.

Perugia war ein exzentrisches Genie mit profundem Wissen auf dem Gebiet der Schuhtechnik. Er war bekannt für Verzierungen und verwendete als Erster exotische Leder, Flechtleder und Lackriemchen. Abendschuhe aus goldfarbenem Ziegenleder, die ohne Stütze für den Mittelfuß auskommen, belegen das Geschick des Designers, Technik und Ästhetik miteinander zu verbinden. Braune Wildlederpumps mit modelliertem Goldabsatz illustrieren seine Sensibilität als Gestalter der Moderne. Getrieben von dem Wunsch, innovative Materialien, Silhouetten und Texturen zu erforschen, kreierte Perugia Zeit seines Lebens Schuhe von frappierender Originalität. —*M.M.A.*

ANDRÉ PERUGIA EST DEVENU L'UN des premiers chausseurs célèbres pendant les années 1920. D'après *Vogue*, il était aux chaussures ce que Gabrielle Chanel et Madeleine Vionnet étaient à la mode. Ce cordonnier et designer hautement compétent a créé des modèles avant-gardistes pour de nombreuses célébrités, dont les meneuses de revue Josephine Baker et Mistinguett ou encore l'actrice Gloria Swanson. Modernes pour l'époque, ses souliers de luxe étaient fortement influencés par le cubisme et le surréalisme. Son expérience d'ingénieur dans une usine d'avions pendant la Première Guerre mondiale a affûté sa capacité à résoudre les problèmes de design et profondément influencé son esthétique créative.

Formé aux aspects techniques du métier par son père cordonnier à Nice, André Perugia a repris l'entreprise familiale en 1913. Après que ses créations ont attiré l'attention de Paul Poiret, il s'est installé rue du Faubourg-Saint-Honoré à Paris en 1922. Il a créé des chaussures pour de nombreux couturiers, notamment Elsa Schiaparelli, Jacques Fath et Hubert de Givenchy. Charles Jourdan, avec qui il travaillait dans les années 1960, a été sa dernière collaboration.

André Perugia était un génie excentrique doté d'une connaissance approfondie des techniques de cordonnerie. Réputé pour ses créations décorées, il a innové dans l'utilisation des cuirs exotiques, des cuirs tressés et des brides vernies. Ses sandales de soirée en chevreau doré dépourvues de tout support au niveau de la cambrure du pied démontrent tout son talent quand il s'agit d'allier technique et esthétique, tandis que ses escarpins en daim marron aux talons dorés sculptés illustrent sa sensibilité moderniste. Mu par le désir d'explorer des matières, des silhouettes et des textures inédites, Perugia a créé des chaussures d'une originalité fascinante tout au long de sa carrière. —*M.M.A.*

Panchromatic pantoufle

Bright multicoloured boot of crocheted string, lined with kid. Key your costume to a stripe or wear it with all-white. Really enough of a shoe to walk in. Padova shoe and bag designed in Paris by Perugia for Saks-Fifth Avenue. Pierre Roy seascape

"André Perugia was an innovator, an original. He made all these designs that designers are still influenced by today."

— ARSHO BAGHSARIAN, DESIGNER

Perugia
Pumps: Green kid
leather, gold pigment
France, 1930–32

Perugia
Sling-back pump:
Red leather, red woven
synthetic fabric
France, *ca.* 1965

Perugia
Evening pump: Brown
suede leather, gold metal
France, *ca.* 1950

FOLLOWING
Perugia
Evening shoes: Gold kid
leather, rhinestones
France, 1940

Pinet

ONE OF THE GREATEST OF all modern footwear creators was Jean-Louis François Pinet, known for his nominative heel. Born in 1817 to a shoemaking family, Pinet was 13 when his father died, and spent a transient adolescence and early adulthood moving around Central France, where he rose from apprentice to master shoemaker. By 1844 he finally settled in Paris where he spent the next decade honing his craft, making prudent financial investments, and studying the kinetics of human locomotion. By 1854 the culmination of his efforts resulted in the patent of a new kind of heel: Inspired by the concave "Louis" heel of the eighteenth century as well as the needs of modern urban dwellers, his "Pinet" heel was less tapered but more solid, sturdy yet elegant.

Jean-Louis François Pinet
(1817–1897)

Pinet opened his firm in 1855, the same year as legendary couturier Charles Frederick Worth. Like Worth, Pinet advanced his artistic designs with a blend of handcraftsmanship and modern technology inspired by the industrial revolution sweeping Europe and the US in the early 1800s — and became the leading shoe designer of his age. The two designers both married women who inspired them creatively and with whom they formed collaborative partnerships — and garnered awards at the Paris world's fair, the 1867 Exposition Universelle. A publication for the event declared that Pinet understood "the true center of the heel . . . and by a mathematical calculation, he fixed it proportionally to its height at the most convenient place for the ease of walking." Pinet is credited with creating the first ankle boot for women in the late 1800s. His distinctive footwear was often covered in an array of vividly colored silks with sumptuous botanical embroidery.

The shoes in The Museum at FIT's collection date to the 1920s and '30s, long after Pinet's death in 1897. Like the house of Worth, which continued to exist for decades after the couturier's passing, shoes from Maison Pinet remained fashionable, relevant, and retained high technical standards. —*P.M.*

LA PREMIÈRE MARQUE DU MONDE

CHAUSSURES
F. PINET DE PARIS

B. SIRVEN, IMP. ÉDIT. TOULOUSE-PARIS.

JEAN-LOUIS FRANÇOIS PINET WAR EINER der größten Schuhdesigner der Moderne und Schöpfer des bekannten, nach ihm benannten Absatzes. Er wurde 1817 in eine Schuhmacherfamilie geboren und verlor als 13-Jähriger seinen Vater. Seine weitere Jugend und Lehrzeit verbrachte er auf Wanderschaft in Zentralfrankreich und wurde vom Schuhmachergesellen zum Meister. 1844 ließ er sich schließlich in Paris nieder. Im folgenden Jahrzehnt perfektionierte er sein Können, tätigte kluge Investitionen und studierte den menschlichen Gang. Seine Bemühungen gipfelten 1854 in dem Patent für einen neuartigen Absatz. Angelehnt an den konkaven Louis-XV-Absatz des 18. Jahrhunderts und an die Bedürfnisse des modernen Großstädters angepasst, lief der „Pinet"-Absatz nicht mehr so spitz zu, war dafür aber stabiler – robust und dennoch elegant.

Pinet gründete seine eigene Firma 1855, im selben Jahr wie der legendäre Couturier Charles Frederick Worth. Genau wie Worth beflügelt von der industriellen Revolution, die seit Anfang des 19. Jahrhunderts Europa und die USA erfasste, trieb Pinet seine kunstvollen Designs in einer Mischung aus handwerklicher Finesse und moderner Technik voran – und wurde so zum führenden Schuhdesigner seiner Epoche. Beide Designer heirateten Frauen, die sie kreativ inspirierten und als Partnerinnen an ihrer Arbeit mitwirkten, und beide erhielten auf der Pariser Weltausstellung 1867 Auszeichnungen. Wie eine damalige Publikation befand, hatte Pinet „die wahre Mitte des Absatzes erkannt ... und mittels mathematischer Berechnung an der proportional zu seiner Höhe geeignetsten Stelle für unbeschwertes Gehen angebracht." Auch die Entwicklung der ersten Damenstiefelette im späten 19. Jahrhundert wird Pinet zugeschrieben. Bezogen waren seine unverkennbaren Kreationen häufig mit unterschiedlichen Seiden in lebhaften Farben und üppigen floralen Zierstickereien.

Die Schuhe in der Sammlung des FIT-Museums entstanden in den 1920er- und 30er-Jahren, lange nach Pinets Tod im Jahr 1897. So wie das Haus Worth nach dem Tod des Couturiers jahrzehntelang weiterbestand, blieb auch die Marke Pinet mit modischen Schuhdesigns relevant und ihrem hohen technischen Standard treu. —*P.M.*

CONNU POUR LE TALON QUI PORTE SON NOM, Jean-Louis François Pinet reste sans conteste l'un des plus grands créateurs de chaussures modernes. Né en 1817 dans une famille de cordonniers, il avait 13 ans à la mort de son père. Il a ensuite consacré sa brève adolescence et ses premières années d'adulte à l'apprentissage en se déplaçant dans le centre de la France pour devenir maître cordonnier. Il s'est installé à Paris en 1844, où il a passé la décennie suivante à perfectionner son art tout en réalisant de prudents investissements et en étudiant la cinétique de la locomotion humaine. En 1854, ses efforts ont porté leurs fruits avec le dépôt d'un brevet pour un nouveau type de talon : inspiré du talon Louis XV concave du XVIIIᵉ siècle et par les besoins des citadines modernes, son talon dit « Pinet » était à la fois fuselé et plus solide, robuste, mais élégant.

Pinet a créé son entreprise éponyme en 1855, la même année que le légendaire couturier Charles Frederick Worth. Comme ce dernier, il inventait ses modèles artistiques en s'appuyant sur le savoir-faire manuel et sur une technologie moderne inspirée par la Révolution industrielle qui déferlait sur l'Europe et les États-Unis depuis le début du XIXᵉ siècle – et il est ainsi devenu le plus grand créateur de chaussures de son époque. Worth et Pinet ont épousé des femmes qui inspiraient leur créativité et avec lesquelles ils formaient un partenariat collaboratif. Ils ont tous deux remporté des prix à l'Exposition universelle de Paris en 1867. Un ouvrage publié à l'occasion de l'événement affirmait que Pinet avait trouvé « le véritable centre du talon » et l'avait « positionné, à l'aide d'un calcul mathématique, proportionnellement à sa hauteur à l'endroit le plus pratique pour faciliter la marche ». Pinet est considéré comme l'inventeur de la première bottine à talon pour dame à la fin du XIXᵉ siècle. Ses chaussures originales étaient souvent revêtues de soies aux couleurs vives brodées de somptueux motifs floraux.

Les exemplaires conservés dans la collection du musée du FIT datent des années 1920 et 1930, soit bien après la mort de Pinet en 1897. Comme la Maison Worth qui a survécu au couturier pendant des décennies, les chaussures de la Maison Pinet sont restées tendance, d'actualité et conformes aux standards techniques de leur créateur. —P.M.

Prada

"UGLY IS ATTRACTIVE, UGLY IS EXCITING. Maybe because it is newer," mused famed designer Miuccia Prada. Under her leadership, the family-owned Italian luxury brand has become synonymous with an offbeat, directional approach to design. Prada's seasonal collections often fuse references to fine art and architecture with more unlikely sources of inspiration, such as hot rod cars and anime. The inventiveness and rejection of conventional beauty that has come to define Prada's clothing also translated to the brand's shoes, which are essential to the complete look of each collection.

Miuccia Prada (b. 1949)

The Prada brand was founded on its designs for fashionable leather goods. In 1913, Miuccia's grandfather, Mario Prada, opened the company's first store in the Galleria Vittorio Emanuele II in Milan. He sold leather bags, steamer trunks, and travel accessories, eventually becoming an official supplier of the Italian royal house. Miuccia Prada joined her family's business in the mid-1970s, and at the close of the decade the brand made its first foray into fashion with a collection of women's shoes. Nearly a decade later, in 1988, Prada presented her first women's ready-to-wear collection, followed by a menswear line in 1993. Although Prada's clothing took center stage during the '90s, stylish and sometimes quirky footwear for both men and women remained integral to the brand's identity.

Prada continues to expand its global presence, and shoes are central to its development. The "Flame" shoes — introduced in 2012 as part of a collection themed around classic 1950s automobiles — were rereleased in 2018, underscoring their lasting desirability. As *Harper's Bazaar* writer Grace O'Neill summarized, "Miuccia Prada knows shoes. Season after season, year after year, the Italian powerhouse manages to release a constant array of cult-like footwear." —*E.M.*

Prada
Mule: Black-and-red
patent leather, metal
Italy, spring 2012

Prada
Boot: Gray leather,
red plastic
Italy, fall 1998

„HÄSSLICH IST ATTRAKTIV, HÄSSLICH IST aufregend. Vielleicht, weil es neuer ist", sinnierte die berühmte Modeschöpferin Miuccia Prada. Unter ihrer Leitung wurde das familiengeführte italienische Luxuslabel zum Synonym für unkonventionelles, richtungweisendes Design. Häufig werden in den Saisonkollektionen der Marke Referenzen an Kunst und Architektur mit eher ungewöhnlichen Inspirationsquellen wie Hot-Rod-Oldtimern und Anime-Trickfilmen verwoben. Einfallsreichtum und die Ablehnung konventioneller Schönheit definieren Prada-Kleidung von heute und prägen auch die Schuhe des Labels, die für den Gesamtlook jeder Kollektion wesentlich sind.

Den Grundstock der Marke Prada bildeten modische Lederwaren. Miuccias Großvater Mario Prada eröffnete 1913 in der Mailänder Galleria Vittorio Emanuele II das erste Ladengeschäft für Ledertaschen, Schiffskoffer und Reiseaccessoires und wurde schließlich ein offizieller Hoflieferant des italienischen Königshauses. Mitte der 1970er-Jahre schloss sich Miuccia Prada dem Familienunternehmen an, und Ende des Jahrzehnts wagte das Label mit einer Damenschuhkollektion seinen ersten Vorstoß in die Modesparte. 1988, fast zehn Jahre später, präsentierte Miuccia ihre erste Prêt-à-porter-Kollektion für Damen, der 1993 eine Herrenlinie folgte. Auch wenn Kleidung in den 1990er-Jahren die Hauptrolle bei Prada spielte, blieb stilvolle und mitunter kuriose Schuhmode für Herren wie Damen ein zentrales Element der Markenidentität.

Heute baut Prada seine globale Präsenz weiter aus, wobei die Schuhsparte ein Kernelement dieser Entwicklung bildet. Die „Flame"-Sandalette, die erstmals 2012 als Teil einer Kollektion vorgestellt wurde, die sich thematisch um Autos aus den 1950er-Jahren drehte, wurde 2018 aufgrund ihrer ungebrochenen Anziehungskraft neu aufgelegt. Grace O'Neill fasste in einem Artikel für *Harper's Bazaar* zusammen: „Miuccia Prada kann Schuhe. Saison für Saison, Jahr für Jahr gelingt es dem italienischen Energiebündel erneut, eine Auswahl an Kultschuhen zu präsentieren." —*E.M.*

« SI LE LAID ATTIRE ET FASCINE, c'est peut-être parce qu'il est nouveau », se demandait la célèbre créatrice Miuccia Prada. Sous sa direction, la marque familiale italienne de luxe est devenue l'incarnation d'une mode décalée qui dicte les tendances. Les collections saisonnières de Prada fusionnent souvent des références artistiques et architecturales avec des inspirations plus improbables, par exemple les voitures *hot-rod* et les mangas. L'inventivité et le rejet de la beauté conventionnelle qui définissent aujourd'hui le style Prada se traduisent aussi dans les chaussures de la griffe, accessoires indispensables pour compléter les looks de chaque collection.

À ses débuts, la marque Prada vendait des produits de maroquinerie à la mode. Mario Prada, le grand-père de Miuccia, proposait des sacs en cuir, des malles et des accessoires de voyage dans sa première boutique ouverte en 1913 dans la Galleria Vittorio Emanuele II à Milan. Il finira par devenir le fournisseur officiel de la famille royale d'Italie. Miuccia Prada a rejoint l'entreprise familiale au milieu des années 1970. À la fin de la décennie, la marque a fait sa première incursion dans la mode avec une collection de chaussures pour femme. Une dizaine d'années plus tard, en 1988, Prada a présenté sa première collection de prêt-à-porter féminin, suivie d'une collection pour homme en 1993. Bien que les vêtements aient occupé une place centrale dans l'offre Prada des années 1990, ses chaussures élégantes et parfois excentriques pour homme et pour femme sont restées un pilier de l'identité de la marque.

Prada continue d'étendre sa présence mondiale et les chaussures jouent un rôle clé dans son développement. Les mules à talons Flame présentées en 2012 dans le cadre d'une collection inspirée par les automobiles vintage des années 1950 ont été relancées en 2018, pour preuve de leur attrait durable. Comme l'a résumé la journaliste Grace O'Neill dans *Harper's Bazaar* : « Miuccia Prada s'y connaît en chaussures : d'une saison à l'autre, année après année, la grande Maison italienne réussit toujours à proposer une sélection de modèles cultes. » —*E.M.*

Prada
Pumps: Brown leather
Italy, fall 1996

Prada
Men's sandals: Black-
and-white cotton,
leather, suede, rubber
Italy, *ca.* 1995

Prada
Men's shoes:
Brown leather
Italy, *ca.* 1987

Prada
Pumps: Black velvet,
leather, wood
Italy, *ca.* 1995

Prada
Pump: Brown patent
leather
Italy, fall 2008

Prada
Pumps: Chartreuse
velvet, purple patent
leather, green
suede, plastic
Italy, spring 2008

Prada
Pump: Black-and-taupe
silk satin, metal
Italy, fall 2007

Saint Laurent

Yves Saint Laurent (1936–2008)

YVES SAINT LAURENT TRANSFORMED THE fashion landscape when he burst on the Paris scene in 1957 as the new head designer for Dior at just 21 years old. When he founded his label in 1961, he established himself as the enfant terrible of French fashion, churning out collections inspired by fine art, youth culture, film, and fashion history, always with a certain romantic sensibility. In each season, shoes completed a look. As French fashion writer Patrick Mauriès explains of Saint Laurent, "For him, shoes fell into the category of discreet complementary details, of light final touches to be applied sparingly." But this did not mean that his shoes were always demure and bourgeois. He frequently experimented with more daring over-the-knee boots and bold color combinations. Shoes would often appear purposely mismatched to ensembles. This was Saint Laurent's rebuke of traditional rules of matching and "proper" etiquette in dress. Indeed, supermodel Iman once recalled to *Vogue* how she "learned from Mr. Saint Laurent the beauty and audacity of clashing colors and how harmoniously beautiful they are in the hands of a master like Mr. Saint Laurent!"

Saint Laurent was born in 1936 in Oran, Algeria. After moving to Paris, he remained deeply connected to North Africa in his designs and often credited his time there to his interest in vibrant colors. In 1966 Saint Laurent launched a ready-to-wear label, Rive Gauche, which gave a wider demographic of women access to his designs, including shoes and accessories. Saint Laurent retired from his house in 2002, and since then a number of designers have acted as creative director. While each head designer has endowed the label with a distinct sensibility, footwear has remained a point of complementary design — a Saint Laurent shoe completes a look rather than steals the show. —*E.M.*

YVESSAINTLAURENT

PREVIOUS
Saint Laurent
Thigh-high boots:
Black crocodile skin
France, *ca.* 1985

A 1990s advertisement
for Yves Saint Laurent
features long legs and
high-heeled pumps.

Saint Laurent
Spectator pumps:
Red-and-white leather
France, *ca.* 1979

ALS YVES SAINT LAURENT 1957 mit gerade einmal 21 Jahren als neuer Chefdesigner des Hauses Dior das Pariser Parkett erstürmte, verwandelte er die Modelandschaft. Mit seinem eigenen, vier Jahre später gegründeten Label etablierte er sich als Enfant terrible der französischen Mode. Kunst und Jugendkultur, Film und Modegeschichte inspirierten ihn zu Kollektionen am laufenden Band, die stets eine gewisse romantische Empfindsamkeit verrieten. Schuhe komplettierten den jeweiligen Look der Saison. Der Modejournalist Patrick Mauriès sagte über Saint Laurent: „Für ihn fielen Schuhe in die Kategorie abrundendes Detail, ein leichter Final Touch, mit dem man sparsam umgehen musste." Was jedoch nicht hieß, dass seine Schuhe immer brav und bieder waren. Häufig experimentierte er mit eher verwegenen Overknee-Stiefeln und kühnen Farbkombinationen. Oft wirkten Schuhe, als passten sie absichtlich nicht zum Ensemble. Das war Saint Laurents Absage an tradierte Kleiderordnungen und „korrekte" Modeetikette. Tatsächlich erklärte das Supermodel Iman einst in einem *Vogue*-Interview, sie habe „durch Saint Laurent die Schönheit und Kühnheit von Farbdissonanzen kennengelernt und erlebt, wie wundervoll sie unter den Händen eines Meisters wie Saint Laurent harmonieren!"

Saint Laurent kam 1936 im algerischen Oran zur Welt und blieb Nordafrika auch nach dem Wegzug nach Paris in seinem Schaffen tief verbunden. Sein Faible für lebhafte Farben rührte, wie er selbst oft bestätigte, von seiner Zeit dort her. Mit Rive Gauche lancierte er 1966 eine Prêt-à-porter-Linie, mit der seine Mode einschließlich Schuhen und Accessoires einer breiteren Schicht von Kundinnen zugänglich wurde. Seit Saint Laurents Rückzug aus seinem Unternehmen im Jahr 2002 sind ihm eine Reihe von Kreativchefs nachgefolgt. Jeder dieser Chefdesigner hat das Label um seine spezielle Sensibilität bereichert, doch die Schuhmode wird nach wie vor als Ergänzung kreiert – ein Schuh von Saint Laurent komplettiert einen Look, anstatt ihn zu übertrumpfen. —*E.M.*

YVES SAINT LAURENT A transformé le paysage de la mode et fait sensation sur la scène parisienne lorsqu'il est devenu directeur artistique de Dior en 1957 à seulement 21 ans. Quand il a créé sa griffe en 1961, il s'est imposé comme l'enfant terrible de la mode française avec des collections toujours empreintes d'une certaine sensibilité romantique qui s'inspiraient de l'art, de la culture de la jeunesse, du cinéma et de l'histoire de la mode. Les chaussures servaient à compléter le look de chaque saison. « Pour lui, les souliers entraient dans la catégorie des détails complémentaires, des touches de finition discrètes à utiliser avec parcimonie », dit l'écrivain français Patrick Mauriès à propos de Saint Laurent. Cela ne signifie pas pour autant que ses chaussures étaient toujours sobres et bourgeoises. Il lui arrivait souvent de proposer des cuissardes plus osées et des combinaisons de couleurs audacieuses. Ses chaussures pouvaient paraître délibérément mal assorties à ses looks, car Saint Laurent rejetait les règles traditionnelles et les conventions vestimentaires consistant à coordonner tous les composants d'un ensemble. En effet, la top-modèle Iman a un jour confié à *Vogue* qu'elle a « appris de Monsieur Saint Laurent que les couleurs qui détonnent peuvent être belles et audacieuses, et qu'entre ses mains de maître, elles peuvent produire une magnifique harmonie ! ».

Yves Saint Laurent est né en 1936 à Oran, en Algérie. Une fois installé à Paris, il exprimait son profond attachement à l'Afrique du Nord à travers ses créations et citait souvent le temps passé dans cette région comme l'origine de sa passion pour les couleurs vives. En 1966, il a lancé la griffe de prêt-à-porter Rive Gauche grâce à laquelle davantage de femmes ont eu accès à ses créations, notamment à ses chaussures et accessoires. Après que Saint Laurent a pris sa retraite en 2002, plusieurs créateurs se sont succédé à la direction de sa Maison. Même si chacun d'eux a insufflé sa propre sensibilité à la marque, les souliers sont restés un accessoire complémentaire : une chaussure Saint Laurent sert à compléter un look, pas à lui voler la vedette. —E.M.

Saint Laurent
Boot: Brown suede,
gold leather, wood
France, *ca.* 1980

Saint Laurent
Ankle boots: Black-
and-brown leather,
shearling, metal
France, fall 2009

"Saint Laurent's women are from harems, castles, and even the suburbs; they are all over the streets, subways, dime stores, and stock exchanges."

— MARGUERITE DURAS, AUTHOR

Saint Laurent
Pumps: brown leather
and suede, wood
France, 1975–76

Saint Laurent
Wedge-heeled sandals:
Black-and-white leather,
black plastic
France, *ca.* 1976

Saint Laurent
Wedge-heeled espa-
drilles: Red canvas,
gold metallic ribbon,
black rickrack
France, 1973–74

Saint Laurent
Sandals: Red, purple,
and green satin,
black rubber
France, fall 1991

Saint Laurent
Sandals: Beige and red
leather, metal, enamel
France, spring 2003

Saint Laurent
Ghillie-style pumps:
Silver snakeskin,
black suede
France, 1977

"Just to pronounce those three special words, 'Yves Saint Laurent,' is to feel something special pass through you, which you know is quintessentially rare, chic, and Parisienne. Yves's rare combination of talent, reinvention, artistic angst, and blurred ideas of sexuality became a perfect storm for his times."

— LINDA FARGO, FASHION EXECUTIVE

Shoe Biz at Henri Bendel

ESTABLISHED IN THE LATE 1960S, Shoe Biz was a specialty footwear brand sold at Henri Bendel, a luxury fashion retailer on Fifth Avenue in New York. Run by shoe designer and magnate Jerrold (Jerry) Miller, Shoe Biz footwear was sold within one of the 12 "Little Shops" at Henri Bendel, which operated as small boutiques. Their designs stood out for their eye-catching, youthful appeal.

Early in his career, Jerry Miller worked in the shoe factories run by his grandfather, Israel Miller. It was there that he met shoe designer Margaret Clark. The couple married in 1954 and started a business under the label Margaret Jerrold in New York City. In a time when heels were either ultra-flat or

Jerry Miller and Margaret Clark (1921–1994)

noticeably high, Margaret Jerrold was known for offering a shoe with a medium heel. Clark is credited with a number of innovations, including a design that prevented shoes from digging into the wearer's heels. Miller spoke highly of his wife's talents in his autobiography, writing "I don't think there is any question that she was the expert on the low heel . . . [and] young, sophisticated shoes." Accordingly, Clark's work also became important to the Shoe Biz line.

Female employees of the Shoe Biz boutique were known as "shoe girls" and were encouraged to dress in miniskirts that emphasized both their legs and their fashionable footwear in a ploy to attract customers. Shoe Biz was especially known for its colorful knee-high boots that laced up the leg and featured provocative cutouts or charming embellishments. During the 1970s Shoe Biz formed manufacturing partnerships with factories in Bulgaria, France, Greece, Italy, and Spain. They also became the first American shoe company to produce shoes in China. Arsho Baghsarian, a shoe designer who worked for the Shoe Biz brand for 15 years before designing for Stuart Weitzman, stated, "Jerry was a pioneer in the industry, and we were real globetrotters." —*M.M.*

Margaret Clark Empire State Bldg New York, N.Y. 4/30/54

Margaret Clark Empire State Bldg New York, N.Y. 6/21/54

PREVIOUS
Shoe Biz at Henri Bendel
Boot: Brown suede, multicolor embroidery
Greece, *ca.* 1970

Sketches by Margaret Clark for Shoe Biz include flats with split toes, citrus embellishments, and playful colors. 1954.

Shoe Biz at Lou Lattimore
Wedge: Black-and-green satin
USA, *ca.* 1974

DAS ENDE DER 1960ER-JAHRE GEGRÜNDETE Label Shoe Biz wurde in einem der zwölf „Little Shops" verkauft, die das New Yorker Luxuskaufhaus Henri Bendel in der Fifth Avenue als kleine Boutiquen betrieb. Kopf der für ausgefallene, jugendliche Looks bekannten Marke war der Schuhdesigner und Großindustrielle Jerrold (Jerry) Miller.

Miller arbeitete zu Beginn seiner Karriere in den Schuhfabriken seines Großvaters Israel Miller, wo er die Schuhdesignerin Margaret Clark kennenlernte. Die beiden heirateten 1954 und gründeten in New York ihre eigene Firma Margaret Jerrold. Zu einer Zeit, in der Absätze entweder ultraflach oder auffallend hoch waren, brachte Margaret Jerrold Schuhe mit halbhohem Absatz heraus. Clark sind eine Reihe von Innovationen zu verdanken, darunter Schuhe mit Fersenschutz. Miller pries ihr Talent in seiner Autobiografie mit den Worten: „Ich denke, es steht außer Frage, dass sie die Expertin für den flachen Absatz war, für den jungen, raffinierten Schuh." Dementsprechend wichtig wurde Clarks Arbeit auch für die Shoe-Biz-Linie.

Als Kniff, um Kunden anzulocken, wurde den „Shoe Girls" genannten Verkäuferinnen der Shoe-Biz-Boutiquen empfohlen, Miniröcke zu tragen, die sowohl ihre Beine als auch ihr modisches Schuhwerk zur Geltung brachten. Ein besonders beliebter Shoe-Biz-Look waren kniehohe Schnürstiefel mit aufreizenden Cut-outs oder farbenfrohen Verzierungen. Im Lauf der 1970er-Jahre ging Shoe Biz Kooperationen mit Herstellern in Bulgarien, Frankreich, Griechenland, Italien und Spanien ein. Zudem ließ das Unternehmen als erstes US-Label Schuhe in China produzieren. Arsho Baghsarian, der als Schuhdesigner 15 Jahre für Shoe Biz tätig war, ehe er zu Stuart Weitzman wechselte, resümierte: „Jerry war ein Pionier der Branche, und wir waren echte Globetrotter." —*M.M.*

CRÉÉE À LA FIN DES ANNÉES 1960, Shoe Biz était une marque de chaussures vendue chez Henri Bendel, un magasin de mode de luxe situé sur la Cinquième Avenue à New York. Dirigée par le créateur de chaussures et magnat Jerrold (Jerry) Miller, elle était vendue dans l'une des douze « petites boutiques » du magasin Henri Bendel. Ses créations séduisaient grâce à leur look jeune et accrocheur.

Au début de sa carrière, Jerry Miller a travaillé dans les usines de chaussures de son grand-père Israel Miller, où il a rencontré la créatrice Margaret Clark. Ils se sont mariés en 1954 et ont créé la marque Margaret Jerrold à New York. À une époque où les talons étaient soit ultra-plats, soit extrêmement hauts, la griffe s'est fait connaître en proposant un talon de hauteur intermédiaire. Margaret Clark est à l'origine de plusieurs innovations, notamment d'un design qui empêchait le talon de creuser le pied. Dans son autobiographie, Jerry Miller ne tarit pas d'éloges sur les talents de son épouse : « Elle était incontestablement l'experte du petit talon, des souliers jeunes et sophistiqués. » Le travail de Margaret Clark jouait donc un rôle important pour la marque Shoe Biz.

Surnommées les *shoe girls*, les employées de la boutique Shoe Biz étaient encouragées à porter des minijupes pour mettre en valeur leurs jambes et leurs chaussures à la mode, un stratagème conçu pour attirer la clientèle. La marque était surtout connue pour ses bottes colorées qui laçaient la jambe avec des découpes provocantes ou de charmants détails décoratifs. Dans les années 1970, Shoe Biz a conclu des partenariats de production avec des usines en Bulgarie, en France, en Grèce, en Italie et en Espagne. C'est aussi le premier chausseur américain à avoir fait fabriquer des modèles en Chine. « Jerry était un pionnier de l'industrie et nous étions de vrais globe-trotters », a déclaré Arsho Baghsarian, un créateur de chaussures qui a travaillé pour Shoe Biz pendant quinze ans avant de rejoindre Stuart Weitzman. —*M.M.*

**Shoe Biz at
Henri Bendel**
Pumps: Pink suede,
pink metallic leather
USA, 1971

**Shoe Biz at
Henri Bendel**
Boots: Red suede
Italy, 1971

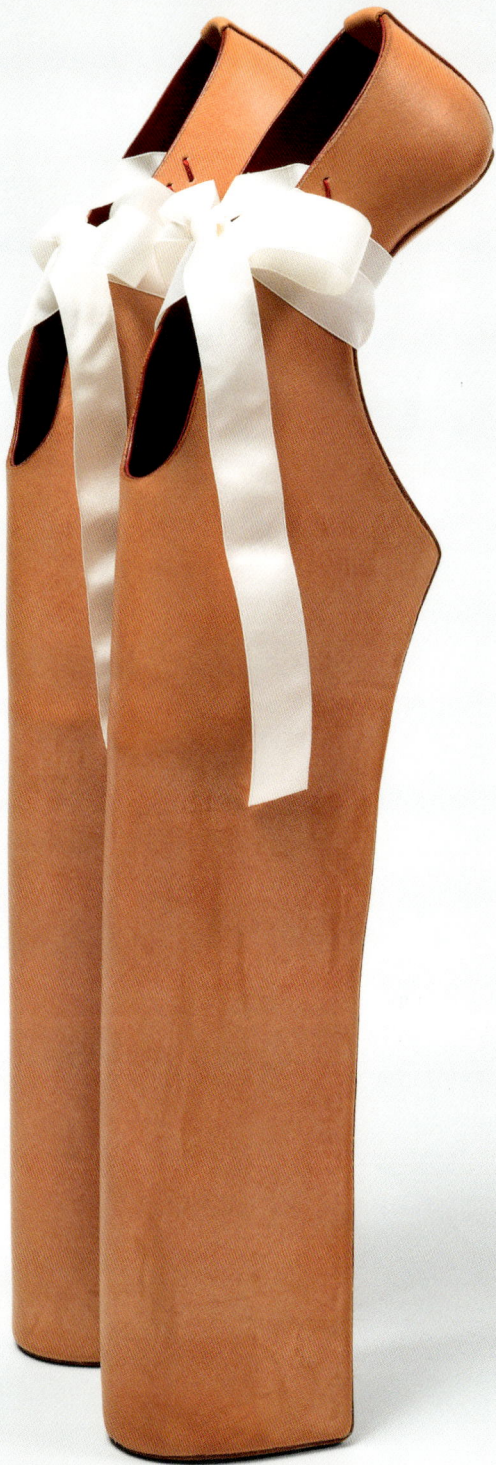

Noritaka Tatehana

THERE'S NO MISTAKING NORITAKA TATEHANA'S signature heelless shoes. Sculptural and arresting, the foot is pitched up and forward, as if floating, on a narrow platform. While his shoes might seem to defy the laws of physics, it *is* possible to walk in them, albeit with a careful gait. Avid collectors of his work Daphne Guinness and Lady Gaga have mastered the precarious balancing act necessary to move in these creations.

Tatehana was born in Tokyo in 1985 and earned his degree at Tokyo University of the Arts where he studied fine art, Japanese craft, dyeing, and weaving. During his studies he became fascinated with the elaborate dress of the Oiran, elite courtesans of the Japanese Meiji period, particularly their elevated shoes known as *geta*. His heelless design grew out of this research — a fusion between the structure of the courtesan's high *geta* and the silhouette of a western high heel.

Today, Tatehana works in Tokyo as an artist, producing his shoes alongside other art projects. He has shown his work in galleries and museums worldwide, making his shoes a perfect hybrid of art object and footwear. —*E.M.*

DER SCHUH OHNE ABSATZ IST Noritaka Tatehanas unverkennbares Markenzeichen: Skulptural und fesselnd hebt sich der Fuß wie auf einem schmalen Podest in die Höhe und nach vorn, als würde er schweben. Obwohl Tatehanas Schuhe den Gesetzen der Physik zu trotzen scheinen, kann man darin gehen, allerdings mit Vorsicht. Den heiklen Balanceakt, den die Fortbewegung in diesen Kreationen erfordert, haben Daphne Guinness und Lady Gaga, beide passionierte Sammlerinnen seiner Designs, gemeistert.

Tatehana, geboren 1985 in Tokio, studierte an der dortigen Kunsthochschule bildende Kunst sowie japanische Handwerkskünste, Färbe- und Webtechniken. Fasziniert von der kunstvollen Kleidung der Oiran genannten Edelkurtisanen der Meiji-Periode, setzte er sich während des Studiums insbesondere mit deren hohen Schuhen auseinander, den als Geta bezeichneten Plateausandalen. Aus dieser Forschungsarbeit resultierte sein absatzloses Design, das die Konstruktion der hohen Geta mit der Silhouette des westlichen High Heels vereint.

Heute arbeitet Tatehana in Tokio als Künstler auch an anderen Projekten und zeigt seine Werke in Galerien und Museen auf der ganzen Welt, was seine Schuhe zum perfekten Hybriden aus Kunstobjekt und Fußbekleidung macht. —E.M.

LES CHAUSSURES SANS TALONS signature de Noritaka Tatehana se reconnaissent au premier coup d'œil. Sculpturales et saisissantes, elles projettent le pied en hauteur vers l'avant, comme s'il flottait sur un socle étroit. Bien qu'elles semblent défier les lois de la physique, on peut les porter à condition de marcher très prudemment. Daphne Guinness et Lady Gaga ont appris à maîtriser le numéro d'équilibriste requis pour se déplacer dans les créations de Noritaka Tatehana qu'elles collectionnent avec ferveur.

Né à Tokyo en 1985, Noritaka Tatehana est diplômé de l'université artistique de sa ville natale où il a étudié les beaux-arts, l'artisanat japonais, la teinture et le tissage. Pendant ses études, il s'est découvert une fascination pour la garde-robe complexe des *oiran*, courtisanes de haut rang sous l'ère Meiji, en particulier pour leurs chaussures à plateforme appelées *geta*. C'est de cette recherche qu'est issu son soulier sans talon qui fusionne la structure de la haute *geta* de courtisane avec la silhouette d'un escarpin occidental à talon haut.

Aujourd'hui, Tatehana travaille en tant qu'artiste à Tokyo, où il produit des chaussures aux côtés d'autres projets artistiques. Son travail a été exposé dans des galeries d'art et des musées à travers le monde entier, preuve que ses créations sont un parfait hybride entre objet d'art et chaussure. —E.M.

Valentino

HAILED AS A MASTER OF Italian design, Valentino Garavani's career has spanned almost half a century. Born in Voghera, Italy, he studied fashion illustration from the age of nine. He moved to Paris in 1949 where he was trained in technical construction, working as an apprentice for couture designers. In 1960, Valentino established his own couture atelier in Rome with his partner, Giancarlo Giammetti. Known for his sophisticated garments, refined tailoring, and elegant use of color and prints, Valentino rose to international recognition. By the mid-1970s, he was one of the first couturiers to show ready-to-wear collections in Paris. Valentino believed, "The things

Valentino Garavani (b. 1932)

that really make a woman elegant are the accessories." In the early 1980s, he debuted a ready-to-wear line called Night by Valentino Garavani, offering matching shoes and handbags designed by René Caovilla.

Valentino's versatile footwear — ranging from sandals, flats, espadrilles, wedges, boots, and sneakers — continues to attract the modern woman looking for a glamorous representation of power, provocation, and elegance in her manner of dressing. A high level of craftsmanship is echoed in Valentino's material choices, whether it be vibrant satin purple knee-high boots, a pair of strappy gold stiletto sandals, or black mules featuring jet beadwork. After Valentino's retirement in 2008, Maria Grazia Chiuri and Pierpaolo Piccioli took over as the label's creative directors. As part of the house's fall / winter 2010 collection, the low heel sling-back "Rockstud" pump was first introduced, becoming a new symbol of Valentino's signature luxury. Metal-studded hardware mixed with patent leather balanced the brand's edge and femininity. Following Maria Grazia Chiuri's departure to Dior womenswear in 2016, Pierpaolo Piccioli served as the sole creative director of the house until 2024, when Alessandro Michele took over the role. The Valentino brand continues to produce haute couture, ready-to-wear, and a full range of accessories, including shoes and bags. —*M.M.*

Valentino Couture
Sandal: Gold metallic
chains
Italy, spring 1998

Valentino Boutique
Boots: Purple satin
Italy, *ca.* 1970

DIE KARRIERE VON VALENTINO GARAVANI, einem gefeierten Meister der italienischen Mode, umspannt nahezu ein halbes Jahrhundert. 1932 im italienischen Voghera geboren, begann Valentino als Neunjähriger mit dem Modezeichnen und ging 1949 nach Paris, um bei dortigen Couturiers eine Ausbildung in Schnitttechnik zu absolvieren. 1960 eröffnete er mit seinem Partner Giancarlo Giammetti einen eigenen Couture-Salon in Rom und erlangte mit raffinierten Kleidern, ausgefeilter Schnitttechnik und seiner eleganten Auswahl von Farben und Mustern internationale Bekanntheit. Mitte der 1970er-Jahre zeigte er als einer der ersten Couturiers Prêt-à-porter-Kollektionen in Paris. Er folgte der Überzeugung: „Die Dinge, die einer Frau wirklich Eleganz verleihen, sind die Accessoires." So bot seine Prêt-à-porter-Linie *Night by Valentino Garavani*, vorgestellt in den frühen 1980er-Jahren, aufeinander abgestimmte Schuhe und Handtaschen nach Entwürfen von René Caovilla.

Valentinos Schuhmode ist mit einer Vielfalt an Modellen - von Sandalen über flache Schuhe, Espadrilles, Wedges und Stiefel bis hin zu Sneakern - nach wie vor anziehend für moderne Frauen, die ihrer Garderobe einen glanzvollen Ausdruck von Stärke, Provokation und Eleganz verleihen möchten. Von hohem handwerklichem Niveau zeugen die von Valentino verwendeten Materialien, etwa bei kniehohen Stiefeln in leuchtend violettem Satin, goldenen Riemchensandaletten oder schwarzen Mules mit Schmuckperlen. Nach Valentinos Rückzug im Jahr 2008 übernahmen Maria Grazia Chiuri und Pierpaolo Piccioli die kreative Leitung des Hauses. Als Teil ihrer Herbst-/Winterkollektion 2010 präsentierten sie die Slingpumps „Rockstud" mit halbhohem Absatz, die zu einem neuen Markenzeichen für Valentino-Luxus avancierten und durch die Kombination von Nietenbesatz und Lackleder die Härte und Weiblichkeit des Labels gleichermaßen widerspiegelten. Nach Maria Grazia Chiuris Wechsel zu Dior im Jahr 2016 war Pierpaolo Piccioli bis 2024, als Alessandro Michele diese Rolle übernahm, alleiniger Leiter des Hauses Valentino, das weiterhin Haute Couture, Prêt-à-porter sowie ein komplettes Accessoire-Sortiment einschließlich Schuhen und Taschen produziert. *—M.M.*

FIGURANT PARMI LES GRANDS MAÎTRES de la mode italienne, Valentino Garavani revendique une carrière de plus d'un demi-siècle. Né à Voghera en Italie, il a étudié l'illustration de mode dès l'âge de 9 ans, puis s'est installé à Paris en 1949, où il a suivi une formation technique et travaillé comme apprenti pour de grands couturiers. En 1960, il a ouvert son propre atelier de couture à Rome avec son associé Giancarlo Giammetti. Valentino a accédé à la reconnaissance internationale grâce à ses vêtements sophistiqués, ses tailleurs raffinés ainsi que son usage élégant de la couleur et des imprimés. Au milieu des années 1970, il comptait parmi les premiers couturiers à présenter des collections de prêt-à-porter à Paris. « Les accessoires sont ce qui rend une femme élégante », estimait-il. Au début des années 1980, il a lancé une ligne de prêt-à-porter appelée Night by Valentino Garavani qui incluait des chaussures et des sacs à main coordonnés conçus par René Caovilla.

La variété de l'offre de chaussures Valentino - sandales, ballerines, espadrilles, compensées, bottes et sneakers - continue d'attirer la femme moderne en quête d'une représentation glamour du pouvoir, de la provocation et de l'élégance. Les choix de matières de Valentino reflètent un haut savoir-faire, qu'il s'agisse de bottes en satin violet brillant, de sandales à lanières dorées et talons aiguilles, ou encore de mules noires ornées de perles de jais. Après que Valentino a pris sa retraite en 2008, Maria Grazia Chiuri et Pierpaolo Piccioli lui ont succédé à la direction de la Maison. L'escarpin à bride arrière Rockstud lancé dans le cadre de la collection Automne/Hiver 2010 s'est imposé comme un nouveau symbole du luxe signature de Valentino : l'alliance des clous en métal et du cuir verni incarnait l'équilibre entre féminité et avant-gardisme qui distingue la marque. Maria Grazia Chiuri est partie diriger la mode pour femme chez Dior en 2016 et Pierpaolo Piccioli a alors été l'unique directeur artistique de la Maison Valentino jusque 2024 lorsqu'Alessandro Michele a repris le poste. La marque continue à produire de la haute couture, du prêt-à-porter et une collection complète d'accessoires incluant des souliers et des sacs à main. *—M.M.*

"The designer's mantra is: 'I always wanted to
make women beautiful,' and his inspiration
was that of a provincial boy in the drab postwar period going to the movies with his sister
and catching the glory days of Hollywood
stars in their silver-screen years."

— SUZY MENKES, JOURNALIST

**Valentino
(Rene Caovilla)**
Stilettos: Black satin,
beaded rose applique
and matching bag
Italy, *ca.* 1981

Valentino Couture
Mules: Black satin, plastic mesh, jet beadwork
Italy, spring 1998

Valentino
Sandals: Brown leather,
pink satin, enameled
metal flowers
Italy, 2005

Iris van Herpen

IRIS VAN HERPEN HAS BEEN heralded as one of the most innovative designers of the twenty-first century and has described fashion as the "engine of progress in our rapidly changing digital age." Her interdisciplinary approach to design is manifested in collaborations with artists, architects, and scientists, introducing new modes of sartorial expression and expanding accepted fashion norms. Like her fashion designs, van Herpen's footwear merges the use of novel methods and materials with traditional handcrafted techniques. Technology has been a guiding principle in van Herpen's work, and she was among the first designers to present 3D-printed garments on the runway.

Iris Van Herpen (b. 1984)

A graduate of the ArtEz Academy of Art & Design in the Netherlands, van Herpen interned under the groundbreaking designer Alexander McQueen and by 2007 founded her own atelier. In 2011 she became a guest member of the Chambre Syndicale de la Haute Couture. Van Herpen's multidisciplinary approach to design has led her to collaborate with notable artists such as Jólan van der Wiel, Neri Oxman, and the architect Philip Beesley. In 2010 van Herpen partnered with United Nude, a shoe company known for unconventional architectural footwear, to produce limited-edition handmade kid leather platform booties. Additional collaborations with United Nude produced leather "crystallization" booties with complex chain detailing (spring 2011), handmade plissé acrylic shoes (spring 2011), and sculptural 3D-printed footwear resembling tree roots for van Herpen's 2013 *Wilderness Embodied* couture collection.

Further exploring unconventional techniques, van Herpen collaborated with Dutch designer Jólan van der Wiel to engineer shoes made of resin mixed with iron filings. Applying magnetic forces to the resin still in its "molten" state, she grew spiky forms, a process that exemplifies her trademark synthesizing of fashion, nature, and technology. —*M.M.A.*

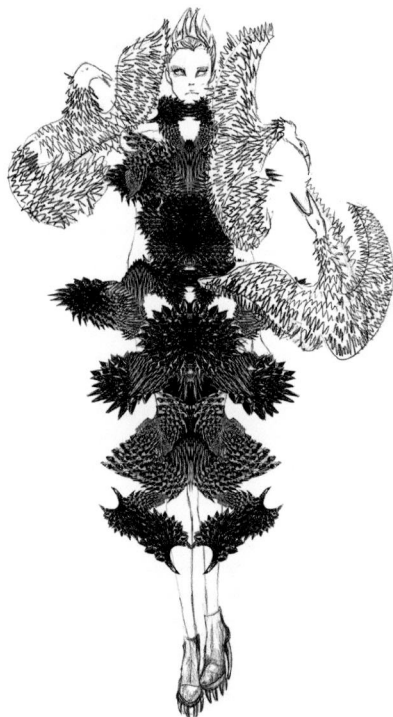

PREVIOUS
**United Nude
(Iris van Herpen)**
"Crystallization" ankle
boot: Black leather,
gold metallic leather
The Netherlands,
fall 2010

A fauna-filled 2014
sketch by van Herpen
depicts clawed platform
booties and an ornamental bird dress.

**United Nude
(Iris van Herpen)**
Ankle boots:
Leather, metal
The Netherlands,
spring 2011

FOLLOWING
**Iris van Herpen and
Jolan van der Wiel**
"Magnetic Motion"
shoes: Gray polyurethane, metal powder,
leather, metal
The Netherlands, 2014

IRIS VAN HERPEN, DIE ALS EINE der innovativsten Designerinnen des 21. Jahrhunderts gilt, beschreibt Mode als den „Motor für Fortschritt in unserer schnelllebigen digitalen Zeit". Ihr interdisziplinärer Designansatz offenbart sich in Kooperationen mit Künstlern, Architekten und Wissenschaftlern, die der Mode neue Ausdrucksmöglichkeiten eröffnen und die gängigen Normen ausweiten. So wie van Herpens Kleiderentwürfe entstehen auch ihre Schuhdesigns aus der Verschmelzung neuartiger Verfahren und Materialien mit traditionellem Handwerk. Der Einsatz moderner Technologien zieht sich als ein Leitprinzip durch ihre Arbeit; so zeigte van Herpen als eine der Ersten Kleider, die im 3-D-Druck-Verfahren hergestellt waren.

Nach ihrem Studium an der niederländischen Kunsthochschule ArtEZ und einem Praktikum bei dem innovativen Modedesigner Alexander McQueen gründete van Herpen 2007 ihr eigenes Atelier. 2011 wurde sie Gastmitglied der Chambre Syndicale de la Haute Couture. Ihr multidisziplinärer Designansatz führte zur Zusammenarbeit mit namhaften Künstlern wie Jólan van der Wiel, Neri Oxman und dem Architekten Philip Beesley. In Kooperation mit dem für unkonventionelle architektonische Schuhe bekannten Label United Nude produzierte sie im Jahr 2010 eine limitierte Serie von handgefertigten Ziegenleder-Booties mit Plateausohle. Als weitere Koproduktionen mit United Nude folgten die „Crystallization"-Lederstiefel mit komplexen Kettendetails (Frühjahr 2011), handgearbeitete Schuhe aus plissiertem Acryl (Frühjahr 2011) und die skulpturalen, an Baumwurzeln erinnernden Entwürfe für van Herpens Couture-Kollektion *Wilderness Embodied* von 2013, die im 3-D-Drucker entstanden.

Eine weitere unkonventionelle Methode entwickelte van Herpen in Zusammenarbeit mit dem niederländischen Designer Jólan van der Wiel. Sie produzierte Schuhe aus Kunstharz, vermischt mit Eisenspänen, die durch Magnetisierung des noch „flüssigen" Harzes gezackte Formen ausbildeten. Dieser Prozess veranschaulicht beispielhaft die für sie charakteristische Synthese von Mode, Natur und Technologie. —*M.M.A.*

IRIS VAN HERPEN EST CONSIDÉRÉE comme l'une des créatrices les plus innovantes du XXIᵉ siècle. Selon elle, la mode est un « moteur de progrès dans notre ère numérique qui évolue à toute vitesse ». Son approche interdisciplinaire de la création s'exprime dans des collaborations avec des artistes, des architectes et des scientifiques qui présentent de nouveaux moyens d'expression vestimentaire et repoussent les frontières de la mode. À l'image de ses vêtements, les chaussures d'Iris van Herpen sont produites à l'aide de méthodes et de matériaux innovants alliés à des techniques artisanales traditionnelles. La technologie a toujours été un principe directeur dans le travail de la créatrice, qui figurait parmi les premiers à présenter des vêtements imprimés en 3D dans ses défilés.

Diplômée de l'ArtEz Academy of Art & Design aux Pays-Bas, Iris van Herpen a fait un stage auprès du couturier avant-gardiste Alexander McQueen avant de créer sa propre marque en 2007. Elle est devenue « membre invité » de la Chambre syndicale de la haute couture en 2011. Son approche multidisciplinaire de la mode l'a amenée à collaborer avec des designers importants comme Jólan van der Wiel et Neri Oxman, ainsi qu'avec l'architecte Philip Beesley. En 2010, elle s'est associée à United Nude, un chausseur réputé pour ses créations architecturales insolites, afin de produire des bottines compensées en cuir de chevreau faites main en édition limitée. Dans le cadre d'autres collaborations avec United Nude, elle a créé les bottines en cuir Crystallization lacées de chaînes complexes (Printemps 2011), des escarpins en acrylique plissé faits main (Printemps 2011) et des chaussures sculpturales imprimées en 3D ressemblant à des racines d'arbre pour *Wilderness Embodied*, sa collection haute couture 2013.

Iris van Herpen poursuit son exploration des techniques non conventionnelles en collaboration avec le designer néerlandais Jólan van der Wiel pour concevoir des chaussures dans un mélange de résine et de limaille de fer. Elle a créé des formes hérissées en appliquant une force magnétique sur la résine à l'état liquide, un procédé qui illustre bien sa synthèse signature entre mode, nature et technologie. —M.M.A.

Versace

A DESIGN BY GIANNI VERSACE was unmistakable: It was
sexy, bold, and brash. His signature aesthetic, described by
The New York Times as embodying the "juxtaposition of
the jungle and court society," featured bright colors and
black, leather, straps and buckles, and metal accents,
including his golden Medusa-head logo and Greek
key patterns. Versace footwear for men and women
was elegantly proportioned and often heavily embellished. It exuded hedonism and pushed the boundaries
of accepted taste. Widely photographed on the top
supermodels of the 1990s, the brand's expanding lines
and boutiques were a testament to its international appeal.

Gianni Versace
(1946–1997)

Gianni Versace was born in 1946 in Reggio di Calabria,
Italy. The city has strong historical links to ancient Greece,
whose motifs would influence Versace's later designs. He learned to sew at an early age
from his mother, a dressmaker, and moved to Milan in 1973 to pursue a career in fashion. He began designing for other Italian labels, including Callaghan and Complice, working continually and producing multiple lines across brands. Versace gained accolades
quickly; in 1974 *Women's Wear Daily* praised not only the modern, unstructured clothes
he designed for Callaghan but also the accessories, including high heel pumps and ghillies.
Partnering with his brother, Santo, Versace launched his own ready-to-wear line in 1978. At
this point, Milan was one of three Italian fashion hubs, but Versace was among the ready-
to-wear designers, including Giorgio Armani, Gianfranco Ferré, and Missoni, who helped
redefine the city as the singular Italian fashion capital. Gianni Versace designed until his
murder in 1997. His sister and frequent collaborator, Donatella Versace, took over the
design of the Versace label, presenting her first collection just 12 weeks after her brother's
death. Her style picked up aspects of Gianni Versace's design philosophy and also evolved
the Versace aesthetic. "Gianni was a genius. He broke barriers," she said to *GQ*. "Some
people said it was vulgar . . . but, you know, women love what Gianni did, not because
they showed skin, but because he empowered women. He told them not to be afraid of
their sexuality." —*E.W.*

EIN GIANNI-VERSACE-DESIGN WAR AUF ANHIEB erkennbar: sexy, gewagt und knallig. Teil seiner Markenästhetik, die die *New York Times* als „Aufeinandertreffen von Dschungel und Hofstaat" beschrieb, waren leuchtende Farben und Schwarz, Riemen, Schnallen, metallische Akzente wie etwa der goldene Medusenkopf in seinem Logo und bekannte griechische Muster. Seine Schuhmode für Herren wie Damen war von eleganten Proportionen und oft überreich verziert. Sie verkörperte Hedonismus und reizte die Grenzen des herrschenden Geschmacks aus. Die ständig wachsende Zahl seiner Boutiquen und Kollektionen, häufig fotografiert an den Supermodels der 1990er-Jahre, bezeugen den internationalen Appeal der Marke.

Gianni Versace kam 1946 in Reggio di Calabria zur Welt. Die süditalienische Stadt hat starke historische Bezüge zur griechischen Antike, deren Ornamentik Versaces spätere Entwürfe beeinflussen sollte. Von seiner Mutter, einer Damenschneiderin, lernte er früh das Nähen und ging 1973 nach Mailand, um eine Laufbahn in der Modebranche einzuschlagen. Zunächst arbeitete er fortlaufend für italienische Labels wie Callaghan und Complice, wobei er quer durch alle Marken eine Vielzahl an Linien entwarf. Schnell erntete Versace viel Lob, so von der *Women's Wear Daily*, die 1974 nicht nur seine modernen weiten Kleiderdesigns für Callaghan pries, sondern auch die Accessoires, etwa hochhackige Pumps und Ghillies. 1978 lancierte Versace zusammen mit seinem Bruder Santo eine eigene Prêt-à-porter-Linie. Zu diesem Zeitpunkt gab es in Italien neben Mailand noch zwei Modemetropolen, doch Versace und eine Reihe weiterer Designer wie Giorgio Armani, Gianfranco Ferré und Missoni verhalfen Mailand zum Aufstieg in den Rang der alleinigen Modehauptstadt. Gianni Versace designte bis zu seinem gewaltsamen Tod im Jahr 1997. Dann übernahm seine Schwester Donatella die Leitung des Labels. Sie hatte bereits häufig mit ihrem Bruder zusammengearbeitet und präsentierte nur zwölf Wochen nach dessen Tod ihre erste Kollektion. Für ihren eigenen Stil griff sie Aspekte seiner Designphilosophie auf und entwickelte die Versace-Ästhetik weiter. „Gianni war ein Genie. Er durchbrach Schranken", sagte sie der *GQ*. „Manche meinten, Giannis Mode sei vulgär … aber Frauen lieben sie nun mal, nicht weil sie Haut zeigte, sondern weil sie die Frauen stark machte. Er sagte ihnen, sie sollten keine Angst vor ihrer Sexualität haben." —*E.W.*

SEXY, AUDACIEUSES ET IMPERTINENTES, LES créations de Gianni Versace étaient inimitables. L'esthétique signature du couturier, décrite comme l'incarnation d'une « rencontre entre la jungle et la société de cour » dans *The New York Times*, misait sur les couleurs vives, le noir, le cuir, les sangles, les boucles et les touches de métal, à l'image de son logo doré à tête de Méduse et de ses clés grecques. Les chaussures Versace pour homme et pour femme présentaient des proportions élégantes. Souvent richement ornées, elles respiraient l'hédonisme et remettaient en question la notion de bon goût. Abondamment photographiées sur les top-modèles des années 1990, les collections sans cesse croissantes de la marque reflétaient son attrait international, tout comme ses boutiques.

Gianni Versace est né en 1946 à Reggio di Calabria en Italie, une ville historiquement associée à la Grèce antique dont les motifs devaient influencer ses créations futures. Il a appris à coudre très tôt auprès de sa mère couturière, puis s'est installé à Milan en 1973 pour se lancer dans la mode. Il a d'abord travaillé pour des griffes italiennes telles que Callaghan et Complice. Il créait en continu et produisait plusieurs lignes pour chaque marque. Il n'a pas tardé à se faire remarquer : en 1974, *Women's Wear Daily* a salué les vêtements modernes et non structurés qu'il concevait pour Callaghan, mais aussi ses accessoires, dont des escarpins à talons hauts et des ghillies. En 1978, Gianni Versace s'est associé avec son frère Santo pour lancer sa propre collection de prêt-à-porter.

À cette époque, Milan était l'une des trois villes d'Italie qui comptaient dans le domaine de la mode. Aux côtés d'autres créateurs de prêt-à-porter tels Giorgio Armani, Gianfranco Ferré et Missoni, Versace a contribué à réimposer la ville comme la seule et unique capitale de la mode italienne. Il a travaillé jusqu'à son assassinat en 1997. Sa sœur et collaboratrice régulière Donatella Versace a ensuite assumé la direction de la création de la griffe, présentant sa première collection douze semaines seulement après le décès de son frère. Son style, qui reprenait certains aspects de la philosophie créative de Gianni Versace, a également fait évoluer l'esthétique de la marque. « Gianni était un génie », a-t-elle confié à *GQ*. « Il a fait tomber des barrières. Certains trouvaient sa mode vulgaire… mais vous savez, si les femmes adorent ce que faisait Gianni, c'est parce qu'il leur donnait du pouvoir, pas parce que ses créations dévoilaient le corps. Il leur disait de ne pas avoir peur de leur sexualité. » —*E.W.*

"Versace posed and provoked the basic issues of fashion's role. Versace tantalized us with vulgarity.

— RICHARD MARTIN, CURATOR

"When Gianni started, fashion was about
being safe, being sophisticated. The word
glamour didn't exist. Gianni invented
glamour. It meant women not being afraid
to embrace femininity and sensuality.
I make sure glamour stays."

— DONATELLA VERSACE

Versace
Sling-back pumps: Black
silk satin, rhinestones,
gold metal medallions
and chains
Italy, 1992

Versace
Mule: Black leather,
gold metal studs and
medallions
Italy, fall 1992

Versace
Mules: Black silk twill,
rhinestones, gold metal
medallions
Italy, 1992

Roger Vivier

JUST AS CHRISTIAN DIOR DEFINED haute couture during the mid-twentieth century, Roger Vivier likewise epitomized the finest in Parisian footwear design. He was aptly called the "Fragonard of the Shoe" and the "Fabergé of Footwear." Opulent, extravagant, and richly ornamented, Vivier's sculpted shoes were also inventive, modernist creations.

A native Parisian, Roger Henri Vivier was born in 1913. In 1924 he began studying sculpture at the École des Beaux-Arts, leaving school two years later to begin a shoe-making apprenticeship. Because of his fascination with theater and music halls, Vivier also began designing stage sets, in the process meeting legendary performers Josephine Baker and Mistinguett, for whom he created custom-made shoes. By 1937 Vivier opened his first shoe boutique on rue Royale in Paris. In 1938 Vivier made his couture debut, creating bold platforms for Elsa Schiaparelli. He designed for Christian Dior starting in 1947, the year of Dior's *New Look* collection. For the next decade, their collaboration marked a golden age in modern shoe design. Vivier "invented" the stiletto in 1954, and the following year his name appeared alongside Dior's on the house's shoe labels. Like the couturier, Vivier used the richest fabrics and an array of luxe trimmings.

After Dior's death in 1957, Vivier continued to design for the house until 1963, the year he created the sinuous "Virgule," or "comma" heel. During the 1960s, he made an array of fashion boots and buckled Pilgrim pumps worn by Catherine Deneuve in the film *Belle de Jour*. Even after his passing in 1998, the company still produced this shoe as well as newer creations by later creative directors such as Bruno Frisoni. —*P.M.*

de haut en bas : une mule en satin tilleul à
shantung rose et broderie anglaise de raphia ;
Vivier pour Christian Dior. Coiffure Carita.

A transparent and
orange plastic striped
boot with a back zipper.
1966.

Known as the
"Fragonard of the Shoe,"
Roger Vivier designed
for Christian Dior from
the 1940s to the 1960s.
Advertisement from
1959–60.

**Christian Dior
(Roger Vivier)**
Pumps: Taupe lizard,
orange silk grosgrain
France, *ca.* 1957

SO WIE CHRISTIAN DIOR ZUR Mitte des 20. Jahrhunderts die Haute Couture prägte, wurde Roger Vivier zum Inbegriff für feinste Pariser Schuhmode und nicht zu Unrecht als „Fragonard des Schuhs" und „Fabergé der Fußbekleidung" bezeichnet. Seine formschönen Schöpfungen waren opulent, extravagant und reich verziert, doch zugleich einfallsreich modern.

Roger Henri Vivier, geboren 1907 in Paris, studierte zwei Jahre lang Bildhauerei an der École des Beaux-Arts, um 1926 in eine Schuhmacherlehre zu wechseln. Fasziniert von Theater und Varietés, begann er zudem, Bühnenbilder zu entwerfen, und lernte dabei die legendären Künstlerinnen Josephine Baker und Mistinguett kennen. Für beide fertigte Vivier Schuhe nach Maß und eröffnete 1937 schließlich seinen ersten Schuhsalon in der Pariser Rue Royale. Im Jahr darauf gab er mit kühnen Plateauschuhen, entworfen für Elsa Schiaparelli, sein Couture-Debüt. Viviers Zusammenarbeit mit

Christian Dior begann 1947 – dem Entstehungsjahr von Diors *New Look*-Kollektion. Das folgende Jahrzehnt markierte ein goldenes Zeitalter im modernen Schuhdesign. 1954 „erfand" Vivier den Stiletto, und ab dem folgenden Jahr trug das Schuhlabel des Hauses Dior auch seinen Namen. Genau wie Dior verwendete Vivier die hochwertigsten Materialien und verzierte die Schuhe mit kostbarem Besatz.

Nach Diors Tod 1957 hielt Vivier dem Haus noch bis 1963 die Treue und kreierte in diesem letzten Jahr den gebogenen „Virgule"- oder auch „Komma"-Absatz. Im Lauf der 1960er-Jahre entwarf er eine Vielzahl modischer Stiefel und jene „Pilgrim"-Pumps mit Schnalle, die Catherine Deneuve in dem Film *Belle de Jour* trug. Selbst nach Viviers Tod 1998 wurde dieser Schuh weiter unter seinem Label produziert, ebenso wie neuere Kreationen von nachfolgenden Designern wie Bruno Frisoni. —*P.M.*

TOUT COMME CHRISTIAN DIOR A défini la haute couture du milieu du XXᵉ siècle, Roger Vivier incarnait l'élite des chausseurs parisiens. C'est à juste titre qu'on le surnommait « le Fragonard de la chaussure » et qu'on qualifiait ses souliers de « Fabergé ». Somptueuses, extravagantes et richement ornées, ses chaussures sculpturales étaient aussi des créations modernistes pleines d'inventivité.

Roger Henri Vivier est né en 1907 à Paris. En 1924, il a entamé des études de sculpture à l'École des beaux-arts, qu'il a quittée deux ans plus tard pour se lancer dans un apprentissage en cordonnerie. Sa fascination pour le théâtre et le cabaret l'a aussi amené à concevoir des décors. Cette expérience lui a permis de rencontrer les légendaires meneuses de revue Josephine Baker et Mistinguett pour lesquelles il a créé des chaussures sur mesure. En 1937, il a ouvert sa première boutique rue Royale à Paris. En 1938, il a fait ses débuts dans la haute couture en créant d'audacieux modèles à semelles compensées pour Elsa Schiaparelli. Il a commencé à travailler pour Christian Dior en 1947, année de la collection New Look du couturier. Pendant dix ans, leur collaboration marquera un âge d'or de l'histoire moderne de la chaussure. Vivier a « inventé » le talon aiguille en 1954, et l'année suivante, son nom est apparu à côté de celui de Dior sur les étiquettes des souliers de la Maison. À l'instar du couturier, Vivier utilisait les tissus les plus chers et toutes sortes de détails décoratifs de luxe.

Après la mort de Dior en 1957, il a continué à créer pour la Maison jusqu'en 1963, année où il a inventé le talon sinueux Virgule. Dans les années 1960, il a créé une série de bottes tendance et d'escarpins ornés d'une large boucle en métal immortalisés par Catherine Deneuve dans le film *Belle de jour*. Après son décès en 1998, son entreprise a continué à produire ces escarpins, mais aussi de nouveaux modèles conçus par les directeurs de la création qui lui ont succédé, notamment Bruno Frisoni. —*P.M.*

Roger Vivier
Sandal: White leather
France, 1970

Roger Vivier
Pumps: Off-white
patent leather, black
plastic buckle
France, *ca.* 1967

Roger Vivier
Wedges: Rust kid,
brown suede
France, 1944–45

Roger Vivier
Pump: Fuchsia-and-
black printed silk
France, 1985–88

**Christian Dior
(Roger Vivier)**
Pumps: Pink satin,
rhinestones
France, 1955–57

Roger Vivier
Pumps: Gold-and-silver
metallic brocade
France, 1963–64

**Christian Dior
(Roger Vivier)**
Pump: Green, purple,
turquoise warp-print silk
France, *ca.* 1957

PREVIOUS
Agnès B. (Roger Vivier)
Pumps: Black crepe,
amber resin
France, 1996

Roger Vivier
"Sexy Choc" pumps:
Red silk satin,
rhinestones
France, spring 2016

**Roger Vivier
(Bruno Frisoni)**
"Sandal Sin Rose 'n
Roll" sandal: Denim,
black leather
France, spring 2017

"It is safe to say that
what Harry Winston is
to fine jewelry, Roger
Vivier is to the business
of shoe design."

— JEFFREY FELNER, WRITER

**Roger Vivier
(Bruno Frisoni)**
"Bootie Sphere Cage
Tiger" boots: Black silk
satin, beads, sequins,
pavé rhinestones
France, spring 2017

**Roger Vivier
(Bruno Frisoni)**
"Bootie Sphere Diamond
Cut" ankle boots:
Black-and-off-white
leather, silver metal
France, fall 2016

**Roger Vivier
(Bruno Frisoni)**
"d'Orsay Sphere
Frilly" heel: Laminated
lambskin leather, pavé
rhinestones
France, fall 2016

Vivienne Westwood

VIVIENNE WESTWOOD STARTED A BUSINESS with then-partner Malcolm McLaren in 1971, initially selling new and used clothes in the 1950s "Teddy Boy" style, as well as fetish-inspired gear. Their wares were marketed in response to the commercialized "flower power" movement that dominated the early 1970s. The success of their subversive styles took Westwood by surprise: "I did not yet regard myself as a fashion designer at that time," she recalled. "We were looking for motifs of rebellion to shock the establishment. The result was punk." Her first catwalk show in 1981 repositioned Westwood into the world of high fashion.

Vivienne Westwood (1941–2022)

Shoes have always played an integral role in Westwood's design aesthetic. Her fall 1982 collection, entitled *Nostalgia of Mud*, included the "Buffalo Sack" boot, a slouchy, flat-soled style made from distressed leather and suede. For the spring 1985 *Mini-Crini* collection, she introduced her "Rocking Horse" platform shoes. Paired with short hooped skirts, Westwood intended the rocking motion created by the shoes to enhance the sway of the garments when the wearer walked.

During the runway presentation for the fall 1993 *Anglomania* collection, supermodel Naomi Campbell famously fell while walking in Westwood's latest style, known as the "Super Elevated" platform shoes. Made from bright-blue imitation crocodile leather, the shoes were 12 inches tall. Her comparatively more wearable version, the "Elevated" platform, measures just over six inches tall. For the fall 1994 Westwood collection *On Liberty*, she continued to design exceptionally high concealed platforms, which were specifically intended to alter the wearer's posture. According to fashion curator Claire Wilcox, "[her] platform shoes began to be acquired by various enthusiasts, not always to wear, but as sculptural objects in their own right." —*M.M.*

Vivienne Westwood
"Elevated Court" pump:
Black patent leather
England, fall 1990

Vivienne Westwood's
nonconformist designs
famously inspired 1970s
punk fashions. Pictured
at London Fashion Week
in 1987, models parade
in burlesque dresses,
hats, and wooden plat-
forms by the designer.

Vivienne Westwood
"Rocking Horse"
shoes: Black leather,
natural wood
England, fall 1987

VIVIENNE WESTWOOD ERÖFFNETE 1971 MIT ihrem damaligen Partner Malcolm McLaren einen Laden, in dem sie anfangs neue und gebrauchte Kleidung im „Teddy Boy"-Stil der 1950er-Jahre sowie Fetischartikel verkaufte. Dieses Sortiment war ihre Reaktion auf den Kommerz der Flower-Power-Bewegung, die die frühen 70er-Jahre dominierte. Der Erfolg ihrer subversiven Mode überraschte Westwood: „Ich selbst sah mich damals noch nicht als Modedesignerin", so ihre Erinnerung. „Wir suchten einfach nach rebellischen Motiven, um das Establishment zu schocken. Das Ergebnis war Punk." Doch ihre erste Laufstegschau 1981 beförderte Westwood in höhere Modesphären.

Schuhe spielen in Westwoods Designästhetik von jeher eine elementare Rolle. Bestandteil ihrer Herbstkollektion 1982, *Nostalgia of Mud*, war der zerknautschte „Buffalo Sack", ein flacher Stiefel aus speckigem Glatt- und Wildleder. Bei *Mini-Crini*, ihrer Frühjahrskollektion 1985, kombinierte sie kurze Reifröcke mit dem Plateauschuh „Rocking Horse" (Schaukelpferd) in der Absicht, durch den wiegenden Gang, den dieser Schuh bewirkte, das Schwingen der Kleidung zu verstärken.

Für Schlagzeilen sorgten ihre „Super Elevated"-Plateauschuhe, als sie bei der Präsentation der *Anglomania*-Herbstkollektion 1993 das Supermodel Naomi Campbell zu Fall brachten. Die Kreation aus leuchtend blauem Krokodilleder-Imitat war gut 30 cm hoch. „Elevated", ein weiteres Modell, war mit gut 15 cm vergleichsweise tragbar. Auch für *On Liberty*, ihre Herbstkollektion 1994, entwarf Westwood Schuhe mit ausnehmend hohem, verstecktem Plateau, die gezielt die Haltung der Trägerin verändern sollten. Der Modekuratorin Claire Wilcox zufolge „wurden [ihre] Plateauschuhe zunehmend von verschiedensten Schuhliebhabern erworben, nicht immer zum Tragen, sondern als eigenständige skulpturale Objekte." *–M.M.*

EN 1971, VIVIENNE WESTWOOD A OUVERT une boutique avec Malcolm McLaren, son compagnon de l'époque, pour vendre des vêtements neufs et d'occasion dans le style Teddy Boys des années 1950, ainsi que des tenues d'inspiration fétichiste. Ils opéraient leur sélection en réaction à la commercialisation du Flower Power qui dominait le début des années 1970. Le succès de leurs vêtements subversifs a pris Vivienne Westwood par surprise : « À l'époque, je ne me considérais pas encore comme une créatrice de mode. Nous cherchions des symboles de rébellion pour choquer l'establishment. C'est ainsi qu'est né le style punk. » Son premier défilé en 1981 l'a néanmoins positionnée dans l'univers de la mode de luxe.

Les chaussures ont toujours fait partie intégrante de l'esthétique créative de Vivienne Westwood. Intitulée Nostalgia of Mud, sa collection de l'automne 1982 présentait la botte Buffalo Sack, un modèle souple à talon plat créé à partir de cuir et de daim usé. Dans la collection Mini-Crini du printemps 1985, elle a introduit ses souliers compensés Rocking Horse à porter avec des mini-jupes à crinoline : la créatrice voulait que le mouvement de bascule créé par les chaussures accentue l'oscillation fluide des vêtements pendant la marche.

Lors du défilé de la collection Anglomania à l'automne 1993, la top-modèle Naomi Campbell a fait une célèbre chute avec les Super Elevated aux pieds, nouvelles créations à semelles compensées de Vivienne Westwood. Habillées d'un faux cuir de crocodile bleu vif, elles culminaient à 30 centimètres de hauteur. Leur version relativement plus facile à porter, le modèle Elevated, mesure un peu de plus 15 centimètres de haut. Pour la collection On Liberty de l'automne 1994, elle a continué à créer des modèles à semelles compensées cachées d'une hauteur vertigineuse spécialement conçus pour modifier la posture. Selon la commissaire d'expositions de mode Claire Wilcox, « toutes sortes d'admiratrices ont commencé à acheter [ses] chaussures compensées, pas toujours pour les porter, mais comme des objets sculpturaux à part entière ». —M.M.

Vivienne Westwood
"Rocking Horse"
boots: Black leather,
natural wood
England, 1987

Vivienne Westwood
"Buffalo Sack" boots:
Brown mottled leather
and suede
England, fall 1982–83

Vivienne Westwood
Pumps: Gold leather,
metal
England, fall 1994–95

Vivienne Westwood
Mules: Black leather
England, spring 2000

FOLLOWING
Vivienne Westwood
"Elevated" pumps:
Tartan silk twill,
black patent leather
England, fall 1993

Giuseppe Zanotti

GIUSEPPE ZANOTTI WAS BORN IN the Italian village of San Mauro Pascoli, an area known for its shoemaking traditions. After an unsuccessful career as a radio DJ, Zanotti turned to shoe manufacturing as an alternate outlet for his creativity. He began to work as a free-lance designer for various fashion houses, including Roberto Cavalli, Christian Dior, Gianfranco Ferré, and Valentino. In 1994 he established his own high-end label.

Zanotti had been in and out of footwear factories since the age of 11, and he was familiar with the shoemakers working in his native village. He acquired Vicini, a small shoe factory located there. While working under his own label, Zanotti created shoes for Balmain, Dsquared2, and Proenza Schouler. Zanotti opened his first fashion store in Milan in 2000, and two years later opened his first store in the United States, located on Madison Avenue in New York. Zanotti introduced his line of luxury sneakers in 2010, blending street style with high-fashion embellishments. He has since become a leader in the luxury sneaker market. Often inspired by hip-hop, he collaborates with multiple musicians, including Beyoncé, Jennifer Lopez, Rihanna, and Kanye West.

Giuseppe Zanotti (b. 1957)

What initially began as an Italian footwear brand has now expanded globally, currently producing bags, jewelry, men's shoes, and ready-to-wear clothing. Looking back at the more than 20 years of his brand, Zanotti stated, "You cannot design shoes if you only think about fashion, it's too realistic. When I design, I dream." —*M.M.*

PREVIOUS
Giuseppe Zanotti
Evening sandal:
Pink leather, silk
Italy, 2003

Giuseppe Zanotti's
designs are handcrafted
in Emilia-Romagna,
Italy. A 2020 watercolor
for a stiletto sandal
features red floral
ornamentation and
ankle straps.

Giuseppe Zanotti
Evening sandal: Gold
leather, metal chains
Italy, 2003

GIUSEPPE ZANOTTI, GEBOREN IM italienischen San Mauro Pascoli, stammt aus einer für ihre Schuhmachertradition bekannten Region. Nachdem er zunächst als Radio-DJ experimentiert hatte, fand Zanotti in der Schuhmacherei ein neues Ventil für seine Kreativität. Anfangs arbeitete er als freier Designer für verschiedene Modehäuser wie Roberto Cavalli, Christian Dior, Gianfranco Ferré und Valentino, um 1994 sein eigenes Luxuslabel zu gründen.

Zanotti, der schon als Junge immer wieder in Schuhfabriken gearbeitet hatte und mit den Schuhmachern seines Heimatdorfs bekannt war, erwarb dort eine kleine Schuhfabrik, Vicini. Während er für seine eigene Firma arbeitete, entwarf Zanotti Schuhe unter anderem für Balmain, Dsquared2 und Proenza Schouler. Auf die Eröffnung seines ersten Modegeschäfts in Mailand im Jahr 2000 folgte zwei Jahre später die erste US-Dependance in der New Yorker Madison Avenue. 2010 stellte Zanotti seine eigene Edel-Sneaker-Linie vor, in der sich Streetstyle und Elemente aus der Haute Couture mischen. Häufig arbeitet er dabei, vom Hip-Hop inspiriert, mit Künstlern wie Beyoncé, Jennifer Lopez, Rihanna und Kanye West zusammen.

Was als italienisches Schuhlabel begann, hat sich zu einer globalen Marke entwickelt, die heute Taschen, Schmuck, Herrenschuhe und Prêt-à-porter-Mode umfasst. Mit Blick auf seine mehr als 20-jährige Firmengeschichte stellte Zanotti fest: „Man kann keine Schuhe entwerfen, wenn man nur an die Mode denkt, das ist zu realistisch. Wenn ich entwerfe, träume ich." —*M.M.*

GIUSEPPE ZANOTTI EST NÉ à San Mauro Pascoli, un village italien situé dans une région traditionnellement réputée pour son savoir-faire cordonnier. Après une expérience de DJ à la radio, il s'est tourné vers la fabrication de chaussures pour exprimer sa créativité. Il a d'abord travaillé en freelance pour différentes Maisons de mode, notamment Roberto Cavalli, Christian Dior, Gianfranco Ferré et Valentino, avant de créer sa propre marque de luxe en 1994.

Comme Giuseppe Zanotti travaillait par intermittence dans les usines de chaussures depuis son plus jeune âge, il connaissait tous les cordonniers de son village natal. C'est là qu'il a acheté la petite manufacture de souliers Vicini. Il créait notamment des modèles pour Balmain, Dsquared2 et Proenza Schouler tout en travaillant pour sa propre griffe. En 2000, il a ouvert sa première boutique à Milan, suivie deux ans plus tard par un premier magasin aux États-Unis sur Madison Avenue à New York. En 2010, Zanotti a lancé une collection de sneakers mêlant *street style* et ornementations issues de la mode haut de gamme. Depuis, il s'est imposé comme l'un des leaders du marché des baskets de luxe. Souvent inspiré par le hip-hop, il collabore avec de nombreux musiciens, dont Beyoncé, Jennifer Lopez, Rihanna et Kanye West.

Ce qui avait commencé comme une marque de chaussures italienne est aujourd'hui une entreprise internationale qui produit également des sacs, des bijoux, des souliers pour homme et du prêt-à-porter. « Je ne peux pas créer de chaussures en ne pensant qu'à la mode : c'est trop réaliste », a un jour déclaré Zanotti alors qu'il évoquait la vingtaine d'années d'existence de sa marque. « Quand je crée, je rêve. » —*M.M.*

A Walk Through Time

Text by Colleen Hill

audree

a new shoe.....in a new colour
"*sonora*"
....a shade that's more rose than beige
18.50

SAKS ~ FIFTH AVENUE
FORTY-NINTH to FIFTIETH STREET, NEW YORK

1600s–1800s

MEN IN HEELS

These men's shoes are the earliest example of footwear in The Museum at FIT collection. They exemplify the high heels favored by upper-class men in Western Europe from the late sixteenth century until the early eighteenth century. The stacked heels and square toes are typical of seventeenth-century footwear styles, as are the open sides, which were meant to highlight trim ankles and expensive hose. The shoes also feature red soles and heels. High heels — particularly those colored red — are indelibly associated with Louis XIV and his court, and a desire for red heels spread throughout Europe. Red pigment was costly, and the eye-catching color signaled the wearer's status.

ENGLISH PRACTICALITY

High-heeled shoes had fallen out of favor with men by the 1740s, but they remained fashionable for women. English shoes from the early to mid-eighteenth century were characterized by their low, sturdy heels, which differed from the French fashion for higher and narrower heel styles. Many upper-class English women resided at estates in the countryside, requiring heels that would not sink easily into the dirt. The practical heel of this example is contrasted by its fabric, a costly and easily soiled silk brocade.

PREVIOUS
A 1927 Saks Fifth Avenue advertisement for Fenton's "Sonora" heel, illustrated by Raymond Loewy.

Men's shoes: Black leather, red painted leather, green silk
Europe, 1640–70

Shoes: Green silk damask and natural linen, England, 1740–45
Buckles: Silver metal and paste
England, early to mid-eighteenth century

Shoes: Ivory silk brocade, silver metal and paste buckles
England, 1775–80

Shoe: Black-and-pale blue leather
England, *ca.* 1800

A TIPTOEING GAIT

Heavy English heels were replaced by higher, more delicate styles by the 1770s. Such designs would have necessitated a tiptoeing gait. Silk brocades in neutral hues or plain satin fabrics had eclipsed the earlier fashion for brightly colored damasks. The fashion for slightly raised petticoats made shoes more visible, but only the most formal occasions required footwear to match a gown. Buckles were introduced during the seventeenth century and initially served a purely functional role. Yet they soon became as decorative as they were useful, often utilizing sparkling stones made from paste or, for the very wealthy, real gemstones.

SENSIBLE SOLES

The impracticality of high heels meant that they were closely associated with the aristocracy. By the late eighteenth century, the fall of the ancien régime in France — and with it, the turn toward a more sensible, egalitarian way of dressing — had resulted in a fashion for flat-soled shoes throughout Europe and North America. Yet even when such shoes were made from durable leather, practicality did not necessarily preclude ornamentation. This style, with insets of pale blue leather, was likely intended for wear with stockings of the same hue. They would have provided the illusion of provocative cutouts while maintaining the wearer's propriety.

1800s

NEOCLASSICAL MOTIFS

The excavation of ancient Roman ruins began in 1738 and awakened interest in classical ideals. Enthusiasm for classicism continued into the early nineteenth century, where it also found expression in fashion. Here, myrtle leaf embroidery — a popular neoclassical motif — emphasizes the period's idealization of antiquity. The myrtle leaf was favored by French Emperor Napoleon Bonaparte, and it was used to decorate his palace following his coronation in 1804. Flat-soled shoes predominated during this era, and the pale yellow leather used to make this example may have been chosen to match other accessories such as a hat or gloves.

THE RED SHOES

The simple design of these shoes — already known as "flats" by the early nineteenth century — belies their role as early nineteenth-century status objects. They are made from Morocco leather, a goatskin that was both supple and durable. Frequently used for footwear and bookbinding, Morocco leather was often tanned black. Made prior to the introduction of chemical dyes in the 1850s, the flats' brilliant red hue would have been both difficult and expensive to achieve. Hans Christian Andersen cited red Morocco leather shoes as a coveted luxury item in his 1845 tale "The Red Shoes."

Shoes: Yellow leather,
gilt embroidery, and gold
metal sequins
France, *ca.* 1808

Shoes: Red Morocco
leather and velvet
England or France,
1800–10

Slippers: Brown glazed
kid leather, pink silk
France, late 1850s–60s

Boots: Black satin
USA, 1860s

CHAMELEON SLIPPERS

These delicate shoes, with their floral-patterned cutouts over the vamp and hand-embroidered stitching, were not meant to be worn outdoors. They would have been paired with a morning dress or a wrapper, both of which were casual garments worn at home. These shoe designs were sometimes referred to as "chameleon" slippers, since they were produced with underlays in a range of vibrant colors to match the wearer's clothing. The pink used for this example was perhaps the most common shade, but examples using silks in blue, green, or red were also prevalent.

BUTTONED-UP BEAUTY

Women's boots had become fashionable by the mid-nineteenth century, and they were available in a variety of styles. This pair exemplifies the button boot, a popular, fitted design that rose just over the ankle and featured scalloped edging around the buttonholes. The buttons required a hook to be fastened — a task that was performed by a maid for wealthy women. The placement of the heel toward the instep created the illusion of a smaller foot, which was an element of the idealized fashionable female body during the nineteenth century.

1890s–1900s

UNUSUAL OXFORDS

Oxford shoes were part of a movement toward more functional women's footwear at the end of the nineteenth century. This example, though typical in silhouette, is remarkable in other ways. Metallic leathers were not common until the 1920s, and the gold hue indicates that the otherwise sensible style was worn in the evening. The shoes were sold at Alfred J. Cammeyer, a prominent, New York–based retailer that specialized in footwear. By the 1860s the United States was known as a leader in the manufacture and marketing of high-quality, ready-made shoes.

EGYPTIAN ELEGANCE

These elegant evening shoes bear an unusual label: "L. Juster, Le Caire, Rue Mousky." Of French or possibly Belgian origin, they were sold in Cairo and underscore the increasingly global reach of European fashion styles by the late nineteenth century. A Belgian commerce report from 1899 stated that Egyptians preferred shoes that were stylish and well-priced, but that the country lacked the factories to mass produce footwear. As the cultural climate of Egypt shifted during this time period, its major cities began to offer more European goods — including shoes — and many upper-class women in Egypt were keen to adopt the latest fashions.

Alfred J. Cammeyer
Evening shoes: Gold
metallic kid leather
USA, *ca.* 1891

L. Juster
Evening shoe: Ivory
satin, silver metallic
thread, and silver beads
French or Belgian (for
export), 1890s

Alfred J. Cammeyer
Boots: Brown corduroy
and leather
USA, *ca.* 1898

Jack Jacobus
Boots: Black-and-brown
leather, red silk
Austria, 1895–1900

WHEELWOMEN ON THE MOVE

These boots were probably worn as part of a woman's bicycling ensemble. Cycling became a popular pastime for women during the late nineteenth century, and it was praised for its health benefits. The sport required specialized attire that allowed for greater freedom of movement while maintaining propriety. Bifurcated garments with hemlines that grazed the mid-calf were ideal, and high boots offered both protection and concealment of a woman's legs. By the turn of the century, however, *The New York Times* reported that wheelwomen found such boots too clumsy. Instead, they were beginning to favor heavy golf stockings worn with regular leather shoes.

A SUGGESTION OF SEDUCTION

As women began to lead more active lives during the late nineteenth century, the high-button walking boot evolved into an essential element of dress. Made from plain black or brown leather with a sturdy heel, the boots were significantly more durable than slippers made from thin leather or silk. This particular style, however — with its high, curved heel, tightly fitted ankle, and scarlet lining — is more seductive and daring than it is practical. The boots were hand-sewn in Vienna but sold at Jack Jacobus in London, a prominent retailer who later supplied shoes for Queen Elizabeth the Queen Mother.

1900s–1910s

EVENING EXTRAVAGANCE

Evening shoes with bows at the throat were fashionable from the 1880s to the end of the century. The bows' dainty design was often enhanced by beading and paired with still more beading over the vamp. The Monquignon shop was prominently located on the Rue Saint-Honoré in Paris, and the high, curved heel and slightly upturned toe is typical of French high fashion at the turn of the century. While there are several other examples of Monquignon shoes featuring lavish beadwork or embroidery in museum collections, little is known about their maker.

ECHOES OF THE EIGHTEENTH CENTURY

The heeled, slip-on shoe is known as a "pump" in the United States and a "court shoe" in Britain. It became a prevalent style in women's dress during the early twentieth century. Historic revivals were common in fashion at this time, and the choice of brocaded fabric, rhinestone buckles, and curved "Louis" heel deliberately echoed the eighteenth century. This style was sold at Peter Yapp Ltd., a prominent, London-based shoemaker whose finely crafted styles were worn by the royal court. In addition to its own designs, the company sold styles imported from France.

Monquignon
Evening shoes:
Black satin, metal
beads, sequins
France, *ca.* 1900

Peter Yapp
Evening pumps: Pale
blue brocaded silk,
metal, rhinestones
England, *ca.* 1910

Walk-Over
Shoes: Black leather
and tan suede
USA, *ca.* 1912

J & J Slater
Tango boot: Black
silk satin
USA, *ca.* 1914

STYLISH AND SENSIBLE

By the late nineteenth century, a variety of practical shoe styles were introduced to address concerns over the health of women's feet. While these were often plainly designed, the aptly named Walk-Over shoes company specialized in styles that were sensible and stylish. The brand advertised its ethos in a 1912 advertisement, emphasizing that "Women who wear Walk-Over shoes know real comfort and real style." The company had stores in major cities across the United States and Europe. In 1933 Elsa Schiaparelli chose Walk-Over shoes to pair with a selection of sporty styles from her new couture collection.

TANGO FEVER

The craze for tango dancing developed during the early twentieth century, when dancers and musicians began to travel from Argentina to Europe to showcase their talents. The dance had taken off in the United States by 1913. Tango fashions included specially marketed women's gowns and men's suits, but footwear for women was especially important. The laced fastenings that characterized tango shoes ensured their snug fit, and they revealed hosiery. Both sheer and brightly colored stockings were fashionable. A 1913 editorial in *Women's Wear Daily* described a pair of black satin tango shoes worn over a pair of "American Beauty" rose-red stockings.

1910s–1920s

A POIRET FANTASY

Paul Poiret began promoting his flat-heeled "Russian" boots in 1913. The style was named for its similarities to Russian military footwear. The lambskin pair, made by the Parisian bootmaker Favereau, was part of the personal wardrobe of Poiret's wife and muse, Denise. A 1915 *New York Times* article mentioned that the boots were initially viewed as a "Poiret fantasy," but they had since found their place in fashion. "There were never such high boots and such short skirts as now," the article explained, describing newly risen hemlines that were as short as 12 inches from the floor.

STURDY IN THE SNOW

Wanamaker's boots are the successor to a style introduced during the mid-nineteenth century, known as a "carriage boot." The fur-trimmed boots were originally designed to be slipped over a woman's shoes, helping to keep her feet warm during travel. Early examples were typically made from velvet and did not have a sturdy sole, which limited their functionality. By the 1920s more practical styles, made from more durable leather, were worn on their own. Rubber galoshes were also fashionable and, when worn unbuckled, made a flapping sound from which the 1920s "flapper" archetype may have taken her name.

**Favereau for
Paul Poiret**
Boots: Olive lambskin
France, *ca.* 1918

John Wanamaker
Boot: Black leather,
brown fur
USA, *ca.* 1922

Pumps: Multicolor
ombré silk, blue stones
USA, *ca.* 1920

Grand Luxe
Mules: Green-and-
metallic gold brocade
silk, purple silk
France, *ca.* 1920

OMBRÉ OPULENCE

As hemlines rose during the 1910s, shoes became much more visible — and as a result, much more colorful and decorative. While the curved "Louis" heel and slightly pointed toe are typical of the early 1920s, the ombré effect of the dyed silk — which gradually transforms from blue at the toe to fuchsia at the heel — is unusual. It is possible that the shoes were purchased to coordinate with multiple evening gowns. By around 1924, the fashion for the slip-on pump was eclipsed by the "bar" shoe, which featured a strap over the instep.

AT-HOME ATTIRE

Boudoir mules are an elegant form of house slippers characterized by their high heels, luxurious fabrics, and ornate embellishments. During the early 1920s, they were paired with new types of at-home attire, including lounging pajamas and smoking ensembles. Boudoir slippers made frequent appearances in fashion magazines, which often suggested the most luxurious examples to be included in a trousseau or given as a gift. This pair, bearing the label "Grand Luxe," originates from a shop on the Boulevard de la Madeleine in Paris.

1920s–
1930s

BEACH DRESS DECORUM

Specialized bathing shoes proliferated during the early twentieth century, as beach-going became a more popular pastime. Their materials were generally not waterproof, but rubber soles enabled walking over sand and stones. Beach-dress decorum was a much-debated topic as bathing costumes became increasingly revealing. In 1922 an American woman described her beach ensemble: "It's made of taffeta, with an artfully fitted waist, a perky little skirt and ruffled knickers peeping out from under it ... I had silk stockings, of course, and satin bathing boots lacing up almost to the knee." While her attire was appropriate on American beaches, she reported that she was embarrassingly overdressed in Britain.

STREAMLINED IN SILVER

Hellstern and Sons was a prominent shoe-maker established during the early 1870s in Paris. First specializing in men's footwear, the company had begun to focus on women's shoes by the early twentieth century. The streamlined silver pumps are an uncharacteristically subdued style for the label, which is best known for its lavish embellishments and vibrant materials. The predominant fashion for shoes with ankle straps was challenged by the late 1920s as strapless shoes provided the appearance of a longer leg. The prominent vertical top-stitching of the design would have heightened the effect of an uninterrupted line from toe to hemline.

Bathing boots:
Green satin, rubber
USA, *ca.* 1922

Hellstern and Sons
Pumps: Metallic silver
leather
France, *ca.* 1928

Fenton Footwear
Evening shoes: Pink silk
faille, gold-and-silver
metallic leather
USA, *ca.* 1933

Frank Brothers
Evening sandals: Olive
and red silk brocade,
gold metallic leather
USA, *ca.* 1932

MODERN RESTRAINT

Shoes from the 1930s often featured a modern, streamlined aesthetic that was enhanced by restrained surface decoration. Narrow strips of metallic gold and silver leather on Fenton's pink heels fan out to accentuate the silhouette of the shoe and draw attention to its cutouts. *Vogue* featured a similar style in its September 15, 1933, issue, where it was described as "festive and restrained at the same time." Fenton Footwear was sold at Saks Fifth Avenue and advertised as a label that offered a high-fashion look at a moderate price. The brand sometimes adapted designs from pre-eminent French shoemakers such as André Perugia.

PROVOCATIVE PEEP-TOES

Advances in footwear manufacturing during the 1930s resulted in more innovative styles. These evening sandals feature multiple cutouts, delicately trimmed in gold leather. Even beneath the long hemlines of 1930s evening gowns, the design would have offered a provocative glimpse of the wearer's toes. As stockings were still an essential part of sartorial decorum, some manufacturers began to market hosiery with less reinforcement at the toe. Lighter stockings looked less unsightly with open shoes and also allowed newly fashionable painted toenails to be visible.

1930s–1940s

PLATFORMS FOR THE BEACH

The fashion for beach sandals developed during the late 1920s. Early styles typically featured a short, sturdy heel. The heel height of beach sandals gradually became more exaggerated during the 1930s, evidenced by this example with a four-inch heel. Although the design appears difficult to walk in, the rocking motion created by the "toe spring" — the upward curvature of the sole toward the toes — would have offered mobility. Platform soles originated for beach shoes, but they had been widely adapted for many types of women's footwear by the end of the 1930s.

COMFORT AND CUTOUTS

Oxford pumps were a ubiquitous 1930s style that were marketed for their qualities of comfort and practicality. Many examples were made in black or brown leather with little embellishment, yet some styles were more daring, exemplified by Napiers' iteration made from crisscrossed bands of material. While the cutouts over the toes and around the vamp were more commonly seen on evening shoes, the use of natural linen and leather clearly indicate that this style was meant to be worn during the day — perhaps paired with a tailored suit.

Beach sandal:
Natural wood, red elastic
USA, 1938–40

I. Miller
Sandals: Pink leather
USA, *ca.* 1939

Napiers
Oxford pumps:
Tan linen, brown leather
USA, *ca.* 1935

**Debutante Fashions
(Saks Fifth Avenue)**
Wedge-heeled pump:
Black suede, red leather
USA, *ca.* 1940

DESIGNED FOR DANCING

The slogan for New York–based footwear manufacturer I. Miller was, quite simply, "beautiful shoes." Polish-born founder Israel Miller moved from London to New York in the 1890s and initially made shoes for dancers and actors before expanding his designs to include high-fashion footwear. This style may have been worn for dancing and features an intriguing fusion of design elements. Alluring cutouts are combined with sporty, nonfunctional front lacing, and the vibrant pink leather is perforated over the vamp. I. Miller shoes boasted practicality as well as beauty, and its line of "airy" shoes made from perforated leather was advertised as early as 1932.

INVISIBLE WEDGES

"Novelty reaches a new high in styles shown for fall; arches emphasized," declared a *Women's Wear Daily* article in 1940. It included two sketches of shoes with cutout heels, described as "invisible wedges." Wedge heels had been popularized by Salvatore Ferragamo several years before, and they offered height and stability. This example, though seemingly precarious, includes a metal shank under the arch that provides support. While Saks' peep-toe take and those described in the article were made from suede — a material most commonly used for dressy daytime or cocktail shoes — the newspaper emphasized that the style was best suited for eveningwear.

1930s– 1940s

MODERN-DAY CHOPINES

These sandals resemble a modern-day version of chopines, a style of platform shoe worn in Europe from the fourteenth to the mid-seventeenth centuries. They were intended to raise their wearers above the dust and mud of city streets and could reach up to an astounding 20 inches in height. This 1940s design, measuring nearly five inches tall, is more novel than it is functional. It was created by Bernard Rudofsky, a designer, writer, architect, and teacher. Rudofsky was an outspoken critic of fashion whose later work focused on creating functional "reform" shoes — a far cry from this exaggerated style, which he made while working in Brazil.

A FLEETING TREND

Although fashion boots had largely fallen out of favor by around 1920, there was a short-lived fad for ankle booties beginning around 1936. Elsa Schiaparelli introduced booties for day and evening, made from materials such as striped red satin, leopard skin, and black suede trimmed with monkey fur. Although this unlabeled example is more subdued, the open back, satin fabric, and metallic leather lining indicate that they were worn for evening. In 1936 *Women's Wear Daily* reported that 75 percent of American women preferred evening shoes made from black materials.

A WARTIME GIFT

"Souvenir" sandals were prevalent during World War II and were commonly purchased by soldiers stationed abroad to send home to their wives or girlfriends. Many such sandals originated in the Philippines, though some were made in Japan. Their fashionable wedge heels were hand-carved and painted and most often depicted palm trees, huts with grass roofs, and vibrantly colored, "exotic" flowers. Sent by a Museum at FIT donor's father to his mother, the colorful wedges were purchased while his father was on tour with the Irving Berlin's popular wartime musical *This Is the Army*. The show was performed in the Philippines in 1944.

FAMOUS "F" Heels

Salvatore Ferragamo's innovative approach to design became especially apparent during World War II, when many materials for footwear — including leather — were strictly rationed. Ferragamo was renowned for his wedge heels, which were carved from unrationed cork or wood. Produced just after the war, his gold sandals feature the sinuously curved wedge that became known as the "F" heel. Although shoemaker Seymour Troy had introduced a similar heel style in 1939, Ferragamo's version became one of his signature designs. Crafting the heel was a technical feat that involved joining two precisely carved pieces of wood and covering them to provide a seamless appearance.

1940s–1950s

PLAYFUL PLATFORMS

Platform shoes predominated during the 1940s. Everyday examples featured sturdy heels, a modest platform, and materials in neutral hues. The stability provided by such shoes was ideal during wartime, since many women spent more time walking or taking public transportation. Yet some platform styles — such as the brightly colored pair featuring a one-and-a-half-inch platform and a four-inch heel — were clearly designed to be more playful than practical. Creations by Henri specialized in styles for the theater and entertainment industries. Although Henri shoes were flashy, they were also beautifully crafted.

CHINESE SILK

Thomas Cort's evening sandals are made from vibrant red silk brocaded with Chinese motifs, indicating that the fabric was imported. In May 1948 *Harper's Bazaar* excitedly announced the availability of "Chinese silk — for the first time since the war." Earlier in the decade, inflation, transportation hazards, and scarcity of materials in China had largely precluded import of its silks to the United States. The desire for Chinese goods during this time was high, due in part to the country's increasingly positive image in America. In 1941, following Japan's attack on Pearl Harbor, China became an ally in the fight against fascism

Creations by Henri
Platform pumps:
Multicolor leather
USA, *ca.* 1948

Seymour Troy Originals
Sling-back pumps: Black
suede, black leather
USA, *ca.* 1950

Thomas Cort
Platform evening pump:
Red silk brocade
USA, *ca.* 1948

Dal Co'
Pumps: Black leather
with white leather piping
Italy, *ca.* 1958

NEW LOOK, NEW SHOES

Fashionable shoes of the early 1950s featured high, narrow heels without a hint of a platform. The shift in style was prompted by the introduction of Christian Dior's highly influential New Look collection in 1947. The fashion for clothing with slender waistlines, rounded shoulders, and long, full skirts made platform shoes appear cumbersome and inelegant. The pumps, by New York–based shoemaker Seymour Troy, alternate in their use of materials — black suede vamps with leather straps on the right shoe and the reverse use of materials on the left. Troy's wife, Ella, donated the shoes and likely commissioned their quirky, custom design.

THE STILETTO

The construction of the stiletto heel — a style named for its resemblance to a sharply pointed dagger — was mastered by the mid-1950s. A thin but strong metal shank was inserted into the center of the heel, which allowed it to bear weight despite its slim silhouette. The stiletto heel was predominant by 1957 and could be seen on nearly every type of shoe. This pair, by the Rome-based shoe designer Alberto Dal Co', showcases the especially high, alluring style that characterized the brand's aesthetic. The company's numerous celebrity clients included Sophia Loren and Marilyn Monroe.

1950s–1960s

FLORAL IS THE NEW BLACK

Stiletto heeled shoes were often made with sharply pointed toes. While the shoes provided a lean, elegant silhouette, they could also be difficult and painful to wear. The potential discomfort of this style is overshadowed by its striking fabric, a silk printed with life-size, naturalistic roses that covers the body of the shoe and its insole. *Vogue* featured similar styles in its August 1957 issue, advising women to "think of a shoe as you would a jewel (it needn't be coal black to go with everything)." Shoes with floral prints in shades of deep blue, gold, and red were recommended for wear during the autumn.

AN ICON'S COUTURIER

More practical alternatives to stiletto heels were appearing by the late 1950s. This example is from the Paris-based label René Mancini, which was established in 1950. Leading designers such as Balenciaga, Cardin, Chanel, and Givenchy paired Mancini's meticulously crafted shoes with their couture creations. Mancini also provided designs for Chanel's personal wardrobe, who included the couturier among other high-profile clients, including Grace Kelly and Jacqueline Kennedy. These shoes were worn and donated by the actress and style icon Lauren Bacall. During the late 1950s, the majority of Bacall's shoes were made by Mancini.

Saks Fifth Avenue
Pump: Printed silk and
black velvet
USA, *ca.* 1957

René Mancini
Pumps: Black-and-
white wool
France, *ca.* 1959

Taj of India
Sling-back pumps: Green
raw silk, gold metallic
snakeskin, brass
USA, *ca.* 1960

Creazioni V. Buso
Pump: Red suede,
green painted metal
Italy, *ca.* 1960

INDIA IN WESTERN TRANSLATION

Taj of India was founded around 1960 and
sold shoes, handbags, and scarves. Although
the shoes were crafted using hand-loomed
silks imported from India, they were
designed and manufactured in the United
States, where the company was managed by
Faïe Joyce. Described in advertisements as
"luxurious occasion shoes" that evoked "the
mood of India in a Western translation,"
Taj of India designs were easily recognizable. They boasted vibrant colors, slightly
upturned toes, and golden soles. The most
ubiquitous styles were flat slippers and host-
ess shoes with brass heels that were made
in Italy.

ITALIAN ARTISTRY

There was a vogue for Italian shoes during the late 1950s, and they were in high
demand at department stores and specialty boutiques across the United States.
While many Italian styles were lauded for
their practicality and craftsmanship, others — such as Creazioni V. Buso's pair with
a sculpted metal heel, crafted to resemble
the thorny stem of a rose — were more
focused on beauty than functionality. A 1958
shopping guide in *Vogue* warned American
buyers against impractical styles, stating:
"Although it seems almost impossible for an
Italian craftsman to turn out an ugly product, he sometimes sacrifices sturdiness to
grace and turns out a flimsy one."

1960s

THE SURVIVAL OF THE SANDAL

Although sandals were worn infrequently during World War II, they made a comeback in the 1950s — and have not been out of fashion since. This example features the fashionable low, curved heel of the early 1960s. It was then referred to as the "tapered heel" or the "demi heel" and is now commonly known as a "kitten" heel. Although lower heels were most often associated with teenagers, they were also worn by older women. Some more mature women intentionally selected the style for its youthful connotations, presaging the impending "youthquake" culture of the 1960s.

SHOES MADE INSIDE-OUT

Henri Bendel (nephew to the luxury accessories store founder of the same name) opened the Belgian Shoes shop in Manhattan in 1956. True to its name, the store specialized in footwear handcrafted in Belgium. While the materials of Belgian Shoes have varied over the years according to trends in fashion, their silhouettes remain unchanged, as does their artisanal craftsmanship. They are made inside-out, and their meticulously hand-stitched insoles are filled with felt for comfort. The signature, delicate bow on each shoe is hand-tied. Belgian Shoes can also be made to order, and customers may provide an outline of their bare foot to ensure an ideal fit.

Saks Fifth Avenue
Evening sandal:
Black patent leather,
metal
Italy, *ca.* 1962

Belgian Shoes
"Midinette" slippers:
Gold brocade, metallic
gold leather
Belgium, *ca.* 1963

Anello & Davide
Boots: Black leather,
elastic
England, 1961–64

Wing-Dings
Shoes: Light-blue cotton
canvas, white rubber
USA, 1964

BEATLES BOOTS

London-based Anello & Davide, established in 1922, initially specialized in shoes for dance and theater. During the early 1960s, the brand became famous for selling boots to the Beatles, whose fashionable appearance received nearly as much attention as their music. "Beatles Boots" were a combination of a classic Chelsea boot (an ankle-high style with elasticized sides) and a high, Cuban heel. John Lennon and Paul McCartney purchased the style in the early 1960s, and it became an icon of "Swinging London." This Anello & Davide pair was worn by the American socialite and fashion leader "Baby" Jane Holzer, highlighting the style's unisex appeal.

POP CULTURE PRINTS

Wing-Dings specialized in inexpensive canvas shoes that were marketed toward teenage girls. The brand released a series of sneakers printed with the likenesses and autographs of the Beatles in 1964 — the same year the band first visited the United States. Most extant examples are low-top, lace-up tennis shoes. This higher slip-on version was perhaps meant to evoke the shape of the famous "Beatles Boots." Although these mass-produced shoes were clearly intended as a novelty style, they epitomize the overlap between youth culture, music, and popular culture that characterized the 1960s.

1960s

WINKLE PICKERS

Men's shoes with deeply pointed toes gained popularity during the 1950s, recalling poulaines, a medieval style with an extreme, pointed toe. Known as "winkle pickers" for their likeness to a sharp tool used to pry snails (winkles) from their shells, the shoes were closely associated with the rock-and-roll subculture in the United Kingdom. During the 1960s, they were adopted as part of the modernist, or "mod" style, which became highly commercialized so that mod shoes with pointed toes could be found at nearly any price point.

A HINT OF HISTORICISM

Designer Margaret Clark and her husband, businessman Jerrold Miller (the grandson of shoe magnate Israel Miller), founded the Margaret Jerrold brand in 1954. The kitten-heeled evening pumps exemplify the quality for which the brand was known — the velvet "stripes" are in fact bands of ribbon individually stitched to the satin backing fabric. Small, curved heels — covered in bright red silk — may reference the style of Louis XIV. Margaret Jerrold shoes appeared regularly in the fashion press, emphasizing that elegance and historicism were not lost among the predominantly youthful, future-forward designs of the 1960s.

Seat Belt
Men's shoes: Black
leather, metal
England (possibly),
1960–65

Margaret Jerrold
Evening pumps: Pale
blue silk satin, gold velvet ribbon, and red silk
USA, *ca.* 1965

Bernardo
"Jingle Bells" sandal:
Gold metallic leather,
brass bells
USA, 1965

Sandal: Clear acrylic
and vinyl
USA, *ca.* 1966

GRECIAN GAIETY

Bernard Rudofsky introduced the Bernardo
label in 1946. His earliest styles, which
he referred to as "elementary foot cov-
erings," were Grecian-inspired sandals
designed to follow the natural shape of the
feet and allow them "complete freedom."
Eva Sonnino took over as head designer
of Bernardo shoes around 1954, and the
brand expanded under her direction. This
style, aptly named "Jingle Bells," featured
41 small, functioning bells on each shoe.
The company's emphasis on sandals was
underscored by its advertisements, many
of which displayed styles near a fragment
of a classical sculpture — a foot wearing a
leather sandal.

THE INVISIBLE SHOE

Shoes crafted from clear acrylic and vinyl
became fashionable during the early 1950s,
when prominent labels such as Delman and
Beth Levine began to experiment with the
materials. A decade later, Roger Vivier's
transparent pumps revived interest in
"invisible" shoes. In 1966 *Women's Wear
Daily* announced that "Boots are so dead,
but naked transparent shoes like Vivier's
for St. Laurent look new." While unlabeled,
these sandals are certainly bare. The straps
of clear vinyl tubing and open cylindrical
heels appear to have been premade indus
trial materials that were cleverly reworked
into high fashion.

1960s

MODERN MONDRIAN

These boots encompass several mid-1960s trends. André Courrèges introduced mid-calf white boots as part of his 1964 *Space Age* collection, and the style was quickly adapted by many manufacturers. The boots also show the influence of Yves Saint Laurent's fall 1965 couture collection, in which shift dresses were adorned with blocks of color to resemble Piet Mondrian's famous grid paintings. The energetic go-go dancers of the era required flat-soled, easy-to-wear shoes, which then became known as go-go boots. Hi-Brows were worn by one of the dancers on the musical variety show *Hullabaloo*.

THE BOUTIQUE EXPERIENCE

"Strident, strippy. Kinetic, Kliegy. Hard-edged, happy. Plastic, powerful. In other words — Paraphernalia," wrote *Vogue* in its March 1967 issue. Founded two years earlier, the Paraphernalia boutique was part of a dynamic, new shopping culture. Boutiques were typically run by young entrepreneurs who sold the experimental fashions designed for and by their peers, and the shops centered as much on experience as merchandise. Paraphernalia boasted a host of up-and-coming talents, including Diana Dew, Betsey Johnson, and Emmanuelle Khanh. Dorian Destenay's velvet shoes would have complemented their future-forward clothing designs, which were often made using shiny silver materials.

Hi-Brow
Boots: White, red, blue,
and black vinyl
USA, 1966

**Dorian for
Paraphernalia**
Pumps: Black velvet,
silver leather
USA, *ca.* 1967

Adige
Evening pumps: White
satin, silver metallic
leather
France, *ca.* 1967

Peter Max by Randy
Men's sneakers:
Multicolor printed
canvas
USA, 1968–69

SNEAKER PSYCHEDELIA

Peter Max launched his graphic design business in 1962. By the end of the decade, he had found tremendous commercial success with his bold, psychedelic-influenced artwork. His work was featured on record album covers, tableware, fabrics, and many other mass-produced goods — including shoes. Max collaborated with footwear manufacturer Randy to create this cheerful design, which showcases the artist's trademark image of a toothy smile over a layer of clouds. This was one of several styles, and the shoes were also sold in children's sizes. Although they are now valuable collectors' items, they originally retailed for the low price of $2.

SOPHISTICATED SPECTATORS

Spectator shoes — designed and named for onlookers at sporting events — were popularized at the beginning of the twentieth century. Spectators are distinguished by their toe caps, which are fashioned from a darker material than the rest of the shoe to disguise mud or dirt. By the mid-century, spectators had inspired high fashion. This pair, with its slender heels and luxurious materials, was possibly made for Chanel. The designer launched her "two-tone" shoes in 1957, and they have come to be a signature of the brand's aesthetic. Although Chanel is best known for working with the shoemaker Massaro, Adige also crafted some of her shoes.

1960s–1970s

MOON BOOTS

The space age ignited the public's imagination in 1957 when Russia launched the first artificial satellite, Sputnik, and lasted through the 1960s. Interest in space made a substantial impact on fashion. Pierre Cardin, a trained couturier who had worked for Christian Dior, began experimenting with futuristic designs as early as 1958. In 1967 he launched his famous *Cosmos* collection, which featured men's and women's clothing described by *Women's Wear Daily* as "astronaut" outfits. Cardin's boots were made slightly later, but they maintain a space age aesthetic. Vinyl and other "wet look" materials had a futuristic appeal.

YOUTH AND VERSATILITY

The Jack Rogers label was founded in 1960 and typically sold shoes in restrained, ladylike styles and neutral colors. For the label's 1969 resort collection, flats were shown alongside a selection of more traditional pumps. Their uncharacteristic vibrancy emphasizes the far-reaching impact of the colorful, youth-influenced aesthetic on 1960s fashion. The shoes were sold with two sets of rosettes that could be changed to match to the wearer's ensemble or simply on a whim. Slip-on flats or pumps with low heels provided an alternative to boots.

Pierre Cardin
Men's boot: Brown patent leather
France, *ca.* 1968

Jack Rogers
Flat: White leather, pink, green, yellow, and orange leather
USA, 1969

Patou by Andrea Pfister
Pumps: Brown-and-black printed pony hair, black leather
France, *ca.* 1970

Alita by Encore
Sandal boots: White leather, metal, brown leather
USA, *ca.* 1970

A NEW STYLE FOR THE '70S

Andrea Pfister moved to Paris from Pesaro, Italy, in 1964. Shortly thereafter, he began to design shoes at the House of Patou under the leadership of Michel Goma. He also launched his own label in 1965. The lace-front closure of Pfister's animal-printed pumps was likely inspired by ghillies, the shoes traditionally worn for Celtic dance. While ghillies are typically made from black leather with a flat sole, Pfister's shoes are crafted from a bold material and incorporate a high, slim heel — two of the designer's signatures. Fashion journalists touted similar designs as being well-suited to the fashions of the early 1970s, which began to incorporate ankle-length hemlines after the long reign of the miniskirt.

ALMOST NO BOOT AT ALL

This hybrid design resembles the "gladiator sandals" that were introduced around 1968 but also incorporates the front-laced closure of a boot. They were an ideal style for an era obsessed with boots. In a February 1971 article, Mary Ann Crenshaw of *The New York Times* fretted, "If summer comes, will boots be left behind?" The answer was no — as this style exemplifies, boots could be adapted for warm weather. Crenshaw's text was accompanied by sketches of boot-sandals that laced up the leg in various ways, which she described as "open toe, open heel, open front — in fact, almost no boot at all."

1970s

THE PLATFORM REVIVAL

Shoes with small platforms began to appear in fashion magazines as early as 1967. Terry de Havilland, the son of a London cobbler, began to make platform styles from the 1940s lasts he found in his father's workshop. His first shoes, made in 1969, were crafted from snakeskin and sold at London's Kensington Market — a hotspot for the latest fashions. De Havilland quickly gained renown for his expert craftsmanship, creativity, and the sense of playfulness he brought to high-end footwear. He went on to make shoes for celebrities such as David Bowie and Cher.

LACED UP THE LEG

Vogue proclaimed shoes and boots that laced up the leg to be a "must have" in 1971. Styles varied from gladiator sandals to pumps with ballet-style ribbons. Paris-based Japanese designer Kenzo Takada's lace-front boots are inspired by espadrilles, a style characterized by its cotton uppers and soles made from, or trimmed with, rope. The style was traditionally worn in parts of France and Spain and has been in existence since at least the fourteenth century. Espadrilles with wedge heels or flat soles provided fashionable and functional alternatives to platform shoes during the early to mid-1970s.

Terry de Havilland
Platform sandals:
Brown snakeskin
England, *ca.* 1970

Albert Durelle
Pumps: Blue, yellow,
tan, and white leather
Spain, *ca.* 1973

Kenzo
Boot: Blue cotton can-
vas, red leather, and rope
Japan, *ca.* 1971

Fiorucci
Boots: Gold metallic
leather, brown leather
Italy, *ca.* 1976

PLATFORMS FOR ALL

Albert Durelle was a shoe designer and buyer at Alexander's department store, a New York–based retailer. Alexander's specialized in affordable, well-made clothing, and advertisements often made note of its imported, or "continental," styles. These Spanish-made shoes represent the availability of fashionable platforms at all price levels. With their swirling bands of color and bold heel, they also illustrate the outlandish platform styles that had become fashionable by 1973. Such designs bore only a passing resemblance to their 1940s predecessors.

FIORUCCI FLASH

Cowboy boots gained popularity during the 1970s for both men and women. High-fashion versions such as Fiorucci's gold example often eschewed traditional styling and materials. Elio Fiorucci, the son of a shoe shop owner, launched his trendy label in Milan in 1967. By the mid-1970s, the brand was well known for its sexy, fitted jeans, but its true moneymaking enterprise was in sales of inexpensive, logo-branded goods. These woman's boots — also available in metallic red, blue, and silver — were one of the brand's highest-priced items. They sold for $110 in 1976, nearly five times the cost of a Fiorucci T-shirt.

1970s–1980s

PROVOCATIVE PATRIOTISM

Manufactured around the time of the bicentennial celebration in the United States, the stars and stripes sneakers may have been as provocative as they were patriotic. In 1971 *Women's Wear Daily* reported on the potential illegality of consumer products that adopted the likeness of the American flag. The use of such imagery on apparel has been a gray area since the passing of a federal law in 1968, which made it a crime to desecrate the American flag. That same year, political activist Abbie Hoffman was arrested for wearing an American flag shirt at a Vietnam protest, and police ripped the shirt from his back.

A DOSE OF COLOR

Platform heels were on the wane by the mid-1970s, replaced by higher, narrower heels. Strappy evening sandals were especially stylish, and fashion editors recommended colorful shoes to wear with all-white or all-black ensembles. By the late 1970s, the American designer Halston had built a veritable empire, with goods ranging from furs to cosmetics. He introduced his first collection of shoes in 1976, and their sleek design complemented his clothing. The line was made in Italy for the brand Garolini. Advertisements for the shoes featured illustrations by Joe Eula, Halston's creative director, and Halston's friend Andy Warhol.

Men's sneakers: Red, white, and blue printed cotton, white rubber
USA, *ca.* 1975

Halston
Evening sandal: Green satin, silver metallic leather
USA, *ca.* 1979

Norma Kamali
Boot: Red suede, white rubber
USA, *ca.* 1983

Carel
Booties: Red, white, and black patent leather
France, 1984

SEXY SNEAKERS

"Norma Kamali's art lies in unerringly transforming traditional staples of American dress into fashion items of high fun," wrote *New York Times* reporter John Duka in 1983. "Take, for example, her successful handling of sweatshirt clothes . . . Or her recent collection of shoes with variations on every generic style of American shoe, including high-heeled sneakers." This design is styled after the rubber-soled, high-top basketball shoe, typified by the "All Star" sneakers introduced by Converse in 1917. Kamali's shoes exemplify the increasing influence of athletic apparel on high fashion during the early 1980s, while the high heel and cherry-red suede provide sex appeal.

A PLAYFUL TAKE ON TRADITION

The first Carel shoe boutique opened in Paris in 1952. By 1974 the brand had sold more than one million pairs of its colorful "Marquis" high heels. Carel is known for its combination of craftsmanship, color, and humor. "Il Topo," a ballet flat with mouse whiskers designed for the brand by Japanese designer Tokio Kumagai in 1978, was followed by this literal, tongue-in-cheek interpretation of the "tuxedo" shoe — traditionally a formal menswear style made from black patent leather. This design corresponds to two mid-1980s trends: flat shoes adorned with large bows and women's suits.

1980s

MONTANA'S MENSWEAR

Claude Montana launched his menswear line in 1981, just two years after he started his own company. Alongside designers such as Jean Paul Gaultier, Thierry Mugler, and Gianni Versace, Montana's provocative, cutting-edge fashions for both men and women helped to define the decade. His menswear was as superbly crafted as his women's clothes, but it relied less on experimental silhouettes and more on color and pattern. His line of men's shoes took a similar direction, evidenced by the choice of boldly printed calf hair for these boots.

A NEW TAKE ON THE IT SCARF

Vogue reported in May 1985 that "classic Hermès scarves have been showing up on trendy young women and worn as a definite fashion 'item.'" Known in Europe as a leading luxury brand, Hermès was also gaining popularity in the United States during the 1980s. The brightly colored silks that were developed for the brand's signature scarves — first introduced in 1937, 100 years after the company's founding — were instantly recognizable and renowned for their durability. They later came to be used for myriad goods, including blouses, neckties, and footwear. The perfect symmetry of these shoes highlights their superb craftsmanship.

Claude Montana
Men's boots: Black leather, black-and-white printed hair calf
France, *ca.* 1983

Hermès
Shoes: Navy, fuchsia, and gold printed silk
France, *ca.* 1984

Diego Della Valle
Evening pumps: Red-and-purple-striped satin
Italy, 1985

Manolo Blahník
Sling-back pumps: Black-and-cream spotted lizard skin, black-and-white-striped ribbon
England, *ca.* 1985

A REVAMPED CLASSIC

Diego Della Valle is best known today as the chairman of Tod's, a business run by the designer's family, which he had reinvigorated in the late 1970s. During the following decade, Della Valle exercised his business prowess not only for Tod's but for a label under his own name. While Tod's specializes in stylish casual shoes, the styles for Della Valle's eponymous label were more fashion forward. This example enlivens the classic stiletto pump with a vibrant, luxurious silk. Della Valle also made footwear for designers such as Azzedine Alaïa, Gianfranco Ferré, and Romeo Gigli.

THE SHOE TAKEOVER

By the mid-1980s, fashion editors were asserting that shoes were the most important accessory of the decade. No longer purchased to simply complete a look, shoes were making the look. As *New York Times* writer Angela Taylor observed in 1983, "Shoes are to the present generation what hats were to their mothers in the '50s." When Manolo Blahník began his career in the early 1970s, his work was best known to fashion insiders. By the mid-1980s, his lively designs had established him as one of the biggest names in footwear, and he became a household name through the regular inclusion of his designs in *Sex and the City* the following decade. Tina Chow, a regular Blahník client, wore these playful Manolos.

1980s–1990s

SUBCULTURAL STYLE

Nancy and Paul Kaufman and a friend, Lynn Tyler, founded NaNa in 1976. Known as an "alternative fashion" brand, the company sold apparel, but it was best known for its shoes. NaNa first sold Dr. Martens imported from England in its store and later introduced its own line of shoes, designed by Paul. Although NaNa's founders were reluctant to identify with labels such as "punk" or "new wave," their designs were clearly inspired by subcultural styles. These shoes bear the influence of 1970s punk designs — which were, in turn, inspired by 1950s winkle pickers. NaNa managed six stores at its peak, but the company folded in 2001.

BOOTS IN EVERY FABRIC

The introduction of "status jeans" during the late 1970s — epitomized by brands such as Fiorucci and Calvin Klein — paved the way for all things denim by the following decade. Denim clothing and accessories were especially popular for juniors' fashion collections. This design was worn by actress Jennifer Connelly in the July 1986 issue of *Seventeen* magazine. Styled after jeans with topstitching, belt loops, and functional pockets, the boots were available in several different denim washes. Boots were especially important to 1980s fashion and designs in nearly every material and silhouette were available.

NaNa
Men's shoes: Black
leather, silver metal
USA, 1984–85

Matake
Boots: Blue denim
USA, 1985–86

Mario Valentino
Bootie: Red suede
Italy, *ca.* 1990

Nike
"Air Jordan I" sneakers:
Red, white, and black
leather
USA, 1985

BRIGHT BOOTIES

Mario Valentino founded his label in 1952 in Naples, Italy. By the following decade, he had established his reputation in the United States by making shoes for I. Miller. Valentino introduced ready-to-wear clothing in the late 1960s, initially designed by Karl Lagerfeld. While he was considered the first footwear designer to successfully expand into apparel, the brand continued to be closely focused on its shoes. This style highlights Valentino's innovative use of leather, which is skillfully folded and shaped like fabric. Ankle-skimming boots were recommended for wear with leggings or the slinky cat suits fashionable during the early 1990s.

THE SNEAKER PHENOMENON

Designed by Peter Moore, Nike's "Air Jordan I" basketball sneakers — named for Chicago Bulls star Michael Jordan — were an instant phenomenon. *The Wall Street Journal* reported on the shoes before their launch, citing that Jordan was contracted to receive $2.5 million dollars a year for five years for his endorsement. Nike quickly recouped its money as sales of the shoe in their first year amounted to an astounding $100 million. The initial style, in black-and-red, did not comply with uniform rules set by the National Basketball Association, prompting Jordan to adopt this tricolor version.

1980s–1990s

INEXPENSIVE INNOVATION

Thierry Mugler's "Apollo" shoes were named for their lightning bolt design. Mugler, Jean Paul Gaultier, and French boutique label Dorothée Bis each designed plastic "jelly" shoes for the 1985 "Designer Collection" of Brazilian manufacturer Grendha (a subsidiary of Grendene), which specialized in inexpensive plastic footwear. Jelly shoes originated in the 1960s, when the development of injection molding techniques allowed for the creation of fun, inexpensive footwear styles. By the 1980s jellies had become fashionable beachwear for adults and children. The Grendene label, now known as Melissa, continues its collaborations with high-fashion designers.

DR. MARTENS REDESIGN

Wayne and Geraldine Hemingway founded the London-based label Red or Dead in 1982. They originally sold their offbeat creations in a stall in Camden Market. The brand's fame grew quickly — by 1989, there were seven Red or Dead shops, and they showed their collections at London Fashion Week. This version of the classic Dr. Martens boot was shown with the brand's *Space Baby* collection, which included men's and women's garments made from clear vinyl and plastered with images of a cheerful baby wearing a space helmet. Alexander McQueen, who was then working at the label, helped to design the collection.

**Thierry Mugler
for Grendha**
"Apollo" shoes:
Green molded plastic
France, 1985

**Red or Dead for
Dr. Martens**
Boot: Clear plastic
England, 1989/1990

Bottega Veneta
Men's sneakers: Black
woven leather and suede
Italy, *ca.* 1993

John Fluevog
Pumps: Black suede
and plastic
Canada, 1995

THE RISE OF SNEAKER CULTURE

In April 1994, *Vogue* editor Charles Gandee wrote an article on the rise of casual fashion. "As the staples of the street become the staples of the runway, it becomes increasingly difficult to identify who the contemporary arbiters of style and taste really are," he wrote. "Whom do we thank for high-top basketball sneakers, rubber flip-flops, and combat boots?" As "sneaker culture" grew under the influence of Air Jordans and other coveted sports shoes, high-fashion brands introduced their own luxury versions. While Bottega Veneta's 1993 sneakers bear no logo, they do feature the brand's distinctive woven leather.

RETRO WITH A TWIST

John Fluevog and Peter Fox opened a store in Vancouver, British Columbia, in 1970, specializing in unique footwear. Fluevog launched his own line in the mid-1980s. While his work consistently appeals to subcultural groups such as punks and goths, it has also found success in high fashion. In the early 1990s, Fluevog worked with fashion designer Anna Sui to create retro designs with a modern twist. This design was part of a mid-1990s trend for Mary Janes, a style named after a character from the early twentieth-century comic strip *Buster Brown*. It features Fluevog's signature chunky, curved heel.

1990s

SLIP-ON SNEAKERS

Dirk Bikkembergs was a member of the famous "Antwerp Six," a group of avant-garde fashion designers who graduated from Antwerp's Royal Academy of Fine Arts in the early 1980s. By 1996 Bikkembergs had acquired what *New York Times* writer Amy Spindler described as a "vast cult following" for his unique men's and women's fashions. His experimental approach to design is evident in these slip-on shoes. Laces are eschewed in favor of a wide elastic band that extends not only over the instep, but also wraps over the sole. The design was intended to fit as closely as possible while still maintaining flexibility.

THE CURVE OF THE HEEL

Sleek boots that were closely fitted to the leg had replaced heavier, grunge-influenced styles by 1996. Square toes and thick high heels were also fashionable and were seen on both shoes and boots. Ann Demeulemeester paired her boots with a layered, asymmetrical ensemble in all-black fabrics, allowing their red soles to stand out. While red-soled shoes would be inextricably associated with Christian Louboutin by the end of the decade, the curved heel became a signature of Demeulemeester's style. She was known for her design juxtapositions, and the rounded silhouette of the heel provided a soft contrast to her sharply tailored clothing.

Dirk Bikkembergs
Men's shoe: White
leather, tan rubber
Belgium, *ca.* 1995

Ann Demeulemeester
Boots: Black suede,
black leather
Belgium, fall 1996

**Vivienne Tam
for Candie's**
Mules: Embroidered
black satin, black plastic
USA, spring 1997

Robert Clergerie
Sandal: Clear vinyl,
silver metallic leather,
silver metal
France, 1998

NOT-SO-CLASSIC CANDIE'S

Candie's introduced its high-heeled mules in 1978 and sold millions of pairs over the next few years. After fading from the spotlight, the brand sought a comeback during the 1990s. Betsey Johnson, Nicole Miller, Vivienne Tam, and Anna Sui were enlisted to add their signature styles to the classic slide. Chinese-born, New York–based designer Tam described her rose-embroidered shoes as "Western classics with an Asian twist." At a considerably higher price point than the general Candie's line, the designer shoes were intended to attract the brand's original customers. The collaboration lasted for several seasons and was part of the trend for retro revivals during the 1990s.

A FEAT OF ENGINEERING

Robert Clergerie established his company in 1981 and quickly achieved notoriety for his practical, high-quality creations. While this style seemingly values form over function, its design is, in fact, meticulously engineered. The curved steel heel is not only eye-catching but also strong and lightweight. In a 1992 *New York Times* profile on the designer, Suzanne Slesin wrote, "Shoes, like buildings, have a mysterious chemistry of proportions. And Clergerie has the alchemy down pat." The designer's knowledge of engineering and mastery of metals was honed prior to becoming a shoe designer, when he worked at a steel plant.

1990s

SANDALS FOR EVERY SEASON

The strappy, high-heeled sandals of the 1990s often resembled their late 1970s predecessors, but the ways in which they were worn were notably different. In a 1994 editorial on summer sandals, *Harper's & Queen* featured styles in metallic leathers, announcing that "high heels are no longer for evenings only." They were also not only for summer — sandals in dark shades such as the deep red of this pair were also proclaimed by fashion magazines to be appropriate for winter. Sergio Rossi, who had begun designing during the late 1960s, was especially well-known for his sexy high heels.

CLASSICAL BALLET FLATS

The classic "ballet" flat of the early nineteenth century evolved to become a staple of the contemporary wardrobe. Following the prevalence of both stiletto and platform heels during much of the 1990s, flat-soled shoes again became fashion news in 1998. Franco Fieramosca — a designer who had worked for Bally, Ferragamo, Gucci, and Cole Haan before starting his own line in 1992 — fashioned this style to mirror the soft pink leather and drawstring bow of the ballet slipper. "Even women who love heels also like to wear flats sometimes," the designer stated. "If done beautifully, flats can be very sophisticated and elegant."

Sergio Rossi
Sandal: Red metallic
patent leather
Italy, 1998

Franco Fieramosca
Flats: Pale pink suede,
gold metallic leather
USA, spring 1998

Emma Hope
Boots: Ivory silk
satin with multicolor
embroidery
England, fall 1998

**Jimmy Choo for
Anya Hindmarch**
Mules: Aqua silk satin,
multicolor beads
England, *ca.* 1998

BRITISH PEDIGREE

Emma Hope began designing what she
called "regalia for feet" during the 1980s.
After studying at London's Cordwainers
Technical College, which specializes in shoemaking, she was named alongside John
Galliano as one of Britain's brightest new
talents in 1984. One of Hope's first jobs
involved designing demure ballet flats for
Laura Ashley, but her signature extravagant, embellished style emerged when she
opened her own boutique in 1985. Hope
was part of a wave of new shoemakers
based in Great Britain — including fellow
Cordwainers graduates Jimmy Choo and
Patrick Cox — who became especially influential during the late twentieth century.

STATEMENT MULES

"Blanhík, Choo and Rossi help make New
York a shoe town," declared *New York Times*
writer Anne-Marie Schiro in 1998. In fact,
women all over the world were clamoring
for the latest designer shoes at previously
unthinkable prices. Choo, who had launched
his brand during the late 1980s, was cited
for his connection to a particularly famous
client: Diana, Princess of Wales. The statement mules — with their bold, comic book-
inspired embellishments — were clearly not
for everyday wear, making their purchase all
the more extravagant.

1990s– 2000s

MINIMALIST MODE

Jil Sander was described by fashion writer Suzy Menkes as a "purist and perfectionist" who was especially known for her impeccable tailoring. Sander reached the height of her fame during the 1990s, when her innate sense of style coincided with a larger trend for minimalism. Later in the decade, Sander paired her restrained clothing styles with equally minimalist sandals. While some examples were colorful, they were always monochromatic, and they featured no embellishment. Shoes with thick platform soles (a style now referred to as "flatforms") provided a more sensible alternative to the parallel fashion for stiletto-heeled sandals.

A PROSPEROUS PARTNERSHIP

Yohji Yamamoto's collaborations with Adidas began in 2001. A dazzling review of the first collection in *Women's Wear Daily* stated, "While other designers have gone *sportif*, few have turned basic athletic stripes and baseball jackets exotic." Originally available in six styles — including these wrestling boots and a pair of kimono-print sneakers — the shoes were a great success. The ongoing collaboration, originally known as Adidas for Yohji Yamamoto, is now sold under the name Y-3. Collaborations between high-fashion designers and athletic shoemakers have become increasingly important during the twenty-first century. Other examples include Maison Martin Margiela x Chuck Taylor and Comme des Garçons x Nike.

Jil Sander
Sandals: White patent
leather
Germany, 1999

Dr. Martens
Boots: Black leather,
rubber
England, 2000

**Adidas for
Yohji Yamamoto**
Boots: Black nylon, red
nylon, black suede, white
reflective tape
Japan, fall 2001

Stella McCartney
Booties: White cork
England, 2009

SUBCULTURAL ESSENTIALS

In 1947 Dr. Klaus Maertens (a medical doctor) and Dr. Herbert Funk (a mechanical engineer) started their handmade shoe company in Seeshaupt, Germany. Maertens had previously devised a sole made of air-filled material, rather than hard leather, which provided better support for the feet. While Dr. Martens footwear was intended as workwear, it was later adopted as part of a subcultural "uniform" by skinheads, punks, and heavy metal enthusiasts. "Doc" Martens also became associated with the grunge look that briefly permeated high fashion during the early 1990s. This is the brand's best-selling "1460" boot, introduced in 1960.

CRUELTY FREE

Stella McCartney launched her own label in 2001. A lifelong vegetarian, she is an advocate for animal rights and eschews the use of all animal products in her collections. "People really don't want to talk about the fact that the fashion industry's biggest impact is its use of leather," explains McCartney, who is regularly interviewed about the environmental concerns surrounding its production. The designer's beliefs are especially pertinent to her designs for bags and shoes, for which she must regularly source alternate materials. In spite of — or perhaps because of — her refusal to use leather, McCartney's accessories are coveted luxury items.

2000s–2010s

PROCESS AND EXPERIMENTATION

Dutch designer Marloes ten Bhömer specializes in conceptual footwear. Her abstract shapes are informed by her research into the cultural significance of women's shoes — particularly high heels — as well as the ergonomics of footwear. This style, which the designer named "Rationalmouldedshoe," was the result of experimentations with pouring, molding, and de-molding polyurethane. Originally created for an installation at the Krannert Art Museum in Illinois, they were displayed alongside a series of test designs to underscore the process of innovation involved in the designer's work. While the final design is recognizable as footwear, it is also evocative of sculpture.

SHOES ON THE CATWALK

Tom Ford's sinuous, curved-wedge heels resemble Ferragamo's "F" heel from the 1940s. Ford is forthright and unapologetic about being inspired by fashion's past. "I'm very classic because what I do is always based on something you've seen before," he explains. Ford's red velvet rendition was produced just after he debuted his womenswear collection for his eponymous label in 2011 — a development that was highly anticipated by fashion aficionados who had followed his earlier tenures at Gucci and Yves Saint Laurent. These eye-catching sandals were made at a time in which extravagant runway shoes were receiving nearly as much attention as the clothing they were worn with.

Marloes ten Bhömer
"Rationalmouldedshoe"
pumps: Pale green
polyurethane rubber,
stainless steel
England, 2009

Tom Ford
Evening sandals:
Red resin, red leather,
red velvet
USA, spring 2012

A Bathing Ape
"Bapesta" sneakers:
White canvas, camou-
flage-printed leather
Japan, 2010

PONY X Colette
Sneakers: Blue-and-
white man-made leather,
white rubber
France, 2013

LIMITED EDITION

Japanese designer, DJ, and record producer
Nigo established A Bathing Ape (Bape)
in 1993, initially selling a small selection
of T-shirts and hoodies. The label soon
expanded to include a full range of fashion and accessories. In 2002 A Bathing Ape
released its "Bapesta" sneaker, a style that
was closely based on Nike's "Air Force 1"
shoe. The Nike "swoosh" was replaced
with Bape's star logo, and the shoe was
available in a remarkable number of color-
ways. Some collectors surmise that only 100
shoes in each colorway were produced. The
"Bapesta" has since become a highly collect-
ible style.

NEW YORK SNEAKERS /
PARISIAN CHIC

These sneakers were designed exclusively
for the Parisian fashion store Colette,
described by Forbes magazine as "the trend-
iest boutique in the world." In operation
from 1997 to 2017, Colette was a hotspot for
unique offerings. The store was perhaps best
known for its collaborations, which set the
standard for similar partnerships across the
industry. Colette's high tops are an updated
version of PONY's "Topstar" basketball
sneakers, first introduced in 1975. PONY
is an acronym for "Product of New York,"
and the sneakers — made in the same bright
blue used on Colette's carrier bags — offered
a unique fusion of New York style and
Parisian chic.

2010s

TOWERING HEELS

"How high can heels go — without killing your feet?" asked *Wall Street Journal* writer Christina Binkley in 2013. She went on to explain the myriad negative effects that high heels can have on the body. Despite this warning — and many others — women in the United States spent $ 38.5 billion on high-heeled shoes in 2012 alone. While Walter Steiger's soaring five-inch heels are well past the maximum of two inches recommended by doctors, their arched shape is anatomically correct, as the tip of the heel lands just under the center of the heel bone.

MEXICAN ARTISTRY

Mexican native Ricardo Seco presented the New Balance sneakers as part of his 2015 *Dreams* collection. He commissioned their design from the Huichol (or Wixáritari), an indigenous people of Mexico renowned for their vibrant and intricate bead art. While these shoes were made for the runway, simplified versions were later produced commercially. Seco's dedication to the culture of his home country is further exemplified by his ongoing *Yo Soy Mexico* initiative, which supports emerging Mexican fashion designers who want to expand their work internationally. Cultural awareness and respect for the art of indigenous peoples has become central to fashion during the twenty-first century.

Walter Steiger
Pumps: Beige cotton,
beige-and-orange
tiger-print cotton,
orange leather
USA, spring 2013

**Ricardo Seco
(Huichol People and
New Balance)**
Sneaker: Black-and-
yellow leather, multi-
color glass beads
Mexico, spring 2015

**Roger Vivier
(Bruno Frisoni)**
"Belle Vivier" pumps:
Patent leather, metal
France, *ca.* 2015

Sophia Webster
"Chiara" sandals: Black
suede, multicolor pavé
crystals
England, 2017

PILGRIM PUMPS

Roger Vivier introduced his buckled "pilgrim pump" in 1965. The shoes were first shown with designs by Yves Saint Laurent, who paired them with dresses from what is referred to as the "Mondrian" collection from the same year. Catherine Deneuve frequently wore the style with her Saint Laurent clothing. When they received a close-up in one of Deneuve's most famous films, *Belle de jour* (1967), the company sold more than 200,000 copies, and the shoes were widely imitated by other manufacturers. They have come to be one of the label's most enduring designs, with regular updates to materials and heel styles providing a fresh appeal.

INSPIRED BY NATURE

English designer Sophia Webster launched her own brand in 2012 after working as an apprentice for Nicholas Kirkwood. She has consistently incorporated a butterfly motif into her work, an idea she initiated for her final collection at the Royal College of Art in London. As Webster explains, "I started looking at butterfly wings close-up, and they have so many amazing patterns and colors going on — like hidden codes." While the designer described her early approach to design as "maximalist," she has expanded her line to include flats, sneakers, and other shoes that are more appropriate for everyday wear.

2010s

SPORTY SENSIBILITY

Thom Browne cleverly reinvented the platform heel for his fall 2017 collection. As models strutted down a runway made to resemble a frozen lake, they balanced on a variety of elegant shoe styles that were perched upon tall metal "blades," reminiscent of antique ice skates. While the whimsical shoes were not designed for commercial production, they were beautifully crafted and underscored Browne's unique design sensibility. As *Women's Wear Daily* noted, "Browne likes to play, but he is extremely serious about his work, the craftsmanship of clothes, and that was really the focus of this extraordinary collection."

GENDER INCLUSIVITY

Hood By Air designer Shayne Oliver frequently challenges standards of race, class, and sexuality with his collections. Oliver's thigh-high boots were paired with an ensemble from the 2016 *Pilgrimage* collection and were worn by a man on the runway. They were made by Pleaser, a brand that describes itself as "the ultimate go-to name in sexy shoes" and specializes in "exotic" footwear. While the fetish-inspired, stiletto-heeled style is overtly provocative, it also coincides with a growing acceptance of high-heeled shoes for men during the twenty-first century.

Thom Browne
Shoes: Black-and-white leather, white metal
USA, fall 2017

Pleaser for Hood By Air
Thigh-high boots: Red synthetic patent leather
USA, fall 2016

Puma #REFORM
"Clyde Court" sneakers: black-and-gray tweed knit, black rubber
USA, 2019

Christian Louboutin
Men's "DandyLove" evening shoes: Black velvet, multicolor leather
France, spring 2019

FUN FOOTWEAR FOR MEN

Statement-making shoes for men have become an important part of contemporary fashion. In a 2012 article on new footwear styles, *Wall Street Journal* reporter Ray Smith noted that "men are showing interest in grown-up shoes that make a distinctive statement. Designers are also hoping men start indulging in a pair of 'just for fun' shoes, the way women bought striking, impractical heels in the 'Sex and the City' days." Christian Louboutin expanded his business to include men's shoes in 2011. This style is a take on the "Love" flat from 1991, one of the designer's earliest creations.

STATEMENT SNEAKERS

The "Clyde Court" sneakers bear an important quote from track-and-field star Tommie Smith: "We had to be seen because we couldn't be heard." Alongside fellow African American athlete John Carlos, Smith had raised a black-gloved fist during the U.S. national anthem at the 1968 Olympic medal ceremony, making a clear statement about civil rights. Puma's #REFORM sneakers build on Smith's legacy. They were made in collaboration with rapper Meek Mill and serve as the brand's "rally cry to stand up against the broken U.S. criminal justice system." All proceeds go directly to a related organization called the Reform Alliance.

INDEX

COLLECTION CREDITS

All shoes featured in the book are from the collection of The Museum at FIT. The accession numbers and collection credits follow.

4: 98.77.2/Gift of Manolo Blahník
7: 2016.46.22/Gift of Ohne Titel
8: 71.202.16/Gift of the Victoria & Albert Museum
11: 2006.61.1/Gift of Judith Neuman-Cantor and Beth Neuman
12: 2003.100.18/Gift of Robert Renfield
15: 94.156.1/Gift of Ms. Phyllis Unroch
16: 2005.53.1/Gift of Louis Vuitton
19: 2013.83.1/Museum purchase
22: 74.32.4/Unknown donor
23: P82.25.8/Museum purchase
26: 2019.85.1/Museum purchase
27: 2004.31.3/Museum purchase
30: 2013.50.1/Museum purchase
31: 71.213.40/Gift of Sally Cary Iselin
34: P91.25.2/Museum purchase
35: 87.16.1/Gift of Richard Martin
40: 99.3.1/Gift of Bella Freud
41: 99.9.1/Gift of Birkenstock Footprint Sandals, Inc.
44: 2012.63.1/Gift of CHANEL
45: 2019.68.1/Gift of Jennifer Loturco
48: 2017.29.3/Gift of Puma
49: 2021.11.1/Gift of Brother Vellies
52: 2012.38.1/Museum purchase
56: 2013.25.9/Gift of Veronica Del Gatto

57 (above): 2017.76.1/Gift of Veronica Webb
57 (below): 2009.71.3/Gift of Veronica Webb
58: 2008.65.1/Gift of Veronica Webb
59: 92.34.1DE/Gift of Azzedine Alaïa
62-63: 2018.48.1/Museum purchase
65: 2007.10.1/Museum purchase
66: 2018.62.1/Gift of Dr. Harriette Kaley
70: 82.52.15/Gift of Bridget Restivo
72 (below): 93.159.20/Gift of Ady Gluck-Frankel
73 (above): 81.145.39/Gift of Naomi Sims
77: 92.225.34/Gift of The Estate of Tina Chow
79: 98.77.3/Gift of Manolo Blahník
80: 92.225.45/Gift of The Estate of Tina Chow
81 (above): 92.225.69/Gift of The Estate of Tina Chow
81 (below): 2017.24.1/Gift of Michèle Gerber Klein
82: 91.186.2/Gift of Carolyne Roehm Inc.
83 (above): 92.225.68/Gift of the Estate of Tina Chow
83 (below): 91.186.14/Gift of Carolyne Roehm Inc.
84: 2002.62.1/Gift of C. Hooper
85: 98.38.4/Gift of Ruffo
86 (above): 2017.72.1/Gift of Virginia Barbato
86 (below): 98.77.2/Gift of Manolo Blahník
87 (above): 2013.11.1/Gift of Manolo Blahníks
87 (below): 98.77.1/Gift of Manolo Blahník
88–89: 2019.88.1/Gift of Manolo Blahník
93: 86.21.48/Gift of David P. Dann
94 (above): 72.61.60CD/Gift of Mr. and Mrs. Adrian McCardell
94 (below): 76.147.8/Gift of Mrs. Adrian McCardell

95: 76.147.2/Gift of Mrs. Adrian McCardell
96 (above): 74.107.153/Gift of Lauren Bacall
96 (below): 80.311.25/Gift of Lauren Bacall
97: 71.254.171/Gift of Lauren Bacall
98: 2018.41.1/Museum purchase
101: 2015.82.2/Gift of Anonymous
102-103: 2015.26.1/Museum purchase
104: 92.225.73/Gift of The Estate of Tina Chow
108: 92.225.50/Gift of The Estate of Tina Chow
109: 86.89.7/Gift of Bridget Restivo
110: 2012.63.3/Gift of CHANEL
111 (above): 2012.63.4/Gift of CHANEL
111 (below): 2018.38.1/Gift of Jean Shafiroff
112-113: 2012.63.2/Gift of CHANEL
114: 80.181.42/Gift of Jane Holzer
116: 80.181.34/Gift of Jane Holzer
117: 80.311.19/Gift of Ms Lauren Bacall
118: 2018.70.3/Gift of Chloé
120: 2017.48.1/Gift of Maison Chloé
121: 2017.48.2/Gift of Maison Chloé
122: 2018.70.3/Gift of Chloé
123: 2018.70.1/Gift of Chloé
124: 2015.39.1CD/Gift of Chloé
125: 2018.70.2/Gift of Chloé
126: 2021.49.3/Gift of Jimmy Choo
130: 2021.49.1/Gift of Jimmy Choo
131: 2021.49.2/Gift of Jimmy Choo
132: 2005.49.2/Museum purchase
134: 98.60.3/Gift of Comme des Garçons

135: 2017.52.1CD/Museum purchase
136 (above): 2008.77.7/Gift of Janet Cooper
136 (below): 87.150.4/Gift of Carole Aizenstark
137 (above): 98.60.1/Gift of Comme des Garçons
137 (below): 98.60.4/Gift of Comme des Garçons
138: 2019.2.1/Museum purchase
139: 2017.73.1/Gift of Jill Hemingway
145: 83.164.2/Gift of Mrs. Sally Iselin
146-147: 77.183.2CD/Gift of Ruth Sublette
148: 96.42.2/Gift of Patrick Cox
150: 99.32.3/Gift of Jeff Fazio
151: 98.13.1/Gift of Patrick Cox New York, Inc.
152: 70.10.21/Gift of Mrs. Sidney G. Bernard
154: 89.94.8/Gift of Mrs. Bartle Bull
157 (above): 81.61.22/Gift of Mrs. Janet Chatfield-Taylor
157 (below): 93.176.1/Gift of Beth Levine
158-159: 71.263.4/Gift of Yeffe Kimball Slatin
160 (above): 71.263.3/Gift of Yeffe Kimball Slatin
160 (below): P89.40.34/Museum purchase
161: 71.263.2/Gift of Yeffe Kimball Slatin
162: P89.55.32/Museum purchase
163 (above): 76.30.229/Gift of Mrs. Henry Rose
164: 98.45.2/Gift of Dolce & Gabbana
167 (above): 2017.44.2/Gift of Mr. Gordon Kendall
167 (below): 2006.62.3/Gift of Linda Tain
168: 89.164.2/Gift of David Evins
172: 75.230.627/Gift of David Evins

173 (above): 89.164.4/Gift of David Evins
173 (below): 89.164.91/ Gift of David Evins
174 (above): 89.164.167/ Gift of David Evins
174 (below): 89.164.152/ Gift of David Evins
175 (above): 89.164.80/ Gift of David Evins
175 (below): 89.164.73/ Gift of David Evins
176: 85.176.1/Gift in memory of Inez Mantiglia Meo
178: P84.35.3/Museum purchase
179: 71.255.36/Gift of Stanley R. Jacobs
180-181: 81.176.4/Gift of Janet A. Sloane
185: 71.213.44/Gift of Sally Cary Iselin
186-187: P91.98.21/ Museum purchase
188: 71.213.55/Gift of Sally Cary Iselin
189: 80.300.6/Gift of Lillian Bartok
190 (above): 81.178.11/ Gift of Mr. Richard J. Kempe
190 (below): 74.37.19/ Anonymous Donor
191 (above): 2006.63.1/ Gift of Flavia Robinson Derossi
191 (below): 2017.51.1/ Gift of Salvatore Ferragamo
192: P89.64.2/Museum purchase
195: P89.64.5/Museum purchase
197 (above): P89.64.7/ Museum purchase
197 (below): 89.62.5/ Gift of Carole Aizenstark
198: 88.50.28/Gift of Barbara Hodes
200: 90.100.11/Gift of Hedy Chew
201: 89.32.10/Gift of Catherine Cahill
202 (above): 96.34.10/Gift of Stephane Kelian of America
202 (below): 93.159.3/ Gift of Ady Gluck-Frankel

203: 93.159.2/Gift of Ady Gluck-Frankel
206: 95.27.1/Gift of Suzanne Steier
207: P89.66.1/Museum purchase
208: 98.123.2/Gift of Romeo Gigli
209 (above): 98.123.1/ Gift of Romeo Gigli
209 (below): 2011.53.2/ Anonymous donor
213: 79.169.16/Gift of Arthur Schwartz
214: 79.169.17/Gift of Arthur Schwartz
215: 2019.13.1BC/Gift of Givenchy
216: 2013.78.1/Gift of Givenchy
217: 2011.8.1CD/Gift of Givenchy by Riccardo Tisci
218: 2013.15.1/Gift of Alberto Guardiani
221: 2013.15.2/Gift of Alberto Guardiani
222: 99.64.2/Gift of Gucci
224: 99.64.2/Gift of Gucci
225: 94.147.32/Gift of Anastasia Hayes Piper
227: 99.64.1/Gift of Gucci
228: 2019.66.1/Gift of David Nash
229 (above): 2017.44.3/ Gift of Mr. Gordon Kendall
229 (below): 2015.7.1/ Gift of Gucci
230: 2016.93.1EF/Gift of Gucci
231 (above): 2017.18.1DE/ Gift of Gucci
231 (below): 2017.17.1/ Gift of Alyson Cafiero
232: 2016.18.1/Gift of Pierre Hardy
235: 2017.17.3/Gift of Alyson Cafiero
236: 2009.71.4/Gift of Veronica Webb
237 (above): 2016.18.3/ Gift of Pierre Hardy
237 (below): 2016.18.4/ Gift of Pierre Hardy
238-239: 2016.18.2/Gift of Pierre Hardy
240: 86.171.8/Gift of Mrs. James Levy
244: 87.109.3/Gift of Ruth Rubinstein

245 (above): 86.61.5/Gift of Mireille Levy
245 (below): 91.210.44/ Gift of Elaine Cohen
246: 90.100.9/Gift of Hedy Chew
247: 84.207.1/Gift of Charles Jourdan
248 (above): P90.31.7/ Museum purchase
248 (below): 83.156.3/ Gift of Bridget Restivo
249: 99.59.8/Gift of Hedy Klineman
250: 98.61.2/Gift of Martine Sitbon
253: 96.34.7/Gift of Stephane Kélian of America
254: 2019.66.2/Gift of David Nash
255 (above): 96.34.13/ Gift of Stephane Kélian of America
255 (below): 91.111.37/ Gift of John Brooks Adams
256: 2013.21.1/Gift of Nicholas Kirkwood
259: 2009.53.2CD/ Museum purchase
260: 2010.20.2/Museum purchase
260 (above): 2018.38.4/ Gift of Jean Shafiroff
260 (below): 2017.17.7/ Gift of Alyson Cafiero
261: 2011.11.1BC/ Museum purchase
263: 2018.38.3/Gift of Jean Shafiroff
264-265: 2010.65.3/ Museum purchase
266: 2002.24.8/Gift of Christine Bridges
270 (above): 99.32.1/Gift of Jeff Fazio
270 (below): 87.150.5/ Gift of Carole Aizenstark
271: 2000.48.3/Gift of Nancy Stanton Knox
272: 2019.4.1/Gift of Masaya Kushino
275: 2013.16.1/Gift of Masaya Kushino
279: 2018.52.8/Gift of Judith Corrente
280: 2017.24.2/Gift of Michèle Gerber Klein

281 (above): 2017.24.3/ Gift of Michèle Gerber Klein
281 (below): 98.67.1/Gift of Christian Lacroix
285: 2019.27.1/Gift of Lanvin
286: 88.2.48/Gift of Carroll Cook
287: 2015.51.3/Gift of Pepper Hemingway
288: 88.2.8/Gift of Carroll Cook
291: 88.2.14/Gift of Carroll Cook
92: 88.2.48/Gift of Carroll Cook
293 (above): 88.2.25/Gift of Carroll Cook
293 (below): 88.2.47/Gift of Carroll Cook
294: 81.167.3/Gift of Mr. Otto Grun
298: 97.60.40/Gift of Hebert and Beth Levine
300: 76.56.6/Gift of Beth Levine
299 (above): 76.56.17/Gift of Beth Levine
299 (below): 76.56.1/Gift of Beth Levine
302-303: 76.56.16/Gift of Beth Levine
304 (above): 2013.52.3/ Gift of the Council of Fashion Designers of America (CFDA)
304 (below): 2013.44.1/ Gift of Anonymous
305 (above): 76.101.4/Gift of Mrs. Gyora Novak
305 (below): 75.165.37/ Gift of Alex Fisher
306: 2009.5.1/Museum purchase
308: 98.12.1/Gift of Christian Louboutin
309: 99.30.8/Gift of Christian Louboutin
310: 2013.57.1/Gift of Deena Aljuhani Abdulaziz
311 (above): 99.30.4/ Gift of Christian Louboutin
311 (below): 2016.97.2/ Gift of Joan Juliet Buck
312: 99.30.6/Gift of Christian Louboutin

313 (above): 98.46.3/ Gift of Christian Louboutin

313 (below): 2005.76.1/ Gift of Christian Louboutin

314: 2005.76.2/Gift of Christian Louboutin

315: 2017.41.1/Gift of Caroline Howard Hyman

316 (above): 2010.20.1/ Museum purchase

316 (below): 2010.65.4/ Museum purchase

317: 2018.38.2/Gift of Jean Shafiroff

319: 2014.35.1/Gift of Christian Louboutin

320: 2021.13.1/Gift of Louis Vuitton

323: 2021.13.2/Gift of Louis Vuitton

324: 2021.13.3/Gift of Louis Vuitton

325: 2012.45.1/Gift of Michèle Gerber Klein

326: 2006.25.2/Gift of Rebecca Pietri

329: 2016.43.2/Gift of Jill Hemingway

330-331: 92.182.1/Gift of Richard Martin

332: 98.36.1/Museum purchase

335: 2008.47.1/Museum purchase

336: 2016.25.1/Gift of Craig Chorney

337: 2017.40.1/Gift of Rebecca Vanyo

338-339: 2009.71.2/Gift of Veronica Webb

340: 2013.7.1/Museum purchase

342: 2018.54.1/Gift of Yliana Yepez

343: 2018.72.1/Gift of Adnan Ege Kutay

344: 2019.23.1BC/Gift of Rick Owens

347: 2012.33.1/Gift of Rick Owens

349: 2019.14.1/Gift of Rick Owens

348: 2016.92.1DE/Gift of Rick Owens Studio

350: 2012.34.2/Gift of Ohne Titel

354: 2010.36.1DE/ Museum purchase

355 (above): 2010.72.1DE/ Gift of Ohne Titel

355 (below): 98.120.4/ Gift of Cesare Paciotti

353: 2012.34.1/Gift of Ohne Titel

356: 2011.20.1/Gift of Joseph and Carole Bascetta

360-361: 2011.20.3/Gift of Joseph and Carole Bascetta

362 (above): 2011.20.2/ Gift of Joseph and Carole Bascetta

362 (below): 2011.20.4/ Gift of Joseph and Carole Bascetta

363: 2011.20.5/Gift of Joseph and Carole Bascetta

364: P83.5.3/Museum purchase

368: 2008.84.5/Gift of Frank Smith Collection

369 (above): 84.191.1/ Gift of Mrs. Molly Millbank

369 (below): 79.166.16/ Gift of Cora Ginsburg

370-371: 2003.100.17/Gift of Robert Renfield

372: 2008.84.2/Gift of Frank Smith Collection

375: 77.133.11/Gift of Mrs. Hill Montague III

376: 2019.35.1/Museum purchase

379: 99.102.2/Gift of Prada

380 (above): 97.83.2/Gift of Prada

380 (below): 2011.56.14/ Gift of Craig Chorney

381 (above): 2013.40.9/ Gift of Craig Chorney

381 (below): 2011.53.1/ Anonymous donor

382: 2011.1.1FG/Gift of Prada

383 (above): 2008.45.1FG/Gift from Prada

383 (below): 2007.20.1/ Gift of Prada

384: 2016.105.1/Gift of Simon Doonan

387: 83.144.34/Gift of Mireille Levy

388: 82.183.38/Gift of Alida Miller

389: 2017.17.8/Gift of Alyson Cafiero

390: 91.221.1/Gift of Roz Braverman

391 (above): 79.169.7/Gift of Arthur Schwartz

391 (below): 88.1.178/ Gift of Marina Schiano

392 (above): 92.74.2/Gift of Yves Saint Laurent

392 (below): 2019.49.3/ Gift of Adnan Ege Kutay

393: 79.169.8/Gift of Arthur Schwartz

394: 88.28.15/Gift of Linda Friedman

397: 81.166.32/Gift of Mrs. Morton Jay Seifter

398: 89.25.2/Gift of Linda Friedman

399: 88.28.17/Gift of Linda Friedman

400: 2012.39.1/Museum purchase

402: 2010.59.1/Museum purchase

403: 2014.52.1/Gift of Noritaka Tatehana

404: 98.69.2/Gift of Valentino

407: 86.136.27/Gift of Ruth Ford

408: 89.69.22/Gift of Mireille Levy, Lausanne

409 (above): 98.69.1/Gift of Valentino

409 (below): 2005.46.2/ Museum purchase

410: 2012.35.1/Museum purchase

413: 2013.22.1/Museum purchase

414-415: 2017.6.2/ Museum purchase

416: 2018.73.1/Museum purchase

419: 2000.10.3/Gift of KCD, Inc.

420: 2018.12.5/Gift of Hans, Kazuko & Siv Nilsson

421: 2018.12.13/Gift of Hans, Kazuko & Siv Nilsson

422: 2008.86.1/Gift of Sandy Schreier

423 (above): 2018.12.9/ Gift of Hans, Kazuko & Siv Nilsson

423 (below): 2003.96.1/ Museum purchase

427: 79.169.3/Gift of Arthur Schwartz

428: 92.202.2/Gift of Ania Kayaloff

429 (above): 80.126.3/ Gift of Ms. Diana Vreeland

429 (below): 83.113.2/ Gift of Beatrice Renfield

430 (above): 91.45.18/Gift of Bonnie K. Gokey

430 (below): 79.169.5/ Gift of Arthur Schwartz

431 (above): 2008.13.1/ Gift of The School of Graduate Studies, FIT

431 (below): 79.169.6/ Gift of Arthur Schwartz

432-433: 99.38.1/Gift of Agnès B.

434: 2019.7.6/Gift of Roger Vivier

435: 2019.7.3/Gift of Roger Vivier

436: 2019.7.10/Gift of Roger Vivier

437 (above): 2019.7.2/Gift of Roger Vivier

137 (below): 2019.7.8/ Gift of Roger Vivier

438: 2019.19.1/Museum purchase

441: 2016.108.3/Gift of Nancy Gewirz

442 (above): 2001.44.13/ Gift of Francois

442 (below): 2003.97.4CD/Museum purchase

443 (above): 2019.19.2/ Museum purchase

443 (below): 2000.30.1/ Museum purchase

444-445: 98.119.1/Gift of Vivienne Westwood

446: 2003.5.1/Gift of Vicini S.p.A.

449: 2003.5.2/Gift of Vicini S.p.A.

452 (left): 74.32.4/ Unknown donor

452 (right): 2013.3.1/ Museum purchase

453 (**left**): 2007.12.1/
Museum purchase
453 (**right**): PL71.2.8/On
Permanent Loan from
The Estate of Ruth H.
K. Fries
454 (**left**): 2008.84.22/
Gift of the Frank
Smith Collection
454 (**right**): 2015.34.1/
Museum purchase
455 (**left**): 2008.84.21/
Gift of the Frank
Smith Collection
455 (**right**): 2008.84.18/
Gift of the Frank
Smith Collection
456 (**left**): 73.40.10/
Gift of Eleanor and
Katherine Park
456 (**right**): 80.1.2/Gift of
Florence Anderson and
Mary A. Seymour
457 (**left**): P84.19.6/
Museum purchase
457 (**right**): 71.202.16/
Gift of the Victoria &
Albert Museum
458 (**left**): 83.105.1/Gift
of J.A. Gregg
458 (**right**): 83.208.2/Gift
of Martin Kamer
459 (**left**): P89.57.15/
Museum purchase
459 (**right**): 2008.84.16/
Gift of Frank Smith
Collection
460 (**left**): 2005.45.1/
Museum purchase
460 (**right**): P89.83.1/
Museum purchase
461 (**left**): 2008.84.33/
Gift of Frank Smith
Collection
461 (**right**): 2009.79.10/
Gift of the National
Trust for Historic
Preservation,
Lyndhurst
462 (**left**): P85.54.5/
Museum purchase
462 (**right**): 2018.51.1/
Gift of Thomas A.
Buckley
463 (**left**): P84.35.3/
Museum purchase
463 (**right**): 89.154.22/
Gift of Maria
Burgaleta-Larson
464 (**left**): P89.55.38/
Museum purchase

464 (**right**): P84.25.7/
Museum purchase
465 (**left**): 81.170.5/
Gift of Mrs. Otto E.
Dohrenwend
465 (**right**): 90.2.1/
Anonymous donor
466 (**left**): 92.86.17/
Gift of Mrs. Berta
Rudofsky
466 (**right**): U.593/
Unknown donor
467 (**left**): 2018.56.2/Gift
of Waverly B. Lowell
in honor of Evelyn
Schwartz Lowell
467 (**right**): 80.300.6/Gift
of Lillian Bartok
468 (**left**): P92.11.13/
Museum purchase
468 (**right**): 70.47.8/Gift
of Robert Pusilo
469 (**left**): 78.263.6/Gift
of Mrs. Seymour Troy
469 (**right**): 86.77.1/Gift
of Beth Levine
470 (**left**): 81.23.58/
Gift of Laurie Vance
Johnson
470 (**right**): 68.143.137/
Gift of Lauren Bacall
471 (**left**): 93.148.1/Gift
of Ms. Ruth Gottfried
471 (**right**): P90.78.2/
Museum purchase
472 (**left**): 80.157.142/
Gift of Mrs. Morrie
Slifkin
472 (**right**): 2019.84.2/
Gift of Belgian Shoes
473 (**left**): 86.144.12/Gift
of Jane Holzer
473 (**right**): P92.57.54/
Museum purchase
474 (**left**): P88.51.10/
Museum purchase
474 (**right**): 96.45.2/Gift
of Abby Goell
475 (**left**): 75.221.5/Gift
of Vera Gawansky
475 (**right**): P92.11.11/
Museum purchase
476 (**left**): P91.11.1/
Museum purchase
476 (**right**): 91.13.3/Gift
of Jeffrey Beuglet
477 (**left**): 78.55.95/
Gift of Dorrance H.
Hamilton
477 (**right**): 89.73.1/Gift
of Michael Fazakerly

478 (**left**): 90.149.63/Gift
of Mr. Jean Francois
Daigre
478 (**right**): 74.112.26/
Gift of Mrs. Burton
Tremaine
479 (**left**): 89.54.20/Gift
of Sylvia Slifka
479 (**right**): P91.98.19/
Museum purchase
480 (**left**): 88.28.5/Gift of
Linda Friedman
480 (**right**): 80.181.43/
Gift of Jane Holzer
481 (**left**): 80.146.2/
Gift of Mrs. Laura
Sinderbrand
481 (**right**): 85.47.14/
Gift of Gregory and
Barbara Reynolds
482 (**left**): 92.171.48/Gift
of Michael Dykeman
482 (**right**): 92.237.28/
Gift of Halston
Borghese, Inc.
483 (**left**): P92.57.39/
Museum purchase
483 (**right**): 84.190.1/Gift
of Tony Carel
484 (**left**): 90.128.5/Gift
of Howard Froman
484 (**right**): 92.225.37/
Gift of The Estate of
Tina Chow
485 (**left**): 86.173.1/Gift
of Gianfranco Ferre
S.p.A.
485 (**right**): 92.225.47/
Gift of The Estate of
Tina Chow
486 (**left**): 2001.98.4/Gift
of Glenn Petersen
486 (**right**): 87.114.1/Gift
of Bob Smith
487 (**left**): 2017.24.4/
Gift of Michèle Gerber
Klein
487 (**right**): 85.196.1/Gift
of Nike, Inc.
488 (**left**): 2000.42.1/Gift
of Chauncie McKeever
Rodzianko
488 (**right**): 93.103.2/Gift
of Red or Dead
489 (**left**): 2018.33.1/Gift
of Craig Chorney
489 (**right**): P93.5.1/
Museum purchase
490 (**left**): 2005.66.17/
Gift of Edward
A. Fling

490 (**right**): 97.71.1EF/
Gift of Ann
Demeulemeester
491 (**left**): 98.59.1/Gift of
Candie's, Inc.
491 (**right**): 98.44.2/Gift
of Robert Clergerie
492 (**left**): 98.35.1/Gift of
Sergio Rossi
492 (**right**): 98.47.2/Gift
of Fieramosca & Co.
493 (**left**): 99.8.1/Gift of
Emma Hope
493 (**right**): 2017.72.2/
Gift of Virginia
Barbato
494 (**left**): 2003.90.2/Gift
of Dorothy Lieberman,
MD
494 (**right**): 2010.1.24/
Anonymous donor
495 (**left**): 2000.51.1/
Gift of The School of
Graduate Studies at
the Fashion Institute
of Technology
495 (**right**): 2010.46.1BC/
Gift of Stella
McCartney
496 (**left**): 2014.53.1/Gift
of Marloes Ten Bhömer
496 (**right**): 2013.10.1/
Gift of Tom Ford
International
497 (**left**): 2010.54.1/
Museum purchase
497 (**right**): 2013.53.7/
Gift of Colette
498 (**left**): 2019.47.5/Gift
of Mia Mayer
498 (**right**): 2015.5.1CD/
Gift of Ricardo Seco
499 (**left**): 2019.7.7/Gift of
Roger Vivier
499 (**right**): 2017.55.2/
Gift of Sophia Webster
500 (**left**): 2019.5.2/Gift
of Thom Browne
500 (**right**): 2016.87.1CD/
Gift of Hood by Air
501 (**left**): 2019.9.1/Gift
of Puma
501 (**right**): 2019.69.1/
Gift of Gordon Kendall
502: 2010.62.1CD/Gift of
Burberry
511: 2012.35.1/Museum
purchase

ENDNOTES *all languages*

1   Julie Benasra, director. *God Save My Shoes*. Caïd Productions, 2011. 1 hr.

2   Karen Weintraub. "Going Barefoot Is Good for the Sole." *Scientific American*, June 26, 2019.

3   Elizabeth Semmelhack. *Heights of Fashion: A History of the Elevated Shoe*. (Pittsburgh/Toronto: Periscope Publishers/The Bata Shoe Museum, 2008), 12, 14.

4   Giorgio Riello. *A Foot in the Past: Consumers, Producers, and Footwear in the Long Eighteenth Century*. (Oxford and New York: Oxford University Press, 2006), 62.

5   Nancy Rexford. "The Perils of Choice: Women's Footwear in Nineteenth-Century America." In *Shoes: A History From Sandals to Sneakers*, edited by Giorgio Riello and Peter McNeil, (Oxford and New York: Berg, 2006), 144.

6   Susan B. Kaiser quoted in Valerie Steele. *Shoes: A Lexicon of Style* (New York: Rizzoli, 1999), 60.

7   Janice West. "The Shoe in Art, the Shoe as Art," and Lorraine Gamman, "Self-Fashioning, Gender Display, and Sexy Girl Shoes: What's at Stake — Female Fetishism or Narcissism?" In *On Fashion*, eds. Shari Benstock and Suzanne Ferriss (New Brunswick: Rutgers University Press, 2001).

8   Robert Baldick, ed. *The Memoirs of Chateaubriand*. (London: Hamish Hamilton, 1961), 107–8.

9   Valerie Steele and Colleen Hill. *Shoe Obsession*. (New Haven and London: Yale University Press, 2013), 16.

10 Elizabeth Semmelhack. *Shoes*. (London: Reaktion Books, 2017), 225.

11 Julia Emberley. "The Ends of Fashion: Or, Learning to Theorize with Shoes in the Bata Shoe Museum." In *Footnotes: On Shoes*. (New Brunswick: Rutgers University Press, 2001), 17.

12 Russell W. Belk. "Shoes and Self," *Advances in Consumer Research*. 2003, Vol. 30 Issue 1, 27–33.

ACKNOWLEDGMENTS

As with any project of this magnitude, many people helped make this book possible. We are grateful to Dr. Joyce F. Brown, president of the Fashion Institute of Technology, for supporting The Museum at FIT. As always, heartfelt thanks to the members of the Couture Council for making it possible to acquire, conserve, and exhibit significant objects, like the shoes depicted herein.

Many thanks to the museum team, especially Eileen Costa, museum photographer, and to Patricia Mears, Melissa Marra-Alvarez, Emma McClendon, Michelle McVicker, and Elizabeth Way, who contributed essays to this book. Other colleagues who provided assistance include Alison Castaneda, Nateer Cirino, Ann Coppinger, Sonia Dingilian, Laura Gawron, Michael Goita, Jill Hemingway, Gladys Rathod, Lynn Sallaberry, Thomas Synnamon, Vanessa Vasquez, and Ryan Wolfe. Thank you also to Lauren Posada and Darnell Lisby.

A very special thank you to all the designers and fashion houses featured in this book, and to the many generous individuals who have donated to the museum over the years. Thanks also to Karen Cannell and April Calahan at the Special Collections Department of the Gladys Marcus Library at FIT, and to Robert Nippoldt for contributing illustrations to this book.

Finally, our sincere gratitude to Benedikt and Marlene Taschen and their team: our editors Nina Wiener and Sarah Southard and designer Anna-Tina Kessler. Our thanks also to Frank Goerhardt, Ute Wachendorf, Kathrin Murr, and Alexi Alario at TASCHEN.

—**Valerie Steele & Colleen Hill**

PAGE 502
Burberry
Boots: Black leather, tan shearling, metal, rubber
England, fall 2010

PAGE 511
United Nude
(**Iris van Herpen**)
"Crystallization" ankle boots: Black leather, gold metallic leather
The Netherlands, fall 2010

EACH AND EVERY TASCHEN BOOK PLANTS A SEED!
Each year, we offset our annual carbon emissions with carbon credits at the Instituto Terra, a reforestation program in Minas Gerais, Brazil, founded by Lélia and Sebastião Salgado. To find out more about this ecological partnership, please check: www.taschen.com/institutoterra.
Inspiration: unlimited.
Carbon footprint: (almost) zero.

Want to see more? Visit taschen.com to view our current publications, browse our latest magazine, and subscribe to our newsletter.

© 2025 TASCHEN GmbH
Hohenzollernring 53, D-50672 Köln
taschen.com

Art Direction: Anna-Tina Kessler, Los Angeles
Editors: Sarah Southard, New York and
Kathrin Murr, Cologne
German Translation: Julia Heller, Munich;
Henriette Zeltner, Munich (Chronology)
French Translation: Claire Le Breton, Paris

Printed in Bosnia-Herzegovina
ISBN 978–3–7544–0465–2

"To wear dreams on one's feet is to begin to give a reality to one's dreams."

— ROGER VIVIER

THE HOLY SPIRIT

Copyright © 2017 by Caesar Benedo

ISBN: 978 - 99919-71-91-9

Note: personal pronouns for God, Jesus and the Holy Spirit are lowercased in keeping with the different Bible versions used in this book.

Scripture quotations marked KJV are taken from the Authorized King James version © 1991 by World Bible Publishers, Inc.

Scripture quotations marked NIV are taken from the New International version © 1973, 1978, 1984 by the International Bible Society

Scripture quotations marked NKJV are taken from the New King James version © 1982 by Thomas Nelson, Inc.

Scripture quotations marked NASB are taken from the New America Standard Bible © 1960, 1962, 1963, 1968, 1971, 1972, 1973, 1975, 1977, 1995 by The Lockman Foundation

Scripture quotations marked NLT are taken from the Holy Bible, New Living Translation ®, copyright © 1996, 2004 by Tyndale Charitable Trust. Used by permission of Tyndale House Publishers. All rights reserved.

Scripture quotations marked ESV are taken from the Holy Bible, English Standard Version Copyright © 2001 by Crossway Bibles, a division of Good News Publishers

Scripture quotations marked AMP are taken from the Amplified Bible © 1954, 1958, 1962, 1964, 1965, 1987 by The Lockman Foundation

Scripture quotations marked THE MESSAGE are taken from THE MESSAGE: The Bible in Contemporary Language © 2002 by Eugene H. Peterson. All rights reserved.

Scripture quotations marked HCSB are taken from the Holman Christian Standard Bible © 1999, 2000, 2002, 2003 by Holman Bible Publishers, Nashville Tennessee.

Scripture quotations marked RSV are taken from the Revised Standard Version of the Bible copyright © 1946, 1952, and 1971 the Division of Christian Education of the National Council of the Churches of Christ in the United States of America. Used by permission. All rights reserved.

THE
HOLY
SPIRIT

Rev. Dr. Caesar O. Benedo

ACKNOWLEDGEMENT

A special thanks to the following people for their love, support and prayer to make this book a reality. Mr. and Mrs. Ononiwu, Mr. and Mrs. Ugwulor, Mrs. Sheyi Bonou, Pastor Fadel Akpiti, Mr. Samuel Fabrice Yomo, Pastor Samuel Kalu, Mr. and Mrs. Odjo, Mr. Kingsley Eme, Mr. and Mrs. Fajemirokun, Mrs. Vivian Asempapa, Mrs. Georgette Gbesset Baffoh, Pastor Veronica Bampoe-Darko, Pastor Maximo Deleon, Rev. Emenike Paul Ezechiluo, Rev. Lucile Sossou, Prophet Holy Joy, Rev. Dr. Nicaise Laleye, Rev. Alphonse Dagnonnoueton, Rev. and Pastor Mrs. Tigo, Rev. Isidore Godonou, Rev. and Mrs. Oluwaseyitan, Rev. Mrs. and Bishop Meshack Okonkwo and so on.

A million thanks to the members of my family for your love, encouragement, care, and support. May God richly bless you all.

I want to use this opportunity to express my appreciation to Pastor Benjamin Opeyemi Olaosebikan, and Pastor Eric Osei Yaw for their brotherly support, encouragement, and prayer.

A special thanks to Bishop Kwesi Adutwum for your love, encouragement, advice, support, and prayer. I'm indeed thankful to God for your life and for the incredible support you gave me. May God richly bless you.

A special thanks to Rev. Mrs Betty N. Coleman for your love, encouragement, support and prayer. May God richly bless and reward you for the great work you are doing for the kingdom.

I want to use this opportunity to express my gratitude to Pastor Zina Pierre for your love, support and prayer. May the Lord continue to bless you.

A special thanks to my Bishop, James Nana Ofori Attah for your love, encouragement, support and prayer. May the Lord continue to bless you.

I want to use this opportunity to express my gratitude to Apostle Michael Adeyemi Adefarasin for bringing out the best in me. I admire your commitment to excellence, your sincere desire to make a difference and your love for good work.

A special thanks to my papa, the archbishop Nicholas Duncan-Williams (founder of Action Chapel International), for your prayers, leadership, and spiritual guidance. May God continue to use you to raise and empower men and women to fulfil their divine purpose.

Words cannot convey how much I appreciate the love, care, support and prayer of senior deacon, and mama Georgina Lamptey for all the investment both of you made in my life. Thank you for standing by me at the very moment I needed it the most. May the Lord richly bless you.

DEDICATION

To everyone who wishes to have a deeper understanding of the nature, divinity, and works of the Holy Spirit, and to those who want to cultivate and maintain a good relationship with him, this is for you.

Table of Contents

PRAYER

Heavenly Father, in agreement with the Scripture that says the entrance of your word gives light and understanding to the simple (Ps.119:130), I beseech you to enlighten the eyes of my heart that I may understand the mystery of the Holy Spirit as I read this book. Grant me insight and the grace to take hold of the truth, just as you did for Lydia in Acts16:14, when you opened her heart to receive the truth spoken by the apostle Paul about your Son Jesus.

By the power of the Holy Spirit, I pull down every imagination, argument and thought that does not conform to biblical truths, concepts and principles that the wicked may want to use to hinder me from accepting the truth in this book. It is written that I shall know the truth, and the truth will set me free (Jn.8:32).

Dear Lord, open my eyes to the truth in this book and deliver me from the spirit of error in Jesus name. Amen!

But I tell you the truth: It is for your good that I am going away. Unless I go away, the Counselor will not come to you; but if I go, I will send him to you. When he comes, he will convict the world of guilt in regard to sin and righteousness and judgment: in regard to sin, because men do not believe in me; in regard to righteousness, because I am going to the Father, where you can see me no longer; and in regard to judgment, because the prince of this world now stands condemned. "I have much more to say to you, more than you can now bear. But when he, the Spirit of truth, comes, he will guide you into all truth. He will not speak on his own; he will speak only what he hears, and he will tell you what is yet to come. He will bring glory to me by taking from what is mine and making it known to you.

(Jn.16:7-14 NIV)

INTRODUCTION

A lot has been said about the Holy Spirit since the beginning of the history of the church. Some say he is the third person in the Trinity, who is co-equal and co-eternal with the Godhead. Others claim the Holy Spirit is one of the manifestations, titles, attributes or functions of God rather than a distinct person. A few others assert he is the active power of God that enables him to do things.

Due to the ways some Bible passages present the Holy Spirit, a lot of people seem to be confused as regards to his true nature. Some ask whether the Holy Spirit is a living being or mere force. A friend once ask, "How can we say the Holy Spirit is an individual being, distinct from the Godhead and Jesus, and claim God is one?" Are there three Gods? Is the Holy Spirit different from Jesus, and the Father? Is he the one true God of the Old Testament? When we say Holy Spirit, is it another name for the Father or Jesus?

There are so many questions people ask about the Holy Spirit that we cannot ignore. In my others books, I spoke briefly on the subject.

But because of the role that the Holy Spirit plays in the Christendom, I decided to write a book on it. My intention is to add to the effort made by other great men and women who the Lord had used over the years to enlighten the church on the subject.

The Lord Jesus said in John16:7-14, that it was to our advantage that he goes away for the Holy Spirit to come. And when he comes, he will convict the world of sin, God's righteousness and eternal judgment. Verses 12 and 13 declare, "I still have things to say to you, but you cannot bear them now. When the Spirit of truth comes, he will guide you into all the truth, for he will not speak of his own authority, but whatever he hears he will speak, and he will declare to you the things that are to come."

But I tell you the truth: It is for your good that I am going away. Unless I go away, the Counselor will not come to you; but if I go, I will send him to you. When he comes, he will convict the world of guilt in regard to sin and righteousness and judgment: in regard to sin, because men do not believe in me; in regard to righteousness, because I am going to the Father, where you can see me no longer; and in regard to judgment, because the prince of this world now stands condemned. "I have much more to say to you, more than you can now bear. But when he, the Spirit of truth, comes, he will guide you into all truth. He will not speak on his own; he will speak only what he hears, and he will tell you what is yet to come. He will bring glory to me by taking from what is mine and making it known to you.
(Jn.16:7-14 NIV)

INTRODUCTION

The above passage clearly reveals the important role that the Holy Spirit plays in the church today, and the world in general. For the Lord Jesus to say it was more profitable for him to go away in order for the Holy Spirit to come, emphasizes the significance of the presence and works of the Holy Spirit in this era. The Bible declares in 1 Corinthians12:3, that no one speaking by the Spirit of God ever says, "Jesus is cursed," and no one can say, "Jesus is Lord," except by the Holy Spirit.

This book focuses on the nature of the Holy Spirit, his existence, works, power, divinity, ministry, gifts, fruit and role in the spiritual life of Christians. It also describes the differences between living and walking in the Spirit, platforms on spiritual pathway and phases in spiritual walk. In addition, it speaks about the law of the Spirit of life, importance of spiritual walk, pitfalls in spiritual walk, stages in spiritual life, manifestation of the Holy Spirit etc.

Now there were in the church at Antioch prophets and teachers, Barnabas, Simeon who was called Niger, Lucius of Cyrene, Manaen a member of the court of Herod the tetrarch, and Saul. While they were worshiping the Lord and fasting, the Holy Spirit said, "Set apart for me Barnabas and Saul for the work to which I have called them." Then after fasting and praying they laid their hands on them and sent them off. So, being sent out by the Holy Spirit, they went down to Seleucia, and from there they sailed to Cyprus.

(Acts 13:1-4 ESV)

CHAPTER ONE

NATURE OF THE HOLY SPIRIT

In my book, "The oneness of God," I explained that the Holy Spirit is God's active power that allows him to do things. Whether we say the "Spirit of the Lord or Holy Ghost," it means the same thing – it is another way of saying the "Holy Spirit."

The Holy Spirit subsisted in the Godhead in the beginning as a distinct being until the bodily ascension of Jesus of Nazareth to the right hand throne of the Majesty where he (Jesus) received him (Holy Spirit) from the Father and poured him out on the sons of men (Acts.2:33) for spiritual regeneration. From that moment, the Holy Spirit moved from the Godhead and resided in the glorified body of Jesus Christ.

The coming together of the Word and Spirit of God in Jesus of Nazareth as a single entity produced the completeness of God's eternal power in bodily form.

That could be the reason Colossians 2:9 declares that in Christ dwells the fullness of the Godhead in bodily form, since the constituents of God comprises his Word, Spirit, and essence. Without the Holy Spirit, God's divine agenda for humankind cannot be accomplished on earth. Likewise, without the human body, the Holy Spirit cannot work legally in this world, because the earth is not intended for spirit beings but humans.

In as much as humans need God to do certain things on earth, God needs us to achieve his plans in this world. The reason for this is that God gave the earth to humans, made it our domain, and excluded himself in the management and governance of earth affairs (Gen.1:26 and Ps.115:16).

The nature of the Holy Spirit has been one of the main questions people ask me whenever I talk about the Godhead. Many want to understand who he really is, what he does, why we need him, why the Lord Jesus said it was more important for him to go so that the Holy Spirit could come, why scripture says the sin against the Holy Spirit is unforgiveable, how to fellowship with him and so forth.

Most dictionaries define the word *nature* as the inherent (intrinsic, integral, inborn, innate, permanent and inseparable, essential constituent) features or quality of a thing. The nature of the Holy Spirit could therefore be referred to as the integral or key constituents of his being (the very thing that makes him who he is). For the benefit of this teaching, I would like to focus on his existence, activities and divinity.

EXISTENCE OF THE HOLY SPIRIT

As earlier mentioned, the Holy Spirit subsisted in the Godhead in eternity as part of the constituents of his eternal power until God allowed his eternal power to subsist independently in him as his Word and Spirit, which commenced the beginning of his works.

The individual subsistence of the Holy Spirit in the Godhead as his active power makes him a living being, and it distinguishes him from every other being that later came into existence. He is not a force, wind or dove but a living being. He exists because he lives, he lives because he has life, and the life he has is eternal, which flows from the Godhead who is the source.

In my book, *The Oneness of God*, under the heading "Eternal Existence of God," I explained how God's eternal life goes beyond an endless life to that which has neither beginning nor end of days because all things whether visible or invisible begin and end in him. I also mentioned that the reason God exists is that he lives. He lives because he has life, which has no beginning or ending. To refer to God as "Eternal Spirit" simply means the one who has neither beginning nor end of days, and this is what constitutes the very essence of his divine nature.

As an individual being, the Holy Spirit possesses the life of the Godhead in whom he subsists. Genesis 1:2 informs us that the earth was formless and emptied, darkness covered the deep waters, and the Holy Spirit (Spirit of God) was hovering over the surface of the waters.

It is evident from the passage that the reason the Holy Spirit hovered over the waters is that he is a living being.

Speaking about the Holy Spirit in John14:17, the Lord Jesus explained why the people in the world could not accept him (Holy Spirit). He said the reason is that they do not see him or know him; but the disciples knew him because he lives with them and he will be in them. This also establishes the fact that the Holy Spirit is a living being as I said before. His eternal life, which has no beginning or ending is the basis for his existence.

ACTIVITIES OF THE HOLY SPIRIT

There are numerous passages in the Bible that point to the works of the Holy Spirit. For this reason, many people think that he (Holy Spirit) is a living being because he works. On the contrary, the Holy Spirit works because he exists, he exists because he lives, and he lives because he possesses eternal life. It is very important we get this right, because one has to be alive before he or she can work.

Nevertheless, I tell you the truth: it is to your advantage that I go away, for if I do not go away, the Helper will not come to you. But if I go, I will send him to you. And when he comes, he will convict the world concerning sin and righteousness and judgment: concerning sin, because they do not believe in me; concerning righteousness, because I go to the Father, and you will see me no longer; concerning judgment, because the ruler of this world is judged. "I still have many things to say to you, but you cannot bear them now.

NATURE OF THE HOLY SPIRIT

When the Spirit of truth comes, he will guide you into all the truth, for he will not speak on his own authority, but whatever he hears he will speak, and he will declare to you the things that are to come. He will glorify me, for he will take what is mine and declare it to you. All that the Father has is mine; therefore I said that he will take what is mine and declare it to you.
(Jn.16:7-15ESV)

One of the main differences between living and nonliving things is that the first lives and acts, while the latter is dead and inactive. The first can move, grow, reproduce, respond to stimuli etc. but the latter cannot. The existence and activities of the Holy Spirit are the two key qualities that distinguish him from other living being whether spiritual or physical. He exists because he lives, and he acts because he has self-ability (auto capability). In addition, he possess the whole trait of a living being since he speaks, moves, interact, gets angry and so on.

However, as it is written: "No eye has seen, no ear has heard, no mind has conceived what God has prepared for those who love him"—but God has revealed it to us by his Spirit. The Spirit searches all things, even the deep things of God. For who among men knows the thoughts of a man except the man's spirit within him? In the same way no one knows the thoughts of God except the Spirit of God. We have not received the spirit of the world but the Spirit who is from God, that we may understand what God has freely given us. This is what we speak, not in words taught us by human wisdom but in words taught by the Spirit, expressing spiritual truths in spiritual words.
(1 Co. 2:9-13 NIV)

THE HOLY SPIRIT

Matthew 12:28 reveals that the miraculous works our Lord Jesus accomplished during his earthly ministry was only possible because of the Holy Spirit. He said, "But if it is by the Spirit of God that I drive out demons, then the kingdom of God has come upon you." This implies he drove out devils by the power of the Holy Spirit.

Acts13:2-4 also recounts how the Holy Spirit spoke about Barnabas and Saul when the people of the church at Antioch were worshiping the Lord and fasting. He said, "Set apart for me Barnabas and Saul for the work to which I have called them. Then after fasting and praying they laid their hands on them and sent them off. So, being sent out by the Holy Spirit, they went down to Seleucia, and from there they sailed to Cyprus."

Now there were in the church at Antioch prophets and teachers, Barnabas, Simeon who was called Niger, Lucius of Cyrene, Manaen a member of the court of Herod the tetrarch, and Saul. While they were worshiping the Lord and fasting, the Holy Spirit said, "Set apart for me Barnabas and Saul for the work to which I have called them." Then after fasting and praying they laid their hands on them and sent them off. So, being sent out by the Holy Spirit, they went down to Seleucia, and from there they sailed to Cyprus.
(ESV)

We notice in the passage above that the Holy Spirit asked the church to set Barnabas and Saul apart for the work he called them to do. Verse 4 declares he sent them out to do the work.

Could the Holy Spirit have done that if he were merely a wind, force, energy, dove and the like as some think, rather than a living being? The truth of the matter is that the Holy Spirit lives and works because he has life, will, intellect, self-ability, self-awareness, emotions, desire and so on.

No rotten talk should come from your mouth, but only what is good for the building up of someone in need, in order to give grace to those who hear. And don't grieve God's Holy Spirit, who sealed you for the day of redemption. All bitterness, anger and wrath, insult and slander must be removed from you, along with all wickedness. And be kind and compassionate to one another, forgiving one another, just as God also forgave you in Christ.
(Eph. 4:29-32 HCSB)

The above passage shows that the Holy Spirit can be grieved. This is so because he has emotion, intellect and self-awareness. He is a living being. Acts 7:51 speaks about resisting him.

Acts 10:9-20 recounts how the apostle Peter became hungry and while the meal was being prepared, he fell into a trance and saw heaven opened. Something like a large sheet, which contained all kinds of animals, reptiles, and birds was let down by its four corners. Then a voice said to him, "Get up, Peter; kill and eat them." No Lord," Peter replied. "I have never eaten anything impure or unclean." The voice spoke to him the second time, "What God has made clean, do not call unclean." This happened three times, and the sheet was taken back to heaven.

THE HOLY SPIRIT

While Peter was wondering and thinking about the meaning of the vision, the Holy Spirit said to him, "Simon, three men are looking for you. Get up and go downstairs. Do not hesitate to go with them, for I have sent them." The Holy Spirit did all these because he lives and acts. The self-ability of the Holy Spirit is what scripture refers to as the power of the Holy Spirit.

The next day, as they were on their journey and coming near the city, Peter went up on the housetop to pray, about the sixth hour. And he became hungry and desired something to eat; but while they were preparing it, he fell into a trance and saw the heaven opened, and something descending, like a great sheet, let down by four corners upon the earth. In it were all kinds of animals and reptiles and birds of the air. And there came a voice to him, "Rise, Peter; kill and eat." But Peter said, "No, Lord; for I have never eaten anything that is common or unclean." And the voice came to him again a second time, "What God has cleansed, you must not call common." This happened three times, and the thing was taken up at once to heaven. Now while Peter was inwardly perplexed as to what the vision which he had seen might mean, behold, the men that were sent by Cornelius, having made inquiry for Simon's house, stood before the gate and called out to ask whether Simon who was called Peter was lodging there. And while Peter was pondering the vision, the Spirit said to him, "Behold, three men are looking for you. Rise and go down, and accompany them without hesitation; for I have sent them."
RSV

POWER OF THE HOLY SPIRIT

The power of the Holy Spirit is the sum of his self-ability, the force that resides in him by virtue of his nature, which allows him to perform the will and purposes of the Godhead. The life and power of the Holy Spirit that enable him to live and act are the two intrinsic constituents of his being. That is to say, he lives because he has life, and he acts because he has the ability (power) to do so.

We cannot speak about the Holy Spirit without these two inherent attributes that makeup his being. Moreover, an in-depth look at the Scriptures highlights these two vital qualities, which are revealed to humans in presence, and through various gifts.

This is the message of Good News for the people of Israel—that there is peace with God through Jesus Christ, who is Lord of all. You know what happened throughout Judea, beginning in Galilee, after John began preaching his message of baptism. And you know that God anointed Jesus of Nazareth with the Holy Spirit and with power. Then Jesus went around doing good and healing all who were oppressed by the devil, for God was with him.
(Acts 10:36-38 NLT)

The above Bible passage shows that God anointed Jesus of Nazareth with two things, namely: the Holy Spirit and Power. For this reason, Jesus went from one place to another doing good and healing all who were oppressed by the devil. When scripture says the Holy Spirit and power, it implies two things. First is the tangible manifestation of his being. Second is the totality of his self-ability, called the power of the Holy Spirit.

The first is revealed in presence, while the latter in power through diverse gifts. The full manifestation of the presence of the Holy Spirit is when he comes in a tangible form or way that could be felt and seen. Like what happened the very day, the Lord Jesus was baptized.

Luke3:21-22, recounts how the Lord Jesus came from Galilee to the Jordan River to be baptized by John. After his baptism, he prayed. As he was praying, the heaven opened, and the Holy Spirit descended on him in bodily form, like a dove; and a voice from heaven said, "You are my Son, whom I love; with you I am well pleased." Just as the name suggests, spirit has no body. For the Holy Spirit to descend in bodily form like a dove on Jesus means that his presence, which is the manifestation of his being was so tangible that it took a form that could be liken to that of a dove. This means he came in person (he was fully present).

Now when all the people were baptized, and when Jesus also had been baptized and was praying, the heavens were opened, and the Holy Spirit descended on him in bodily form, like a dove; and a voice came from heaven, "You are my beloved Son; with you I am well pleased."
(ESV)

Another good example is what happened in Acts2:1-4. The passage says when the day of Pentecost arrived, all the believers were together in one place when the Holy Spirit suddenly came like a violent wind from heaven and filled the house where they were sitting.

Then, what looked like flames of fire (some versions used tongues of fire) appeared and settled on each of them. All of them were filled with the Holy Spirit, and they began to speak in other tongues as the Spirit gave them utterance.

When the day of Pentecost came, they were all together in one place. Suddenly a sound like the blowing of a violent wind came from heaven and filled the whole house where they were sitting. They saw what seemed to be tongues of fire that separated and came to rest on each of them. All of them were filled with the Holy Spirit and began to speak in other tongues as the Spirit enabled them.

(NIV)

We see here that the presence of the Holy Spirit was so tangible that it took the form of flames or tongues of fire that settled on the Apostles. The Holy Spirit fully came in person and filled both the house and the people. His presence was so real that the people could see and feel it as he filled every one of them and gave them the ability to speak in other languages. That is not to say that the Holy Spirit is a wind, fire or dove. He is spirit.

Luke4:1 says Jesus was full of the Holy Spirit after the encounter at the River Jordan. The reason is that the Holy Spirit fully came and settled on him, and when Jesus left the Jordan, scriptures declares that he was led by the Holy Spirit into the wilderness, where Satan tempted him for forty days, and since he did not eat anything during the time, he became very hungry. Verse 13 says when the devil had finished tempting him and did not succeed; he left him until an opportune time.

Verse 14 declares that Jesus returned to Galilee in the power of the Spirit. He entered the desert in the fullness of the Holy Spirit and returned in the power of the Holy Spirit. This brings me to the second point, which is the power of the Holy Spirit.

When the Holy Spirit descended on him at the River Jordan, the presence was so tangible that it took a bodily shape (form), which scripture liken to a dove. After which he went in the fullness of the Holy Spirit to the desert, where he fasted forty days and he was tempted by the devil during the time. At the end of the fasting, and temptation, he returned home in the power of the Holy Spirit. The power of the Holy Spirit is the sum of the self-ability of the Holy Spirit.

Jesus, full of the Holy Spirit, returned from the Jordan and was led by the Spirit in the desert, where for forty days he was tempted by the devil. He ate nothing during those days, and at the end of them he was hungry. The devil said to him, "If you are the Son of God, tell this stone to become bread." Jesus answered, "It is written: 'Man does not live on bread alone.'" The devil led him up to a high place and showed him in an instant all the kingdoms of the world. And he said to him, "I will give you all their authority and splendor, for it has been given to me, and I can give it to anyone I want to. So if you worship me, it will all be yours." Jesus answered, "It is written: 'Worship the Lord your God and serve him only.'" The devil led him to Jerusalem and had him stand on the highest point of the temple. "If you are the Son of God," he said, "throw yourself down from here. For it is written: "'He will command his angels concerning you to guard you carefully;

they will lift you up in their hands, so that you will not strike your foot against a stone.'" Jesus answered, "It says: 'Do not put the Lord your God to the test.'" When the devil had finished all this tempting, he left him until an opportune time. Jesus returned to Galilee in the power of the Spirit, and news about him spread through the whole countryside. (Lk.4:1-14NIV)

In the testimony of John the Baptist about Jesus, he said in John 3:34 that God gives him the Spirit without measure – that is, in full. Since the fullness of the Holy Spirit comprises his being and self-ability, which manifest in presence and power, it was necessary for Jesus to have both the tangible presence and power of the Holy Spirit because he was entitled to the fullness of the Holy Spirit.

In my opinion, I think the main reason he had to go into the wilderness, fast forty days and be tempted by the devil is that he had to pay the price tag before the legitimate right to exercise the power could be given to him. That is to say, when the Holy Spirit settled on him at the Jordan River, he came in fullness (presence and power), but stayed with Jesus and watched him go through the lawful righteous requirements of the Godhead before conferring on him, the lawful right to exercise the power. This means nothing comes freely, you have to pay the price to get the prize.

A good analogy is a police or an army officer in uniform with their arms. The uniform is their authority that distinguishes them from the park, while their gun is their force or power that allows them to do certain things when the need arises.

THE HOLY SPIRIT

The presence of the Holy Spirit is like the uniform, while his power is like the weapons. Whenever he manifests, he comes in presence and power. However, he doesn't grant humans both his presence and power at the same time. A person must meet the price tag to each of the two components before receiving them. When a person meets the conditions tagged to only one of the two components, the Holy Spirit would reveal himself to the individual only in that area, and deny him access to the other.

The same way an officer could go to certain places in uniform without a gun, because the law forbids him to take arm for the occasion, the Holy Spirit can manifest in a person's life only in presence without giving the person his power because of the different conditions and requirements tagged to his presence and power that the individual must fulfil in order to be granted both. Unless the person accomplishes both conditions, the Holy Spirit would only grant the individual access to the one he or she fulfils and restrict the person access to the other component until the conditions are met.

When the Holy Spirit came on Jesus in bodily form (both in presence and in power), the Bible says Jesus was full of the Holy Spirit. He had the tangible presence that led him into the wilderness, but the legitimate right to exercise the power (sum of the self-ability) of the Holy Spirit was not given to him until he fulfilled the lawful requirements of God by fasting forty days, resisting and defeating the devil, abiding in the wilderness throughout the period.

As soon as he met all these requirements, God granted him the right to the tangible presence and power of the Holy, and he returned to Galilee in the power of the Holy Spirit doing incredible works that caused his fame to spread through the whole countryside.

The book of Acts 10:38 says God anointed Jesus with the Holy Spirit and power. If the fullness of the Holy Spirit comprises his tangible presence and power, it means the Lord Jesus had the Holy Spirit in full because the Father gave him the Spirit without measure.

In Acts1:8, the Lord promised his disciples that they would receive power when the Holy Spirit comes on them, so they could be his witnesses in Jerusalem, Judea, Samaria, and to the ends of the earth.

Acts2:1-4, recounts how the Holy Spirit came mightily on them on the Pentecost day and filled every one of them. Verses14-47 relates how Peter stood and addressed the crowd, which lead to the salvation of about three thousand people and the Lord added to their number daily those who were being saved. Chapter 3 tells how Peter healed the crippled beggar and spoke to the crowd again, which caused the number of the believers to increase to about five thousand. Chapter 4 describes how the priests, the captain of the temple guard and the Sadducees arrested Peter and John and put them in jail until the next day. When the members of the Sanhedrin had met the following day, they had Peter and John brought before them for questioning. They asked the apostles, "By what power or what name did you do this?"

Then Peter filled with the Holy Spirit, said to them: "Rulers and elders of our people! If we are being called to account today for an act of kindness shown to a man who was lame and are being asked how he was healed, let it be known to all of you that this man was healed by the name of Jesus Christ of Nazareth whom you crucified, but whom God raised from the dead. He is the stone that was rejected by you, which has become the cornerstone. Salvation is found in no one else, for there is no other name under heaven given to men by which we must be saved."

The members of the council were astonished when they saw the boldness of Peter and John, for they could see that they were ordinary men who had no special training as it relates to the Scriptures. They recognized them as men who had been with Jesus.

In an attempt to stop them from continuing the work, they commanded them not to speak or teach at all in the name of Jesus. Then, Peter and John replied, "Which is right in God's eyes: to listen to you, or to him? You be the Judges! We cannot but speak of what we have seen and heard." When they had further threatened them, they let them go, because they could not find a way to punish them since all the people were praising God for what had happened.

On their release, Peter and John reported all that the chief priest and the elders had said to them to their own people. When they heard it, they lifted their voices together in prayer to God. After the prayer, the place they were meeting shook, and they were all filled with the Holy Spirit again and spoke the word of God with boldness.

I recounted the whole story to show you the gradual process the disciples went through for an infilling with the Holy Spirit from one measure to another. Beginning from when the Lord breathed on them in John20:22-23, and said, "Receive the Holy Spirit. If you forgive anyone his sins, they are forgiven; if you do not forgive them, they are not forgiven." Through Acts2:1-4 when they were all filled with the Holy Spirit, to Acts4:23-31 where they prayed and the Holy Spirit filled them again so they could speak the word of God with boldness.

The reason for this is that the infilling of the Holy Spirit comes in measure from one level to another, unlike Jesus to whom the Father gave the Holy Spirit without measure (he had the Spirit in full).

DIVINITY OF THE HOLY SPIRIT

Numerous passages in the Bible highlight the divinity of the Holy Spirit, and the most famous of it all is Acts5:4, which equate him to God. However, the verse remains silent on how the Holy Spirit is equal to God.

Several attempts have been made to explain the basis for the equality between the Holy Spirit and the Godhead. Some say it is because the Holy Spirit possess all the attributes that makeup the being we call God, others claim he is co-equal and co-eternal with the Godhead because he is God the Holy Spirit. "There is nothing that God is that the Holy Spirit is not. All of the essential aspects of deity belong to the Holy Spirit." says Evangelist Billy Graham.

THE HOLY SPIRIT

In his book, *The Holy Spirit*, Evangelist Graham writes, "This is a terribly difficult subject – far beyond the ability of our limited minds to grasp fully. Nevertheless, it is extremely important to declare what the Bible holds, and be silent where the Bible is silent. God the Father is fully God. God the Son is fully God. God the Holy Spirit is fully God. The Bible presents this as fact. It does not explain it. Nevertheless, many explanations have been suggested, some of which sound logical, but they do not preserve the truth of Scriptural teaching." [*]

But a man named Ananias, with his wife Sapphira, sold a piece of property, and with his wife's knowledge he kept back for himself some of the proceeds and brought only a part of it and laid it at the apostles' feet. But Peter said, "Ananias, why has Satan filled your heart to lie to the Holy Spirit and to keep back for yourself part of the proceeds of the land? While it remained unsold, did it not remain your own? And after it was sold, was it not at your disposal? Why is it that you have contrived this deed in your heart? You have not lied to men but to God." When Ananias heard these words, he fell down and breathed his last. And great fear came upon all who heard of it. The young men rose and wrapped him up and carried him out and buried him.
(Acts 5:1-6 ESV)

In the above passage, the apostle Peter told Ananias in verse 3 that his action was against the Holy Spirit. Then in verse 4, he clearly made it known to him that it was not man he lied to but God, meaning the Holy Spirit is God from the Apostle's point of view.

* Billy Graham, The Holy Spirit, (Word Books Publishers, 1978) pp. 22-3

NATURE OF THE HOLY SPIRIT

I think everyone would want to know why the apostle Peter equates the Holy Spirit to God. Second, why he didn't explain the basis for the equality. Third, whether the Holy Spirit is the one true God of Israel, or a distinct being from the God of the Bible who created the heaven and earth. Fourth, whether the words the Apostle used here suggest plurality of persons in the Godhead or just a mere use of the same word for God to highlight the fact they were not doing man's work but Gods.

In my book, *The Oneness of God*, I explained that God is indivisibly one in essence, while his eternal power and divine nature were the two key constituents of his being in eternity past. His works began in eternity when he caused his eternal power to subsist independently, and it subsisted in him as his Word and Spirit (distinct in being, but one in essence).

After the incarnation, death, resurrection and bodily ascension of Jesus of Nazareth to the right hand of God, the Holy Spirit moved from the Godhead and resided in the glorified body of Jesus to form a single entity with the incarnate Word of God, because it pleased the Godhead to have all his fullness dwell in Christ. Key scriptures (Rom.1:20, Pro.8:22-36, Ps.33:6, Jn.1:1-4, Acts2:32-36, Col.1:15-20, 2:9, Heb.1:1-4).

Prior to the beginning, the Word, and Spirit of God constitute his eternal power. The beginning started when his eternal power transitioned to individual subsistence in him (Godhead) as his Word and Spirit.

THE HOLY SPIRIT

At the appointed time, the Word emanated from the Godhead to be incarnated, and after his death and resurrection, he ascended back to heaven, sat at the right hand of the Godhead, and obtained the Holy Spirit from him. This caused the Holy Spirit to emanate from the Godhead as the Word did, and resided in the glorified body of Jesus.

Since the Word of God (Jesus of Nazareth) and the Holy Spirit constitute God's eternal power, they are both equal to the Godhead based on their preexistence. There is no God without his Word, and Spirit because they make-up his eternal power, which is the first constituent of his being, and there is no Christ without God, for the Godhead is his source (please go to my book, *The Oneness of God*, for more information).

Since the Holy Spirit subsists in the glorified body of the incarnate Word (Jesus of Nazareth) as a distinct divine being, but with one essence with the Godhead and the Word, he is one with the Father and Son. That is to say, though the Godhead is one eternal Spirit in essence, he subsists in three distinct beings as God the Father, Jesus his Son and his Spirit (Holy Spirit), not as God the Father, God the Son and God the Holy Spirit. Thus, the divinity of the Holy Spirit is based on the oneness he shares with the Godhead as one of the constituents of his being, even though he subsists in him (Godhead) as independent being.

In summary, the Holy Spirit is a divine being. His existence and activities are the two key qualities (attributes) that make him unique and distinguish him from other living being.

He exists because he lives, and the life he has is eternal. He acts because he possesses self-ability, and the sum of his ability is called the power of the Holy Spirit. He is not a mere force, wind, dove, fire or energy.

The Holy Spirit is an individual divine being distinct from the Father, Son and the angels. He shares equality and union with the Father and Son because he is one of the constituents of the Godhead. He has no physical body since he is spirit, but he possess the whole trait of a living being because he speaks, moves, interact, gets angry and so on. He has life, intellect, will, plans, desires, self-awareness, and self-ability. His divine being comprises his eternal life and power that allows him to live and act forever.

That is what the Scriptures mean when they say, "No eye has seen, no ear has heard, and no mind has imagined what God has prepared for those who love him." But it was to us that God revealed these things by his Spirit. For his Spirit searches out everything and shows us God's deep secrets. No one can know a person's thoughts except that person's own spirit, and no one can know God's thoughts except God's own Spirit. And we have received God's Spirit (not the world's spirit), so we can know the wonderful things God has freely given us. When we tell you these things, we do not use words that come from human wisdom. Instead, we speak words given to us by the Spirit, using the Spirit's words to explain spiritual truths.

(1Co.2:9-13 NLT)

CHAPTER TWO

OPERATION OF THE HOLY SPIRIT

The Holy Spirit is the sole executor of all divine agenda on earth. Without him, God's will and purposes for humanity cannot be achieved. To accomplish his works, he uses his gifts, fruit and ministry. These three fields of activities of the Holy Spirit is what I call the "Operation of the Holy Spirit." It is all about the general works that he accomplishes in the body of Christ to regenerate a living soul for a newness of life in Christ, and then transforms the person into Christ perfect image in words and deeds, by faith and revelation knowledge of the word of God.

I believe the main reason Christ poured the Holy Spirit out on humanity is to draw us to him, change our lives and transform us to his glorious image. Each of the three different fields of activities of the Holy Spirit does a specific work in us. Together, it regenerates our spirit, renews our minds, changes our actions, and our characters.

In my book, *Strategic prayer*, under the heading "Battle of the mind," which I defined as the repeated struggle, fight, and contention that goes on daily in our mind between the Spirit and the flesh, truth and falsehood, good and evil, light and darkness, the list goes on and on.

I explained that the human mind is the battlefield for spiritual warfare between the forces of light and darkness, and that whatever controls the mind controls the person, because the condition of one's mind determines his words and actions. I also described how God uses the operation of the Holy Spirit, which consists of his ministry, gifts, and fruit to transforms us into the very image of Christ in words and deeds. For the benefit of those who have not read the book, below is an excerpt:

"Genesis 6:5 informs us that the Lord saw how great the wickedness of humanity had become on the earth and that every inclination of the thoughts of their hearts was only evil all the time. The human mind is the battlefield for spiritual warfare between the forces of light and darkness. And whatever controls the mind controls the person, because the condition of one's mind determines his words and actions.

Matthew 12:34 says whatever is in the heart determines what comes out of the mouth, and verse 35 declares that a good person produces good things out of the good stored up in him, and an evil person brings forth evil things from the treasury of an evil heart. This could be the reason why the prophet Jeremiah says in chapter 17:9 that the human heart is deceitful above all things and desperately wicked. Who can understand it?

OPERATION OF THE HOLY SPIRIT

In Romans 12:2, the great apostle Paul asks us not to conform to the pattern of this world, but to be transformed by the renewing of our mind, that we may be able to discern what is good, perfect, and pleasing to God. The human mind is made up of memory, thought or contemplation, and imagination. These three components deal with past, present, and future events. The memory keeps mental images of past experiences, the thought deals with the now, while the imagination enables you to project into the future and generates mental pictures that play on the screen of your mind.

Our education, experiences, practices, beliefs, perception, and so on, which determine our attitudes are stored in the mind. Both God and Satan engage humans in the mind to gain control over our lives. This is why the mind is the center for spiritual warfare, the struggle that goes on daily within, between truth and falsehood, good and evil, light and darkness. Each party uses strategic plan and weapons to gain control over the human mind, for no spirit can operate legally in this world without a body. And there is no way a spirit can successfully use the human body unless it controls the person's mind.

James 4:4 makes it clear that friendship with the world is enmity with God, for whomever chooses to be a friend of the world makes himself an enemy of God. Satan uses worldly principles, systems, beliefs, customs, traditions, or ways to entice and enslave people to do his will.

Romans 8:7 says the sinful mind is hostile to God because it does not submit to his law and it will never do so. Verse 8 declares that those who are controlled by the flesh cannot please God. The apostle John writes, "Do not love the world or the things in the world. If anyone loves the world, the love of the Father is not in him. For all that is in the world – the desires of the flesh and the desires of the eyes and pride of life – is not from the Father but is from the world. And the world is passing away along with its desires, but whoever does the will of God abides forever." (1 Jn.2:15-17)

You, however, are controlled not by the sinful nature but by the Spirit, if the Spirit of God lives in you. And if anyone does not have the Spirit of Christ, he does not belong to Christ. But if Christ is in you, your body is dead because of sin, yet your spirit is alive because of righteousness. And if the Spirit of him who raised Jesus from the dead is living in you, he who raised Christ from the dead will also give life to your mortal bodies through his Spirit, who lives in you.
(Rom.8:9-11 NIV)

The scripture above says if anyone does not have the Spirit of Christ, he does not belong to him. I believe the reason is that the Godhead uses the Holy Spirit to infuse his eternal life into the spirit of humans in Christ Jesus, the savior of humanity, for new birth, so the person can be one with Christ in spirit and become member of the universal body of Christ – the church, according to scripture (1Co. 6:17, 12:13). Through the operation of the Holy Spirit, which consists of his ministry, gifts, and fruit, God transforms us into the very image of Christ in words and deeds.

OPERATION OF THE HOLY SPIRIT

The Holy Spirit uses his ministerial work to perform two works in us. First, to regenerate our spirit from the spiritual death that came on humankind through the sin of Adam the father of human race and make us a new creation in Christ at new birth (2 Co.5:17). Second, to renew our mind in light of biblical truths, concepts, and principles (revelation knowledge of the word [Col. 3:10] in order to change our belief system, thought pattern, perception, and words. The ministerial function of the Holy Spirit produces an inward change (spirit and mind) in us and this manifests in words, because words are the expression of thought.

Next, he uses his gifts to change our actions by strengthening our weak zones and reinforcing our areas of excellence for moral activities. He empowers us through his gifts to do things that we wouldn't do on our own, such as fasting, prayer, true love, giving, living for Christ, and so on. This whole process produces a change in our deeds. The last thing he does is to use his fruit to change our character, and this manifested in the way we behave.

In the end, the Holy Spirit produces a new lifestyle in words and actions that reflects the nature of Christ in us through his ministry that changes our spirit and mind (inward transformation), gifts that change our actions (works), and his fruit that changes our character (conduct).

The result that the ministry, gifts, and fruit of the Holy Spirit produce in us is a new way of life in words and actions that reflect Christ (Eph. 4:13).

This is why Christianity is not just a religious activity but a standard of living. Have you ever wondered why the Lord Jesus said in John 16:7 that it was to our advantage for him to go away, so that the Holy Spirit will come to be with us and abide with us forever?

I say then, walk by the Spirit and you will not carry out the desire of the flesh. For the flesh desires what is against the Spirit, and the Spirit desires what is against the flesh; these are opposed to each other, so that you don't do what you want. But if you are led by the Spirit, you are not under the law.
(Gal. 5:16-18 HCSB)

The repeated struggle, fight, and contention in our mind between the Spirit and the flesh is what I call the *battle of the mind*. On one end is the desires of the Spirit, and on the other end is the desires of the flesh, and the two are opposed to each other so that no one can do both simultaneously. God uses the desires of the Spirit to draw us to himself, while Satan uses the desires of the flesh to draw us to himself. Romans 8:5 says those who live by the dictates of the Spirit set their minds on spiritual things, while those who live according to the desires of the flesh set their minds on things that please and satisfy the flesh.

When the Holy Spirit gets a person's spirit and mind through his ministerial work — which consists of witnessing, reproving, teaching and reminding — he regenerates the person's spirit and begins a renewing work on their mind that is tripartite in nature. That is, memory, thought, and imagination.

He starts by deprogramming whatever has been stored in the memory through negative past experiences, practices, customs, beliefs, education, or events, and replacing it with new experiences, values, beliefs, principles, practices, truths, concepts, or events.

He also focuses the person's attention on things that relate to Christ and the kingdom of heaven in order to shape their thought pattern. Lastly, he constantly plays mental images of the envisioned future promised by God on the screen of the person's mind so as to give the person hope and faith about the future, both in this life and the world to come. With this, he produces a new mindset that craves spiritual things in the person. To accomplish this, the Holy Spirit starts a spiritual walk with us by faith and revelation knowledge of the word of God (Eph.4:11-16)."

MINISTRY OF THE HOLY SPIRIT

The ministry of the Holy Spirit deals specifically with his office or the role he plays on earth to accomplish God's will and agenda for humanity. He uses it to work on the inner man of a person, that is to say, the spirit and mind. Through this office, he draws a person to Christ, regenerates their spirit from the spiritual death that came on humankind through the sin of Adam, (who is the father of all human race according to scripture), renews the person's mind and changes their mindset from worldly things to that which relates to God and the kingdom of heaven.

To achieve this, the Holy Spirit witnesses to us about God's offer for the salvation of our souls, reproves us of our sins, teaches us the ways of God, and he also reminds us of who we are in Christ and the hope we have in him. This is why the ministry of the Holy Spirit is divided into four departments namely: witnessing, reproving, teaching and reminding.

Concise Oxford Dictionary (tenth edition), includes in its definition of ministry, the following: "A government department headed by a minister, the work, vocation, or office of a minister of religion, the action of ministering to someone."

The Holy Spirit ministers to humans by witnessing to us about Christ, reproving the world of sin, righteousness and eternal judgment, teaching us the ways of God, and by reminding us God's promises in his word. That is to say, the ministry of the Holy Spirit is grouped into four categories namely: witnessing, reproving, teaching and reminding.

WITNESSING

Most dictionaries define a witness as someone who gives evidence, testifies or makes a statement about what he knows or has seen. Speaking about the Holy Spirit in John15:26, the Lord Jesus said when he comes, he would bear witness (some versions used testify) about him (Christ). Nobody understands the life, mission, ministry, and works of Christ than the Holy Spirit.

OPERATION OF THE HOLY SPIRIT

The apostle Peter also says in Acts 15:31-32 that the Holy Spirit bears witness about the death and resurrection of Jesus Christ the same way they do, and that God raised Jesus from the dead, and exalted him to his own right hand as Prince and Savior to give repentance and forgiveness of sins to Israel.

As a faithful and truthful witness, the Holy Spirit uses this department of his ministerial activity to give evidence about the incarnation, death, resurrection and ascension of the Lord Jesus to the right hand of the Godhead in heaven, the same way the disciples of the Lord did to those around them. He enlightens people about the sacrificial work Jesus accomplished on the cross for the sins of humanity to draw them to God, for none can come to Christ unless the Father draws them through the operation of the Holy Spirit.

All that the Father gives me will come to me, and whoever comes to me I will never cast out. For I have come down from heaven, not to do my own will but the will of him who sent me. And this is the will of him who sent me, that I should lose nothing of all that he has given me, but raise it up on the last day. For this is the will of my Father, that everyone who looks on the Son and believes in him should have eternal life, and I will raise him up on the last day." So the Jews grumbled about him, because he said, "I am the bread that came down from heaven." They said, "Is not this Jesus, the son of Joseph, whose father and mother we know? How does he now say, 'I have come down from heaven'?" Jesus answered them, "Do not grumble among yourselves. No one can come to me unless the Father who sent me draws him.

And I will raise him up on the last day. It is written in the Prophets, 'And they will all be taught by God.' Everyone who has heard and learned from the Father comes to me.
(Jn. 6:37-45 ESV)

Apart from the fact that the Holy Spirit uses this aspect of his ministry to draw people to Christ, he also uses it to affirm those who are born again as we observe in the passage below by joining with our own spirit to assure us of our salvation, inheritance and hope in Christ. He provides evidence and backs it up with several references from the truth revealed in the Bible about God and the kingdom of heaven in order to establish our faith in Christ.

For [the Spirit which] you have now received [is] not a spirit of slavery to put you once more in bondage to fear, but you have received the Spirit of adoption [the Spirit producing sonship] in [the bliss of] which we cry, Abba (Father)! Father! The Spirit Himself [thus] testifies together with our own spirit, [assuring us] that we are children of God. And if we are [His] children, then we are [His] heirs also: heirs of God and fellow heirs with Christ [sharing His inheritance with Him]; only we must share His suffering if we are to share His glory.
(Rom. 8:15-17 AMP)

REPROVING

According to *Cambridge Advanced Learner's Dictionary* (3rd edition), reprove means to tell someone that you disapprove of their bad or silly behaviour. Other dictionaries used the word criticize, rebuke, reprimand, caution, correct, admonish, convince, tell a fault, call to account and so on.

OPERATION OF THE HOLY SPIRIT

The Holy Spirit uses this area of his activities to convict humankind of sin, righteousness, and eternal judgement by showing us the consequences of our actions both in this life and in the world to come as it is written in the Bible. He is the only one who can speak effectively to human hearts and convicts us of our misconduct because of the human nature.

The Bible declares in Jeremiah 17:9 that the human heart is deceitful above all things and desperately wicked. Genesis 6:5 says every inclination of the human thought is evil all the time. For this reason, the Lord was grieved in Genesis that he had made humans on the earth, so he decided to wipe humankind from the face of the earth (Gen.6:5-7). Without the Holy Spirit who reproves us of sin, not a single person is able to admit their wrong deeds.

In John16:8, the Lord Jesus clearly points out three major things that the Holy Spirit does through his reproving ministerial activity. First, he reproves the world of sin. Second, he reproves the world of righteousness. Third, he reproves the world of eternal judgment. These are the three major reasons the Holy Spirit reproves the world according to the Lord Jesus.

But now I am going away to the One who sent me, and not one of you is asking where I am going. Instead, you grieve because of what I've told you. But in fact, it is best for you that I go away, because if I don't, the Advocate won't come. If I do go away, then I will send him to you. And when he comes, he will convict the world of its sin, and of God's righteousness, and of the coming judgment. The world's sin is that it refuses to believe in me.

Righteousness is available because I go to the Father, and you will see me no more. Judgment will come because the ruler of this world has already been judged.
(Jn. 16:5-11 NLT)

Albert Barnes writes, "The word translated "reprove" means commonly to demonstrate by argument, to prove, to persuade anyone to do a thing by presenting reasons. It hence means also to convince of anything, and particularly to convince of crime. This is its meaning here. He will convince or convict the world of sin. That is, he will so apply the truths of God to men's own minds as to convince them by fair and sufficient arguments that they are sinners, and cause them to feel this. This is the nature of conviction always."[*]

Since to convict someone means to declare him or her guilty of wrong doing, the Holy Spirit reproves people to bring them to Christ by convicting them of eternal condemnation for not accepting God's offer for the salvation of their souls as the only way to eternal life (paradise).

I like the way Matthew Henry puts it, "The Spirit is sent to convince sinners of sin, not barely to tell them of it; in conviction there is more than this; it is to prove it upon them, and force them to own it, as they (ch. 8:9) that were convicted of their own consciences. Make them to know their abominations. The Spirit convinces of the fact of sin, that we have done so and so; of the fault of sin, that we have done ill in doing so; of the folly of sin, that we have acted against right reason,

* John 16:8 (from Barnes' Notes, Electronic Database Copyright © 1997, 2003, 2005, 2006 by Biblesoft, Inc. All rights reserved.)

and our true interest; of the filth of sin, that by it we are become odious to God; of the fountain of sin, the corrupt nature; and lastly, of the fruit of sin, that the end thereof is death. The Spirit demonstrates the depravity and degeneracy of the whole world, that all the world is guilty before God."[*]

Romans 3:23 says all have sinned and fall short of the glory of God, while chapter 6:23 declares that the wages of sin is death, but the gift of God is eternal life in Christ Jesus our Lord. Hebrew 9:22 makes it clear that without the shedding of blood, there is no forgiveness of sin. Acts4:12 reveals there is no other name under heaven given among humans by which we must be saved.

To be at peace with God, you must first obtain his righteousness, which scripture declares comes through faith in Jesus Christ. Without faith in Christ, none is justified by the Godhead because he (Jesus) paid the price and fulfilled the lawful righteous requirements of God's law for the redemption of the human souls from eternal condemnation.

The Holy Spirit uses this tool to show us what sin really is, its consequences, how to obtain forgiveness, God's provision for the remission of sins, the need to accept Jesus as Lord and Savior. He does this to make us understand we are in danger of eternal condemnation unless we accept Christ offer for salvation as the only way to paradise.

* John 16:7-15 (from Matthew Henry's Commentary on the Whole Bible, PC Study Bible Formatted Electronic Database Copyright © 2006 by Biblesoft, Inc. All Rights reserved.)

THE HOLY SPIRIT

The first thing specified of which the world would be convinced is sin. Sin, in general, is any violation of a law of God, but the particular sin of which men are here said to be convinced is that of rejecting the Lord Jesus. This is placed first, and is deemed the sin of chief magnitude, as it is the principal one of which men are guilty. This was particularly true of the Jews who had rejected him and crucified him; and it was the great crime which, when brought home to their consciences by the preaching of the apostles, overwhelmed them with confusion, and filled their hearts with remorse. It was their rejection of the Son of God that was made the great truth that was instrumental of their conversion. Acts 2:22-23,37: 3:13-15; 4:10,26-28 [*]

The second thing the Holy Spirit does is to convict and convince the world of righteousness. About this, Adam Clark writes,

Christ was treated by the Jews as an impostor; as a magician; as one possessed by the Devil; as a wicked person, seducer, and destroyer of the law. His vindication from these charges he chiefly referred to the Holy Spirit, the Advocate, who, by his influences on the minds of the people, and by his eloquence and energy in the ministry of the apostles, convinced both the Jews and the Gentiles that the sentence of the Jewish rulers was unjust and infamous, and that the very person whom they had crucified was both Lord and Christ-Lord, the great governor of the universe; and Christ, the Lord's anointed, the promised Messiah.

* John 16:9 (from Barnes' Notes, Electronic Database Copyright © 1997, 2003, 2005, 2006 by Biblesoft, Inc. All rights reserved.)

OPERATION OF THE HOLY SPIRIT

It was a matter of the utmost consequence to the Christian cause to have the innocence and holiness of its founder demonstrated, and the crime of the Jews in putting him to death made manifest to the world.[*]

Righteousness means to be in right standing with the Godhead. Nobody can be at peace with God without Christ because of the human nature that causes us to go against the will and desires of God. Though Jesus was falsely accused and called a sinner, glutton, lawbreaker, blasphemer by the religious leaders of his time, who also condemned and killed him, God vindicated him (Jesus) by raising him from the dead and exalting him to his right hand.

The Holy Spirit convicts those who speak negative things about Jesus, and convinces them that Jesus is just, holy and he is the only way to the Father. He is righteous, faithful and good, not a lawbreaker or sinner as the religious leaders of his time called him. He shows them how to obtain God's righteousness, which is by faith in Jesus Christ in order to be at peace with God. To have the peace of God, we must first be at peace with him according to the written word of God.

Therefore, since we have been justified by faith, we have peace with God through our Lord Jesus Christ. Through him we have also obtained access by faith into this grace in which we stand, and we rejoice in hope of the glory of God.

* John 16:10 (from Adam Clarke's Commentary, Electronic Database. Copyright © 1996, 2003, 2005, 2006 by Biblesoft, Inc. All rights reserved.)

More than that, we rejoice in our sufferings, knowing that suffering produces endurance, and endurance produces character, and character produces hope, and hope does not put us to shame, because God's love has been poured into our hearts through the Holy Spirit who has been given to us. For while we were still weak, at the right time Christ died for the ungodly. For one will scarcely die for a righteous person—though perhaps for a good person one would dare even to die— but God shows his love for us in that while we were still sinners, Christ died for us. Since, therefore, we have now been justified by his blood, much more shall we be saved by him from the wrath of God. For if while we were enemies we were reconciled to God by the death of his Son, much more, now that we are reconciled, shall we be saved by his life. More than that, we also rejoice in God through our Lord Jesus Christ, through whom we have now received reconciliation.
(Rom.5:1-11ESV)

The third thing the Bible tells us the Holy Spirit does is to convict the world of eternal condemnation. In his notes, Barnes writes,

The death of Christ was a judgment or a condemnation of Satan. In this struggle Jesus gained the victory and subdued the great enemy of man. This proves that God will execute judgment or justice on all his foes. If he vanquished his great enemy who had so long triumphed in this world, he will subdue all others in due time. All sinners in like manner may expect to be condemned. Of this great truth Jesus says the Holy Spirit will convince men. God showed himself to be just in subduing his great enemy.

OPERATION OF THE HOLY SPIRIT

He showed that he was resolved to vanquish his foes, and that all his enemies in like manner must be subdued. This is deeply felt by the convicted sinner. He knows that he is guilty. He learns that God is just. He fears that he will condemn him, and trembles in the apprehension of approaching condemnation. From this state of alarm there is no refuge but to flee to Him who subdued the great enemy of man, and who is able to deliver him from the vengeance due to his sins. Convinced, then, of the righteousness of Jesus Christ, and of his ability and willingness to save him, he flees to his cross, and seeks in him a refuge from the coming storm of wrath. [*]

Hell is real, and just as the devil has been condemn to eternal destruction, so will anyone who rejects God's offer and provision for salvation. Hebrew 9:27 says it is appointed to man to die once and after that, he faces judgment. Romans 14:10 declares we will all stand before the judgment seat of God, while 2Corinthians5:10 makes it clear that we must all appear before the judgment seat of Christ, that each one may receive what is due him for the things done while in the body, whether good or bad.

The apostle John writes, "I saw the dead, both great and small, standing before God's throne. And the books were opened, including the Book of Life. And the dead were judged according to what they have done, as recorded in the books. The sea gave up its dead, and death and the grave gave up their dead. And all were judged according to their deeds.

* John 16:11 (from Barnes' Notes, Electronic Database Copyright © 1997, 2003, 2005, 2006 by Biblesoft, Inc. All rights reserved.)

Then death and the grave were thrown into the lake of fire. This lake of fire is the second death. Anyone whose name was not found recorded in the Book of Life was thrown into the fire." (Rev.20:12-15)

The Holy Spirit uses these truths in the written word of God to convict the human souls in order to save us from eternal destruction.

One general exposition may be given of these three verses. The Holy Spirit will convince the world of sin committed, and guilt and condemnation thereby incurred. Of righteousness-of the necessity of being pardoned, and made righteous through the blood of the Lamb, who, after being offered up for sin, went to the Father, ever to appear in his presence as our intercessor: and of judgment-of the great day thereof, when none shall be able to stand but those whose sins are pardoned, and whose souls are made righteous. In all that our Lord says here, there seems to be an allusion to the office of an advocate in a cause, in a court of justice; who, by producing witnesses, and pleading upon the proof, convicts the opposite party of sin, demonstrates the righteousness of his client, and shows the necessity of passing judgment upon the accuser. [*]

TEACHING

Apart from witnessing and reproving, another thing the Holy Spirit accomplishes through this office is teaching.

* John 16:11 (from Adam Clarke's Commentary, Electronic Database. Copyright © 1996, 2003, 2005, 2006 by Biblesoft, Inc. All rights reserved.)

OPERATION OF THE HOLY SPIRIT

In John16:13, the Lord Jesus calls him the Spirit of truth. John 17:17 says the word of God is truth. No one knows the word of God than the Holy Spirit who searches the deep things of God and reveals them to us according to the Scriptures.

But it was to us that God revealed these things by his Spirit. For his Spirit searches out everything and shows us God's deep secrets. No one can know a person's thoughts except that person's own spirit, and no one can know God's thoughts except God's own Spirit. And we have received God's Spirit (not the world's spirit), so we can know the wonderful things God has freely given us. When we tell you these things, we do not use words that come from human wisdom. Instead, we speak words given to us by the Spirit, using the Spirit's words to explain spiritual truths. But people who aren't spiritual can't receive these truths from God's Spirit. It all sounds foolish to them and they can't understand it, for only those who are spiritual can understand what the Spirit means.
(1 Co. 2:10-15 NLT)

As a teacher, he leads, guides, instructs, informs, corrects, explains, and reveals spiritual things to us. No human can understand the things of God without the help of the Holy Spirit. Holy men of old were inspired by God through the Holy Spirit to write the Scripture.

2Timothy 3:16 says all scripture is breathed out (some versions use inspired) by God and is useful for teaching, rebuking, correcting and training in righteousness.

The apostle Paul writes in Ephesians 3:2-6 about the mystery God made known to him by revelation, which was not shown to the previous generations. The mystery about the gentiles becoming children and heirs of God through the gospel of Christ was revealed to him and the other apostles and prophets by the Holy Spirit.

And see, now I go bound in the spirit to Jerusalem, not knowing the things that will happen to me there, except that the Holy Spirit testifies in every city, saying that chains and tribulations await me. But none of these things move me; nor do I count my life dear to myself, so that I may finish my race with joy, and the ministry which I received from the Lord Jesus, to testify to the gospel of the grace of God. (Acts20:22-24NKJV)

I have yet many things to say to you, but you cannot bear them now. When the Spirit of truth comes, he will guide you into all the truth; for he will not speak on his own authority, but whatever he hears he will speak, and he will declare to you the things that are to come. He will glorify me, for he will take what is mine and declare it to you. All that the Father has is mine; therefore I said that he will take what is mine and declare it to you. (Jn.16:12-15RSV)

The Holy Spirit teaches us the will of God, and he helps us to understand biblical truths, concepts and principles. He uses the written word of God to reprogram our minds and thought pattern by deprogramming whatever has been stored in our memory through negative past experiences, practices, customs, beliefs, education, or events. He then replaces it with new experiences, values, beliefs, principles, practices, truths, concepts that are in line with the Scriptures.

REMINDING

The fourth thing the Holy Spirit uses his ministerial work to accomplish is to remind us of the promises of God and the hope we have in Christ. To remind means to bring to mind, call to mind, refresh ones memories, or tell. The Holy Spirit helps us to remember things that relate to Christ and the kingdom of heaven.

All this I have spoken while still with you. But the Counselor, the Holy Spirit, whom the Father will send in my name, will teach you all things and will remind you of everything I have said to you.
(Jn.14:25-26NIV)

The Lord Jesus promised in the above scripture that the Holy Spirit will teach us all things and remind us of everything he said in his word. The great apostle Paul also admonished his son Timothy to guard the good deposit that was entrusted to him by the help of the Holy Spirit (2Tim.1:14).

What the Holy Spirit does is to always play mental pictures of the envisioned future promised by God on the screen of our mind in order to give us hope and faith about the future, both in this life and the world to come. He reminds us of who we are in Christ (our divine identity), God's promises in his word, and he helps us to stay focus regardless of what the enemies might throw at us as we walk the path of faith.

The Holy Spirit uses his ministerial activities — which consists of witnessing, reproving, teaching and reminding — to regenerate our spirits before beginning a renewing work on our minds, which is tripartite in nature. That is, memory, thought, and imagination.

He does it by deprogramming whatever is stored in the memory through negative past experiences, practices, customs, beliefs, education, or events, and he replaces it with new experiences, values, beliefs, principles, practices, truths, concepts and so on, in accordance with the written word of God. He then focuses our attention on spiritual things in order to produces a new mindset that craves spiritual things in us.

In other words, the Holy Spirit uses his ministerial works to bring a person to the knowledge of Christ. Second, he convicts the person of sin. Third, he convinces him or her to repent for remission of sin. Fourth, he encourages the individual to accept Christ's offer for salvation by confessing him as Lord and Savior. Fifth, he starts renewing the person's mind for an inward transformation.

In the end, the ministerial work of the Holy Spirit that focuses on regenerating our spirit and renewing our mind, manifest in words or the way we speak and what we talk about. The Bible declares in Matthew 12:34, that whatever is in our heart determines what we say.

FRUIT OF THE SPIRIT

Most dictionaries define "fruit" as the result that comes from works or activities. Some include in their definition of the word, "The part of plant that has seed and can be eaten as food."

Matthew 7:15-20 warns against false prophets who come in sheep clothing, but inwardly they are ferocious wolves.

The passage says we can identify them by their fruit or the way they do things, because every tree produces fruit after its kind. A good tree cannot bear bad fruit, neither can a bad tree bear good fruit.

The same way a tree is known by the kind of fruit its produces, people can be identified by the kind of things they do. Fruit becomes the primary means by which a tree or person is known, recognized or identified. It reveals the true nature and being of whatever it represents. A tree or person is not different from the kind of fruit them produce. Show me a fruit and I will tell you the tree that produces it.

Watch out for false prophets. They come to you in sheep's clothing, but inwardly they are ferocious wolves. By their fruit you will recognize them. Do people pick grapes from thornbushes, or figs from thistles? Likewise every good tree bears good fruit, but a bad tree bears bad fruit. A good tree cannot bear bad fruit, and a bad tree cannot bear good fruit. Every tree that does not bear good fruit is cut down and thrown into the fire. Thus, by their fruit you will recognize them.
(Matt 7:15-20NIV)

Just as every tree bears fruit after their kind, and humans produce after their nature, the Holy Spirit also bears fruit after his nature. The different fruits each one produces allows us to identify the bearer, because the fruit reveals the true nature and identity of the thing that produces it – a fruit is not different from the tree that bears it.

The main difference amongst the fruit that trees, humans and the Holy Spirit produce is that the first and second bear their fruits in themselves, while the latter bears his fruit in humans.

The Lord Jesus said in the above passage that one can identify a tree or person by the nature of fruit them produce. This means that fruit reveals the true nature, character, identity and so on of a person or tree that produces it. Mainly looking at a fruit, you can identify, categorize, and classify the very thing that bears it, because it reveals their true nature, character, and identity.

The fruit of the Holy Spirit, therefore, has to do with what he produces in us that reveals his nature, character, identity, which allows us to know he lives in a person. It is his personal character and nature that he manifest in the life of Christians, that causes us to reflect the true nature of God. So that when people look at us, they see God through us, by reason of the fruit that the Holy Spirit bears in our lives. The fruit of the Holy Spirit is the physical evidence that God lives in us.

Ephesians2:20-22 declares that we are joined together in Christ Jesus to become a dwelling in which God lives by his Spirit. The Lord lives in us by his Spirit, and he causes us to manifest the character of the Holy Spirit, which scripture calls the "Fruit of the Spirit." The degree to which the fruit manifest is determined by the measure of the presence and power of the Holy Spirit that dwells in us.

But now in Christ Jesus you who once were far off have been brought near by the blood of Christ. For he himself is our peace, who has made us both one and has broken down in his flesh the dividing wall of hostility by abolishing the law of commandments and ordinances,

that he might create in himself one new man in place of the two, so making peace, and might reconcile us both to God in one body through the cross, thereby killing the hostility. And he came and preached peace to you who were far off and peace to those who were near. For through him we both have access in one Spirit to the Father. So then you are no longer strangers and aliens, but you are fellow citizens with the saints and members of the household of God, built on the foundation of the apostles and prophets, Christ Jesus himself being the cornerstone, in whom the whole structure, being joined together, grows into a holy temple in the Lord. In him you also are being built together into a dwelling place for God by the Spirit.
(Eph.2:13-22ESV)

In his book, *WHY YOU ACT THE WAY YOU DO*, Dr. Tim LaHaye defines temperament as the combination of traits we inherited from our parents. He adds, "Humanly speaking, nothing has a more profound influence on your behavior than your inherited temperament. The combination of your parent's genes and chromosomes at conception, which determined your basic temperament nine months before you drew your first breath, is largely responsible for your actions, reactions, emotional responses, and, to one degree or another, almost everything you do."[*]

According to him, it is a person's temperament that makes him outgoing and extroverted or shy and introverted. There are four basic temperaments namely: Sanguine, Choleric, Melancholy and Phlegmatic.

* [pp.20, 21 Tyndale House Publishers, Inc. © 1984]

These different temperaments that are passed on from parents to offspring, which makes us to act the way we do, have strengths and weaknesses. Since the fruit of the Holy Spirit is the physical manifestation of his attributes and nature that he uses to transform us on the outside (outward transformation) by changing and making us stronger in the area of weakness while reinforcing, affirming and solidifying our strength zone.

The Holy Spirit uses this to change our character, and replace it with his nature that manifest in nine ways (one fruit with nine manifestations). The fruit of the Holy Spirit helps to regulate our temperament issues by solidifying our strength zones and strengthening our weakness.

But I say, walk by the Spirit, and do not gratify the desires of the flesh. For the desires of the flesh are against the Spirit, and the desires of the Spirit are against the flesh; for these are opposed to each other, to prevent you from doing what you would. But if you are led by the Spirit you are not under the law. Now the works of the flesh are plain: fornication, impurity, licentiousness, idolatry, sorcery, enmity, strife, jealousy, anger, selfishness, dissension, party spirit, envy, drunkenness, carousing, and the like. I warn you, as I warned you before, that those who do such things shall not inherit the kingdom of God. But the fruit of the Spirit is love, joy, peace, patience, kindness, goodness, faithfulness, gentleness, self-control; against such there is no law. And those who belong to Christ Jesus have crucified the flesh with its passions and desires.
(Gal.5:16-24RSV)

OPERATION OF THE HOLY SPIRIT

The above portion of scriptures describes the struggle and fight between the desires of the Spirit and that of the flesh. It says the two forces are in conflict with each other, to keep you from doing the things you want to do. The Holy Spirit engages the flesh with its desire and passion in order to subdue it, and liberate us from its grips and control. So that he can freely produce his own fruit in the person.

What then? Shall we sin because we are not under law but under grace? By no means! Don't you know that when you offer yourselves to someone to obey him as slaves, you are slaves to the one whom you obey — whether you are slaves to sin, which leads to death, or to obedience, which leads to righteousness? But thanks be to God that, though you used to be slaves to sin, you wholeheartedly obeyed the form of teaching to which you were entrusted. You have been set free from sin and have become slaves to righteousness. I put this in human terms because you are weak in your natural selves. Just as you used to offer the parts of your body in slavery to impurity and to ever-increasing wickedness, so now offer them in slavery to righteousness leading to holiness. When you were slaves to sin, you were free from the control of righteousness. What benefit did you reap at that time from the things you are now ashamed of? Those things result in death! But now that you have been set free from sin and have become slaves to God, the benefit you reap leads to holiness, and the result is eternal life. For the wages of sin is death, but the gift of God is eternal life in Christ Jesus our Lord. (Rom.6:15-23NIV)

When this happens, the person's character changes as he or she begins to manifest the nature of the Holy Spirit. Instead of fornication, impurity, debauchery, idolatry, sorcery, enmity, strife, jealousy, anger, selfishness, dissension, party spirit, drunkenness, and carousing, the person begins to manifest love, joy, peace, kindness, goodness, faithfulness, gentleness, self-control. This kind of change can only take place in a person's life through the operation of the Holy Spirit.

When this happens, it resolves any temperament weakness problem that the person may have, by enabling the individual to behave in certain manner that is somewhat different from the usual way. For example, when a person who used to steal, lie, fornicate, drink alcohol, and so on, suddenly begins to do the opposite, it causes those who live around the individual to wonder and start asking questions about the change the individual is experiencing.

Many schools of thoughts have emerged over the years, regarding the true nature of the fruit of the Holy Spirit. Some say that the fruit of the Spirit is one. And that the one fruit is love. According to them, all the other components are the characteristics of true love that God pours in our hearts at new birth.

The second group believe that the oneness of the fruit of the Spirit is based on the whole or entirety that is made up of nine components, which makes it impossible to separates. To them, the unification of the different components makes it a single fruit, which means you can't separate one part from the other because it all works together to achieve a single goal, and the result it produces is the character of God in us.

The last group claim that to maintain the integrity of scripture, there is one fruit with nine manifestation. However, they do not state what the very one fruit is, but they emphasize on its nine manifestations.

According to the written word of God, there is one fruit with nine manifestations. The fruit of the Spirit is the very nature, character and identity of God that the Holy Spirit manifest in the life of a Christian. It is used by God to produce outward transformation or changes in the person's character.

The fruit allows the other people living around the person to identify the nature and character of the Holy Spirit dwelling in the individual. It reveals the true nature of the spirit that inhabits a person.

The fruit of the Holy Spirit is the indicator that shows the measure of the presence and power of the Holy Spirit that a person has on the inside. It produces an outward transformation on the character of a person, and it manifest in the way we behave. Nonetheless, the degree to which this change manifest is determine by the measure of the presence and power that the individual has through the constant infilling of the Holy Spirit. The more of his presence, and power that a person has, the more intense the change or transformation the individual will see and experience.

GIFTS OF THE SPIRIT

Many great books have been written on the "Gifts of the Holy Spirit" since the beginning of the history of the church by famous authors, preachers and teachers that clearly explain the different gifts, and their roles. I do not intend to focus on the different gifts that the Holy Spirit gives, but on the work he uses the gifts to accomplish in the life of a true Christian.

The great apostle Paul writes in 1 Corinthians 12:4, that there are different kinds of spiritual gifts, but the same Spirit distributes them all. Verse 7 says the manifestation of the Spirit is given to each of us for the common good or to profit everyone. Some Bible versions use "The manifestation of the Spirit," others call it the "The showing forth of the Spirit," a few others use "The evidence of the Spirit's presence, appearance of the Spirit or revelation of the Spirit."

There are different kinds of working, but the same God works all of them in all men. Now to each one the manifestation of the Spirit is given for the common good. To one there is given through the Spirit the message of wisdom, to another the message of knowledge by means of the same Spirit, to another faith by the same Spirit, to another gifts of healing by that one Spirit, to another miraculous powers, to another prophecy, to another distinguishing between spirits, to another speaking in different kinds of tongues, and to still another the interpretation of tongues. All these are the work of one and the same Spirit, and he gives them to each one, just as he determines.
(1 Co. 12:4-11 NIV)

OPERATION OF THE HOLY SPIRIT

This suggests that the gifts of the Spirit is the means through which the Holy Spirit reveals, shows forth, demonstrates, presents, or manifests an aspect of his being to humans for the common good of all. And the part of his being that is manifested through this gifts is his self-ability also known as the "Power of the Holy Spirit," which is the force that resides in him by virtue of his nature that allows him to perform the will and purposes of the Godhead.

I did mentioned earlier, under the heading, "The power of the Holy Spirit," that the life and power of the Holy Spirit that enables him to live and act are the two intrinsic constituents of his being. That is to say, he lives because he has life, and he acts because he has the ability (power) to do so. Thus, we cannot speak about the Holy Spirit without these two inherent attributes that make up his being.

While commenting on this particular verse of the Bible (that is, 1Co.12:7), Adam Clarke writes, "This is variably understood by the fathers; some of them rendering phaneroosis by illumination, others demonstration, and others operation. The apostle's meaning seems to be this: Whatever gifts God has bestowed, or in what various ways soever the Spirit of God may have manifested himself, it is all for the common benefit of the church. God has given no gift to any man for his own private advantage, or exclusive profit. He has it for the benefit of others as well as for his own salvation." [*]

*. 1 Corinthians 12:7 (from Adam Clarke's Commentary, Electronic Database. Copyright © 1996, 2003, 2005, 2006 by Biblesoft, Inc. All rights reserved.)

THE HOLY SPIRIT

The word "manifestation" [fanerootis] means properly that which makes manifest, conspicuous, or plain; that which illustrates, or makes any thing seen or known. Thus, conduct manifests the state of the heart; and the actions are a manifestation, or "showing forth" of the real feelings. The idea here is, that there is given to those referred to, such gifts. endowments, or graces as shall "manifest" the work and nature of the Spirit's operations on the mind; such endowments as the Spirit makes himself known by to people. All that he produces in the mind is a manifestation of his character and work, in the same way as the works of God in the visible creation are a manifestation of his perfections. [*]

The power of the Holy Spirit is the sum of his self-ability, and it is given to humans in measure through different gifts to profit the body of Christ – the church. Whenever you exercise spiritual gifts, you demonstrate, manifest or show forth the ability of the Holy Spirit because the gifts of the Spirit is the manifestation of his power or auto capability that he distributes to men in portion, measure or fraction as he wills.

Just as the Holy Spirit uses his ministerial function to regenerate our spirit and renew our mind in order to produce an inward transformation in our mindset and words, while he uses his fruit to change our characters to produce an outward transformation in the way we behave, he uses his gifts to transform our actions in order to change our works.

*. 1 Corinthians 12:7 (from Barnes' Notes, Electronic Database Copyright © 1997, 2003, 2005, 2006 by Biblesoft, Inc. All rights reserved.)

OPERATION OF THE HOLY SPIRIT

In the end, he produces in us a new way of life in words and deeds through his threefold activities namely: ministry, fruit and gifts. The first focuses on human spirit and mind, while the second focuses on our character and behavior, the last focuses on our actions and works. The first manifest in the way we think and speak, the second manifest in the way we behave, while the last manifest in the way we do things or act.

The gifts of the Holy Spirit is given to strengthen our weak zones and solidify our area of excellence. It turns our weakness to strengthen to make us strong in areas we were initially weak so that we can do moral activities that we couldn't do on our own, such as fasting, prayer, giving, living for Christ and working to advance the kingdom of God on earth. It is through his gifts that the Holy Spirit manifest his power in this world.

I believe this is one of the reasons scriptures refer to the gifts of the Spirit as the demonstration, showing forth, evidence, revelation or manifestation of the Spirit. My reason is that it reveals and manifests the power of the Holy Spirit, which is one of the basic constituents of his being.

To have the complete or all the gifts of the Holy Spirit in full measure means to be clothed with the totality of his power (auto-capability). When this happens, you will become like God on earth. Because you will do the impossible, and work wonders.

In my book, *The Oneness of God*, I explained that the Holy Spirit is the active power of the Godhead, and that he is one of the constituents of God's eternal power that enables him to do as he pleases at any time. To be clothed with the power of the Holy Spirit would make you do things that would cause people to marvel.

Perhaps, this is why the Holy Spirit gives it to us by measure through diverse gifts. Verse 11 of our key scripture says he alone decides the kind of gift each person should have, as he distributes it amongst us for the common good depending on how he wants you to manifest his power, and the kind of work he chooses to accomplish through you. On the other hand, he may decide to give you the whole gifts in full measure and envelope you with his power for a special mission.

The gifts strengthen our weak zones and manifest in works i.e. in what we do and how we do them on daily basis. It enlarges our capacity (ability to receive or accommodate) and our capability (ability to give, produce and do things). The full manifestation of these gifts is the physical demonstration of the power of the Holy Spirit.

To summarize, the operation of the Holy Spirit, which comprises his Ministry, Fruit, and Gifts, produces the following in a believer: regenerated spirit, renewed mind, transformed character and changed actions.

CHAPTER THREE

SPIRITUAL LIFE CYCLE

According to *Merriam-Webster Dictionary*, life cycle is the series of stages through which a living thing passes from the beginning of its life until its death. Just as we have physical life cycle, we also have spiritual life cycle more especially as it relates to Christianity.

From biblical perspective, a spiritual life cycle means a series of stages that the Holy Spirit takes a person through in Christ, beginning from regeneration to spiritual perfection in order to effect both an inward and outward changes in the person's life. These changes usually manifest in words, behaviors, and works.

This process of spiritual transformation begins when God's eternal life is infused into the spirit of a person by the Holy Spirit, at the hearing of the word of faith that is preached in the name of Jesus – the Son of the living God. The word of faith is the gospel message that produces the faith needed for the salvation of human souls in Christ Jesus, the author of salvation.

This spiritual phenomenon is called new birth or the baptism by one Spirit into the one body of Christ – the universal church (I'll expand on this as we proceed).

Once the eternal life is given to a person in Christ by faith, the spirit of the individual is made alive from the spiritual death that came on humans through the sin of Adam, who is the father of human race. The new life brings the individual into oneness with the Godhead in Christ.

In 1John5:11-12, the great apostle John writes, "And this is the testimony: God has given us eternal life, and this life is in His Son. The one who has the Son has life. The one who doesn't have the Son of God does not have life." According to him, God's eternal life can only be given to humans in Christ, so that whoever does not have Christ – the Son of the living God – cannot have God's eternal life that brings humans to oneness with the Father.

God lives in us by the Holy Spirit. 1John4:13-15, says "This is how we know that we live in him, and he in us: He has given us of his Spirit. And we have seen and testify that the Father has sent his Son to be the Savior of the world. If anyone acknowledges that Jesus is the Son of God, God lives in them and they in God."

The Holy Spirit who dwells in us is the proof that the Godhead lives in us and we in him, because without the Holy Spirit, the eternal life that brings us to oneness with him in Christ cannot be infused into our spirit for regeneration.

Spiritual life cycle is basically in two stages namely: living and walking in the Spirit.

The first denotes spiritual existence in Christ by faith, through the operation of the Holy Spirit; while the latter, signifies a walk with the Holy Spirit by faith, and revelation knowledge of God's word. Meaning that for a person to enjoy the fullness of a new life in Christ, the individual must go through this two phases of spiritual life, because it takes both to transform a living soul into the very image of Christ the Son of the living God.

Many in the body of Christ often use these two words interchangeably, when speaking on the subject. The truth is that they are not. There is a great difference between living and walking in the Spirit. It is one thing to be spiritually alive, another is to begin a spiritual walk with the Holy Spirit.

1Corinthians12:13 says, by one Spirit, we are all baptized into one body, whether Jews or Gentiles, slaves or free, and we are all given the one Spirit to drink. The difference between living and walking in the Spirit is the baptism by one Spirit into the body of Christ, and drinking of the same Spirit. The first introduces you to the first phase of spiritual life, while the latter commences the second phase. Both make up the full cycle of spiritual life in Christ.

According to the *King James Version* of the Holy Bible, Galatians5:25 declares, "If we live by the Spirit, let us also walk by the Spirit." I also like the way the *New Living Bible* puts it, "Since we are living by the Spirit, let us follow the Spirit's leading in every part of our lives." The *New International Version* says it this way, "Since we live by the Spirit, let us keep in step with the Spirit."

In my opinion, walking by the Spirit, following the Spirit's leading or keeping in step with the Spirit suggest one thing, to be led by the Holy Spirit. There is no way the Holy Spirit can lead us or cause us to walk at the same level and speed with him without taking us on spiritual walk or journey (I will speak more on this as we continue).

LIVING IN THE SPIRIT

The apostle Paul informs us in the Bible passage below that spiritual life is by faith in Christ. Living in the Spirit is the first phase of spiritual life in Christ Jesus, and it is made possible by faith through the power of the Holy Spirit who infuses the spirit of humans with God's eternal life. This is done in accordance with the written word of God.

I have been crucified with Christ; and it is no longer I who live, but Christ lives in me; and the life which I now live in the flesh I live by faith in the Son of God, who loved me and gave Himself up for me. (Gal.2:20 NASB)

The Bible declares in James 1:18 that God chose to give birth to us through the word of truth, so that we might be a kind of first fruits of all that he created. The word of truth plays a very important role in the regeneration process, because it produces the faith needed for salvation to take place. It is the gospel message that is preached in the name of Jesus.

Romans 1:16 says, it is the power of God for the salvation of everyone who believes: first for the Jews, then for the Gentiles. The Holy Spirit uses it to convict the world of sin, righteousness, eternal destruction, and the need to accept Christ sacrificial work on the cross of Calvary as the only offer God made available for the salvation of human souls from eternal destruction.

When He comes, He will convict the world about sin, righteousness, and judgment: about sin, because they do not believe in Me; about righteousness, because I am going to the Father and you will no longer see Me; and about judgment, because the ruler of this world has been judged.
(Jn.16:8-11 HCSB)

He also points out to them, the consequence of rejecting the offer to be wash by the blood of the eternal covenant, and the awaiting judgment for all who turn down the offer of Christ for eternal life with the Father on the last day.

Anyone who rejected the law of Moses died without mercy on the testimony of two or three witnesses. How much more severely do you think a man deserves to be punished who has trampled the Son of God under foot, who has treated as an unholy thing the blood of the covenant that sanctified him, and who has insulted the Spirit of grace? For we know him who said, "It is mine to avenge; I will repay," and again, "The Lord will judge his people." It is a dreadful thing to fall into the hands of the living God.
(Heb.10:28-31 NIV)

This is done to bring a living soul to the place of repentance, confession and acceptance of the Lordship of Jesus Christ in their lives for salvation.Having done that, the Holy Spirit releases the faith to accept the message of salvation in the person's heart by making him or her to believe in the death and resurrection of Christ for the sins of humankind so that the individual can be justified by faith, and be at peace with the Father who imputes his righteousness to the person.

Even the righteousness of God which is by faith of Jesus Christ unto all and upon all them that believe: for there is no difference: For all have sinned, and come short of the glory of God; Being justified freely by his grace through the redemption that is in Christ Jesus: Whom God hath set forth to be a propitiation through faith in his blood, to declare his righteousness for the remission of sins that are past, through the forbearance of God; To declare, I say, at this time his righteousness: that he might be just, and the justifier of him which believeth in Jesus. (Rom.3:22-26KJV)

In addition, the Holy Spirit helps the individual to confess the Lordship of Christ by accepting and openly declaring him Lord and Savior. At this point, God's eternal life, which scripture affirms to be in Christ is infused into the person's spirit for a new life in Christ Jesus.

And this is the testimony: that God has given us eternal life, and this life is in His Son. He who has the Son has life; he who does not have the Son of God does not have life. (1Jn.5:11-12 NKJV)

If you confess with your mouth, "Jesus is Lord," and believe in your heart that God raised Him from the dead, you will be saved. With the heart one believes, resulting in righteousness, and with the mouth one confesses, resulting in salvation. Now the Scripture says, No one who believes on Him will be put to shame, for there is no distinction between Jew and Greek, since the same Lord of all is rich to all who call on Him. For everyone who calls on the name of the Lord will be saved. But how can they call on Him in whom they have not believed? And how can they believe without hearing about Him? And how can they hear without a preacher? So faith comes from what is heard, and what is heard comes through the message about Christ.
(Rom.10:9-14,17HCSB)

This then means that, whenever a living soul hears the word of truth, that is, the good news and believes, the person would be justified by the Father who forgives the person's sins and causes him to be in right standing with himself by faith, so that the individual can have peace with him (Godhead), in Christ.

When the person confesses by the help of the Holy Spirit that Jesus is Lord, the eternal life of the Father that is in Christ Jesus is infused (injected) into the spirit of the individual by the power of the Holy Spirit who works inwardly with the word of life to regenerate the person's spirit from spiritual death that was passed on humankind from the beginning as a result of the sin of Adam, which brought death and condemnation to humanity. This spiritual occurrence is referred to as "new birth or the baptism by one Spirit into the one body of Christ— the church."

THE HOLY SPIRIT

For by grace you have been saved through faith, and that not of yourselves; it is the gift of God.
(Eph.2:8NKJV)

As a result, the individual becomes a member of the universal body of Christ – the church. Christ the author of salvation, inscribes the person's name in the book of life in heaven as a guarantee for a life with him in the New Jerusalem, when the Lord Jesus finally comes to take his church home. In addition, the Holy Spirit begins to witness to the person's spirit that he is justified and redeemed by the blood of the eternal covenant. Consequently, he is a child of God and co-heir with Christ of all that the Father gave him.

The Spirit himself testifies with our spirit that we are God's children. Now if we are children, then we are heirs—heirs of God and co-heirs with Christ, if indeed we share in his sufferings in order that we may also share in his glory.
(Rom.8:16-17 NIV)

Therefore I am informing you that no one speaking by the Spirit of God says, "Jesus is cursed," and no one can say, "Jesus is Lord," except by the Holy Spirit.
(1Co.12:3 HCSB)

In the process of spiritual rebirth or regeneration, the Holy Spirit plays a major role in the life of an individual for the salvation of one's soul, because no one can respond to the message of salvation unless the person is under the influence of his divine operation.

This we observe in the life of Lydia, whose heart the Lord opened to accept the message that the apostle Paul preached. A full account of the story is in the passage below.

On the Sabbath we went a little way outside the city to a riverbank, where we thought people would be meeting for prayer, and we sat down to speak with some women who had gathered there. One of them was Lydia from Thyatira, a merchant of expensive purple cloth, who worshiped God. As she listened to us, the Lord opened her heart, and she accepted what Paul was saying. She was baptized along with other members of her household, and she asked us to be her guests. "If you agree that I am a true believer in the Lord," she said, "come and stay at my home." And she urged us until we agreed.
(Acts 16:13-15NLT)

When the gospel message is preached, it is the Holy Spirit, who opens a person's heart to understand the word, convicts and convinces the individual of sin and the need for salvation, he also releases the faith through the word to accept, believe and confess Christ as Lord and Savior. After which he infuses the person's spirit with the eternal life of the Godhead. This is why scripture says that we are baptized or born again by one Spirit, that is, the Holy Spirit, into the one body of Christ.

Jesus answered and said to him, "Most assuredly, I say to you, unless one is born again, he cannot see the kingdom of God." Nicodemus said to Him, "How can a man be born when he is old? Can he enter a second time into his mother's womb and be born?" Jesus answered, "Most assuredly, I say to you, unless one is born of water and the Spirit, he cannot enter the kingdom of God.

That which is born of the flesh is flesh, and that which is born of the Spirit is spirit. Do not marvel that I said to you, 'You must be born again.' The wind blows where it wishes, and you hear the sound of it, but cannot tell where it comes from and where it goes. So is everyone who is born of the Spirit.

(Jn.3:3-8 NKJV)

From the above passage of the Bible, we notice in the response of the Lord Jesus to Nicodemus – a Pharisees and member of the Jewish ruling counsel – who came to him secretly at night with pertinent question regarding the kingdom of heaven. The Lord told him that he must be born again to see the kingdom of God. At this, the man was confused and frustrated because he couldn't grasp the sense of what Jesus was saying, when he asked him to be born again in order to see the kingdom of God.

Similarly, even with all that has been said about new birth by different people, at different time since the beginning of the history of the church, many in the body of Christ still haven't come to true understanding of what it means to be born again and the different dynamics involve in the regeneration process.

As a result, some simply say, "It's a mystery." While others quotes a portion of scripture that says, "We are born of water and the Spirit," from the book of John3:5. Still, a few others seem to hold on to the book of James 1:18, which says God has caused us to be born again to a living hope through the resurrection of Jesus Christ from the dead, and 1Peter1:3, that says God gave birth to us by the word of truth.

Blessed be the God and Father of our Lord Jesus Christ, who according to His great mercy has caused us to be born again to a living hope through the resurrection of Jesus Christ from the dead.
(1Pet.1:3 NASB)

By His own choice, He gave us a new birth by the message of truth so that we would be the first fruits of His creatures.
(Jas.1:18 HCSB)

With these in mind, I think it is necessary to take a closer look at the subject from a different angle and establish a common ground for better understanding. Back to the book of John3:5, the Lord Jesus said to Nicodemus, "Most assuredly, I say to you, unless one is born of water and the Spirit, he cannot enter the kingdom of God." It is obvious from this declaration made by the Lord Jesus that new birth is somehow tied to water and Spirit. Flesh gives birth to flesh, but the Spirit gives birth to spirit.

However, the question we really need to ask ourselves is whether the water the Lord Jesus talked about here refers to ordinary water or something else. My reason is that Ephesians5:26, says that he might sanctify her (talking about the church), having cleansed her by the washing of water with the word. James1:18, says that God gave us a new birth by the word of truth, which is the word of life that is preached in the name of Jesus that produces the faith needed for the regeneration of our spirit, through the operation of the Holy Spirit, who infuses it with God's eternal life in Christ Jesus.

From this point of view, I would say that new birth is tied to water, which signifies the word of God, and Spirit that speaks of the Holy Spirit, because of the role that both play in the regeneration process. The word produces the faith, while the Spirit brings us to oneness with the Godhead in Christ by injecting our spirit with the eternal life of God.

For this reason, our sonship in relation to the Godhead is not of natural descent, nor of human decision but of God through grace, by faith in Christ that is born out of the word of life, under the influence of the Holy Spirit.

Yet to all who did receive him, to those who believed in his name, he gave the right to become children of God— children born not of natural descent, nor of human decision or a husband's will, but born of God.
(Jn.1:12-13 NIV)

Let all the house of Israel therefore know for certain that God has made him both Lord and Christ, this Jesus whom you crucified." Now when they heard this they were cut to the heart, and said to Peter and the rest of the apostles, "Brothers, what shall we do?" And Peter said to them, "Repent and be baptized every one of you in the name of Jesus Christ for the forgiveness of your sins, and you will receive the gift of the Holy Spirit. For the promise is for you and for your children and for all who are far off, everyone whom the Lord our God calls to himself." And with many other words he bore witness and continued to exhort them, saying, "Save yourselves from this crooked generation."

So those who received his word were baptized, and there were added that day about three thousand souls.
(Acts2:36-41ESV)

In a nutshell, we are born again by the Godhead in Christ by grace, through faith that is born out of the word of life (the Bible), at the hearing of the message of salvation, which is preached under the influence and operation of the Holy Spirit for the salvation of our souls. The different factors that go into the process of regeneration include the following:

Therefore if any person is [ingrafted] in Christ (the Messiah) he is a new creation (a new creature altogether); the old [previous moral and spiritual condition] has passed away. Behold, the fresh and new has come!
(2Co.5:17AMP)

First, the word of life – this is the gospel message that is preached in the name of Jesus Christ, which produces the faith that is needed for the salvation of our souls.

Second, faith – Hebrews11:6 says, without faith, it is impossible to please God. Whoever comes to God must first believe the Lord lives and that he rewards those who trust in him.

Third, operation of the Holy Spirit – the inward ministerial activities of the Holy Spirit helps to convict and convince an individual of their sinful state and the need to accept the offer of God in Christ for salvation.

Fourth, the blood of Jesus – the Bible declares in Hebrews9:22 that without the shedding of blood, there is no remission.

The blood of Jesus was shed for the cleansing of our sins. The blood cleanses us from sins and iniquities.

Fifth, the name of Jesus – Acts4:12, declares that there is no other name under heaven given among men by which we can be saved except the name of Jesus. The name saves us from the wrath of God.

Sixth, believe and open confession – the Bible declares in Romans10:9-10, that if we confess with our mouth that Jesus is Lord and believe in our heart that God raised him from the dead, we will be saved. For with the heart one believes and is justified, and with the mouth one confesses and is saved. To believe in Christ's redemptive work for humanity brings justification. When one confesses the Lordship of Christ, it brings salvation.

Seventh, justification – when the word is preached, it produces the faith that causes a person to believe and accept the redemptive work of Christ, and obtain forgiveness of sins from the Godhead who imputes his righteousness that is by faith to the individual by bringing him to a right standing with himself, so that the person can have peace with him. You have to be at peace with God before you can have the peace of God.

Eight, salvation – when the person opens his mouth by the help of the Holy Spirit, and confesses the Lord Jesus as savior, God's eternal life will be infused into his spirit for a new life in Christ. Once this is done, the Lord Jesus writes the person's name in the book of life as a guarantee for a life with him in paradise.

SPIRITUAL LIFE CYCLE

The right to inscribe the names of humans in the book of life was given to him when he met the lawful righteous requirements of the Godhead that was tagged to the salvation of human souls, by the offering up of himself on the cross of Calvary as sin offering for humanity. This made the Father to exalt him above the heavens and earth by making him both Christ and Lord over all things whether spiritual or physical.

On the next day their rulers and elders and scribes gathered together in Jerusalem, with Annas the high priest and Caiaphas and John and Alexander, and all who were of the high-priestly family. And when they had set them in the midst, they inquired, "By what power or by what name did you do this?" Then Peter, filled with the Holy Spirit, said to them, "Rulers of the people and elders, if we are being examined today concerning a good deed done to a crippled man, by what means this man has been healed, let it be known to all of you and to all the people of Israel that by the name of Jesus Christ of Nazareth, whom you crucified, whom God raised from the dead—by him this man is standing before you well. This Jesus is the stone that was rejected by you, the builders, which has become the cornerstone. And there is salvation in no one else, for there is no other name under heaven given among men by which we must be saved." Now when they saw the boldness of Peter and John, and perceived that they were uneducated, common men, they were astonished. And they recognized that they had been with Jesus. (Acts4:5-13ESV)

In addition, the Holy Spirit bears witness together with the spirit of the person that he is saved from the wrath of God and eternal condemnation that is reserved for the wicked and ungodly people.

The priests and the captain of the temple guard and the Sadducees came up to Peter and John while they were speaking to the people. They were greatly disturbed because the apostles were teaching the people, proclaiming in Jesus the resurrection of the dead. They seized Peter and John and, because it was evening, they put them in jail until the next day. But many who heard the message believed; so the number of men who believed grew to about five thousand.
(Acts4:1-4NIV)

Giving thanks to the Father, who has qualified you to share in the inheritance of the saints in light. He has delivered us from the domain of darkness and transferred us to the kingdom of his beloved Son, in whom we have redemption, the forgiveness of sins.
(Col.1:12-14ESV)

In my book, *The Oneness of God*, under the heading, "Divine sonship of a Christian," I explained the process of new birth in details. For the sake of those who haven't read the book, let me repeat what I said here.

"… the sonship of a Christian in connection with the Godhead denotes oneness (union) with the eternal Father based on eternal life that is given to the person in Christ Jesus, through the operation of the Holy Spirit who infuses the spirit of the individual with it. This is done in the light of the gospel message that is preached in the name of Jesus the Son of God.

A divine activity that is put to effect by the Godhead in Christ, through the ministerial activity of the Holy Spirit also called the Spirit of adoption. This operation brings a person into oneness with the Father in Christ. That is why our divine sonship as believers is not of natural descent, nor of a human decision, but of God through the power of his Spirit in Christ Jesus.

We accept man's testimony, but God's testimony is greater because it is the testimony of God, which he has given about his Son. Anyone who believes in the Son of God has this testimony in his heart. Anyone who does not believe God has made him out to be a liar, because he has not believed the testimony God has given about his Son. And this is the testimony: God has given us eternal life, and this life is in his Son. He who has the Son has life; he who does not have the Son of God does not have life.

(1Jn.5:9-12 NIV)

The Scripture above reveals that the life of the Father that brings a living soul to oneness with him, resides in Jesus of Nazareth. Romans 8:11, says God gives us the life through the Holy Spirit, while 1Corinthians 6:17, declares that we become one in spirit with the Lord when we are joined to him. The joining with the Lord in spirit occurs when the Holy Spirit infuses (injects) God's eternal life in the spirit man of whoever believes in Christ, and confesses him as Lord and Saviour. Once this is done, the person's spirit is saturated with God's eternal life, which brings the person to oneness with the Father in Christ, through the operation of the Holy Spirit. For without him (Holy Spirit) the life of the Father cannot be given to humans.

This is how we know that we remain in Him and He in us: He has given to us from His Spirit. And we have seen and we testify that the Father has sent the Son as Savior of the world. Whoever confesses that Jesus is the Son of God —God remains in him and he in God.
(1Jn.4:13-15 HCSB)

The divine sonship of a Christian is by adoption, through the ministerial activity of the Holy Spirit who infuses the spirit man of a living soul with the eternal life of the Godhead in Christ Jesus because of Christ atoning sacrifice for the sins of humankind, and his resurrection by which he purchased eternal salvation for humanity. It is through this that he became the author of our salvation and having obtained from the Father the promised Holy Spirit, he poured him out on humans for the salvation of our souls, and the regeneration of our spirit from spiritual death passed on humankind from the beginning through the sin of Adam.

But the gift is not like the trespass. For if the many died by the trespass of the one man, how much more did God's grace and the gift that came by the grace of the one man, Jesus Christ, overflow to the many! Again, the gift of God is not like the result of the one man's sin: the judgment followed one sin and brought condemnation, but the gift followed many trespasses and brought justification. For if, by the trespass of the one man, death reigned through that one man, how much more will those who receive God's abundant provision of grace and of the gift of righteousness reign in life through the one man, Jesus Christ.

Consequently, just as the result of one trespass was condemnation for all men, so also the result of one act of righteousness was justification that brings life for all men. For just as through the disobedience of the one man the many were made sinners, so also through the obedience of the one man the many will be made righteous.
(Rom.5:15-19 NIV)

    Nelson's Illustrated Bible Dictionary defines adoption as, "The act of taking voluntarily a child of other parents as one's child." It says the Greek word translated in the New Testament as adoption literally means, "Placing as a son." It adds, "It is a legal term that expresses the process by which a man brings another person into his family, endowing him with the status and privileges of a biological son or daughter." [h]

    According to the *International Standard Bible Encyclopaedia*, adoption means, "The legal process by which a man might bring into his family, and endow with the status and privileges of a son, one who was not by nature his son or of his kindred." [I]

    Legal process whereby one person receives another into his family and confers upon that person familial privileges and advantages. The "adopter" assumes parental responsibility for the "adoptee." The "adoptee" is thereby considered an actual child, becoming the beneficiary of all the rights, privileges, and responsibilities afforded to all the children of the family. [j]

THE HOLY SPIRIT

If adoption means the legal process of granting family rights, privileges and benefits to an individual in order to make the person a recipient of all the advantages given to the children of the family (as shown above), it then implies that our rights as sons of God is bestowed on us through adoption because our divine sonship is by adoption. The Bible declares that we were chosen by God before the creation of the world to be holy and blameless in his sight in love and at the same time predestined to be adopted as his sons through Jesus Christ in order to confer on us the full rights of sons.

Blessed be the God and Father of our Lord Jesus Christ, who has blessed us in Christ with every spiritual blessing in the heavenly places, even as he chose us in him before the foundation of the world, that we should be holy and blameless before him. In love he predestined us for adoption through Jesus Christ, according to the purpose of his will, to the praise of his glorious grace, with which he has blessed us in the Beloved. In him we have redemption through his blood, the forgiveness of our trespasses, according to the riches of his grace, which he lavished upon us, in all wisdom and insight making known to us the mystery of his will, according to his purpose, which he set forth in Christ as a plan for the fullness of time, to unite all things in him, things in heaven and things on earth.

(Eph.1:3-10ESV)

When Christ ascended to heaven, he obtained from the Father, the promised Holy Spirit by whom we are baptized into his body – the church. Hence the name "Spirit of adoption" because through his operation, a living soul is engrafted in Christ by faith.

For it is written, "If a man confesses with his mouth that, 'Jesus is Lord,' and believe in his heart that God raised him from the dead, he will be saved. For it is with the heart that a man believes in the sacrificial work of Christ to obtain justification, while with the mouth, confession is made to salvation." (Paraphrased – Romans 10:9-10)

This then means that whenever a person believes in their heart that Christ died and rose from the dead for the sins of humankind, the individual will be justified by the Father who imputes his righteousness that is by faith to the person so that he or she can have peace with God in Christ. Now, when the person confesses by the help of the Holy Spirit that Jesus is Lord, the eternal life of the Father will be infused into the spirit of the individual in Christ Jesus. This is done by the power of the Holy Spirit also called the Spirit of Christ for the regeneration of the person's spirit from spiritual death that came on humanity in the beginning through the sin of Adam. This spiritual phenomenon is called "New birth or the baptism by one Spirit into the one body of Christ— the church."

The body is a unit, though it is made up of many parts; and though all its parts are many, they form one body. So it is with Christ. For we were all baptized by one Spirit into one body– whether Jews or Greeks, slave or free – and we were all given the one Spirit to drink. (1Co.12:12-13 NIV)

Therefore, if a person does not have the Spirit of Christ also called the "Spirit of adoption or sonship," he or she does not belong to him according to Scripture (Rom.8:9).

Because the life of the Father that brings us to oneness with him resides in Christ but is infused into our spirit through the operation of the Holy Spirit.

> *By this you know the Spirit of God: Every spirit that confesses that Jesus Christ has come in the flesh is of God, and every spirit that does not confess that Jesus Christ has come in the flesh is not of God. And this is the spirit of the Antichrist, which you have heard was coming, and is now already in the world.*
> *(1Jn.4:2-3 NKJV)*

Many in the body of Christ do not agree with the above point of view on the process of salvation. To them, salvation demands repentance from dead works, water baptism in the name of Jesus and Holy Ghost baptism with the evidence of speaking in other tongues. Thus, the "Sinner's Prayer" commonly practiced by majority in the Christendom as the means by which a person is regenerated to enter into the kingdom of God based on Romans 10:9-10 is erroneous because it does not involve water baptism and Holy Spirit baptism.

In his book, *Restoration of the New Testament Church,* Dr. Henry B. Alexander (founder and presiding bishop of the *Shield of Faith Fellowship of Churches, International, Inc.*), explains that for a person to be saved he or she must repent and be baptized both in water and spirit. He writes, "In order for a person to be saved he or she must experience a two-part baptism consisting of both water and spirit. A person who believes the gospel and repents, and subsequently accepts water baptism is forgiven of his sins, and a person who asks for the Holy Ghost in faith will be given it. That person, having repented, been water baptized and then Spirit-filled has then been born into the Kingdom of God." [k]

He adds, "Some people falsely teach that a person is born again the instant they pray a prayer, because they fundamentally misunderstand the meaning and context of Romans 10:9-10. Scripture never says that a person is reborn simply by prayer: On the contrary, Jesus insists on "water and Spirit." Scripture ties "rebirth" to both water and Spirit." [l] Although, he emphasizes that there is nothing negative about the practice of verbal confession, establishing it as the means for new birth is biblically not correct. "While there is nothing negative in or about the practice of verbal confession, yet it *alone* can never be construed as the means by which a person enters into the Kingdom of God." [m]

In effect, a closer look at Romans10:8-10 reveals that the "word of faith," "confession," and "believe" play distinct roles in the process of salvation. The word of faith produces the faith we need to please God (Heb.11:6), believing that God raised Jesus from death causes him to impute his righteousness that is by faith to us (Rom.4:22-25). Confessing the lordship of Jesus makes God to infuse our spirit with his life for rebirth. To say that salvation comes by merely verbalizing the "Sinner's Prayer" without faith in Christ atoning sacrifice that comes from hearing the gospel message, repentance from dead works and openly confessing Jesus as Lord and Savior is biblically incorrect.

In conclusion, we are born again or given a newness of life by the Godhead in Christ Jesus his Son, through the operation of the Holy Spirit. A spiritual activity that is done in the light of the word of truth, which is the gospel massage preached in the name of Jesus Christ.

The Bible declares that he chose to give us birth through the word of truth that we might be a kind of firstfruits of all he created (Jas.1:18). Without the help or divine operation of the Holy Spirit, nobody can ever admit and confess that Jesus is Lord, which are the basic requirements for the salvation of a living soul (1Co.12:3).

The eternal life of the Godhead that resides in Christ cannot be infused into the spirit man of a living soul by the Holy Spirit unless the individual acknowledges the atoning sacrificial work of Christ on the cross of Calvary and confesses his lordship. "For in Christ Jesus you are all sons of God, through faith." (Gal.3:21ESV)"

WALKING IN THE SPIRIT

As earlier said, a spiritual life from biblical point of view does not end with been born again, it rather begins with it and continues through the second phase, which is known as "walking in the Spirit." And unless a person is born again, he cannot experience the second phase of spiritual life cycle.

Galatians5:25 says if we live in the Spirit, let us also walk in the Spirit. To walk in the Spirit simply means to be led or guided by the Holy Spirit, by faith and revelation knowledge of the word of God, through the path of faith also called the strait gate with narrow pathway.

Matthew7:13-14 admonishes us to enter the kingdom through the narrow gate, because the road that leads to destruction is broad and wide. Only a few number of people ever find the narrow path, while majority walk the broad and wide road that leads to destruction.

Enter ye in at the strait gate: for wide is the gate, and broad is the way, that leadeth to destruction, and many there be which go in thereat: Because strait is the gate, and narrow is the way, which leadeth unto life, and few there be that find it.
(Matt.7:13-14 KJV)

I say then: Walk in the Spirit and you shall not fulfill the lust of the flesh. For the flesh lusts against the Spirit, and the Spirit against the flesh; and these are contrary to one another, so that you do not do the things that you wish. But if you are led by the Spirit, you are not under the law.
(Gal.5:16-18 NKJV)

The apostle Paul says in the above portion of scriptures that the only way to avoid doing the things that the flesh craves and lust after, is to allow the Holy Spirit to guide you. Because the desires of the Spirit is contrary to the flesh, and the desires of the flesh is contrary to the Spirit. They are both in conflict with each other so that no one can satisfy the two at the same time. But when the Spirit takes the lead, and controls your life, you are free from the influence and dictates of the flesh.

2Corinthians10:3 informs us that though we live in the world, we are not of the world, and we do not act the way the people of the world do. The principles and concepts of the world contradict biblical truths, concepts and principles that we live by as Christians.

James4:4 declares that whoever embraces the pattern and practices of the world makes himself an enemy of God. In the same vein, the apostle John warns us in 1John2:15-17 that if anyone loves the world or cherishes the things that are in the world, the love of God is not in him. Worldly values, concepts, principles, practices, beliefs, mindsets, and so on, go against what God recommend for his children. The worldly mindset focuses on the lust of the flesh, lust of the eyes and the pride of life, while the spiritual mindset is focused on things that relate to Christ, and the kingdom of heaven.

Do not love or cherish the world or the things that are in the world. If anyone loves the world, love for the Father is not in him. For all that is in the world--the lust of the flesh [craving for sensual gratification] and the lust of the eyes [greedy longings of the mind] and the pride of life [assurance in one's own resources or in the stability of earthly things]--these do not come from the Father but are from the world [itself]. And the world passes away and disappears, and with it the forbidden cravings (the passionate desires, the lust) of it; but he who does the will of God and carries out His purposes in his life abides (remains) forever.
(1Jn.2:15-17AMP)

The walk with the Holy Spirit that produces an incredible changes in the life of a person begins at a stage called the "Spirit upon us," which is the third level in the manifestation of the Holy Spirit to humans. The first phase of spiritual life cycle begins at new birth, while the second phase starts when the Holy Spirit comes on a living soul.

As I explained under the heading, "The ministry of the Holy Spirit," the Holy Spirit works in us prior to new birth to draw us to Christ, and deliver us from the wrath of God. Starting from the moment we allow Christ to dwell in our hearts, the Holy Spirit begins to live in us until the day he moves from within to be upon. This last phase in the manifestation of the Holy Spirit to humans is what I call the "Spirit upon us." In most cases, it is usually marked with the initial sign of speaking in tongues. Some call it the baptism with the Holy Spirit or the Holy Ghost Baptism. However, there are many point of view about the subject.

In my previous book, *Understanding the Art of Prayer*, under the heading, "Prayer Language," I explained this subject in detail. To further illustrate my point, I would like to repeat what I said in the other book here.

"Prayer language is the ability given by the Holy Spirit to God's people that enables us to say deep and hidden things that cannot be expressed in any known human language. Some call it "tongue talking" or "speaking in tongues" while others call it "praying in the Spirit".

It is a spiritual phenomenon that usually occurs at the baptism with the Holy Spirit, which is accompanied with the initial sign of speaking in tongues.

It is a language that is exclusively reserved for prayer. This makes Christianity the only religion on earth that has a special language for prayer that no one can understand or interpret. It is not meant for buying or selling, but for communicating with God. The language is given to the body of Christ to secure our line and improve our communication with our father in heaven. It is a spiritual language that connects us to the spirit world (heaven). Since prayer is a private and personal thing, the prayer language allows us to put everyone else, including Satan out of our communication with God (Matt.6:6).

Other religions use human languages and dialects in prayers, but we Christians have a unique spiritual language that is solely for prayer. A language that the Lord Jesus gives to his body – the church to enable us talk to him in private, since no body on earth understands it. When you pray in tongues, your line is secure!

However, there are many controversies about the subject among Christians. Some believe it is mandatory for all believers to speak in tongues, while others claim it no longer exists (this is known as the cessation theory). A few others believe it is a sign given to few individuals, while certain groups believe it is of the devil.

SPIRITUAL LIFE CYCLE

A person's position regarding speaking in tongues depends on the knowledge or teaching he has about the subject, which establishes his belief and determines his attitude as it relates to tongue speaking. If you hang out with those who believe in the cessation theory, or with those who believe it is special gift given to some people in the body of Christ, or with those who think it is of the devil, you will never speak in tongues. Knowledge is power! This is why the prophet Hosea says people are destroyed from lack of knowledge (Hos. 4:6).

God gave man free will to choose whatever he wants, and he won't violate it. The Holy Spirit will not force a person to speak in tongues, either. When he comes on an individual, he normally expresses himself by enabling the person to speak in an unknown language. The Spirit comes, and then the tongues follow. Tongues enable you to articulate words in the Spirit to God. It is not meant for communicating among humans, but with God.

People always ask me whether it is possible for a person to be baptized with the Holy Spirit and not speak in tongues. My response has always been this: God gave man the right of choice in the beginning. We have the choice to either let the Holy Spirit express himself freely or to silence him by resisting the urge he puts in our hearts when he comes on us.

Acts 7:51 talks about resisting the Holy Spirit, Ephesians 4:30 warns against grieving the Holy Spirit — by whom we have been sealed for the day of redemption — while 1 Thessalonians 5:19 says we should not quench the Holy Spirit.

When people resist, oppose, or forbid the Holy Spirit from expressing himself through them, they grieve or sadden him, and if it continues, they will quench or completely silence him.

None can say Jesus is Lord without the help of the Holy Spirit, and it is the Holy Spirit who makes us one with the Lord in the spirit (1 Co.12:3, 6:17). Romans 8:9 says if anyone does not have the Spirit of Christ, he does not belong to him, for without the Holy Spirit, God's eternal life that brings us into oneness with the Godhead in Christ cannot be infused into our spirit at new birth for regeneration from spiritual death that came on humanity through the sin of Adam (for more information on this, please go to my book *The Oneness of God*).

This then implies that the fact someone doesn't speak in tongues does not mean they don't have him in their lives. There are stages in the manifestation of the Holy Spirit to every child of God (for more on this, please go to chapter nine, under the heading "The Holy Ghost and man.") The main reasons people silence the Holy Spirit includes the following:

First: the cessation theory, which asserts that spiritual gifts and speaking in tongues ceased with the twelve Apostles after the church was firmly established (1 Co. 13:8). They believe that since the completion of the canon of Scripture, tongues and other supernatural phenomenon that were evident in the primitive church ended.

Second: the belief that speaking in tongues is of the devil. Some believe that speaking in an unknown tongue is a diabolical practice, since they do not understand what they say.

Third: the belief that speaking in tongues is one of the gifts of the Holy Spirit that he gives to whoever he wills, which means that if a person doesn't speak, it is an indication that the Holy Spirit chooses not to give him the gift.

Fourth: misinterpretation of some Bible verses such as 1 Corinthians 14:13, which says that anyone who speaks in a tongue should pray that he may interpret what he says. They feel one must understand what he says before speaking in tongues. In verse 19 of the same chapter, Paul declares that he would rather speak five understandable words to help others than ten thousand words in an unknown tongue, while verse 23 says that if people who don't understand tongues come in your midst and hear everyone speaking in an unknown language, will they not think you are out of your mind?

We have to understand the difference between the gift of tongues and tongues as a sign. The Holy Spirit uses the first to unfold the mind of God to the people, and so it has to be interpreted in order that the people can understand what God is saying to the church. It is used for prophesying or declaring the mind of God to the church in order to edify and give the people direction (to strengthen, encourage, and comfort the church).

But the second is used to convey the mind of the people to God, some deep secrets that none can understand except God. This is why it is called a prayer language, because it connects men to God. Prayers are not offered to humans but God, and the second tongue serves this purpose. Verse 2 declares that anyone who speaks in tongue does not speak to people but to God, for none understands him as he utters mysteries by the Spirit. The first is God to man (brings God's words to humans), while the second is man to God (conveys man's words to God in a coded language that only God understands).

For anyone who speaks in a tongue does not speak to men but to God. Indeed, no one understands him; he utters mysteries with his spirit. But everyone who prophesies speaks to men for their strengthening, encouragement and comfort. He who speaks in a tongue edifies himself, but he who prophesies edifies the church. I would like every one of you to speak in tongues, but I would rather have you prophesy. He who prophesies is greater than one who speaks in tongues, unless he interprets, so that the church may be edified. Now, brothers, if I come to you and speak in tongues, what good will I be to you, unless I bring you some revelation or knowledge or prophecy or word of instruction?
(1 Co. 14:2-7 NIV)

Fifth: some doubt whether it is the Holy Spirit urging them to speak in an unknown tongue or their imagination. Unless you are clear about this, you may never speak in tongues. When the Holy Spirit is the one urging you, it burns and glows in your heart.

The Bible tells us what happened to the disciples when the Lord Jesus spoke with them on the road to Emmaus after his resurrection. They said their hearts burned within them while he talked with them on the road and opened their eyes to scripture, even though they could not recognize him until he broke bread and gave them to eat (Lk. 24:30-32). When the people heard the message of Peter on the day of Pentecost, scripture says the word cut or pierced their heart (Acts 2:37). The word of God burns like fire and pierces the heart.

Sixth: some are just too concerned about what people might say if they speak in a new tongue. Shame is a killer disease! The Lord said in Luke 9:26 that whoever is ashamed of him and his word, he too will be ashamed of that person when he returns in his glory and in the glory of the Father and the holy angels. You have to take your eyes off what others think and stay focused on what God wants you to do in order to be effective in spiritual things.

Seventh: others are held captive and hindered from speaking because of fear of being mocked or ridiculed by others. The fear of the unknown has caused many not to speak no matter how they feel about it in their mind. King Saul lost the kingdom because he feared the people and obeyed their voice rather than following the instruction God gave him.

Saul answered Samuel, "I have sinned. I have transgressed the Lord's command and your words. Because I was afraid of the people, I obeyed them. Now therefore, please forgive my sin and return with me so I can worship the Lord." Samuel replied to Saul, "I will not return with you.

Because you rejected the word of the Lord, the Lord has rejected you from being king over Israel." When Samuel turned to go, Saul grabbed the hem of his robe, and it tore. Samuel said to him, "The Lord has torn the kingship of Israel away from you today and has given it to your neighbor who is better than you. Furthermore, the Eternal One of Israel does not lie or change His mind, for He is not man who changes his mind." (1 Sam 15:24-29 HCSB)

Eighth: lack of true knowledge about speaking in tongues has been the main reason many don't speak. Ignorance is a killer disease! Matthew 22:29 says we make mistakes because we don't know the scripture or the power of God. Knowledge is very important. Faith comes through the knowledge you have about the written word of God. The knowledge you have about spiritual things determines your actions.

Ninth: the environment in which a person lives could also cause a person to silence the urge, because we share the views of those with whom we hang out. You cannot hang out with those who openly criticize and condemn speaking in tongues and expect to speak it one day.

Tenth: some people have made up their mind not to speak as a result of their belief system. Such people can never break out until the stronghold in their mind is demolished.

Something happened to me the very first time I spoke in tongues. It was in a church meeting, during Bible study. I had listened to the late Archbishop Benson Idahosa speaking in tongues on a TV program as he preached before I went to church.

On my way, I started having a strong desire to speak in tongues just like the archbishop did when he was praying.

Suddenly, a passage I had read earlier in Mark 16:17 that says, "And these signs will accompany those who believe: in my name they will drive out demons; they will speak in new tongues" popped up in my mind. Having prayed for the Holy Spirit to baptize me, the urge to say something similar to what I heard on TV became very strong in my heart. I started comparing the new tongues promised in the Bible to what papa Idahosa was speaking.

When I finally got to church, the urge to speak grew stronger in my heart. I was so focused on the desire that I couldn't hear what the man of God was saying anymore, even though I was in the church. I heard myself saying Holy Spirit fill me. All of a sudden, I started screaming and speaking in tongues. My whole body shook violently as I leaped to my feet and continue to speak uncontrollably for some minutes before going down on my knees. When I came to myself, I noticed everyone in the service was looking at me. I was so ashamed that I felt like leaving the place.

The pastor called me out because it was a small church, spoke about what had happened to the congregation, and then encouraged me to maintain it by praying regularly in tongues before he prayed for me. I didn't wait for the service to end before leaving because I was so ashamed.

When you silence the Holy Spirit by refusing him the right to express himself through you in an unknown tongues, it limits your effectiveness in prayer.

Ephesians 6:18 encourages us to pray in the Spirit on all occasions with all kinds of prayers and requests.

We only talk about what we know. There are things the human eyes don't see. The only way we can fully cover all grounds in prayer is by praying in the Spirit. Using the language of the spirit in prayer enables you to offer all kinds of prayers and requests at all times. It takes you beyond the limits of human knowledge and words to a dimension where you can deal with several things at the same time.

The Bible declares in 1 Corinthians 14:2 that anyone who speaks in tongues does not talk to humans but to God, because no one understands him except God alone. True tongues is a coded heavenly language that Satan and his cohorts cannot decode. Verse 4 says he who speaks in tongue strengthens or edifies himself, while the one who prophesies edifies the entire church. Jude 20 also encourages us to build ourselves up in our most holy faith and praying in the Holy Spirit. Praying in tongues builds us up in Christ.

The apostle Paul declares in 1 Corinthians 14:5 that he would like everyone to speak in tongues. At the same time, he would rather have them prophecy because the one who prophesies strengthens, encourages, and comforts the whole church. This is what makes the gift of tongues greater than the tongue that is for signs and prayer. In fact, the first is given to selected individuals as the Spirit wills (1 Co. 12:7, 10-11), while the second is for everyone who desires and asks for it (Mk. 16:17, Acts 2:4)."

SPIRITUAL LIFE CYCLE

The point I am trying to make with the above explanation is that the fact a person doesn't speak in tongues does not necessarily mean such a one is not baptize in the Holy Spirit. There could be many out there who are at the second phase of their spiritual life, which normally begins at the Holy Ghost baptism with the initial sign of speaking in tongues. But because they don't speak in tongues, we assume they don't have the Holy Spirit.

Nonetheless, when you take a closer look at their daily actions, you could tell they are been guided or led by the Spirit. The Holy Spirit could be upon them, but because of their belief system, they refuse him the right to freely express himself through them and make his presence known. Let's not also forget the Lord respects the principles he puts in place and the right of choice he gave humans in the beginning.

In most cases, what God does is to either orchestrate a situation that would cause the person to speak in tongues or bring the individual to a place where he could receive vital information and knowledge that would demolish the stronghold in their mind.

For if you live according to the flesh you will die, but if by the Spirit you put to death the deeds of the body, you will live. For all who are led by the Spirit of God are sons of God. For you did not receive the spirit of slavery to fall back into fear, but you have received the Spirit of adoption as sons, by whom we cry, "Abba! Father!" The Spirit himself bears witness with our spirit that we are children of God.
(Rom.8:13-16 ESV)

Once the Holy Spirit comes on a person, and begins to lead the individual, the person would start living in accordance with biblical truths, concepts and principles. The above passage says those who are led by the Spirit of God are the sons of God. It takes the leading of the Holy Spirit to really manifest our true identity in Christ for those around who do not share our faith to see.

Acts11:24-26, relates how Barnabas – a good man who was full of the Holy Spirit, and faith – brought Saul of Tarsus to the church at Antioch. Both of them stayed there with the church for a whole year, teaching the people. So it happened that at the end, the believers were first called Christians at Antioch. Because others saw the way they behave, and liken them to Christ himself.

Some of them, however, men from Cyprus and Cyrene, went to Antioch and began to speak to Greeks also, telling them the good news about the Lord Jesus. The Lord's hand was with them, and a great number of people believed and turned to the Lord. News of this reached the ears of the church at Jerusalem, and they sent Barnabas to Antioch. When he arrived and saw the evidence of the grace of God, he was glad and encouraged them all to remain true to the Lord with all their hearts. He was a good man, full of the Holy Spirit and faith, and a great number of people were brought to the Lord. Then Barnabas went to Tarsus to look for Saul, and when he found him, he brought him to Antioch. So for a whole year Barnabas and Saul met with the church and taught great numbers of people. The disciples were called Christians first at Antioch. (Acts 11:20-26NIV)

SPIRITUAL LIFE CYCLE

The baptism with the Holy Spirit opens the spiritual door and introduces us to an awesome life changing experience in Christ. Without the baptism with the Holy Spirit, a living soul cannot enter the second phase of a spiritual life, no matter how long the person might have been born again. The reason is that new birth only allows you to have life in Christ like a new born child. Being spiritually alive in Christ is not the ultimate, you need to grow and develop in order to enjoy all the rights and privileges God gives us as joint-heir with Christ of all things.

Think of it this way. If a father dies and leaves an inheritance for his young children, those children are not much better off than slaves until they grow up, even though they actually own everything their father had. They have to obey their guardians until they reach whatever age their father set. And that's the way it was with us before Christ came. We were like children; we were slaves to the basic spiritual principles of this world. But when the right time came, God sent his Son, born of a woman, subject to the law. God sent him to buy freedom for us who were slaves to the law, so that he could adopt us as his very own children. And because we are his children, God has sent the Spirit of his Son into our hearts, prompting us to call out, "Abba, Father." Now you are no longer a slave but God's own child. And since you are his child, God has made you his heir.
(Gal. 4:1-7NLT)

THE HOLY SPIRIT

The passage above informs us that as long as the heir, who by virtue of birth and according to law, owns everything in the house, remains a child, he is no different from a servant. The heir is subject to custodians who tell him how to live his life. He could be manipulated, abuse or denied his privileges until he grows and comes to the knowledge of who he really is and his position in the house. If he doesn't know the true identity of his father, what the father kept for him, his position, rights and privileges in the house as the heir, a servant that is supposed to attend him, could order him around. We don't have to remain baby Christians all the time. Spiritual growth and maturity is most assured in a walk with the Holy Spirit.

Like newborn babies you should crave (thirst for, earnestly desire) the pure (unadulterated) spiritual milk, that by it you may be nurtured and grow unto [completed] salvation, Since you have [already] tasted the goodness and kindness of the Lord.
(1Pet.2:2-3 AMP)

The first phase of spiritual life, which is living in the Spirit, could be liken to a newly born child who though is alive, is unaware of most of the things that happen around him. He would need certain things to be able to go through the different level of changes, growth and development in normal life, in order to understand and adapt to the world he is living in.

Likewise, a life in the Spirit involves different level of changes and procedure before a regenerated person can fully understand spiritual things and adapt to it with the aim of attaining to the fullness of Christ perfect image in words and deeds.

To do this, the Holy Spirit takes us on a spiritual walk, by faith and revelation knowledge of the written word in order to transform us in words and deeds to the very image of Christ perfect stature.

This begins when he comes on us, and takes the lead to guide our lives in light of biblical truths, concepts and principles, as he takes us through the different phases of spiritual walk, and the different platforms on a spiritual pathway, by faith and revelation knowledge of the written word of God.

The different phases in a walk with the Holy Spirit determines the measure of his presence and power that a person could have, while the platforms in spiritual pathway determines how far a person could go on a spiritual pathway. However, both effect changes in the daily lifestyle of the individual in words and actions.

In the end, the person's entire way of life, whether his mindset, belief system, desires, actions, words, conduct and so forth would be entirely transformed by the Holy Spirit, in light of biblical truths, concepts, and principles.

There is therefore now no condemnation to those who are in Christ Jesus, who do not walk according to the flesh, but according to the Spirit. For the law of the Spirit of life in Christ Jesus has made me free from the law of sin and death. For what the law could not do in that it was weak through the flesh, God did by sending His own Son in the likeness of sinful flesh, on account of sin: He condemned sin in the flesh, that the righteous requirement of the law might be fulfilled in us who do not walk according to the flesh but according to the Spirit.

For those who live according to the flesh set their minds on the things of the flesh, but those who live according to the Spirit, the things of the Spirit. For to be carnally minded is death, but to be spiritually minded is life and peace. Because the carnal mind is enmity against God; for it is not subject to the law of God, nor indeed can be. So then, those who are in the flesh cannot please God. But you are not in the flesh but in the Spirit, if indeed the Spirit of God dwells in you. Now if anyone does not have the Spirit of Christ, he is not His.
(Rom.8:1-9 NKJV)

IMPORTANCE OF SPIRITUAL WALK

1. A walk with the Holy Spirit helps a living soul to resist the lust and desire of the flesh, which is constantly in conflict with that of the Spirit. This then implies that without this walk, a living soul would give-in to the craving of the flesh, according to the written word of God.

I say then: Walk in the Spirit and you shall not fulfill the lust of the flesh. For the flesh lusts against the Spirit, and the Spirit against the flesh; and these are contrary to one another, so that you do not do the things that you wish. But if you are led by the Spirit, you are not under the law.
(Gal.5:16-18 NKJV)

2. A walk with the Holy Spirit helps an individual to understand biblical truths, concepts and principles. The Bible declares that he (the Holy Spirit) teaches us all things as regards to God and the kingdom of heaven, and reminds us of everything the Lord Jesus said in the Scripture.

All this I have spoken while still with you. But the Advocate, the Holy Spirit, whom the Father will send in my name, will teach you all things and will remind you of everything I have said to you.
(Jn.14:25-26 NIV)

3. In a walk with the Holy Spirit, a living soul is guided into all truth as it relates to Christ and the kingdom of heaven, in order to protect the person against doctrinal errors and deception, which the wicked often use in leading people astray.

There is so much more I want to tell you, but you can't bear it now. When the Spirit of truth comes, he will guide you into all truth. . He will not speak on his own but will tell you what he has heard. He will tell you about the future.
(Jn.16:12-13 NLT)

4. In a walk with the Holy Spirit, access to the deep things of God is given to an earthen vessel. The wicked fears anyone who understands the deep things of the kingdom. When you have appropriate knowledge and understanding of spiritual issues, it gives you advantage in the things of the Spirit.

But as it is written: What no eye has seen and no ear has heard, and what has never come into a man's heart, is what God has prepared for those who love Him. Now God has revealed them to us by the Spirit, for the Spirit searches everything, even the deep things of God. For who among men knows the concerns of a man except the spirit of the man that is in him? In the same way, no one knows the concerns of God except the Spirit of God. Now we have not received the spirit of the world, but the Spirit who is from God, in order to know what has been freely given to us by God.

We also speak these things, not in words taught by human wisdom, but in those taught by the Spirit, explaining spiritual things to spiritual people. But the natural man does not welcome what comes from God's Spirit, because it is foolishness to him; he is not able to know it since it is evaluated spiritually. The spiritual person, however, can evaluate everything, yet he himself cannot be evaluated by anyone.
(1Co.2:9-15HCSB)

5. A walk with the Holy Spirit transforms a person into the very image of Christ in words and deeds, by faith and revelation knowledge of the word of God. Whoever desires to be like Christ on this planet must be consistent in spiritual walk.

CHAPTER FOUR

STAGES IN SPIRITUAL LIFE

There are different stages in spiritual life, which means that all Christians are not at the same stage. Some are just starting, while others are at a very advanced stage. The stages in spiritual life has to do with the different phases that the Holy Spirit takes us through in Christ, by faith and revelation knowledge of the written word of God, in order to bring us to the full measure of Christ's perfect stature in words and deeds.

There are basically four major stages in spiritual life namely: birth, growth, maturity and perfection. The apostle Paul writes in Galatians4:19, "Oh, my dear children! I feel as if I'm going through labor pains for you again, and they will continue until Christ is fully developed in your lives." Some Bible versions say until Christ is formed in you.

The process that the Holy Spirit uses to develop the nature and attributes of Christ in us comes in different stages.

The stage a person is at determines the level of spiritual growth and development that the individual has attained by faith and revelation knowledge of the word of God.

Ephesians4:11-15 says, Christ gave the apostles, prophets, evangelists, pastors and teachers to the church to equip his people for works of service, so that his body – the church, may be built up until we all reach unity in the faith and knowledge of the Son of God and become mature in the Lord, attaining to the full measure of Christ. So that we may no longer be children tossed back and forth by every wind of new teaching that some people use to trick and deceive others. Instead, we are to speak the truth in love and grow up in every area of our lives to the full measure of Christ, in words and actions.

We have much to say about this, but it is hard to explain because you are slow to learn. In fact, though by this time you ought to be teachers, you need someone to teach you the elementary truths of God's word all over again. You need milk, not solid food! Anyone who lives on milk, being still an infant, is not acquainted with the teaching about righteousness. But solid food is for the mature, who by constant use have trained themselves to distinguish good from evil.
(Heb.5:11-14NIV)

Therefore let us leave the elementary doctrine of Christ and go on to maturity, not laying again a foundation of repentance from dead works and of faith toward God, and of instruction about washings, the laying on of hands, the resurrection of the dead, and eternal judgment. And this we will do if God permits.
(Heb.6:1-4ESV)

The above portion of scriptures shows that there are stages in spiritual life. The first says when the people ought to have been teachers, they still need someone to teach them the basic things about God's word. For this reason, the writer compare them to babies who need milk and cannot eat solid food, which is meant for mature people. Given that those who live on milk are still infants and unskilled in spiritual things. But solid food is for those who are mature, who through training and constant practice could distinguish between good and evil.

In the second passage, he encourages them to move from the stage they are at, and grow to maturity in the things of God. To understand how this works, let's take a look at the different stages of spiritual life, which are birth, growth, maturity and perfection.

SPIRITUAL BIRTH

Much has already been said about new birth, also known as rebirth, regeneration, born-again or the baptism by one Spirit into the one body of Christ, both in my previous book, *The Oneness of God*, and chapter three of this book, under the heading, "Living in the Spirit."

As I explained earlier, the baptism by one Spirit into the one body of Christ, occurs when the Holy Spirit gives God's eternal life to an individual through his spirit man in Christ, at the preaching and hearing of the gospel message, which produces the faith that is needed for rebirth.

Once we are born again, we become a part of the true vine, which is Christ, and a member of the universal body of Christ regardless of the denomination or local church that we go to as long as it is a Spirit filled church or one that holds to biblical truths, concepts and principles.

New birth brings spiritual justification and reconciliation to humans. It delivers us from the kingdom and power of darkness. It saves us from eternal death and condemnation. It brings us to oneness with the Godhead, and it rescues us from his wrath. It introduces us to a new world, and lifestyle that is lived by faith and revelation knowledge of the written word of God.

New birth makes us joint-heir with Christ of all the things he inherited from the Father. It also makes us part of those who are accredited by heaven to exercise divine authority on earth. In other words, it makes us God's law enforcement agents on earth. As members of the universal body of Christ, we have the legal authority to challenge, resist, and rebuke the devil by the word of God and prayer. Christ gave us divine warrant and authority to destroy the works of the wicked, enforce God's judicial counsel for mankind, and birth his will on earth.

SPIRITUAL GROWTH

Cambridge Advanced Learner's Dictionary – 3rd edition, includes in its definition of growth, the following "The growth of a person, animal or plant is its process of increasing in size. 2. An increase in the size or the importance of something."

STAGES IN SPIRITUAL LIFE

We can say that a person, animal or plant is said to have grown when they increase in size or importance.

Likewise, spiritual growth being the second stage in spiritual life is the process of change that the Holy Spirit takes us through by faith and revelation knowledge of the word of God, to transform us into the image of Christ in words and actions. The size of spiritual growth that a person experiences is reflected in the way the individual speaks and acts. Just like when a child is born in the natural, everyone expects him to grow and develop from one stage of life to another. Similarly, in a spiritual life we go through series of spiritual changes that enhance growth and development, and this is reflected in our daily life style.

There is a difference between physical and spiritual growth. The first require physical food for growth and development, while the latter demands spiritual nourishment for proper growth and development. Without appropriate nourishment, growth and development could be hindered in both cases. Many spend more time nourishing their physical body than they do with their spirit and soul. For this reason, they grow and develop in the physical, but remain babies in the Spirit.

The apostle Peter encourages us in 1Peter2:2 to crave pure spiritual milk like newborn babies that we might grow in the Spirit. What the spirit needs to grow is different from the desires of the flesh. And unless we feed ourselves with spiritual food that enhances growth and development, we would remain babies in the things of God regardless of how many years we spend in church.

Most Christians are more concern about their physical look than their spiritual growth. Romans8:5, says those who live according to the flesh set their minds on what the flesh desires, but those who live in accordance with the Spirit set their mind on what the Spirit desires.

John6:5-27 relates how the Lord Jesus fed the multitudes with five bread and two fish. When the people saw the miraculous sign that he performed, they said, "Surely this is the Prophet who is to come into the world." For this reason, they planned to make him king by force. But when he perceived that the people were ready to make him king by force, he withdrew and went into the mountain alone.

The next day, the people got into the boat and went to Capernaum to look for Jesus, because they couldn't find him at the place he fed them with bread and fish, and when they found him on the other side of the sea, they said to him, "Rabbi, when did you get here?" The Lord answered them, "Truly I say to you, you are not looking for me because you saw the miraculous signs I performed, but you are looking for me because you ate the loaves and had your fill. Do not work for food that perishes, but for the food that endures to eternal life, which the Son of Man will give you. For on him God the Father has placed his seal of approval."

Like the multitudes in the above portion of scriptures, many people seek God merely for material blessings, what they will eat, wear and drink. They give more attention to their body than their spirit. While their flesh is been nourished and satisfied, their spirit starve.

In 1 Corinthians 13:11, the apostle Paul writes, "When I was a child, I spoke and thought and reasoned as a child. But when I grew up, I put away childish things." From this Bible passage, we notice that the only way for Paul to do away with childish things was by means of spiritual growth. As a child, he thought, reasoned and spoke in a certain way, but when he grew up, his reasoning, thinking and speaking changed.

When I was a child, I talked like a child, I thought like a child, I reasoned like a child; now that I have become a man, I am done with childish ways and have put them aside.
(1Co.13:11 AMP)

Our mindset, thought pattern, and words are basically the first area that the Holy Spirit works on in our lives for spiritual growth and development. Proverbs23:7 declares that as a man thinks in his heart, so is he. While Matthew12:34 says out of the abundance of the heart, the mouth speaks. Words are expression of thought.

Romans12:2 states clearly that we should not conform to the pattern of this world, but be transformed by the renewing of our mind. In order to know what God's will is, that is to say, what is good, pleasing and perfect in his sight. It takes spiritual renewal of our mind, which comes through growth and development for us to discern God's perfect will. According to 1Crinthians2:14, the natural mind does not accept the things that come from the Spirit of God because it sounds foolish to them. It is only those who are spiritual that can discern the things of the Spirit. To be skilled in the things of the Spirit, one has to grow.

Galatians4:1-2, declares that as long as the heir remains a child, he is no different from a slave, even though he owns everything that the father had. It takes spiritual growth for you to have and enjoy certain things in the kingdom of God. The Lord will not entrust you with some spiritual things unless you grow up.

Think of it this way. If a father dies and leaves an inheritance for his young children, those children are not much better off than slaves until they grow up, even though they actually own everything their father had. They have to obey their guardians until they reach whatever age their father set.
(Gal 4:1-3 NLT)

But speaking the truth in love, we are to grow up in all aspects into Him who is the head, even Christ, from whom the whole body, being fitted and held together by what every joint supplies, according to the proper working of each individual part, causes the growth of the body for the building up of itself in love.
(Eph.4:15-16 NASB)

SPIRITUAL MATURITY

Spiritual maturity is an advanced level of growth and development in the Spirit. This stage of spiritual life is marked with increase measure of faith and revelation knowledge of the written word of God.

According to Ephesians4:13, spiritual maturity is a precise level of growth in faith, and revelation knowledge of the word of God concerning Christ, the Son of the living God.

The Bible encourages us in Hebrews6:1 to move beyond the basic teachings about Christ and go on to maturity. Chapter 5:14 of Hebrews also says, "Solid food is for those who are mature, who through training have the skill to recognize the difference between right and wrong." Everyone can't distinguish between good and evil. It takes spiritual maturity to discern the crafty works of the devil.

Until we all reach unity in the faith and in the knowledge of the Son of God and become mature, attaining to the whole measure of the fullness of Christ. Then we will no longer be infants, tossed back and forth by the waves, and blown here and there by every wind of teaching and by the cunning and craftiness of people in their deceitful scheming. (Eph.4:12-14 NIV)

Spiritual maturity is characterized by an advanced level of knowledge and understanding of the written word of God. In this stage, a living soul can exegetically interpret and apply scriptures. When the knowledge of the word of God increases, faith increases also because faith comes through the word. The ministerial activities, gifts and fruit of the Holy Spirit becomes so clear in the person's life.

Brethren, do not be children in understanding; however, in malice be babes, but in understanding be mature. (1Co.14:20 NKJV)

So let those [of us] who are spiritually mature and full-grown have this mind and hold these convictions; and if in any respect you have a different attitude of mind, God will make that clear to you also. (Phil.3:15 AMP)

A spiritually matured man or woman is a full-grown person, who is not a novice in the things of the Spirit. 2Timothy2:15 says, "Do your best to present yourself to God as one approved, a worker who does not need to be ashamed and who correctly handles the word of truth." When you are spiritually mature, you handle the written word of God correctly. You analyze things in the light of biblical truths, concepts and principles.

SPIRITUAL PERFECTION

Merriam-Webster Dictionary, include in its definition of perfection, the following: "the state or condition of being perfect, the act of making something perfect or better, the act of perfecting something, something that cannot be improved, something that is perfect." Similarly, *Cambridge advanced Leaner's Dictionary*, (3rd Edition), defines it as "the state of being complete and correct in every way."

According to the Bible, a living soul is said to be spiritually perfect when he or she attains to the very height of Christ glorious stature by faith and revelation knowledge of the word, being conformed to his suffering and death. That is to say, spiritual perfection is being made like Christ in every way.

In his epistle to the Philippians, the apostle Paul mentions that in spite of the great works he accomplished in the body of Christ, the deep revelation knowledge and understanding of biblical truths, concepts and principles he had, and the astounding miraculous signs and wonders he performed through the power of the Holy Spirit, he still didn't reach perfection or attain to the fullness of Christ stature in any way as we observe in the passage below.

I want to know Christ and experience the mighty power that raised him from the dead. I want to suffer with him, sharing in his death, so that one way or another I will experience the resurrection from the dead! I don't mean to say that I have already achieved these things or that I have already reached perfection. But I press on to possess that perfection for which Christ Jesus first possessed me. No, dear brothers and sisters, I have not achieved it, but I focus on this one thing: Forgetting the past and looking forward to what lies ahead, I press on to reach the end of the race and receive the heavenly prize for which God, through Christ Jesus, is calling us.
(Phil.3:10-14 NLT)

He also points out how he earnestly strive to achieve it. He writes, "I press on to possess that perfection for which Christ Jesus first possessed me." By leaving the past behind, and putting aside everything that could hinder him from making it to the end. Spiritual perfection is the utmost desire of every spirit filled Christian. As we await the return of the Lord, we all want to be exactly like him in every way, when he comes.

Ephesians5:25-29, informs us that the reason Christ so much loves the church – his body and washes her by the cleansing of God's word, is to present her to himself as a glorious church without a spot or wrinkle or any other blemish, making her holy and blameless (a perfect church).

Since he is holy, righteous, blameless, and pure, he works through the Holy Spirit to make the church like himself in every way.

Husbands, love your wives, just as also Christ loved the church and gave Himself for her, to make her holy, cleansing her in the washing of water by the word. He did this to present the church to Himself in splendor, without spot or wrinkle or any such thing, but holy and blameless. In the same way, husbands should love their wives as their own bodies. He who loves his wife loves himself. For no one ever hates his own flesh, but provides and cares for it, just as Christ does for the church.

(Eph.5:25-29HCSB)

The portion of scriptures below says clearly that we are not yet sure what we will be like when Christ appears in glory. But we know that we will be like him, because we will see him as he is. If spiritual perfection is all about attaining to the fullness of Christ perfect image in holiness, purity, righteousness and the like, and the passage below says we don't know yet how it will be like, it stands to reason that spiritual perfection would only be attain when we meet with the Lord. Because that is the only way to tell whether or not we attained it.

Dear friends, now we are children of God, and what we will be has not yet been made known. But we know that when Christ appears, we shall be like him, for we shall see him as he is. All who have this hope in him purify themselves, just as he is pure.

(1Jn.3:2-3NIV)

CHAPTER FIVE

SPIRITUAL PATHWAY

S piritual pathway is the path of life in Christ that a born again Christian walks through by faith and revelation knowledge of the written word of God. The Bible declares that though this road leads to life, only a small number of people walk the path. The reason could be that many people prefer the easy way, which leads to destruction.

When God created all things in the beginning, he gave humans the right of choice, which means we can choose whatever we want. Since the spiritual pathway is not the easy one, most people choose to walk the broad road that leads to death.

Enter by the narrow gate; for wide is the gate and broad is the way that leads to destruction, and there are many who go in by it. Because narrow is the gate and difficult is the way which leads to life, and there are few who find it.
(Matt.7:13-14 NKJV)

According to the above passage, the way of life in Christ is narrow and difficult. It is the hard but the only way to eternal life. A lot of people don't walk this path because it is hard to go in by it. It is the path of faith, and holiness. The prophet Isaiah calls it the "Highway of Holiness," which is reserved for those who are redeemed. He says no lion or any ravenous beast will be found there, and that the unclean will not journey on it. The path is exclusively reserved for those who are saved because it takes faith and revelation knowledge of God's word to walk the path.

And an highway shall be there, and a way, and it shall be called The way of holiness; the unclean shall not pass over it; but it shall be for those: the wayfaring men, though fools, shall not err therein. No lion shall be there, nor any ravenous beast shall go up thereon, it shall not be found there; but the redeemed shall walk there: And the ransomed of the LORD shall return, and come to Zion with songs and everlasting joy upon their heads: they shall obtain joy and gladness, and sorrow and sighing shall flee away.
(Is.35:8-10 KJV)

The Holy Spirit leads us through this path by faith and revelation knowledge of the written word of God, to transform us into the very image of Christ in words and deeds. It begins in the second phase of spiritual life cycle called "Walking in the Spirit," when the Holy Spirit comes on us. Although, spiritual pathway opens to every child of God at new birth, a walk on it begins at the baptism with the Holy Spirit. The Holy Spirit has to first come on us before he starts leading us on the path. New birth causes us to live in the Spirit, while the baptism with the Holy Spirit officially commences the spiritual walk.

It is the path of truth, where the Holy Spirit reveals the truth about Christ and the kingdom of heaven to a regenerated soul to enhance his or her spiritual growth and maturity. This pathway could also be referred to as "the desert way, the path of the Spirit, the hard but the only way, and the path of truth."

The Holy Spirit uses the truths, concepts, and principles revealed in the written word of God to transform humans into the image of Christ, on this path. As earlier mentioned, the revealed word of God produces faith, which the Holy Spirit uses to transform our lives. Spiritual walk with the Holy Spirit is by faith and revelation knowledge of the written word of God.

I say then: Walk in the Spirit, and you shall not fulfill the lust of the flesh. For the flesh lusts against the Spirit, and the Spirit against the flesh; and these are contrary to one another, so that you do not do the things that you wish. But if you are led by the Spirit, you are not under the law. Now the works of the flesh are evident, which are: adultery, fornication, uncleanness, lewdness, idolatry, sorcery, hatred, contentions, jealousies, outbursts of wrath, selfish ambitions, dissensions, heresies, envy, murders, drunkenness, revelries, and the like; of which I tell you beforehand, just as I also told you in time past, that those who practice such things will not inherit the kingdom of God. But the fruit of the Spirit is love, joy, peace, longsuffering, kindness, goodness, faithfulness, gentleness, self-control. Against such there is no law. And those who are Christ's have crucified the flesh with its passions and desires. If we live in the Spirit, let us also walk in the Spirit. (Gal.5:16-25 NKJV)

On this path, a regenerated person lives under the control of the law of the Spirit of life in Christ Jesus, which sets him or her free from the yoke and influence of the law of sin and death. Verse 18 of the above passage says that if a person is led by the Spirit, he is not under the law. It takes the leading by the Holy Spirit to be free from the grips of the law of sin and death.

When the people of Israel left Egypt to the promise land, the Bible declares that God did not lead them through the easy short way of the Philistine. Instead, He led them through the desert way, which is the equivalence of today's spiritual pathway in order to prepare and equip them for the new life ahead. The Lord gave them the law in the desert through Moses; he taught them his ways, and caused them to live by his word rather than on bread, which was their usual ways of life in Egypt. By so doing, he changed their mindset, words and manners, through the different trials he brought their way. He used the whole process to reprogram their mind, and establish their faith in his name throughout the time they spent in the wilderness.

When Pharaoh let the people go, God did not lead them by way of the land of the Philistines, although that was near. For God said, "Lest the people change their minds when they see war and return to Egypt." But God led the people around by the way of the wilderness toward the Red Sea. And the people of Israel went up out of the land of Egypt equipped for battle.
(Ex.13:17-18ESV)

He humbled you and let you be hungry, and fed you with manna which you did not know, nor did your fathers know, that He might make you understand that man does not live by bread alone, but man lives by everything that proceeds out of the mouth of the LORD.
(Deut.8:3HCSB)

Just as there was the easy short way, and the long hard way in the Exodus of the Israelites from Egypt to Canaan land, there exists two ways today that lead to eternity. The first is the strait gate with narrow pathway, while the second is the broad way. The first leads to eternal life in Christ Jesus – the savior of humanity, while the latter leads to eternal destruction according to the written word of God.

The same way the Mosaic Law was given to the Israelites to live by as they travel to the promise land, the law of the Spirit of life is given to believers in Christ to guide us on the pathway, through the operation of the Holy Spirit – the initiator of the walk.

And thine ears shall hear a word behind thee, saying, This is the way, walk ye in it, when ye turn to the right hand, and when ye turn to the left.
(Is.30:21 KJV)

Then he brought me out by way of the north gate, and led me round on the outside to the outer gate, that faces toward the east; and the water was coming out on the south side. Going on eastward with a line in his hand, the man measured a thousand cubits, and then led me through the water; and it was ankle-deep. Again he measured a thousand, and led me through the water; and it was knee-deep. Again he measured a thousand, and led me through the water; and it was up to the loins. Again he measured a thousand, and it was a river that I could not pass through, for the water had risen; it was deep enough to swim in, a river that could not be passed through.

(Ezek. 47:2-5 RSV)

CHAPTER SIX

PLATFORMS ON SPIRITUAL PATHWAY

The platforms on spiritual pathway are the different stages on the path of the Spirit that indicate the spiritual position of a regenerated soul in Christ, and how far he could go about attaining the goal set by the Godhead, in order to win the prize for which he is called – that is, fulfilling their prophetic destiny. It is based on a sure word of promise from the Godhead, a specific goal to be attained and a price tag. The price tag is the lawful righteous requirements of God that the person must fulfil as part of the rites of consecration that he must complete to secure his position.

Whenever the Lord gives a sure word of promise concerning a thing, it comes with a specific goal, and a price tag that must be met in order to activate, validate and secure it. At new birth, the Godhead gives a sure word of promise to a living soul, in the light of the person's prophetic destiny. Nevertheless, with the sure word of promise also comes a specific goal and a price tag that the individual in question must live up to. The degree to which the person can devote himself to the sure of promise would determine how well he fulfills his prophetic destiny.

When the Lord called Abram out of the land of the Chaldeans to live in Canaan land, he promised to give him the land to possess. Genesis15:7-18 relates how the Lord said to him, "I am the Lord who brought you out of Ur of the Chaldeans to give you this land as your possession." On hearing this, father Abraham asks, "O Sovereign Lord, how can I be sure that I will actually possess it?" In response to his question, God told him, "Bring me a heifer, a goat and a ram, each three years old, along with a dove and a young pigeon." The Lord demanded a sacrifice from him as a requirement he must meet in order to secure his possession, and failure to meet this demand would have disqualified him.

And he said to him, "I am the Lord who brought you from Ur of the Chalde'ans, to give you this land to possess." But he said, "O Lord God, how am I to know that I shall possess it?" He said to him, "Bring me a heifer three years old, a she-goat three years old, a ram three years old, a turtledove, and a young pigeon." And he brought him all these, cut them in two, and laid each half over against the other; but he did not cut the birds in two. And when birds of prey came down upon the carcasses, Abram drove them away.
(Gen 15:7-11RSV)

A closer look at the above passage highlights the fact that to every sure word of promise is tagged a sacrificial demand that authenticates it. Failure to meet the sacrificial demand nullifies a sure word of promise. Scripture records how father Abraham brought the different items God demanded from him. He also stood to protect and defend it against the birds of prey (vultures) that attempted to devour his sacrifice.

The wicked knew the importance of the sacrifice to the fulfilment of the sure word of promise, which God gave to father Abraham. A vulture (devourer) was deploy to devour his sacrifice and frustrates his efforts to secure his prophetic destiny, because they knew the role and significant of sacrifice to a sure word of promise.

As the sun was setting, Abram fell into a deep sleep, and a thick and dreadful darkness came over him. Then the Lord said to him, "Know for certain that your descendants will be strangers in a country not their own, and they will be enslaved and mistreated four hundred years. But I will punish the nation they serve as slaves, and afterward they will come out with great possessions. You, however, will go to your fathers in peace and be buried at a good old age. In the fourth generation your descendants will come back here, for the sin of the Amorites has not yet reached its full measure." When the sun had set and darkness had fallen, a smoking firepot with a blazing torch appeared and passed between the pieces. On that day the Lord made a covenant with Abram and said, "To your descendants I give this land, from the river of Egypt to the great river, the Euphrates
(Gen.15:12-18NIV)

Verse 17 says when the sun had set and darkness fell, a smoking firepot with a blazing torch appeared and passed between the pieces (sacrifice) that father Abraham offered. Verse 18 concludes by saying that the Lord made a covenant with father Abraham that day and said, "I have given this land to your descendants, all the way from the border of Egypt to the great Euphrates River.

THE HOLY SPIRIT

I believe one of the reasons the Lord passed between the pieces or sacrifice before making a covenant with father Abraham is that the pieces represent the price tag God placed on the promise, and since father Abraham fulfilled his part of the deal, God had to accomplish his own part of the deal.

He hath remembered his covenant for ever, the word which he commanded to a thousand generations. Which covenant he made with Abraham, and his oath unto Isaac; And confirmed the same unto Jacob for a law, and to Israel for an everlasting covenant: Saying, Unto thee will I give the land of Canaan, the lot of your inheritance.
(Ps.105:8-11KJV)

The above passage shows how the spiritual pathway, which led to the fulfillment of the promise given by God to his servant Abraham with reference to the land of Canaan, ran through four major stages. It started with father Abraham, then to Isaac, and then to Jacob, before Israel. These four individuals had the same promise at different level and time, with different sacrificial demand that added more weight to it as they carried it along the set path to fulfillment.

When it came to father Abraham, it was a conditional promise with a price tag he had to accomplish to authenticate the sure word of promise. By the time it got to Isaac, it became an Oath. During Jacob's time, it became a law. When it got to the fourth stage, it turned into an everlasting covenant. From a conditional promise to an oath, then to a law, and lastly to an everlasting covenant. These are the four stages on a spiritual pathway.

a) In the first stage, the promise came as a "Covenant or Agreement" with its sacrificial demand and set goal, which father Abraham accomplished.

128

b) In the second stage, the same sure word of promise concerning the land of Canaan became an "Oath" with its sacrificial demand and set goal, which Isaac fulfilled.

d) In the fourth stage, the word became an "Everlasting Covenant" with its sacrificial demand and set goal that the twelve tribes of Israel fulfilled.

c) In the third stage, the promise became a "Law" with its sacrificial demand and set goal, which Jacob accomplished

Just as the sure word of promise that the Lord gave to his servant Abraham – the father of faith according to the Scripture, moved from one stage to another, beginning from the level of a simple agreement or covenant to an oath, then to a law and finally to an everlasting covenant, so is every sure word of promise on a spiritual pathway as regard to a prophetic destiny in Christ. Whoever makes it through the four stages enjoys an everlasting covenant with the almighty God.

A closer look at the life of David – the man after God's heart, also highlights this principle. The Bible reveals in 1 Samuel 13:14b, that God chose David and appointed him leader over his people before the prophet Samuel came to anoint him with oil in the presence of his brothers. In chapter 16 verse 1, God said to Samuel, "…Fill your horn with oil and be on your way; I am sending you to Jesse of Bethlehem. I have chosen one of his sons to be King." Verse 13 relates how the Prophet Samuel anointed him in the presence of his brothers, with the horn of oil he had brought.

The Lord said to Samuel, "How long will you grieve over Saul, since I have rejected him from being king over Israel? Fill your horn with oil, and go.

THE HOLY SPIRIT

*I will send you to Jesse the Bethlehemite, for I have provided for myself a king among his sons." And Samuel said, "How can I go? If Saul hears it, he will kill me." And the Lord said, "Take a heifer with you and say, 'I have come to sacrifice to the Lord.' And invite Jesse to the sacrifice, and I will show you what you shall do. And you shall anoint for me him whom I declare to you." Samuel did what the Lord commanded and came to Bethlehem. The elders of the city came to meet him trembling and said, "Do you come peaceably?" And he said, "Peaceably; I have come to sacrifice to the Lord. Consecrate yourselves, and come with me to the sacrifice." And he consecrated Jesse and his sons and invited them to the sacrifice. When they came, he looked on Eliab and thought, "Surely the Lord's anointed is before him." But the Lord said to Samuel, "Do not look on his appearance or on the height of his stature, because I have rejected him. For the Lord sees not as man sees: man looks on the outward appearance, but the Lord looks on the heart." Then Jesse called Abinadab and made him pass before Samuel. And he said, "Neither has the Lord chosen this one." Then Jesse made Shammah pass by. And he said, "Neither has the Lord chosen this one." And Jesse made seven of his sons pass before Samuel. And Samuel said to Jesse, "The Lord has not chosen these." Then Samuel said to Jesse, "Are all your sons here?" And he said, "There remains yet the youngest, but behold, he is keeping the sheep." And Samuel said to Jesse, "Send and get him, for we will not sit down till he comes here." And he sent and brought him in. Now he was ruddy and had beautiful eyes and was handsome. And the Lord said, "Arise, anoint him, for this is he." Then Samuel took the horn of oil and anointed him in the midst of his brothers. And the Spirit of the Lord rushed upon David from that day forward. And Samuel rose up and went to Ramah.
(1 Sam.16:1-13ESV)*

I believe God promised David the kingship while he was in the desert taking care of his father's sheep. However, he had to take this sure word of promise through different platforms on a spiritual pathway before attaining the set goal as follow: First, God met him in the desert and gave him a promise to make him a king over his people Israel as revealed in the book of 1Samuel13:14b and 16:1. Second, the prophet Samuel was sent to anoint him as king over Israel in the book of 1Samuel16:13. Third, the men of Judah anointed him over the southern kingdom in the book of 2Samuel2:4. Fourth, the men of Israel anointed him king over the northern kingdom in the book of 2Samuel5:3. David went through four stages before he was firmly established as king over Israel.

Another good example of someone who successfully went through the four stages on spiritual pathway is the Lord Jesus Christ. Before he was born, the Godhead sent the angel Gabriel to Nazareth, a town in Galilee to a virgin called Mary, who was pledged to be married to a man named Joseph, a descendant of David. When the angel arrived, he told her she would conceive and give birth to a son, who she would name Jesus. He adds, "He will be great and be called the Son of the Most High. And the Lord God will give him the throne of his father David, and he will reign over the house of Jacob forever, and of his kingdom there will be no end."

When he was born, he stayed thirty years before starting his ministry. On the day John baptized him, the Godhead spoke with a loud voice from heaven to confirm his divine sonship. He said, "This is my beloved Son, in whom I am well pleased."

On another occasion, as he was about to end his earthly ministry, the Godhead spoke again to confirm the same word while he was on the mountain of transfiguration by saying, "This is my Son in whom I am well pleased. Listen to him!"

Then again, when he had paid the ultimate price on the cross of Calvary, the Godhead raised him from the grave and declared him with power to be his Son. It first came through the mouth of the angel Gabriel before he was born. The second took place on the day he was baptized. The third happened on the mountain of transfiguration, while the fourth took place at his resurrection.

When it all started, the Angel simply said he would be called the Son of God. Second, having been tried and tested for about thirty years on earth, the Father openly declared him his Son. Third, having successfully accomplished his full time ministry for about three and half years, the Father again confirmed his sonship, and instructed everyone to listen or obey him. Fourth, after he successfully accomplished the lawful righteous requirements of the Father, which was tagged to the redemption of human souls, he was raised from death and declared with power to be the Son of God.

Abraham got the sure word of promise about Canaan land as a conditional promise (first stage). Isaac got the same promise as an oath from God (second stage). Jacob got it as a law from the same God (third stage). While Israel had it as an everlasting covenant (fourth stage).

David got the promise of kingship from God (1sam.13:14b – first stage). The prophet Samuel came and confirm the same word he got from God by anointing him with oil in the presence of his brothers (1Sam.16:13 – second stage).

The men of Judah anointed him king over Judah (2Sam.2:4 – third stage). The men of Israel also anointed him king over Israel (2Sam.5:3 – fourth stage).

Jesus divine sonship promised by God through the angel Gabriel ((Lk.1:35 – first stage). the Godhead openly declared him his Son (Matt.3:17 – second stage). The Godhead again confirmed his sonship, and instructed everyone to listen to him (Matt.17:5 – third stage). He was raised from death and declared with power to be the Son of God (Rom.1:4 – fourth stage).

The platforms on spiritual pathway begins at the first phase of spiritual life cycle, which is living in the Spirit, but a living soul is granted access to it in the second phase, which is also known as walking in the Spirit. The different platforms on spiritual pathway determine the phases in a walk with the Holy Spirit while a walk with the Holy Spirit determines the level of anointing.

STAGE ONE
CONDITIONAL PROMISE

This is the first platform on spiritual pathway in Christ, and it consists of a sure word of promise, a specific goal and a price tag. The sure word of promise is the reveal mind, will or counsel of God that is given to a living soul in light of the written word concerning a specific thing. The set goal refers to the main plan or target in the mind of God that he wants to use the person to accomplish, while the price tag has to do with the cost of attaining the fixed goal – that is, the sacrificial demand.

It is a bilateral agreement between God and a living soul regarding a particular thing that is well defined and divinely established. Both parties have a role to play in the accomplishment of the set goals. God is the master planner who works all things in accordance with his eternal purpose. The divinely established plans of God become the prophetic destiny of the person in Christ, because we were created in view of his eternal purpose, and predestined to do his will. The Scripture declares in Ephesians2:10 that we are God's handiwork, created in Christ to do good works, which he planned in advance for us to do.

For we are God's handiwork, created in Christ Jesus to do good works, which God prepared in advance for us to do.
(NIV)

Now the word of the LORD came to me saying, "Before I formed you in the womb I knew you, And before you were born I consecrated you; I have appointed you a prophet to the nations.
(Jer.1:4-5 NASB)

In Him also we have obtained an inheritance, being predestined according to the purpose of Him who works all things according to the counsel of His will.
(Eph.1:11 NKJV)

According to the passages above, the divinely established plans of God, which he prearranged before we were born, becomes our primary assignment or prophetic destiny. It is the big picture, and the main target we must attain to be fulfilled in life.

The second passage declares, "I knew you before I formed you in your mother's womb. Before you were born I set you apart and appointed you as a prophet to the nations," says the Lord.

The degree of one's success in fulfilling the divine purpose is determined by how well the person understands it and how far he or she can go on the path of the Spirit.

A sure word of promise from God brings enlightenment, joy, optimism, confidence, direction, motivation and so forth to a living soul as the person walks the pathway of the Spirit. Hebrew 12:1-2, says since we are surrounded by a great cloud of witnesses, let us strip off everything that slows us down, especially the sin that so easily entangles us that we may run with endurance the race God has set before us. To do this, it admonishes us to keep our eyes on Jesus the author and finisher of our faith, who for the joy that was set before him endured the cross, disregarding its shame, and is seated at the right hand of the throne of God.

Therefore, since we are surrounded by so great a cloud of witnesses, let us also lay aside every weight, and sin which clings so closely, and let us run with endurance the race that is set before us, looking to Jesus, the founder and perfecter of our faith, who for the joy that was set before him endured the cross, despising the shame, and is seated at the right hand of the throne of God.
(Heb. 12:1-2 ESV)

The Lord Jesus got an incredible promise from the Godhead concerning the right hand throne. But, before he could obtain the promise, he had to pay the price tag and attain the set goals, which amounted to atoning sacrifice and the redemption of human souls from eternal destruction.

Whenever God gives a sure word of promise to a person regarding a particular thing or purpose, a condition is always attached to it.

The condition becomes the terms of agreement between the two parties – that is, God and the living soul. The person must respect and fulfil his own side of the agreement before he can obtain the promise. In addition, God also uses it to measure the person's loyalty to divine instructions.

When a person successfully live up to the terms of agreement by meeting the price tag to the sure word of promise, by faith and revelation knowledge of the word of God, there would be a change in the platform. At this level, the person begins to enjoy some measure of grace that the Holy Spirit gives as he leads the individual to the next platform.

STAGE TWO

OATH

This is the second platform on spiritual pathway. It has to do with a solemnly pledge from God to a given cause, in view of a divinely established set goal with the aim of authenticating and adding more weight (importance) to the sure word of promise, as a guarantee to its fulfillment. It is used by God to demonstrate his steadfastness, and good will toward the fulfillment of a divine purpose revealed through a sure word of promise, once a person live up to the terms of agreement. This occurs when the person accomplishes the price tag to the divine purpose, which is a sacrificial demand that may be very hard and difficult though not impossible to fulfil.

For when God made a promise to Abraham, since he had no one greater by whom to swear, he swore by himself, saying, "Surely I will bless you and multiply you." And thus Abraham, having patiently waited, obtained the promise. For people swear by something greater than themselves, and in all their disputes an oath is final for confirmation. So when God desired to show more convincingly to the heirs of the promise the unchangeable character of his purpose, he guaranteed it with an oath, so that by two unchangeable things, in which it is impossible for God to lie, we who have fled for refuge might have strong encouragement to hold fast to the hope set before us. We have this as a sure and steadfast anchor of the soul, a hope that enters into the inner place behind the curtain
(Heb. 6:13-19ESV)

Until a living soul meets the sacrificial demand tagged to a sure word of promise in one platform on spiritual pathway; the person cannot have access to the next platform irrespective of who the individual may be. The only way to advance on this path is to live up to the sacrificial demand in words and deeds, by faith and revelation knowledge of the word of God.

Whenever a sure word of promise move from one platform to another, its spiritual state and importance change because a superior platform further establishes and authenticates the divine plan. Second, it guarantees the person's position as regards to the fulfillment of the divine purpose.

The prophet Isaiah asks, "For the Lord Almighty has purposed, and who will annul it? His hand is stretched out, and who can turn it back?" The purpose of God stands forever.

The Lord of hosts has sworn: "As I have planned, so shall it be, and as I have purposed, so shall it stand, that I will break the Assyrian in my land, and upon my mountains trample him under foot; and his yoke shall depart from them, and his burden from their shoulder." This is the purpose that is purposed concerning the whole earth; and this is the hand that is stretched out over all the nations. For the Lord of hosts has purposed, and who will annul it? His hand is stretched out, and who will turn it back?

(Is. 14:24-27RSV)

In the passage below, we notice that an oath is added to a sure word of promise by God to confirm the unchanging nature of his divine purpose concerning a thing. Once a person makes it to this very platform, the possibility of that person accomplishing the divine purpose is very high if the individual continues the race, and remain loyal to the cause for which God called him or her.

And it was not without an oath! Others became priests without any oath, but he became a priest with an oath when God said to him: "The Lord has sworn and will not change his mind: 'You are a priest forever.'" Because of this oath, Jesus has become the guarantee of a better covenant.

(Heb. 7:20-22 NIV)

When a person successfully live up to the terms of agreement by meeting the price tag to the sure word of promise, by faith and revelation knowledge of the word of God, there would be a change in the platform. At this level, the person begins to enjoy and exercise some level of spiritual abilities or power that the Holy Spirit gives as he leads the individual to the next platform.

STAGE THREE

LAW

The next platform on spiritual pathway after the "Oath" is called a "Law." The sure word of promise becomes formally binding in this platform. For this reason, it becomes an obligation for both parties – that is, God and human to fulfill the set goals. Once the sure word becomes a law, it is irreversible regardless of what may happen along the line, the divinely set goals will certainly stand. Not only will the purpose remain unchanged, fulfilling it becomes inevitable because of its legally binding force that compels and commits both parties to the cause. Deuteronomy27:26 declares, "'Cursed is anyone who does not uphold the words of this law by doing them.' And all the people will reply,' Amen." Whoever refuses to obey the law, will face the wrath of the law.

Whoever will not obey the law of your God and the law of the king, let judgment be strictly executed on him, whether for death or for banishment or for confiscation of his goods or for imprisonment. (Ezra7:26 ESV)

We notice in the above Bible passages that it is a curse to break a sure word of promise once it becomes a law. The law has a legally binding force that obliges those involve in the process whether God or human to keep and respect the terms of agreement regarding a set goal.

When a person successfully live up to the terms of agreement on this platform by meeting the price tag to the sure word of promise, by faith and revelation knowledge of the word of God, the Holy Spirit leads the individual to the next platform. Once the change occurs, the person begins to enjoy and exercise some level of spiritual authority that the Holy Spirit gives as he continues to direct and lead the individual to the next platform.

STAGE FOUR

EVERLASTING COVENANT

The next platform on spiritual pathway after the "Law" is called an "Everlasting Covenant." On this platform, the sure word of promise and the divine purpose becomes eternally established. The effect of this platform is trans-generational and eternal.

When a person successfully live up to the terms of agreement by meeting the price tag to the sure word of promise, by faith and revelation knowledge of the word of God, the person becomes fully established. One of the main benefits of this platform is that the blessings becomes trans-generational.

At this level, the person begins to enjoy and exercise dominion through the power of the Holy Spirit. Even when the person dies, the generations after him or her would continue to enjoy the benefits. The blessings rest and remain on the family from one generation to another. It has no end.

CHAPTER SEVEN

PHASES IN SPIRITUAL WALK

The phases in spiritual walk consists of the different levels in the continuous infilling of a Christian with the presence and power of the Holy Spirit, by faith and revelation knowledge of God's word. The presence and power of the Holy Spirit determine the amount of spiritual power and authority that a person receives to achieve a task or set goal.

This normally happens when the Holy Spirit leads a person through the strait gate with narrow pathway, which is also known as the path of righteousness, holiness, faith, etc. It generally begins at the third stage of the manifestation of the Holy Spirit to a person, which is also known as the Spirit upon us or the baptism with the Holy Spirit – a spiritual phenomenon that marks the beginning of the second stage of spiritual life cycle in Christ.

There are many in the body of Christ who believe in what some call "Onetime experience of the Holy Spirit." To them, the infilling of the Holy Spirit only occurs once at new birth when a person is joined to the universal body of Christ.

A few others believe that the onetime infilling usually happens at the baptism with the Holy Spirit. According to Scriptures, the infilling of the Holy Spirit is not a onetime experience as some claim, but a gradual process that involves different levels and dimensions.

The phases in spiritual walk is a subject that explains the step-by-step process that the Holy Spirit takes us through by faith, and revelation knowledge of God's word in order to fill our inner being with his presence, and power with the aim of transforming us to Christ perfect image, in words and deeds. The measure of the presence and power of the Holy Spirit that a person receives is determine by the phase the individual attains. The willingness and eagerness of the person to go all the way with the Holy Spirit plays a major role in the process because it determines how far the individual could go on the path.

There are several verses in the Bible that prove the infilling of the Holy Spirit is not a onetime experience. Under the heading "Walking in the Spirit," I explained that to walk with the Holy Spirit means to be led or guided by him. The Holy Spirit leads us by faith and revelation knowledge of the word of God, through the path of faith (strait gate with narrow pathway), from one platform to another. When the platform changes, the phase changes also, and this increases the amount of the presence and power of the Holy Spirit we receive. The farther we walk with him, the more he fills us.

As we move from one phase to another, the measure of the presence and power of the Holy Spirit in our inner being increases. This is one of the reasons we all operate at different levels and dimensions, even though we all walk the same path.

PHASES IN SPIRITUAL WALK

Where you are at in a walk with the Holy Spirit determines the platform, and phase you are in. The platforms on spiritual path establish, confirm and authenticate the sure word of promise God gives to a person regarding a specific thing, while the phases determine the amount of the presence and power of the Holy Spirit that God gives to you.

The measure of the presence and power of the Holy Spirit that one has determines the amount of spiritual power and authority that is needed for the fulfilment of the set goal and task that God assigned to the person.

In a nutshell, the platforms on spiritual path establish a person's position as regards to the fulfilment of a divine assignment. The phases in spiritual walk determine the measure of the presence and power of the Holy Spirit God gives to the person. The measure of the presence and power of the Holy Spirit that the person receives determines the amount of spiritual power and authority that the individual needs to fulfil the divine purpose.

The knowledge you have about spiritual walk and the different factors that could either enhance or impede your commitment, consistency, willingness, eagerness, loyalty, obedience and so forth to the Holy Spirit as he leads you on the path is very important. Knowledge is key! Ignorance is no excuse! The knowledge you have about a thing, determines your attitude towards that very thing.

Similarly, the knowledge you have about the phases in spiritual walk determines your attitude towards the subject.

I love the words of the apostle Peter in his second epistle chapter 1:2-4, which says God has given us everything we need for life and godliness by his divine power, through the knowledge of him who called us by his own honor and glory.

May you have more and more grace and peace through the knowledge of God and Jesus our Lord. By his divine power the Lord has given us everything we need for life and godliness through the knowledge of the one who called us by his own honor and glory. Through his honor and glory he has given us his precious and wonderful promises, that you may share the divine nature and escape from the world's immorality that sinful craving produces.
(2Pet.1:2-4CEB)

"My people are destroyed for lack of knowledge. Because you have rejected knowledge, I will reject you from serving as My priest. Since you have forgotten the law of your God, I will also forget your sons."
(Hos.4:6HCSB)

Knowledge is very essential. Those without appropriate knowledge about spiritual walk often fall victims of the pitfall in a walk with the Holy Spirit. The knowledge you have about spiritual walk makes it easy to remain focus and consistent in this walk. The more you know about the different factors that either enhance or hinder spiritual walk, the easier it is to walk with the Holy Spirit.

Let's use one of the experiences of the prophet Ezekiel to illustrate this point.

Chapter 47:1-6 recounts how a certain man with a measuring rod led him to the river that flows from the temple, and asked him to wade through from one level to another until it became too deep for him to cross.

Apart from the differences in depth, there was also a distance of about 1,750 feet between each level that the prophet Ezekiel walked through. The man kept measuring the distance between each level as he led the man of God through the water.

First, the water was about an ankle-deep when he started the journey. After about one thousand seven hundred and fifty feet, the water was up to his knees. As he continues the journey, the water came up to his waist after walking the same distance. The man again measured 1,750 feet, but the river was now too deep for him to walk through because the water had risen and become very deep.

The man brought me back to the entrance of the temple, and I saw water coming out from under the threshold of the temple toward the east (for the temple faced east). The water was coming down from under the south side of the temple, south of the altar. He then brought me out through the north gate and led me around the outside to the outer gate facing east, and the water was flowing from the south side. As the man went eastward with a measuring line in his hand, he measured off a thousand cubits and then led me through water that was ankle-deep. He measured off another thousand cubits and led me through water that was knee-deep. He measured off another thousand and led me through water that was up to the waist.

He measured off another thousand, but now it was a river that I could not cross, because the water had risen and was deep enough to swim in — a river that no one could cross. He asked me, "Son of man, do you see this?"

(Ezek.47:1-6 NIV)

The above passage shows how the water gradually increased both in depth, and height after some distances as the prophet Ezekiel walks through. The water increased from an ankle-deep to the knees, then to the waist, and finally to overflowing that he could not walked through because the water had risen so high, and gone too deep that none could walk across it.

The man of God experienced the continuous infilling in four different phases namely: ankle, knees, waist, and the overflow, with a distance of about a thousand cubits between the phases. The prophet had to wade through the stream from one level to another until he got to a point he couldn't stand or walk but had to swim, yielding to the force of the water that immersed him as it continues to rise.

In verses 7 to 9, the man with the measuring line told the prophet that wherever the river flows, there will be swarms of living things there, and that the water makes the salty water of the Dead Sea fresh. The prophet Ezekiel saw many trees growing on both sides of the river. I think the reason the water gives life to everything on its way is that it is a living water. It turns a dead and barren land to a fruitful field.

The apostle John records an instance when the Lord Jesus referred to the Holy Spirit as the river of living water that will flow from the heart of his believers. He says whoever is thirsty may come to him and drink. And that rivers of living water will flow from within them. The passage says when he said "living water," he meant the Holy Spirit, whom those who believed in him would later receive, because no one had received the Holy Spirit at the time, since Jesus had not yet been glorified.

On the last day of the feast, the great day, Jesus stood up and cried out, "If anyone thirsts, let him come to me and drink. Whoever believes in me, as the Scripture has said, 'Out of his heart will flow rivers of living water.'" Now this he said about the Spirit, whom those who believed in him were to receive, for as yet the Spirit had not been given, because Jesus was not yet glorified.
(Jn.7:37-39ESV)

Since the Lord Jesus spoke of the Holy Spirit as living water, we can liken him (Holy Spirit) to the living water that flows from the temple, which the prophet Ezekiel was asked to walk through. We can also use the different stages in his experience to explain the different phases in the infilling of the Holy Spirit that a believer goes through.

Just as the prophet Ezekiel's experience in the river that flows from the temple came in different stages, beginning from the ankle-deep to the knees, then to the waist and finally to overflow, a believer in Christ also experiences the infilling of the Holy Spirit in stages once the person drinks from him. 1 Corinthians 12:13 says we were all baptized into one body, whether Jews or Gentiles, slaves or free, and we were all given the one Spirit to drink.

THE HOLY SPIRIT

The body is a unit, though it is made up of many parts; and though all its parts are many, they form one body. So it is with Christ. For we were all baptized by one Spirit into one body– whether Jews or Greeks, slave or free – and we were all given the one Spirit to drink. (1Co.12:12-13 NIV)

Once a person is given a drink from the one Spirit of Christ, the rivers of living water begins to flow from within the person. And once that commences, the individual begins a walk with the Holy Spirit by faith, and revelation knowledge of the Scriptures.

In the experience of the prophet Ezekiel, we notice that the more he walked, the farther he went, and the further he went, the deeper became the river. The more the distance he walked, the deeper he went in the river. The farther he went, the more the water covered him.

Equally, the more we walk with the Holy Spirit, the more we are filled with his presence and power, and the more of his presence and power we receive, the more spiritual power and authority we exercise. Each phase in spiritual walk comes with a measure of the presence and power of the Holy Spirit that a person receives, while the measure of the presence and power of the Holy Spirit determines the amount of spiritual power and authority a Christian can have and exercise. The more we go with him, the more he fills us, and the more he fills us, the more powerful we become spiritually.

Jesus answered and said unto her, If thou knewest the gift of God, and who it is that saith to thee, Give me to drink; thou wouldest have asked of him, and he would have given thee living water.

The woman saith unto him, Sir, thou hast nothing to draw with, and the well is deep: from whence then hast thou that living water? Art thou greater than our father Jacob, which gave us the well, and drank thereof himself, and his children, and his cattle? Jesus answered and said unto her, Whosoever drinketh of this water shall thirst again: But whosoever drinketh of the water that I shall give him shall never thirst; but the water that I shall give him shall be in him a well of water springing up into everlasting life."
(Jn.4:10-14KJV)

The above portion of Scriptures relates the dialogue between the Lord Jesus and the Samaritan woman when he asked her for a drink. The preceding verses say the Lord was tired from the long walk, and he sat down by the well at about noon when the Samaritan woman came to draw water from the well.

The woman was surprised when the Lord asked her for a drink because Jews don't associate with the Samaritans. She said to him, "You are a Jew and I am a Samaritan woman. How can you ask me for a drink?" Jesus answered her, "If you knew the gift of God and who it is that asks you for a drink, you would have asked him and he would have given you living water."

As the dialogue continues, the Lord made a profound statement about the living water in verse 14 that draws my attention. He said whoever drinks the water he gives, will never thirst. In addition, the water will become a spring in the person welling up to eternal life, which implies that when the Lord Jesus gives the living water to a person to drink, the water will become a well that continues to flow, increase or rise to fullness within the person, before it starts running over. That is to say, from a drink or infilling to well, then to fullness, and finally to overflow. These are the four different phases in spiritual walk, and it corresponds with the four stages in the prophet Ezekiel's experience – ankle, knees, waist and the overflow.

First, it begins with an infilling with the Holy Spirit from the Lord Jesus. This later settles as a well of living water within the person's spirit man. As the person continues to walk with the Holy Spirit, the living water would mount up to fullness. What follows is that it starts overflowing because of the continuous inflow from the throne of grace. The continuous infilling causes a rise in the amount of the presence and power of the Holy Spirit that the person receives from the Lord. Focus, commitment, consistency and the like, ensures constant rise in the volume of the living water (presence and power of the Holy Spirit) that a person would have at the end of the day.

ANKLE-DEEP LEVEL (INFILLING)

This is the first phase in a walk with the Holy Spirit that every believer must experience. It could also be referred to as a "drink into the one Spirit of Christ." This phase marks the beginning of the second phase of a spiritual life cycle in Christ. It commences when a person is given a drink into the one Spirit of Christ according to scripture. This very phase ushers a person into a life changing experience with the Holy Spirit that will transform the individual into the very image of Christ in words and deeds.

PHASES IN SPIRITUAL WALK

In the dialogue between the Lord Jesus and the Samaritan woman, he said something very important that in my opinion, explains the appropriate and easiest way to receive an infilling from him. First, he spoke about knowing the gift of God. Second, he talked about knowing him (Jesus). Third, he spoke about asking him the gift. Fourth, he talked about him giving you living water. It all begins with knowing about the gift (Holy Spirit), to knowing about Jesus (the giver of the gift), to asking the Lord for the gift (prayer), and then finally receiving it from Jesus (Holy Ghost baptism).

Jesus answered and said to her, "If you knew the gift of God, and who it is who says to you, 'Give Me a drink,' you would have asked Him, and He would have given you living water."
(Jn.4:10 NKJV)

KNOWING ABOUT THE GIFT OF GOD – knowledge is very vital as regard to the gift of God. The knowledge you have about the Holy Spirit, his operation and the need for you to have him in your life is very important.

In John14:17, the Lord Jesus explained some reasons those in the world cannot receive the Holy Spirit. The first is that they do not see him, while the second reason is that they do not know him. The passage says the Holy Spirit would be in the disciples because they knew him and he lived with them. The knowledge the disciples had about the Holy Spirit gave they advantage over those in the world.

Knowing about the Holy Spirit, and his works is the very first step towards receiving an infilling from him. We have to learn about the Holy Spirit, his ministry, gifts and fruit.

We need to know why he is the sole executor of all divine activities on earth. And why the Lord Jesus said it was to our advantage that he leaves for the Holy Spirit to come. Finally, why every sin and blasphemy can be forgiven, but blasphemy against the Spirit will not be forgiven.

For anyone reading this book who has not been baptize with the Holy Spirit, and who really desires to be filled with his presence and power, the first thing to do is to acquire appropriate knowledge about him. I encourage you to prayerfully read this book, and open your heart to receive the truth revealed about the Holy Spirit in it.

KNOWING THE LORD JESUS – the second thing the Lord spoke about in the passage is knowing him (Jesus). Knowing who Jesus really is, the works he accomplished for humanity, accepting and confessing him as Lord and Savior are the basic requirements for new birth that gives us access to the kingdom. Jesus is the author of salvation, the Lord of all things, the possessor of the sevenfold Spirit of God, and the only one who can give the Holy Spirit to humans.

I baptize you with water for repentance. But after me comes one who is more powerful than I, whose sandals I am not worthy to carry. He will baptize you with the Holy Spirit and fire.
(Matt.3:11NIV)

For more information about who the Lord Jesus really is, his preexistence, incarnation, human and divine sonship, sacrificial offering (atonement), the works he accomplished for humans, why the Father made him both Lord and Christ, why the fullness of the Godhead dwells in him bodily, why you have to accept him as Lord and Savior, why he is the possessor of the sevenfold Spirit of God, and the only one who can give the Holy Spirit to humans, go to my book, "The Oneness of God."

ASKING FOR THE GIFT – with the right knowledge about the Holy Spirit, the faith to ask for the gift from the Lord is activated and established in one's heart. This gives us the courage to approach God in prayer and ask for the infilling of the Holy Spirit, in the name of his Son, Jesus Christ of Nazareth.

And I tell you, ask, and it will be given to you; seek, and you will find; knock, and it will be opened to you. For everyone who asks receive, and the one who seeks finds, and to the one who knocks it will be opened. What father among you, if his son asks for a fish, will instead of a fish give him a serpent; or if he asks for an egg, will give him a scorpion? If you then, who are evil, know how to give good gifts to your children, how much more will the heavenly Father give the Holy Spirit to those who ask him!
(Lk.11:9-13ESV)

The above portion of Scriptures gives us the assurance that if ask God for the gift of the Holy Spirit by faith, in the name of Jesus, he will grant our request. He says if we humans who are evil know how to give good gifts to our children, how much more will he give the Holy Spirit to those who ask him. The key word here is asking by faith.

RECEIVING AN INFILLING – the final stage is that of receiving an infilling from the Lord. When the Lord finally gives you the Holy Spirit at the Holy Ghost baptism, it is usually and often marked with the physical sign of speaking in tongues. According to the Lord Jesus, speaking with new tongues is one of the signs that follows those who believe in him (Mark16:17).

A friend once said that the tongues the Lord Jesus spoke about here refers to languages that would be different from the normal language spoken by the disciples at the time (spiritual language).

When the Holy Spirit comes, he gives you the ability to speak with new tongues or languages. This only happens to people who do not have controversial view and stand about tongue speaking. There are some in the Christendom who teach against Holy Ghost baptism and tongue speaking. I explained some of the reasons they do that in chapter three, under the heading, "Walking in the Spirit."

Tongue speaking is the language of the Spirit that none can understand except God. The Holy Spirit uses it to reveal his presence in our lives. When we oppose tongue speaking, we refuse the Holy Spirit the legitimate right to audibly express himself in our lives. Resisting the Holy Spirit could result in grieving him, and when you constantly grieve him, it leads to quenching or completely silencing him.

This very phase in spiritual walk is often characterize with an incredible zeal for the work of the ministry, the hunger and thirst for the Lord, and the desire to pursue things of the kingdom of heaven. Here, you start speaking with new tongues as the Spirit enables. A language that differs from your mother tongue.

When the prophet Ezekiel got to the entrance of the temple, he saw water coming out from under the threshold of the temple. By the time the man with the measuring line brought him through the water, it was at the ankle-deep level. This was after he had walked about a thousand cubits down the river. None could imagine from the beginning that the water would become that deep after flowing through a distance of about 1,750 feet. The continuous flow from the source cause the water to rise from ankle-deep to the next level.

KNEES-DEEP LEVEL (WELL)

This is the second phase in a walk with the Holy Spirit. It is often marked with an increase in the measure of the presence and power of the Holy Spirit that a person receives from the Lord. The increase is due to the continuous inflow of living water from the throne room of God into the spirit man of the person. This only occurs when the person meets the spiritual requirement or price tag, as I explained in chapter six.

In fact, this phase is not different from the second platform on spiritual pathway that the Holy Spirit takes us through to establish and authenticate our divine purpose. As the sure word of promise move from one platform to another, its spiritual state and importance changes because a superior platform further establishes and authenticates the divine plan. While the person's position regarding the fulfillment of the divine purpose is reaffirm, through the different platforms, the amount of spiritual power and authority, which comes through the presence and power of the Holy Spirit that is needed to achieve the set goal and task, is released and given to the person through the different phases.

As the sure word of promise turns to an "OATH" on the second platforms, it further establishes the divine purpose, and enhances the person's likelihoods of fulfilling it. At the same time, the phases change also to release the amount of the presence and power of the Holy Spirit, which determine the measure of spiritual power and authority the person needs to accomplish the task and reach the set goal.

In order words, the platforms establish and secure the divine purpose, and the person's chances of fulfilling it, while the phases release the spiritual power and authority that the person needs to achieve the purpose.

According to the experience of the prophet Ezekiel, the walking distance between the first and second phase is about 1,750 feet. This implies that for a person to enjoy a continuous inflow, he or she must keep walking by faith and revelation knowledge of God's word. Just as the prophet Ezekiel maintained a steady and continuous walk with the man who led him through the water in order to experience the different phases, we must abide in Jesus and follow the leading of the Holy Spirit to experience the different phases in spiritual walk.

As the Holy Spirit continues to fill us with his presence and power, it will form a well of living water in our inner man that increases both in depth and height as long as we remain consistent to his leading until it attains the next level call the "Waist-deep level."

WAIST-DEEP LEVEL (FULLNESS)

Just as the water level increased from the knees-deep level to waist in the prophet Ezekiel's experience, the living water flowing from the throne of grace that speaks of the presence and power of the Holy Spirit continuous to rise on the inside of us until it attains fullness.

At this level, the sure word of promise becomes a "Law" as the platform changes and reaffirms the divine purpose or set goal. When this happens, the measure of infilling of the presence and power of the Holy Spirit that the person receives rises to fullness. In the end, it increases the amount of spiritual power and authority that the person receives to accomplish the task that he or she has been assigned.

Just as the prophet Ezekiel experienced the waist-deep level after walking through a distance of about 1,750 feet, we must go through the first two phases, meet the whole requirements before the Holy Spirit could lead us to this phase.

In chapter one, under the heading, "The Power of the Holy Spirit," I explained how the Lord Jesus came from Galilee to the Jordan River to be baptized by John. After his baptism, he prayed. As he was praying, the heaven opened, and the Holy Spirit descended on him in bodily form, like a dove; and a voice from heaven said, "You are my Son, whom I love; with you I am well pleased." Just as the name suggests, spirit has no body. For the Holy Spirit to descend in bodily form like a dove on Jesus means that his presence, which is the manifestation of his being was so tangible that it took a form that could be liken to that of a dove. That is to say, he came in person (he was fully present).

Now when all the people were baptized, and when Jesus also had been baptized and was praying, the heavens were opened, and the Holy Spirit descended on him in bodily form, like a dove; and a voice came from heaven, "You are my beloved Son; with you I am well pleased."
(Lk.3:21-22 ESV)

I also mentioned that Luke4:1 says Jesus was full of the Holy Spirit after the encounter at the River Jordan. The reason is that the Holy Spirit fully came and settled on him, and when Jesus left the Jordan, scriptures declares that he was led by the Holy Spirit into the wilderness, where Satan tempted him for forty days, and since he did not eat anything during the time, he became very hungry. Verse 13 says when the devil had finished tempting him and did not succeed; he left him until an opportune time. Verse 14 declares that Jesus returned to Galilee in the power of the Spirit. He entered the desert in the fullness of the Holy Spirit and returned in the power of the Holy Spirit.

And Jesus, full of the Holy Spirit, returned from the Jordan, and was led by the Spirit for forty days in the wilderness, tempted by the devil. And he ate nothing in those days; and when they were ended, he was hungry. The devil said to him, "If you are the Son of God, command this stone to become bread." And Jesus answered him, "It is written, 'Man shall not live by bread alone.'"

PHASES IN SPIRITUAL WALK

And the devil took him up, and showed him all the kingdoms of the world in a moment of time, and said to him, "To you I will give all this authority and their glory; for it has been delivered to me, and I give it to whom I will. If you, then, will worship me, it shall all be yours." And Jesus answered him, "It is written, 'You shall worship the Lord your God, and him only shall you serve.'" an, the presence was so tangible that it took a bodily shape (form), *And he took him to Jerusalem, and set him on the pinnacle of the temple, and said to him, "If you are the Son of God, throw yourself down from here; for it is written, 'He will give his angels charge of you, to guard you,' and 'On their hands they will bear you up, lest you strike your foot against a stone.'" And Jesus answered him, "It is said, 'You shall not tempt the Lord your God.'" And when the devil had ended every temptation, he departed from him until an opportune time. And Jesus returned in the power of the Spirit into Galilee, and a report concerning him went out through all the surrounding country.*
(Lk.4:1-14 RSV)

When the Holy Spirit descended on him at the River Jordwhich scripture liken to a dove. After which he went in the fullness of the Holy Spirit to the desert, where he fasted forty days and he was tempted by the devil during the time. At the end of the fasting, and temptation, he returned home in the power of the Holy Spirit. The power of the Holy Spirit is the sum of the self-ability of the Holy Spirit.

We notice in the above passages that even though the Lord Jesus had the fullness of the Holy Spirit before being led to the desert, it wasn't the sum of the presence and power of the Holy Spirit he received.

It was the third phase in a walk with the Holy Spirit, and using the word "fullness" may cause some people to think it means the totality or sum of the presence and power of the Holy Spirit. The truth is, it is not.

The Holy Spirit had to lead him (Jesus) to the wilderness, where he fasted forty days and was tempted by the devil before he could attain the next level, and received the totality of the presence and power of the Holy Spirit. He first had the presence of the Holy Spirit in full, and he needed also to have his power in full. He got the latter after meeting the specified requirements.

OVERFLOW LEVEL

At this phase, a living soul becomes overshadow and envelop with the presence and power of the Holy Spirit. The person's spirit man gets inundated with the living water. The platform turns to everlasting covenant, and the phase moves to the overflow. The individual begins to walk in the power of the Holy Spirit, rather than just being led as we observed in the life of the Lord Jesus.

When the Lord Jesus received the presence of the Holy Spirit in full, he was led by him to the wilderness.But after he moved to the next level and received the power of the Holy Spirit in full, he returned in the power of the Holy Spirit, and reports about him spread throughout the surrounding country.

For better understanding, let me use the example of a total Solar Eclipse to illustrate this point.

Total eclipse normally occurs when the moon completely covers the sun light or passes between the sun and earth. This makes the moon to cast its shadow on the earth's surface. Those within the region that is covered and traveled by the shadow of the moon would see the moon enveloped with the sun light, while the sun becomes totally invisible to them. The moon glows and shines as the sun light encircles it. People watching from the zone or region that the moon cast its shadow don't see the sun light directly because the moon covers it and shines with its light.

Just as the moon covers the sun light and shines by reason of the sun behind it, a living soul glows and radiate the glory of God at this level. The presence and power of the Holy Spirit completely overshadows the person and causes him or her to reflect the glory of God. Anyone who wishes to see God, sees him through the person. And as the glory of the sun encircles the moon when view from the zone its shadow covers, the person would be envelop by God's glory and power.

The same way the sun light causes the moon to cast its shadow on the earth surface and cover those within the zone that it travels, the person would impact people wherever he or she goes. This could possibly be one of the reasons people brought out their sick into the streets and laid them on beds and mats so that Peter's shadow might fall across some of them as he went by. The Bible says people gathered from the villages around Jerusalem, bringing their sick and those possessed by unclean spirits, and they were all healed.

THE HOLY SPIRIT

Now many signs and wonders were regularly done among the people by the hands of the apostles. And they were all together in Solomon's Portico. None of the rest dared join them, but the people held them in high esteem. And more than ever believers were added to the Lord, multitudes of both men and women, so that they even carried out the sick into the streets and laid them on cots and mats, that as Peter came by at least his shadow might fall on some of them. The people also gathered from the towns around Jerusalem, bringing the sick and those afflicted with unclean spirits, and they were all healed.
(Acts5:12-16 ESV)

Acts10:38 says how God anointed Jesus of Nazareth with the Holy Ghost and power, who went about doing good and healing all who were oppressed by the devil, for God was with him. John3:34 declares that God gave the Spirit to him (Jesus) without measure (in full). He had both the presence and power of the Holy Spirit in full. The Godhead was with him wherever he went, and did wonders through him. This is what happens when a person attains this phase in a walk with the Holy Spirit. The Lord will be with the individual wherever he or she goes doing wonders through the person, by the power of the Holy Spirit that will overshadow him or her.

Meanwhile Moses was shepherding the flock of his father-in-law Jethro, the priest of Midian. He led the flock to the far side of the wilderness and came to Horeb, the mountain of God. Then the Angel of the Lord appeared to him in a flame of fire within a bush. As Moses looked, he saw that the bush was on fire but was not consumed. So Moses thought: I must go over and look at this remarkable sight.

Why isn't the bush burning up? When the Lord saw that he had gone over to look, God called out to him from the bush, "Moses, Moses!" "Here I am," he answered. "Do not come closer," He said. "Take your sandals off your feet, for the place where you are standing is holy ground." Then He continued, "I am the God of your father, the God of Abraham, the God of Isaac, and the God of Jacob." Moses hid his face because he was afraid to look at God.

(Ex.3:1-6 HCSB)

In the passage above, we see how the Lord raised an ordinary tree to a dimension where the trees in the bush reflected his glory. It says the Angel of the Lord appeared to Moses in a flame of fire from the midst of the bush. Although the bush was engulfed in flames, it did not burn up. When Moses saw the scene, he was amazed. He said, "Why isn't that bush burning up? I must go and see it.

When the Angel appeared in flames and enveloped the trees, it caused the whole trees to reflect the glory of the Lord and shine. As Moses approached the scene, all he heard was the voice of the Lord speaking from the midst of the bush. The Lord was behind the trees doing his works and manifesting his glory, same way the sun hides behind the moon at total Solar Eclipse and envelop it, causing it to radiate its glory.

The moon comes into perfect alignment and reaches the dimension of the sun, which causes it to shin and reflect its glory. At this point, the moon is engulfed in the sun light, same way the trees were engulfed in the flames of the Angel.

Likewise, when a person reaches the overflow level in the phases in spiritual walk, he or she comes to the dimension of God, and be overshadowed by the presence and power of the Holy Spirit. This would make the individual shine, and glow in the presence, power, and glory of the Lord.

CHAPTER EIGHT

LAW OF THE SPIRIT OF LIFE

The Bible declares in Romans8:1-2, that there is no condemnation for those who are in Christ Jesus, because through him the law of the Spirit of life has set us free from the law of sin and death. Verses three and four add that what the law was unable to do because it was weakened by the flesh, God did it by sending his own Son in the likeness of sinful flesh to be a sin offering. Through this, he condemned sin in the flesh, in order that the just requirements of the law might be fully met in us, who do not live according to the flesh but according to the Spirit.

There is therefore now no condemnation for those who are in Christ Jesus. For the law of the Spirit of life in Christ Jesus has set me free from the law of sin and death. For God has done what the law, weakened by the flesh, could not do: sending his own Son in the likeness of sinful flesh and for sin, he condemned sin in the flesh, in order that the just requirement of the law might be fulfilled in us, who walk not according to the flesh but according to the Spirit.
(Rom. 8:1-5RSV)

The law of the Spirit of life, which sets us free from the law of sin and death is the truths, concepts and principles born out of the written word of God, that the Holy Spirit engraves in the heart of a born again child of God. He (Holy Spirit) uses it to renew the person's mind and liberate it from the influence, dictates, lust and unholy desires of the flesh in order to transform him or her to the image of Christ in words and deeds. After which he focuses it on things that pertain to Christ and the kingdom of heaven.

In my book, *Strategic Prayer,* under the heading "Intercession Strategy", I explained:

"Biblical truth is the real facts from God's perspective. It is constant, firm, and reliable (it never changes). There are many things the human eyes and mind cannot see or comprehend, and the fact we can't see it does not mean it doesn't exist. The Lord sees what we don't see and he knows what we don't know. When he speaks, he says it the way it really is.

Biblical concepts are notions revealed in the Bible that give us insight to spiritual things. There are key concepts in the Bible that we have to understand, and knowing them gives you confidence. The following are few examples: covenant, faith, sin, redemption, justification, salvation, baptism, confession, anointing, etc.

Biblical principles never change. They work everywhere. The principle of sowing and reaping, giving and receiving, birth and death, and day and night are constant. Understanding biblical principles helps you to know how God works."

LAW OF THE SPIRIT OF LIFE

Colossians3:1-2, encourages us to set our mind on things that are above, not on earthly things, since we have been raised with Christ, who is seated at the right hand of God in heaven. The Holy Spirit uses the biblical truths, concepts and principles from the written word of God to direct our minds and focus it on heavenly things.

If then you have been raised with Christ, seek the things that are above, where Christ is, seated at the right hand of God. Set your minds on things that are above, not on things that are on earth.
(ESV)

In his epistle to the Romans, the apostle Paul writes that those who live according to the flesh set their mind on what the flesh desires, but those who are controlled by the Holy Spirit have their minds set on things that please the Spirit. When the mind is control by the flesh, it leads to death; but when the Spirit governs the mind, it leads to life and peace. The mind that focuses on the lusts and desires of the flesh is hostile to God because it cannot obey the law of God. For this reason, those who live in accordance with the desires of the flesh cannot please God.

For those who live according to the flesh think about the things of the flesh, but those who live according to the Spirit, about the things of the Spirit. For the mind-set of the flesh is death, but the mind-set of the Spirit is life and peace. For the mind-set of the flesh is hostile to God because it does not submit itself to God's law, for it is unable to do so. Those who are in the flesh cannot please God.
(Rom. 8:5-8 HCSB)

Romans12:2, says do not conform to the pattern of this world, but be transformed by the renewing of your mind. That you may be able to discern the will of God, that which is good, acceptable and perfect. No one can live a successful Christian life without renewing their mind because of the continuous fierce struggle that goes on in our mind daily, between good and evil, truth and falsehood, light and darkness, love and hatred, and so on.

The Holy Spirit uses the truths, concepts and principles of the written word of God to renew our minds and change our lives. He also uses it to judge our thoughts and intentions. If what we purpose in our heart to do, and the way we intend doing it contradicts biblical truths, concepts, and principles, the Holy Spirit would resist it and then teach us the right way to do it.

The Bible declares in Hebrew4:12-13, that the word of God, from which the law of the Spirit of life is born, is alive and active. It is sharper than any two-edged sword, cutting between soul and spirit, between joint and marrow; it judges the thought and intentions of the heart.

For the word of God is living and effective and sharper than any double-edged sword, penetrating as far as the separation of soul and spirit, joints and marrow. It is able to judge the ideas and thoughts of the heart. No creature is hidden from Him, but all things are naked and exposed to the eyes of Him to whom we must give an account. (HCSB)

The Holy Spirit uses it to judge our thoughts and intentions in order to keep us on track and stop us from living a disorderly life in this era of grace that many seems to live and do as them please, *all in the name of liberty.* Some hide under the umbrella of "grace" to fulfil their evil desires, while others simply quote the popular passage that says where sin increased, grace increased all the more (Rom.5:20). A few interpret this to mean that as long as grace abides, sin is not accounted for. To them, we can live the way we want and do whatever pleases us, because we in the era of grace.

It is true we have been called out of the world and from all its ways and practices to live freely in Christ Jesus. However, the Scripture warns us not to use our liberty as an opportunity for unruly living. In Galatians3:13, the apostle Paul made it clear that even though we were called to freedom, we are not to use the freedom as an opportunity to fulfil the desires of the flesh. I think one of the reasons he had to place some sorts of restriction to how we use the freedom Christ gave to us is so that we don't live as lawless people – doing whatever we want.

For freedom Christ has set us free; stand firm therefore, and do not submit again to a yoke of slavery. Look: I, Paul, say to you that if you accept circumcision, Christ will be of no advantage to you. I testify again to every man who accepts circumcision that he is obligated to keep the whole law. You are severed from Christ, you who would be justified by the law; you have fallen away from grace. For through the Spirit, by faith, we ourselves eagerly wait for the hope of righteousness. For in Christ Jesus neither circumcision nor uncircumcision counts for anything, but only faith working through love. For you were called to freedom, brothers. Only do not use your freedom as an opportunity for the flesh, but through love serve one another.
(Gal.5:1-6, 13 ESV)

A friend once said that any Christian that obeys the law, be it written or oral, has fallen from grace. He stresses that in Christ, we are free from all kinds of laws. To him, a child of God should not submit to any law. He often defends his opinions and stands with the passage below. According to him, the passage makes it clear that we should not submit to any form of regulations as Christians because they are commands and doctrines of men. "A child of God who follows any kind of rules or regulations that prohibits them from eating, doing, or touching certain things still belong to the world" he said.

And when you were dead in trespasses and in the uncircumcision of your flesh, He made you alive with Him and forgave us all our trespasses. He erased the certificate of debt, with its obligations, that was against us and opposed to us, and has taken it out of the way by nailing it to the cross. He disarmed the rulers and authorities and disgraced them publicly; He triumphed over them by Him. Therefore, don't let anyone judge you in regard to food and drink or in the matter of a festival or a new moon or a Sabbath day. These are a shadow of what was to come; the substance is the Messiah. . Let no one disqualify you, insisting on ascetic practices and the worship of angels, claiming access to a visionary realm and inflated without cause by his unspiritual mind. He doesn't hold on to the head, from whom the whole body, nourished and held together by its ligaments and tendons, develops with growth from God. If you died with the Messiah to the elemental forces of this world, why do you live as if you still belonged to the world? Why do you submit to regulations: "Don't handle, don't taste, don't touch"? All these regulations refer to what is destroyed by being used up; they are commands and doctrines of men.

Although these have a reputation of wisdom by promoting ascetic practices, humility, and severe treatment of the body, they are not of any value in curbing self-indulgence.
(Col.2:13-23HCSB)

The same apostle Paul who wrote the above epistle, also writes in 1Corinthians9:21 that whenever he is with the Gentiles who do not follow or live according to the Jewish law and customs, he also live and do things like them, so he can win them to Christ. However, he does it within the parameters that the law of Christ establishes.

To those outside the law I became as one outside the law (not being outside the law of God but under the law of Christ) that I might win those outside the law.
(1Co.9:21ESV)

We notice in the passage that in his attempt to win those outside the law (lawless people) to Christ, the apostle Paul himself became like one of them, by doing what they do. However, he adds that even though he presented himself as someone who is not follow the rules of the law and customs of the Jews, his life is control by the law of Christ. This means that apart from the Law of Moses, which the Jew live by, there is another law that a Christian must submit to. We were delivered from the law of sin and death, to live by the law of Christ.

The law of the Spirit is another name for the law of Christ. It defines the parameters and sets boundaries for the freedom we enjoy in this era of grace. It determines what is lawful or unlawful, and it helps us to stay on track.

This means that though we have been set free from the law of sin and death, we are not lawless people who can do whatever they want at any time. There are sets of rules and regulations that the Holy Spirit uses to guide us on the spiritual pathway as he leads us through the different platforms and phases for spiritual growth, maturity and perfection.

This body of rules that is established and revealed in the written word of God through biblical truths, concepts and principles, which the Holy Spirit uses to renew the mind and change the character of a born again child of God is what I call "The law of the Spirit of life or the law of Christ." It highlights the dos and don'ts rules of conducts that Christians must live by.

There are some in the Christendom who have corrupted the gospel of grace and made people think that Christianity is a license for uncontrollable behavior stating that Christ died once and paid the price for all our sins, and that no other sacrifice is required for whatever sins we might commit because we are under grace. "Were sins abound, grace also abound," they say. A few others add that God forgives every manner of sins a Christian commit even before the person does the act, and that we don't have to ask for the forgiveness of whatever sins we commit because grace covers it all. Many Christians have been entrap and led into terrible sins by this distorted and deceitful gospel of grace.

It is true that we are in the era of grace, and that Christ does not have to die every day for our sins, because he met the lawful righteous requirement of the Godhead for the redemption of human souls when he offered himself as sin offering on the cross to save humanity from eternal condemnation.

Once saved, we must work out our salvation with fear and trembling, according to the written word of God (Phi.2:12). To achieve this, the Lord laid a body of rules and regulations down in the Scripture that establishes the parameters and boundaries regarding what is allow or disallow, lawful or unlawful, profitable or unprofitable in the Christendom. It is called the law of the Spirit of life or the law of Christ.

In my book, *The Origin and Purpose of Prayer*, under the heading, "Family Altar," I explained how God sought a neutral ground to introduce his ways and practices to the Israelites, because of the following reasons. First is that they were all born and raised according to the pattern and belief system of Egypt, which is totally contrary to his ways. Second, the ways and pattern of the land he was leading them to contradict his own way. Third, he had to reveal himself, and his ways to them in the desert, which was a neutral ground between Egypt and Canaan land. For the sake of those who have not read the book, below is an excerpt.

"When God visited the Israelites in Egypt, and delivered them from the hand of the Egyptians, they were all born, raised, educated and trained according to the pattern, belief system, mentality, practices, culture, and traditions of Egypt, which was totally different from God's ways, standard and pattern of doing things.Second, the land of Canaan he promised to their fathers for an inheritance was occupied by a different people with culture, belief system, mentality, tradition, mode of worship, characters, and habits that is also different from what he intend for his people.

Having redeemed them from Egypt, God had to find a neutral ground, where he could introduce his ways, principles, concepts, standard, practices, and the central truth about himself to his people in order to create a paradigm shift in their mind by deprogramming all that they learned in Egypt, and reprogram it with the law he gives to Moses as a way of protecting them against what the people in the land of Canaan prepared to offer them.

The systems both in Egypt and Canaan land allow the people to believe in the worship of multiple gods, and indulge in certain practices that God disallows. To correct the error and pattern of Egypt, he revealed his laws to Moses, laid down principles, precepts, and pattern that is totally different from that of Egypt, which the people were used to. He also built the Tabernacle and introduced a new way of worship with all its utensils and requirements. The Lord used this to establish new parameters, lines, and boundaries as to what is allowed or unlawful in accordance with his laws and principles.

God started a whole new process of transformation to deliver his people from the grips of Egypt, and also to protect them against the snare of Canaan land. He took them through different kinds of things to build new experiences that would shape their belief systems with new references. Actions produce experiences, which establish references that build and strengthen beliefs.

When you go through something, it becomes an experience that you could sometime refer to along the line, and when such experience reoccurs, it becomes a reference point and a lens through which you examine and view other similar issues.

For example, when the Lord told them human does not live by bread alone as they have always done in Egypt, but by the word that proceeds from his mouth, he proves it by allowing them to hunger, before giving them manna to eat. He gave them strict instruction regarding the manna to obey before they could have it for food (Deut.8:3).

For this process of reformation and transformation to be successful, God didn't initiate it in Egypt neither did he wait for them to arrive Canaan land before introducing it. Both Egypt and Canaan are types of the World that surround us today, while the camp in the wilderness represents our respective homes and families. To effect his purpose in their lives, God came and dwelled amongst them in the camp. And gave them the following instruction, through the mouth of his servant Moses.

And you must love the Lord your God with all your heart, all your soul, and all your strength. And you must commit yourselves wholeheartedly to these commands that I am giving you today. Repeat them again and again to your children. Talk about them when you are at home and when you are on the road, when you are going to bed and when you are getting up. Tie them to your hands and wear them on your forehead as reminders. Write them on the doorposts of your house and on your gates.
(Deut. 6:5-9 NLT)

The Lord commanded the Israelite in the above scripture to teach their children all the things they learned about him, including his laws and principles, when they are in the house, on the road, when going to bed, and when getting up in the morning.

So that the younger generation can learn about his works and ways, laws and principles, patterns, culture and practices.

When this becomes part of them, it will give them a sense of who they really are, why they exist, and what they stand for. The laws and principles of God establish values, lines and boundaries that allow us to stay on track wherever we found ourselves.

The same way God chose the camp, where all members of the family of the Israelites met and discus about his works, to introduce his laws and principles, the family altar is the most suitable place for establishing moral values and principles that shape the life and destinies of the members of the family. An easy way to do this is to choose a time that is convenient for the members of the family to gather for a quality time in the presence of God, through Bible study, meditation, worship and prayer."

The same way God used the law of Moses to deliver the Israelites from the grips of Egypt, shaped their manners, and reprogrammed their mindset in the wilderness, he uses the law of the Spirit of life in Christ to renew our mind, change our character, maintain order, and produce the fruits of righteousness in the Christendom, as he works out his eternal purpose in our lives. He uses it to transform us into the very image of his one and only begotten Son Jesus Christ, through the working power of the Holy Spirit.

This very law is mainly characterized by two things. First is a genuine love for God, and the latter is an unfeign love for one another. The Lord Jesus commands us in John13:34-35, to love one another, just the same way he loves us. For by this, all people will know that we are his disciples.

A new commandment I give to you, that you love one another, even as I have loved you, that you also love one another. By this all men will know that you are My disciples, if you have love for one another.
(Jn.13:34-35 NASB)

Jesus replied: "'Love the Lord your God with all your heart and with all your soul and with all your mind. This is the first and greatest commandment. And the second is like it: 'Love your neighbor as yourself. All the Law and the Prophets hang on these two commandments.
(Matt.22:37-40 NIV)

Owe no one anything, except to love each other, for the one who loves another has fulfilled the law. For the commandments, "You shall not commit adultery, You shall not murder, You shall not steal, You shall not covet," and any other commandment, are summed up in this word: "You shall love your neighbor as yourself." Love does no wrong to a neighbor; therefore love is the fulfilling of the law.
(Rom.13:8-10 ESV)

For the whole law can be summed up in this one command: "Love your neighbor as yourself."
(Gal.5:14 NLT)

This new law was instituted because of the changes in the order of things as regard to the covenant, mode of worship and the era we are in – that is, from the dispensation of the Law of Moses, which was merely a shadow of the real thing to the dispensation of grace that came through Jesus Christ according to the written word of God. The Bible declares in John1:17 that the law was given through Moses, but grace and truth came through Jesus Christ.

The old system under the law of Moses was only a shadow, a dim preview of the good things to come, not the good things themselves. The sacrifices under that system were repeated again and again, year after year, but they were never able to provide perfect cleansing for those who came to worship.
(Heb.10:1NLT)

God put the Law of Moses in place in the old era to prepare, guide and lead the Jews to faith – by which we are all save – that was destine to be revealed by Christ in the new era according to Scripture.

Is the Law then contrary and opposed to the promises of God? Of course not! For if a Law had been given which could confer [spiritual] life, then righteousness and right standing with God would certainly have come by Law. But the Scriptures [picture all mankind as sinners] shut up and imprisoned by sin, so that [the inheritance, blessing] which was promised through faith in Jesus Christ (the Messiah) might be given (released, delivered, and committed) to [all] those who believe [who adhere to and trust in and rely on Him]. Now before the faith came, we were perpetually guarded under the Law, kept in custody in preparation for the faith that was destined to be revealed (unveiled, disclosed), So that the Law served [to us Jews] as our trainer [our guardian, our guide to Christ, to lead us] until Christ [came], that we might be justified (declared righteous, put in right standing with God) by and through faith. But now that the faith has come, we are no longer under a trainer (the guardian of our childhood).
(Gal.3:21-25 AMP.)

The changes occurred because God found fault with the old covenant.

He wasn't pleased with the manner and attitude of those who worshipped him as we observe in Hebrew8:7-13. Verse 7 asserts that if the first covenant had been faultless, there wouldn't have been any need for a second covenant to replace it. Apart from the fact God found fault with the first covenant, he also found fault with the people.

The passages says, "The days are coming, declares the Lord, when I will make a new covenant with the people of Israel and Judah. It will not be like the covenant that I Made with their ancestors when I took them by the hand to lead them out of Egypt, because they did not remain faithful to my covenant, and I turned away from them, says the Lord. This is the covenant that I will make with the house of Israel after those days, declares the Lord; I will put my laws into their minds and write them on their hearts, and I will be their God, and they shall be my people. And they will no longer teach their neighbors, or say to one another, 'Know the Lord,' because everyone from the least to the greatest will all know me. I will forgive their wickedness and remember their sins no more." Verse 13 says when God speaks of a new covenant, it means he has made the first one obsolete. Since it is now outdated, it will soon disappear.

For if there had been nothing wrong with that first covenant, no place would have been sought for another. But God found fault with the people and said: "The time is coming, declares the Lord, when I will make a new covenant with the house of Israel and with the house of Judah. It will not be like the covenant I made with their forefathers when I took them by the hand to lead them out of Egypt, because they did not remain faithful to my covenant, and I turned away from them, declares the Lord.

This is the covenant I will make with the house of Israel after that time, declares the Lord. I will put my laws in their minds and write them on their hearts. I will be their God, and they will be my people. No longer will a man teach his neighbor, or a man his brother, saying, 'Know the Lord,' because they will all know me, from the least of them to the greatest. For I will forgive their wickedness and will remember their sins no more." By calling this covenant "new," he has made the first one obsolete; and what is obsolete and aging will soon disappear.
(Heb.8:7-13NIV)

A time will come, however, indeed it is already here, when the true (genuine) worshipers will worship the Father in spirit and in truth (reality); for the Father is seeking just such people as these as His worshipers. God is a Spirit (a spiritual Being) and those who worship Him must worship Him in spirit and in truth (reality).
(Jn.4:23-24 AMP.)

Since God was no longer pleased with the old ways, he sought a time to change it. For this reason, he sent his Son Jesus to die for the sins of humanity and inaugurate a new era of his kingdom on earth. The birth, death, resurrection, and bodily ascension of Jesus of Nazareth to the right hand of God in heaven, made the reformation plan a reality. It brought about a change in the order of priesthood, the Law, covenant, mode of worship and so on.

The Lord had spoken by the Holy Spirit, through the mouth of his servant, the prophet Jeremiah that a time will come when he would make a new covenant with the house of Israel and Judah. A covenant that will differs from the one he made with their forefathers when he brought them out of Egypt, because they did not respect the terms of the covenant.

One of the main differences between the old and new covenant is that the latter will be written in the minds and hearts of humans.

The time is coming," declares the LORD, "when I will make a new covenant with the house of Israel   and with the house of Judah. It will not be like the covenant I made with their forefathers when I took them by the hand to lead them out of Egypt, because they broke my covenant, though I was a husband to them," declares the LORD. "This is the covenant I will make with the house of Israel   after that time," declares the LORD. "I will put my law in their minds and write it on their hearts. I will be their God, and they will be my people. No longer will a man teach his neighbor, or a man his brother, saying, 'Know the LORD,' because they will all know me, from the least of them to the greatest," declares the LORD. "For I will forgive their wickedness and will remember their sins no more."
(Jer.31:31-34NIV)

The new covenant God promised in the above passage is that which Christ made and established through his death and resurrection, while the new law is the "Law of the Spirit of life" that is engraved in the heart of a born again child of God, through the operation of the Holy Spirit. It came about as a result of the changes in the order of priesthood, which also led to a change in the law when Christ became the high priest of God after the order of Melchizedek.

For this reason He is the mediator of a new covenant, so that, since a death has taken place for the redemption of the transgressions that were committed under the first covenant, those who have been called may receive the promise of the eternal inheritance. For where a covenant is, there must of necessity be the death of the one who made it.

For a covenant is valid only when men are dead, for it is never in force while the one who made it lives. Therefore even the first covenant was not inaugurated without blood.
(Heb.9:15-18NASB)

The writer of the book of Hebrew asks, "So if the priesthood of Levi, on which the law was based, could have achieved the perfection God intended, why did God need to establish a different priesthood, with a priest in the order of Melchizedek instead of the order of Levi and Aaron?" Verse 12 says if the priesthood is changed, the law must also be changed.

The priesthood cannot change without the law that authorizes it been changed also. The first priests came from the tribe of Levi according to the Law of Moses. But the Lord Jesus who became the priest of God after the order of Melchizedek came from the tribe of Judah, and according to the Law of Moses, no member of this tribe has ever served at the altar as priest. In fact the Law of Moses forbids any member of this tribe to serve at the altar as priest.

Since the priesthood of Jesus, on which the new law is based came by an oath, after the order of Melchizedek, the first law had to be changed and replaced by the new one. A change in the priesthood also necessitates a change in the law that allows and validates it.

Now if perfection had been attainable through the Levitical priesthood (for under it the people received the law), what further need would there have been for another priest to arise after the order of Melchizedek, rather than one named after the order of Aaron? For when there is a change in the priesthood, there is necessarily a change in the law as well.

For the one of whom these things are spoken belonged to another tribe, from which no one has ever served at the altar. For it is evident that our Lord was descended from Judah, and in connection with that tribe Moses said nothing about priests. This becomes even more evident when another priest arises in the likeness of Melchizedek, who has become a priest, not on the basis of a legal requirement concerning bodily descent, but by the power of an indestructible life. For it is witnessed of him, "You are a priest forever, after the order of Melchizedek." For on the one hand, a former commandment is set aside because of its weakness and uselessness (for the law made nothing perfect); but on the other hand, a better hope is introduced, through which we draw near to God. And it was not without an oath. For those who formerly became priests were made such without an oath, but this one was made a priest with an oath by the one who said to him: "The Lord has sworn and will not change his mind, 'You are a priest forever.'"
(Heb.7:11-21 ESV)

The change that occurred in the order of the priesthood from the tribe of Levi to that of Judah, also caused a change in the law from the one of Moses to that of the Spirit of life in Christ. Verse 18 says the former regulation about the priesthood was set aside because it was weak and useless. While verses 20 and 21 declare that the new system was established with an oath. For he became a priest with an oath when God said to him, "The Lord has sworn and will not change his mind, 'You are a priest forever.'"

This makes Jesus the guarantor of a better covenant. The former priests were many in number, because they were prevented by death from continuing in office, but he holds his priesthood permanently, because he continues forever.

Consequently, he is able to save to the uttermost those who draw near to God through him, since he always lives to make intercession for them. For it was indeed fitting that we should have such a high priest, holy, innocent, unstained, separated from sinners, and exalted above the heavens.

(Heb.7:11-26 ESV)

In the old priesthood system, many priests served at the altar because death prevented them from remaining in office. But in the new system, Jesus holds a permanent priesthood because he lives forever. Just as the former priesthood system differs from the new, the Law of Moses that certifies it also differs from the law of the Spirit that confirms the latter.

The first law was written on tablets of stones by humans, but the law of the Spirit of life is inscribed in the minds of Christians by the Holy Spirit, through his ministerial activities, with the aim of transforming us into the very image of Christ who is the head and bridegroom of the church. The law consists of divine truths, concepts, and principles born out of the written word of God, which the Holy Spirit uses to effect a gradual and progressive change in the mind-set, actions and character of a born again child of God.

Now ye are clean through the word which I have spoken unto you. (Jn.15:3KJV)

Put to death therefore what is earthly in you: sexual immorality, impurity, passion, evil desire, and covetousness, which is idolatry. On account of these the wrath of God is coming. In these you too once walked, when you were living in them. But now you must put them all away: anger, wrath, malice, slander, and obscene talk from your mouth.

Do not lie to one another, seeing that you have put off the old self with its practices and have put on the new self, which is being renewed in knowledge after the image of its creator.
(Col.3:5-10NIV)

The Godhead uses this new law to transform Christians in words and deeds, from inside out through the operation of the Holy Spirit with the aim of producing a new generation in Christ, without stain or wrinkles but holy and blameless. It is the only "road safety code" so to say, along the pathway of the Spirit that a born again child of God must live by in order to walk successfully with the Holy Spirit. The law of the Spirit of life could also be referred to as the following:

LAW OF CHRIST – the apostle Paul refers to this law as that law of Christ in his epistle to the Galatians. While encouraging those who are matured among them to assist and gently restore anyone caught in sin to the right path, he warns they to be careful not to fall into the same temptation. In verse 2, he asks they to bear one another's burden, and that in this way, they will fulfil the law of Christ.

Bear ye one another's burdens, and so fulfil the law of Christ.
(Gal.6:2KJV)

The Lord Jesus Christ, the Son of the living God is the author and establisher of this law. As earlier mentioned, it came about as a result of the changes that occurred in the order of the priesthood, which also demands that the law be changed. The former system operates by the law of Moses, while the new order functions by the law of Christ. From the tribe of Levi, and the law of Moses to the tribe of Judah, and the law of Christ.

A new commandment I give to you, that you love one another, even as I have loved you, that you also love one another. By this all men will know that you are My disciples, if you have love for one another. (Jn.13:34-35 NASB)

PERFECT LAW OF LIBERTY – the apostle James says anyone who hears the word and does not obey it is like someone who looks at his face in a mirror and afterwards goes away, and immediately forgets what he looks like. In verse 25, he declares that whoever looks into the perfect law that gives freedom, and continues in it, not forgetting what he hears but doing it, will be blessed.

But one who looks intently at the perfect law, the law of liberty, and abides by it, not having become a forgetful hearer but an effectual doer, this man will be blessed in what he does. (Jas.1:25NASB)

It is the only law that has the power to set us free from the grip and influence of the law of sin and death, which the prince of this age uses to keep people under captivity to do his will – that is, yield their body to the passion, lust and unholy desires of the flesh.

LAW OF GOD – when God spoke about this law through the mouth of his prophet Jeremiah, he said, "… I will put my law within them and write it on their hearts. I will be their God, and they will be my people."

But this is the covenant which I will make with the house of Israel after those days, says the Lord: I will put my law within them, and I will write it upon their hearts; and I will be their God, and they shall be my people. (Jer.31:33RSV)

It is the law of the Godhead that is inscribed in the mind of Christians, through the operation of the Holy Spirit. It produces the fruits of righteousness, and distinguishes us from others.

The Bible recounts what happened when the disciples were first called Christians. According to Acts 11:19-26, some of the believers who had been scattered during the persecution that arose when Stephen was killed preached to the Gentiles about the Lord Jesus. This led to the salvation of many Gentiles at Antioch.

When the church at Jerusalem heard about what happened, they sent Barnabas. Upon his arrival at Antioch, he saw the great things God did for the people. So, he encouraged them to remain true to the Lord. He then went on to Tarsus and look for Saul, brought him back to Antioch, where both of they stayed and taught the people for a whole year. Because of the effect of their teaching on the disciples for one year, those who were not part of the believers called them Christians. The transformation was so obvious and evident that others liken them to Christ. The word they heard positively changed their entire lives and produced the fruits of righteousness in them.

Now those who were scattered because of the persecution that arose over Stephen traveled as far as Phoenicia and Cyprus and Antioch, speaking the word to no one except Jews. But there were some of them, men of Cyprus and Cyrene, who on coming to Antioch spoke to the Hellenists also, preaching the Lord Jesus. And the hand of the Lord was with them, and a great number who believed turned to the Lord. The report of this came to the ears of the church in Jerusalem, and they sent Barnabas to Antioch.

When he came and saw the grace of God, he was glad, and he exhorted them all to remain faithful to the Lord with steadfast purpose, for he was a good man, full of the Holy Spirit and of faith. And a great many people were added to the Lord. So Barnabas went to Tarsus to look for Saul, and when he had found him, he brought him to Antioch. For a whole year they met with the church and taught a great many people. And in Antioch the disciples were first called Christians.
(Acts 11:19-26ESV)

WORD OF FAITH – another name for the law of the Spirit is the word of faith because it produces the faith we need in this era of grace. Ephesians2:8 says we are saved by grace, through faith. According to Romans10:17, faith comes from what we hear about Christ.

So faith comes from what is heard, and what is heard comes through the message about Christ.
(Rom.10:17HCSB)

The law of the spirit of life, also known as the word of faith produces faith in the mind of the hearer, by the working power of the Holy Spirit, who uses it to achieve God's eternal purpose in the life of an individual in Christ.

WORD OF LIFE – the Lord Jesus made it clear in the Scripture that the word he speaks gives life. It is the only word that saves, and gives life to whoever hears it. john6:63 says it is the Spirit that gives life, and that the flesh accomplishes nothing. The words that proceed from the mouth of the Lord Jesus are spirit and life.

It is the Spirit who gives life; the flesh is no help at all. The words that I have spoken to you are spirit and life.
(Jn.6:63ESV)

The word of life gives life to humans in Christ Jesus, the Son of the living God. It is another name for the law of the Spirit of life that sets us free from the law of sin and death. It energizes, enlightens, strengthens and awakens our inner man.

REVEALED OR RHEMA WORD – unlike the first law that was written in tablets of stones by humans, this one is revealed or born out of the written word of God by the Holy Spirit, and then engraved in our minds. The Bible declares that when the Lord Jesus came to the region of Caesarea Philippi, he asked his disciples the following question, "Who do people say the Son of man is?"

In reply, they said, "Some say John the Baptist, others say Elijah, and still others, Jeremiah or one of the prophets." He said to them, "But who do you say that I am?" then Simon Peter answered, "You are the Messiah, the Son of the living God." The Lord commended Peter for his wise response. He also made it clear that it was revealed to Peter by the Godhead.

Now when Jesus came into the district of Caesarea Philippi, he asked his disciples, "Who do people say that the Son of Man is?" And they said, "Some say John the Baptist, others say Elijah, and others Jeremiah or one of the prophets." He said to them, "But who do you say that I am?" Simon Peter replied, "You are the Christ, the Son of the living God." And Jesus answered him, "Blessed are you, Simon Bar-Jonah! For flesh and blood has not revealed this to you, but my Father who is in heaven.

And I tell you, you are Peter, and on this rock I will build my church, and the gates of hell shall not prevail against it. I will give you the keys of the kingdom of heaven, and whatever you bind on earth shall be bound in heaven, and whatever you loose on earth shall be loosed in heaven." Then he strictly charged the disciples to tell no one that he was the Christ.

(Matt.16:17-18ESV)

The law of the Spirit of life is the revealed word of God that illuminates a believer in Christ. It is the revealed mind of God born out of the Scripture, and engraved in our minds. It teaches us how to live daily in accordance with God's will. The letter kills, but the revelation knowledge of the word of God produces spiritual life and direction. The Psalmist says the word of God is a lamp to his feet and a light to his path. The revelation knowledge of the word of God gives understanding and direction.

And the disciples came and said to Him, "Why do You speak to them in parables?" He answered and said to them, "Because it has been given to you to know the mysteries of the kingdom of heaven, but to them it has not been given. For whoever has, to him more will be given, and he will have abundance; but whoever does not have, even what he has will be taken away from him. Therefore I speak to them in parables, because seeing they do not see, and hearing they do not hear, nor do they understand. But blessed are your eyes for they see, and your ears for they hear; for assuredly, I say to you that many prophets and righteous men desired to see what you see, and did not see it, and to hear what you hear, and did not hear it.

(Matt.13:10-13,16-17NKJV)

CHAPTER NINE

HOLY GHOST AND MAN

In this section, we shall be looking at the different stages in the manifestation of the Holy Spirit to humans. It consists of three major ways in which the Holy Spirit reveals himself to a person in Christ. The Bible passages below prove that the early disciples encounter the Holy Spirit in different stages, beginning with the level of him "being with them," to that of "being in them," and finally to "being upon them."

The Spirit of truth, whom the world cannot receive, because it neither sees Him nor knows Him; but you know Him, for He dwells with you and will be in you.

(Jn.14:17NKJV)

Again Jesus said, "Peace be with you! As the Father has sent me, I am sending you." And with that he breathed on them and said, "Receive the Holy Spirit. If you forgive anyone's sins, their sins are forgiven; if you do not forgive them, they are not forgiven.

(Jn.20:21-23NIV)

And while staying with them he ordered them not to depart from Jerusalem, but to wait for the promise of the Father, which, he said, "you heard from me; for John baptized with water, but you will be baptized with the Holy Spirit not many days from now." So when they had come together, they asked him, "Lord, will you at this time restore the kingdom to Israel?" He said to them, "It is not for you to know times or seasons that the Father has fixed by his own authority. But you will receive power when the Holy Spirit has come upon you, and you will be my witnesses in Jerusalem and in all Judea and Samaria, and to the end of the earth.

(Acts1:4-8ESV)

In order words, they first knew him as the Spirit with them, latter as the Spirit in them, and finally as the Spirit upon them. In the first passage, the Lord Jesus told his disciples that the Holy Spirit dwells with them because they know him, and that he will be in them. This happened after the Lord had spent about three years with them, during his earthly ministry. He made it clear in the passage that the people in the world cannot receive the Holy Spirit for two reasons. The first is that they do not see him, while the second is that they do not know him.

In my opinion, the statement of the Lord in the above passage reveals two important facts about the manifestation of the Holy Spirit. The first is that the Holy Spirit dwelt with them at the time because they knew him, while the second is that he will be in them. For the Holy Spirit to be with them at one point in time, and then be in them at a different time, means there is a difference between the Spirit being with someone, and the Spirit being in someone.

Another important thing I would like to point out is that the Lord Jesus made this declaration before his sacrificial death on the cross of Calvary for the sins of humanity, and his triumphant resurrection for our justification. Having paid the ultimate price for human redemption, he came back to the same disciples and breathed on them saying, "receive the Holy Spirit" according to the book of Jn.20:22. Then again, before he ascended to heaven, he commanded them not to leave Jerusalem until the Holy Spirit comes upon them according to the book of Acts1:4-8. This spiritual phenomenon was destined to release power on the disciples, and launch them into a new phase in ministry.

The Spirit with, in and upon are the different stages in the manifestation of the Holy Spirit to a living soul in Christ – the head of the church. Just as it was with the early disciples of the Lord Jesus, these three different stages do not occur on a single day or at once. Instead, it takes time and series of activities for an individual to experience it in full, because each stage has its role and spiritual significant to the body of Christ.

The Bible declares that whatever happens in the days of the Bible was written for our instruction, so that we can learn from it (1Co.10:11). We can examine the different stages in which the early disciples experience the manifestation of the Holy Spirit, learn from it, and use the knowledge and understanding we get to position ourselves for an incredible encounter with the Holy Spirit in fullness.

SPIRIT WITH US

This is the first stage in the manifestation of the Holy Spirit to an individual in Christ, and it takes place prior to new birth. Here, the Holy Spirit lives with a person, not in a person to draw him or her to Christ, through his ministerial activities by convicting the individual of his or her sin, eternal condemnation, and the need to accept the offer made by Christ for the salvation of human souls. This is done in the light of the gospel truth, being the word of faith that produces the faith by which a person is save in Christ.

But what does it say? "The word is near you, in your mouth and in your heart" (that is, the word of faith which we preach): that if you confess with your mouth the Lord Jesus and believe in your heart that God has raised Him from the dead, you will be saved. For with the heart one believes unto righteousness, and with the mouth confession is made unto salvation.
(Rom.10:8-10NKJV)

Nevertheless, I am telling you the truth. It is for your benefit that I go away, because if I don't go away the Counselor will not come to you. If I go, I will send Him to you. When He comes, He will convict the world about sin, righteousness, and judgment: About sin, because they do not believe in Me; about righteousness, because I am going to the Father and you will no longer see Me; and about judgment, because the ruler of this world has been judged.
(Jn.16:7-11HCSB)

He does this to draw an individual to Christ because the Lord Jesus himself said that no one could come to him unless the Father who sent him draws the person.

This work is accomplished through the operation of the Holy Spirit, who is the sole executor of all divine activities on earth.

> *No one is able to come to Me unless the Father Who sent Me attracts and draws him and gives him the desire to come to Me, and [then] I will raise him up [from the dead] at the last day.*
> *(Jn.6:44AMP)*

The major activity of the Holy Spirit in the life of an individual at this stage is to capture his or her mind, and then subject it to the will of the Godhead in Christ, by developing the seed of faith, that is, the imperishable seed of God's word in the person's mind in the light of the gospel message that is preached in the name of Jesus. Once the seed of God's word is sown and nurtured in the person's mind by the Holy Spirit, he then uses it to draw the individual to Christ for new birth.

I keep asking myself why the Lord Jesus would tell his disciples that the Holy Spirit was with them at the time he spoke, rather than being in them having worked together with them for about three and a half years.

> *Even the Spirit of truth, whom the world cannot receive, because it neither sees him nor knows him. You know him, for he dwells with you and will be in you.*
> *(Jn.14:17ESV)*

The Bible reveals in John7:37-39 that the Holy Spirit could not be given to anyone until Jesus had entered his glory. That is to say, he had to first meet the righteous demand of the Godhead for the redemption of human souls by offering himself as sin offering on the cross for humanity.

This means that at the time he spoke to the disciples, the right to baptize or give the Holy Spirit to a person was not yet given to him, because he has not paid the ultimate price that the Father tagged to it, which amounted to an atoning sacrifice for the redemption of human souls from eternal death.

> *Now on the last day, the great day of the feast, Jesus stood and cried out, saying, "If anyone is thirsty, let him come to Me and drink. He who believes in Me, as the Scripture said, 'From his innermost being will flow rivers of living water.'" But this He spoke of the Spirit, whom those who believed in Him were to receive; for the Spirit was not yet given, because Jesus was not yet glorified.*
> *(Jn.7:37-39NASB)*

This then mean that even though the Holy Spirit was with the disciples at that moment, working out the eternal purpose of the Father in their lives, he could not live in them because the right to do so was not yet given by the Father.

Similarly, until a person is born again, the Holy Spirit cannot live in him or her because the right to do so is only given in the second stage of his manifestation to humans in Christ – the head of the church. However, he can live with the person to draw him or her to Christ, through his ministerial activities, in light of the gospel message that is preached in the name of Jesus, the author and finisher of our faith.

SPIRIT IN US

The second stage in the manifestation of the Holy Spirit to humans in Christ is called the Spirit in us. Here, the Holy Spirit comes and lives in a born again child of God.

This spiritual phenomenon usually takes place at new birth or the baptism by one Spirit into the one body of Christ – the church, according to the written word of God.

For we were all baptized by one Spirit into one body—whether Jews or Greeks slave or free—and we were all given the one Spirit to drink.
(1Co.12:12-14 NIV)

At this point, the Holy Spirit infuses the spirit man of a person who believes, and confesses the Lordship of Christ, by faith at the hearing of the word of life, with the eternal life of the Godhead for a newness of life in Christ Jesus. This is why scripture declares that if a person does not have the Spirit of Christ, he or she does not belong to him.

You, however, are controlled not by the sinful nature but by the Spirit, if the Spirit of God lives in you. And if anyone does not have the Spirit of Christ, he does not belong to Christ.
(Rom.8:9NIV)

The reason is that we are adopted by the Godhead as sons and daughters in Christ, through the Spirit of adoption (Holy Spirit), who infuses us with the eternal life of God in Christ. Just as I explained in my previous book, *The Oneness of God*, under the heading, "Divine Sonship of a Christian", we were chosen by the Godhead before the creation of the world to be holy and blameless in his sight in love. And at the same time, we were predestined to be adopted as his sons and daughters, through the same Spirit, in order to confer on us the full rights of sons in Christ according to scripture.

THE HOLY SPIRIT

Blessed be the God and Father of our Lord Jesus Christ, who has blessed us in Christ with every spiritual blessing in the heavenly places, even as he chose us in him before the foundation of the world, that we should be holy and blameless before him. In love, he predestined us for adoption as sons through Jesus Christ, according to the purpose of his will, to the praise of his glorious grace, with which he has blessed us in the Beloved. In him we have redemption through his blood, the forgiveness of our trespasses, according to the riches of his grace. (Eph.1:3-7 ESV)

Therefore, if a living being does not have the Spirit of Christ who is also referred to as the "Spirit of adoption or sonship", he or she is not of Christ. Because the life of the Father that brings us into oneness and union with him, resides in Christ but it is infused into our spirit man through the operation of the Holy Spirit.

1Corinthians6:17, says whoever is joined to the Lord becomes one with him in spirit. The Holy Spirit joins our spirit with the Lord, and makes it one with him by uniting himself with our spirit as he infuses us with God's eternal life for new birth.

For the benefit of those who have not read *The Oneness of God*, below is an excerpt on the subject from the book.

"As earlier mentioned, the sonship of a Christian in connection with the Godhead denotes oneness (union) with the eternal Father based on eternal life that is given to the person in Christ Jesus, through the operation of the Holy Spirit who infuses the spirit of the individual with it. This is done in the light of the gospel message that is preached in the name of Jesus the Son of God.

A divine activity that is put to effect by the Godhead in Christ, through the ministerial activity of the Holy Spirit also called the Spirit of adoption. This operation brings a person into oneness with the Father in Christ. That is why our divine sonship as believers is not of natural descent, nor of a human decision, but of God through the power of his Spirit in Christ Jesus.

We accept man's testimony, but God's testimony is greater because it is the testimony of God, which he has given about his Son. Anyone who believes in the Son of God has this testimony in his heart. Anyone who does not believe God has made him out to be a liar, because he has not believed the testimony God has given about his Son. And this is the testimony: God has given us eternal life, and this life is in his Son. He who has the Son has life; he who does not have the Son of God does not have life.
(1Jn.5:9-12 NIV)

The Scripture above reveals that the life of the Father that brings a living soul to oneness with him, resides in Jesus of Nazareth. Romans 8:11, says God gives us the life through the Holy Spirit, while 1Corinthians 6:17, declares that we become one in spirit with the Lord when we are joined to him. The joining with the Lord in spirit occurs when the Holy Spirit infuses (injects) God's eternal life in the spirit man of whoever believes in Christ, and confesses him as Lord and Saviour. Once this is done, the person's spirit is saturated with God's eternal life, which brings the person to oneness with the Father in Christ, through the operation of the Holy Spirit. For without him (Holy Spirit) the life of the Father cannot be given to humans in Christ.

THE HOLY SPIRIT

This is how we know that we remain in Him and He in us: He has given to us from His Spirit. And we have seen and we testify that the Father has sent the Son as Savior of the world. Whoever confesses that Jesus is the Son of God —God remains in him and he in God.
(1Jn.4:13-15 HCSB)

The divine sonship of a Christian is by adoption, through the ministerial activity of the Holy Spirit who infuses the spirit man of a living soul with the eternal life of the Godhead in Christ Jesus because of Christ atoning sacrifice for the sins of humankind, and his resurrection by which he purchased eternal salvation for humanity. It is through this that he became the author of our salvation and having obtained from the Father the promised Holy Spirit, he poured him out on humans for the salvation of our souls, and the regeneration of our spirit from spiritual death passed on humankind from the beginning through the sin of Adam.

But the gift is not like the trespass. For if the many died by the trespass of the one man, how much more did God's grace and the gift that came by the grace of the one man, Jesus Christ, overflow to the many! Again, the gift of God is not like the result of the one man's sin: the judgment followed one sin and brought condemnation, but the gift followed many trespasses and brought justification. For if, by the trespass of the one man, death reigned through that one man, how much more will those who receive God's abundant provision of grace and of the gift of righteousness reign in life through the one man, Jesus Christ. Consequently, just as the result of one trespass was condemnation for all men, so also the result of one act of righteousness was justification that brings life for all men.

For just as through the disobedience of the one man the many were made sinners, so also through the obedience of the one man the many will be made righteous.
(Rom.5:15-19 NIV)

   Nelson's Illustrated Bible Dictionary defines adoption as, "The act of taking voluntarily a child of other parents as one's child." It says the Greek word translated in the New Testament as adoption literally means, "Placing as a son." It adds, "It is a legal term that expresses the process by which a man brings another person into his family, endowing him with the status and privileges of a biological son or daughter." [h]

   According to the *International Standard Bible Encyclopaedia,* adoption means, "The legal process by which a man might bring into his family, and endow with the status and privileges of a son, one who was not by nature his son or of his kindred." [I]

   Legal process whereby one person receives another into his family and confers upon that person familial privileges and advantages. The "adopter" assumes parental responsibility for the "adoptee." The "adoptee" is thereby considered an actual child, becoming the beneficiary of all the rights, privileges, and responsibilities afforded to all the children of the family. [j]

   If adoption means the legal process of granting family rights, privileges and benefits to an individual in order to make the person a recipient of all the advantages given to the children of the family (as shown above), it then implies that our rights as sons of God is bestowed on us through adoption because our divine sonship is by adoption.

THE HOLY SPIRIT

The Bible declares that we were chosen by God before the creation of the world to be holy and blameless in his sight in love and at the same time predestined to be adopted as his sons through Jesus Christ in order to confer on us the full rights of sons.

Blessed be the God and Father of our Lord Jesus Christ, who has blessed us in Christ with every spiritual blessing in the heavenly places, even as he chose us in him before the foundation of the world, that we should be holy and blameless before him. In love he predestined us for adoption through Jesus Christ, according to the purpose of his will, to the praise of his glorious grace, with which he has blessed us in the Beloved. In him we have redemption through his blood, the forgiveness of our trespasses, according to the riches of his grace, which he lavished upon us, in all wisdom and insight making known to us the mystery of his will, according to his purpose, which he set forth in Christ as a plan for the fullness of time, to unite all things in him, things in heaven and things on earth.
(Eph.1:3-10ESV)

When Christ ascended to heaven, he obtained from the Father, the promised Holy Spirit by whom we are baptized into his body – the church. Hence the name "Spirit of adoption" because through his operation, a living soul is engrafted in Christ by faith. For it is written, "If a man confesses with his mouth that, 'Jesus is Lord,' and believe in his heart that God raised him from the dead, he will be saved. For it is with the heart that a man believes in the sacrificial work of Christ to obtain justification, while with the mouth, confession is made to salvation." (Paraphrased – Romans10:9-10)

This then means that whenever a person believes in their heart that Christ died and rose from the dead for the sins of humankind, the individual will be justified by the Father who imputes his righteousness that is by faith to the person so that he or she can have peace with God in Christ. Now, when the person confesses by the help of the Holy Spirit that Jesus is Lord, the eternal life of the Father will be infused into the spirit of the individual in Christ Jesus. This is done by the power of the Holy Spirit also called the Spirit of Christ for the regeneration of the person's spirit from spiritual death that came on humanity in the beginning through the sin of Adam. This spiritual phenomenon is called "New birth or the baptism by one Spirit into the one body of Christ—the church."

The body is a unit, though it is made up of many parts; and though all its parts are many, they form one body. So it is with Christ. For we were all baptized by one Spirit into one body– whether Jews or Greeks, slave or free – and we were all given the one Spirit to drink. (1Co.12:12-13 NIV)

Therefore, if a person does not have the Spirit of Christ also called the "Spirit of adoption or sonship," he or she does not belong to him according to Scripture (Rom.8:9). Because the life of the Father that brings us to oneness with him resides in Christ but is infused into our spirit through the operation of the Holy Spirit.

By this you know the Spirit of God: Every spirit that confesses that Jesus Christ has come in the flesh is of God, and every spirit that does not confess that Jesus Christ has come in the flesh is not of God.

And this is the spirit of the Antichrist, which you have heard was coming, and is now already in the world.
(1Jn.4:2-3 NKJV)

Many in the body of Christ do not agree with the above point of view on the process of salvation. To them, salvation demands repentance from dead works, water baptism in the name of Jesus and Holy Ghost baptism with the evidence of speaking in other tongues. Thus, the "Sinner's Prayer" commonly practiced by majority in the Christendom as the means by which a person is regenerated to enter into the kingdom of God based on Romans 10:9-10 is erroneous because it does not involve water baptism and Holy Spirit baptism.

In his book, *Restoration of the New Testament Church*, Dr. Henry B. Alexander (founder and presiding bishop of the *Shield of Faith Fellowship of Churches, International, Inc.*), explains that for a person to be saved he or she must repent and be baptized both in water and spirit. He writes, "In order for a person to be saved he or she must experience a two-part baptism consisting of both water and spirit. A person who believes the gospel and repents, and subsequently accepts water baptism is forgiven of his sins, and a person who asks for the Holy Ghost in faith will be given it. That person, having repented, been water baptized and then Spirit-filled has then been born into the Kingdom of God." [k]

He adds, "Some people falsely teach that a person is born again the instant they pray a prayer, because they fundamentally misunderstand the meaning and context of Romans 10:9-10. Scripture never says that a person is reborn simply by prayer:

On the contrary, Jesus insists on "water and Spirit." Scripture ties "rebirth" to both water and Spirit." [l] Although, he emphasizes that there is nothing negative about the practice of verbal confession, establishing it as the means for new birth is biblically not correct. "While there is nothing negative in or about the practice of verbal confession, yet it *alone* can never be construed as the means by which a person enters into the Kingdom of God."[m]

In effect, a closer look at Romans10:8-10 reveals that the "word of faith," "confession," and "believe" play distinct roles in the process of salvation. The word of faith produces the faith we need to please God (Heb.11:6), believing that God raised Jesus from death causes him to impute his righteousness that is by faith to us (Rom.4:22-25). Confessing the lordship of Jesus makes God to infuse our spirit with his life for rebirth. To say that salvation comes by merely verbalizing the "Sinner's Prayer" without faith in Christ atoning sacrifice that comes from hearing the gospel message, repentance from dead works and openly confessing Jesus as Lord and Savior is biblically incorrect.

In conclusion, we are born again or given a newness of life by the Godhead in Christ Jesus his Son, through the operation of the Holy Spirit. A spiritual activity that is done in the light of the word of truth, which is the gospel massage preached in the name of Jesus Christ.

The Bible declares that he chose to give us birth through the word of truth that we might be a kind of firstfruits of all he created (Jas.1:18).

Without the help or divine operation of the Holy Spirit, nobody can ever admit and confess that Jesus is Lord, which are the basic requirements for the salvation of a living soul (1Co.12:3).

The eternal life of the Godhead that resides in Christ cannot be infused into the spirit man of a living soul by the Holy Spirit unless the individual acknowledges the atoning sacrificial work of Christ on the cross of Calvary and confesses his lordship. "For in Christ Jesus you are all sons of God, through faith." (Gal.3:21ESV)"

Immediately after the triumphant resurrection of the Lord Jesus, by which he met the lawful righteous requirements of God that was tagged to the redemption of human souls, he ascended to the heavenly courtroom and presented his hands and sides, which represented his atoning sacrifice on the cross of Calvary. This was done in order to obtain from the Godhead, the lawful rights to infuse with eternal life those he has chosen and spent about three and a half years to prepare for the work that was entrusted to his charge by the Father.

Then I saw in the right hand of him who sat on the throne a scroll with writing on both sides and sealed with seven seals. And I saw a mighty angel proclaiming in a loud voice, "Who is worthy to break the seals and open the scroll?" But no one in heaven or on earth or under the earth could open the scroll or even look inside it. I wept and wept because no one was found who was worthy to open the scroll or look inside. Then one of the elders said to me, "Do not weep! See, the Lion of the tribe of Judah, the Root of David, has triumphed. He is able to open the scroll and its seven seals."

Then I saw a Lamb, looking as if it had been slain, standing in the center of the throne, encircled by the four living creatures and the elders. He had seven horns and seven eyes, which are the seven spirits of God sent out into all the earth. He came and took the scroll from the right hand of him who sat on the throne. And when he had taken it, the four living creatures and the twenty-four elders fell down before the Lamb. Each one had a harp and they were holding golden bowls full of incense, which are the prayers of the saints. And they sang a new song: "You are worthy to take the scroll and to open its seals, because you were slain, and with your blood you purchased men for God from every tribe and language and people and nation. You have made them to be a kingdom and priests to serve our God, and they will reign on the earth."
(Rev.5:1-10NIV)

In the evening of that same day, he came and stood among his disciples and showed them his hands and sides as a sign that the price for their salvation has been paid. Having done that he breathed on them and said, "Receive the Holy Spirit" if you forgive anyone his or her sins, he or she will be forgiven; if you do not forgive anyone his or her sins, the person's sin will be retain against him or her.

Jesus said to her, "Do not cling to Me, for I have not yet ascended to My Father; but go to My brethren and say to them, 'I am ascending to My Father and your Father, and to My God and your God.'" Mary Magdalene came and told the disciples that she had seen the Lord, and that He had spoken these things to her. Then, the same day at evening, being the first day of the week, when the doors were shut where the disciples were assembled, for fear of the Jews,

Jesus came and stood in the midst, and said to them, "Peace be with you." When He had said this, He showed them His hands and His side. Then the disciples were glad when they saw the Lord. So Jesus said to them again, "Peace to you! As the Father has sent Me, I also send you." And when He had said this, He breathed on them, and said to them, "Receive the Holy Spirit. If you forgive the sins of any, they are forgiven them; if you retain the sins of any, they are retained."
(Jn.20:17-23NKJV)

This then implies that before the Lord Jesus finally ascended to heaven and sat at the right hand throne of the Majesty, the disciples where born again or rather baptized by the one Spirit into the one body of Christ. This implies that the early disciples did not get born again on the day of Pentecost as many think, but on the day the Lord breathed on them, before he ascended bodily to heaven. This point of view may contract the belief of many people. More especially those who believe the early disciples of Christ got born again on the day of Pentecost (Acts2:1-4). The only question I want to ask you is: why did the Lord Jesus breathed on the disciples and asked them to receive the Holy Spirit before he ascended to heaven?

The Holy Spirit came into them, and infused their spirit man with the eternal life of the Godhead that resides in Christ. However, the right to make himself know in an audible way was not given to him (Holy Spirit) in this stage, but that is not to say he wasn't in them.

In fact, the Bible declares that God lives in us through the Holy Spirit, because the Holy Spirit carries his eternal life, and infuses our spirit man with it in Christ.

And in him you too are being built together to become a dwelling in which God lives by his Spirit.
(Eph.2:22NIV)

Very often, we think that the fact someone does not speak in tongues is a sign that he or she is not born again. On the contrary, one could be born again and not speak in tongues, because the right to speak in tongues is only given in the third stage of the manifestation of the Holy Spirit to humans in Christ. Nevertheless, the baptism by one Spirit into the one body of Christ that occurs in this second stage of the manifestation of the Holy Spirit in Christ, guarantees the following things:

Forgiveness and Sanctification by the blood of the eternal covenant
The Righteousness of God that is by faith is imputed to us
Our names are written in the book of life
Eternal life of the Godhead is given to us

The Lord Jesus did not wait until he finally ascended to the right hand throne of the majesty, before granting the disciples eternal life by giving the Holy Spirit to regenerate their spirit man. He only went to present himself in the heavenly courtroom, and came back to earth the same day, showed himself to them for over a period of forty days, and spoke to them about the kingdom of God, with many convincing proof that he lives according to scripture.

To them also He showed Himself alive after His passion (His suffering in the garden and on the cross) by [a series of] many convincing demonstrations [unquestionable evidences and infallible proofs], appearing to them during forty days and talking [to them] about the things of the kingdom of God.
(Acts1:3AMP)

SPIRIT UPON US

This has to do with the third stage in the manifestation of the Holy Spirit to humans in Christ that normally takes place at the baptism with the Holy Spirit. It is marked with the customary sign of speaking in new tongues, a promise the Lord Jesus made to all who will believe in him. Here, the Holy Spirit expresses himself, and makes his presence known by giving the person ability to articulate words in the language of the Spirit, usually known as tongue speaking. This is why believers in Christ speak with new tongues or language once baptized with the Holy Spirit.

These signs will accompany those who have believed: in My name they will cast out demons, they will speak with new tongues. (Mk.16:17NASB)

The baptizing with the Holy Spirit is a noticeable experience that marks the beginning of the second stage of spiritual life cycle, known as walking in the Spirit (for more information on this, please go to chapter three).

In the first stage of his manifestation, the Holy Spirit works to conquer our mind in order to regenerate our spirit man with God's eternal life. Although, this mission is accomplished in the second stage of his manifestation, known as the Spirit in us. This allows the Holy Spirit to gain partial control of the human mind, and bring it under subjection to the will of God in Christ, through his ministerial operation by which the word of faith that brings liberty is continuously developed for the renewal of the person's mind.

In this third stage of the manifestation of the Holy Spirit, known as the Spirit upon us, the Holy Spirit inundates a believer's inner man, and overshadows it with his presence, as a deposit from the Father to gain absolute control of it, and then lead the person in a spiritual walk.

But it is God Who confirms and makes us steadfast and establishes us [in joint fellowship] with you in Christ, and has consecrated and anointed us [enduing us with the gifts of the Holy Spirit]; [He has also appropriated and acknowledged us as His by] putting His seal upon us and giving us His [Holy] Spirit in our hearts as the security deposit and guarantee [of the fulfillment of His promise]. (2Co.1:21-22AMP)

Just like what happened on the day of Pentecost, when a sound like the blowing of a violent wind came from heaven and filled the whole house where they were all sitting. Then what looked like tongues of fire appeared and settled on each of them. And they were all filled with the Holy Spirit and began to speak in other tongues as the Spirit gave them utterance, according to the book of Acts2:1-4.

When the day of Pentecost had arrived, they were all together in one place. Suddenly a sound like that of a violent rushing wind came from heaven, and it filled the whole house where they were staying. And tongues, like flames of fire that were divided, appeared to them and rested on each one of them. Then they were all filled with the Holy Spirit and began to speak in different languages, as the Spirit gave them ability for speech. (HCSB)

THE HOLY SPIRIT

When the Holy Spirit fully manifest in presence and rest on a person, he controls the individual and takes him on a walk. He leads the person through spiritual pathway, and uses the different activities and events on the path to renew the person's mind, work on his character and transform the individual into the very image of Christ in words and deeds, by faith and revelation knowledge of the word of God.

Using the life and experience of the early disciples of the Lord Jesus as case study, the story shows us how the Holy Spirit took full control of the apostles and used they to accomplish incredible things. The Lord Jesus had told them in Acts1:5-8 that they will receive power after the Holy Spirit has come upon them, and that they will be his witness in Jerusalem, Judea, Samaria, and to the utter most parts of the earth.

For John baptized with water, but you will be baptized with the Holy Spirit not many days from now." So when they had come together, they asked him, "Lord, will you at this time restore the kingdom to Israel?" He said to them, "It is not for you to know times or seasons that the Father has fixed by his own authority. But you will receive power when the Holy Spirit has come upon you, and you will be my witnesses in Jerusalem and in all Judea and Samaria, and to the end of the earth. (Acts1:5-8ESV)

On the day of Pentecost, they were all filled by the Holy Spirit and spoke in other languages as the Spirit enable them. After being empowered by the Holy Spirit, the apostle Peter stood with the other apostles and addressed the crowd.

He explained the meaning and significance of the experience that they just had with the Holy Spirit to the people. By the time Peter finished his message, about three thousand people got born again that day.

The same Peter who denied the Lord Jesus when a servant girl looked at him, and said he was one of Jesus' followers, according to Luke22:56, became so powerful and courageous that he could publicly confess his faith before thousands of people, minister to them, and won about three thousand new members. This happened because the Holy Spirit came on him, and gave him power to do what he couldn't do before. Beginning from that very day, the life and ministry of Peter moved from one level of glory to another as he walked with the Holy Spirit.

This stage of the manifestation of the Holy Spirit is very important to the Christendom, because it gives a believer in Christ an access to the strait gate with narrow pathway for a walk with the Holy Spirit, by faith and revelation knowledge of the word of God. In that, it produces a change in the person's state of being, by transforming him or her into the very image of Christ, in words and deeds. In addition, it releases on the person the right and ability to communicate with the Godhead, using the language of the Spirit (spiritual language) in prayer.

For one who speaks in an [unknown] tongue speaks not to men but to God, for no one understands or catches his meaning, because in the [Holy] Spirit he utters secret truths and hidden things [not obvious to the understanding].
(1Co.14:2 AMP)

The "Spirit upon us" is a stage that all believers must endeavor to attain. It commences the second stage of a spiritual life cycle in Christ. Unlike the first stage of the manifestation of the Holy Spirit that occurs prior to new birth, and the second stage that takes place at the baptism by one Spirit into the universal body of Christ, this last stage usually occurs at the Holy Ghost baptism with the initial sign of speaking in tongues.

Although, the Spirit upon us is the last stage in the manifestation of the Holy Spirit to humans, it begins the second stage of spiritual life cycle known as walking in the Spirit. Once this commences, the Holy Spirit begins to lead the person through the different phases in spiritual walk, and the various platforms on the spiritual pathway.

There are diverse pitfalls on this path that the enemy uses to hinder our progress as we embark on the journey by faith, and revelation knowledge of God's word. We have to be sensitive, obedience, and submissive to the Holy Spirit as he leads us.

CHAPTER TEN

PITFALLS IN SPIRITUAL WALK

As earlier mentioned, there are things that could jeopardize or hinder our walk with the Holy Spirit. The knowledge and understand you have about these things, and how you can avoid them, would save you from falling into any of them.

Concise Oxford Dictionary – Tenth Edition, include in its definition of pitfall, the following: a hidden or unsuspected danger or difficulty; a covered pit for use as a trap. *Merriam-Webster*, defines it as a danger or problem that is hidden or not obvious at first.

The pitfalls in a walk with the Holy Spirit are hidden or unsuspected danger that frustrate and hinder a progressive and successful walk with the Holy Spirit. It is the only thing that destroys good relationship, and fellowship between the Holy Spirit, and humans.

There are basically three major pitfalls in a walk with the Holy Spirit that all believers must avoid in order to succeed in the journey of faith. The pitfalls include the following: resisting, grieving, and extinguishing the Holy Spirit.

RESISTING THE HOLY SPIRIT – under the heading, "Ministry of the Holy Spirit", I explained how the Holy Spirit uses his ministerial activities, which comprises witnessing, reproving, teaching and reminding to work on the inner man of a person, that is to say, the spirit and mind. To achieve this, he witnesses to us about God's offer for the salvation of our souls, reproves us of our sins, teaches us the ways of God, and he also reminds us of who we are in Christ and the hope we have in him.

You stiff-necked people, with uncircumcised hearts and ears! You are just like your fathers: You always resist the Holy Spirit! (Acts 7:51 NIV)

To resist means to withstand, fight, repel, fend off, ward off, deter, drive back, prevent, and so forth. When you resist the prompting of the Holy Spirit, you make him very unhappy and sad. The prompting of the Holy Spirit could come in form of warning, command, encouragement, direction, conviction and so on. The Holy Spirit speaks to us in diverse ways, and at different times.

GRIEVING THE HOLY SPIRIT – when a person continues to resist the Holy Spirit through words and actions, he (Holy Spirit) becomes grieved. To be grieved means to become unhappy, distress, sadden, sorrowful and the like.

The prophet Isaiah relates what happened to the Israelites when they rebelled and grieved the Holy Spirit. He says the Lord became their enemy and fought against them as we observe in the passage below.

For he said, "Surely they are my people, children who will not deal falsely." And he became their Savior.

In all their affliction he was afflicted, and the angel of his presence saved them; in his love and in his pity he redeemed them; he lifted them up and carried them all the days of old. But they rebelled and grieved his Holy Spirit; therefore he turned to be their enemy, and himself fought against them.

(Is.63:8-10 ESV)

Just as the Lord tuned his back on the ancient nation of Israel when they rebelled and grieved the Holy Spirit in the above Bible passage, he does the same to whoever grieved his Spirit in this era.

Let no corrupting talk come out of your mouths, but only such as is good for building up, as fits the occasion, that it may give grace to those who hear. And do not grieve the Holy Spirit of God, by whom you were sealed for the day of redemption. Let all bitterness and wrath and anger and clamor and slander be put away from you, along with all malice. Be kind to one another, tenderhearted, forgiving one another, as God in Christ forgave you.

(Ep.4:29-32 ESV)

The apostle Paul advises us in the passage above not to grieve the Holy Spirit of God, by whom we were sealed for the day of redemption. Grieving the Holy Spirit has a lot of consequences. It is one of the pitfalls we must avoid at all cost to succeed in a walk with the Holy Spirit.

ESTINGUISHING THE HOLY SPIRIT – some may ask whether a person can really put out the Holy Spirit. According to Scripture, the Holy Spirit can be extinguished after a series of activities that obliged him to withdraw from ones' life.

THE HOLY SPIRIT

For although they knew God, they neither glorified him as God nor gave thanks to him, but their thinking became futile and their foolish hearts were darkened. Although they claimed to be wise, they became fools and exchanged the glory of the immortal God for images made to look like mortal man and birds and animals and reptiles. Therefore God gave them over in the sinful desires of their hearts to sexual impurity for the degrading of their bodies with one another. They exchanged the truth of God for a lie, and worshiped and served created things rather than the Creator — who is forever praised. Amen. Because of this, God gave them over to shameful lusts. Even their women exchanged natural relations for unnatural ones. In the same way the men also abandoned natural relations with women and were inflamed with lust for one another. Men committed indecent acts with other men, and received in themselves the due penalty for their perversion. Furthermore, since they did not think it worthwhile to retain the knowledge of God, he gave them over to a depraved mind, to do what ought not to be done. They have become filled with every kind of wickedness, evil, greed and depravity. They are full of envy, murder, strife, deceit and malice. They are gossips, slanderers, God-haters, insolent, arrogant and boastful; they invent ways of doing evil; they disobey their parents; they are senseless, faithless, heartless, ruthless. Although they know God's righteous decree that those who do such things deserve death, they not only continue to do these very things but also approve of those who practice them.
(Rom.1:21-32NIV)

The passage above clearly reveals that certain actions or conducts would make God turn his back on people.

Verse 24 talks about God abandoning them to do whatever shameful things their hearts desired, while verse 28 speaks about God giving them over to a depraved mind, and letting them do things that should never be done.

When a person keeps resisting and grieving the Holy Spirit, he will quietly leave that person without the individual knowing about it. Unlike, when the Holy Spirit comes on a person at the Holy Ghost baptism with the initial signs of speaking in tongues, vibration and sound that everyone around could hear, see or notice. The individual may not even know that the Holy Spirit has left him or her because he (Holy Spirit) doesn't give any sign when he leaves, apart from the emptiness that the person later feels.

The story of Samson perfectly illustrates this point. When the Holy Spirit came mightily on Samson, he turned him to a superman, and used him to accomplish great things. But the day he (Holy Spirit) left him, the Bible declares that Samson did not know that the Lord had departed from him. He said, "I will go out as before and shake myself free." But he didn't realize the Lord had left him.

When Delilah saw that he had told her all his heart, she sent and called the lords of the Philistines, saying, "Come up again, for he has told me all his heart." Then the lords of the Philistines came up to her and brought the money in their hands. She made him sleep on her knees. And she called a man and had him shave off the seven locks of his head. Then she began to torment him, and his strength left him. And she said, "The Philistines are upon you, Samson!" And he awoke from his sleep and said, "I will go out as at other times and shake myself free." But he did not know that the Lord had left him.

And the Philistines seized him and gouged out his eyes and brought him down to Gaza and bound him with bronze shackles. And he ground at the mill in the prison. But the hair of his head began to grow again after it had been shaved.
(Judg.16:18-22ESV)

The passage says Samson's enemies (Philistines) captured him, and gouged out his eyes and took him to Gaza, where he was bound with bronze chains and forced to grind grain in the prison.

Just as the enemies captured Samson, gouged out his eyes, bind him with chains, and forced him to grind grains in the prison simply because the presence of the Lord departed from him, a Christian would go through many horrible things than Samson if the Holy Spirit withdrawals from him or her. The final state of such a person would be a dormant spirit, depraved mind, dead conscience, and faith because the Holy Spirit who does the interior spiritual works has departed.

One who continually resists the Holy Spirit, would end up grieving him, and when the Holy Spirit is constantly and repeatedly grieved, he would be put out. When he leaves, the divine activities he is doing in the person's life stops.

IMPORTANT
ABBREVIATIONS

Gen..Genesis
Ex. ....Exodus
Lev. .... Leviticus
Num. ....Numbers
Deut. ....Deuteronomy
Josh. ....Joshua
Judg. ....Judges
1Sa. 1Samuel
2Sa. 2Samuel
1Ki. 1Kings
2Ki. ....2 Kings
1Ch. 1Chronicles
2Ch. 2Chronicles
Neh. ....Nehemiah
Esth. ....Esther
Ps. .... Psalms
Pr. ....Proverbs
Ecc. ....Ecclesiastics
SoS.. Song of Songs
Is. ....Isaiah
Jer..Jeremiah
Lam. ....Lamentations
Ezek. ....Ezekiel
Dan....... ....Daniel
Hos. ....Hosea
Jon. ....Jonah
Mic. ....Micah
Nah. ....Nahum
Hab. .... Habakkuk
Zeph. .... Zephaniah
Hag. .... Haggai
Zec...Zechariah

Matt. ....Matthew
Mk. ....Mark
Lk. ....Luke
Jn. ....John
Rom. ....Romans
1Co. 1Corinthians
2Co. 2Corinthians
Gal. ....Galatians
Eph. ....Ephesians
Phi. ....Philippians
Col. ....Colossians
1Thes. 1Thessalonians
2Thes. 2Thessalonians
1Tim. 1Timothy
2Tim. 2Timothy
Heb. .... Hebrews
Jas. ....James
1Pet. 1Peter
2Pet. 2Peter
1Jn. 1John
2Jn. 2John
3Jn. 3John
Rev. ....Revelation

PRAYER OF SALVATION

The gospel message also known as the word of faith, belief and open confession play distinct roles in the salvation process, according to Romans10:8-10. The word of faith produces the faith we need to please God and be at peace with him (Heb.11:6), believing that God raised Jesus from death causes him to impute his righteousness that is by faith to us (Rom.4:22-25). Confessing the lordship of Jesus makes God to infuse our spirit with his eternal life for rebirth.

Salvation does not come by merely verbalizing the *Sinner's Prayer* without faith in Christ atoning sacrifice that comes from hearing the gospel message, repentance from dead works, and open confession of Jesus Christ as Lord and Savior.

1. Believe in your heart that Christ is the Son of the living God.

2. Believe he died on the cross for your sins and iniquities.

3. Believe that God raised him from the dead after three days for your justification.

4. Believe he is at the right hand of the Father in heaven interceding for you.

5. Believe that only Christ has the legitimate right to give eternal life to humans.

6. Ask him to forgive your sins and wash you by his blood.

7. Openly declare him lord of your life from the depth of your heart.

8. Invite him to come and dwell in you.

9. Ask him to write your name in the book of life.

And this is the testimony: God has given us eternal life, and this life is in his Son. He who has the Son has life; he who does not have the Son of God does not have life. I write these things to you who believe in the name of the Son of God so that you may know that you have eternal life.
(1 Jn. 5:11-14 NIV)

If you confess with your mouth the Lord Jesus and believe in your heart that God has raised Him from the dead, you will be saved. For with the heart one believes unto righteousness, and with the mouth confession is made unto salvation.
(Rom.10:9-10NKJV)

Salvation is found in no one else, for there is no other name under heaven given to men by which we must be saved.
(Acts 4:12NIV)

If we confess our sins, He is faithful and righteous to forgive us our sins and to cleanse us from all unrighteousness.
(1Jn.1:9-10 HCSB)

Once you finish reading the above portion of scriptures, you can make the following confession with me from the depth of your heart. Believe it as you speak, and you shall be saved in Jesus name.

Dear Jesus,

I believe that you died on the cross for my sins, and rose on the third day for my justification. You took away my sins, iniquities, infirmities and blotted out the handwriting of ordinances that were against me by your blood. You were bruised for my transgressions, and became a curse for me in order to redeem my soul from death.

I beseech you Lord to come into my life today, and make my heart your dwelling place. I confess you now as my Lord and Savior. Write my name in the book of life, and make me a new person. Thank you Lord Jesus for saving me. Amen

Congratulation!

For John baptized with water, but you will be baptized with the Holy Spirit not many days from now." So when they had come together, they asked him, "Lord, will you at this time restore the kingdom to Israel?" He said to them, "It is not for you to know times or seasons that the Father has fixed by his own authority. But you will receive power when the Holy Spirit has come upon you, and you will be my witnesses in Jerusalem and in all Judea and Samaria, and to the end of the earth.

(Acts 1:5-8 ESV)

Follow me on f Caesar Benedo
Email.caesben11@yahoo.com

Dépot Légal N° 9605 du 07 / 09 / 2017
Bibliothèque National Du Bénin, 3ème Trimestre

www.ingramcontent.com/pod-product-compliance
Lightning Source LLC
LaVergne TN
LVHW051625080426

835511LV00016B/2184